# Geographies of Sound: Sounding and Listening to the Urban Space of Early Modern Italy with a Contemporary Perspective

# STUDIES ON ITALIAN MUSIC HISTORY

EDENDUM CURAVIT
FULVIA MORABITO

VOLUME 17

PUBLICATIONS OF THE CENTRO STUDI OPERA OMNIA LUIGI BOCCHERINI
PUBBLICAZIONI DEL CENTRO STUDI OPERA OMNIA LUIGI BOCCHERINI
PUBLICATIONS DU CENTRO STUDI OPERA OMNIA LUIGI BOCCHERINI
VERÖFFENTLICHUNGEN DES CENTRO STUDI OPERA OMNIA LUIGI BOCCHERINI
PUBLICACIONES DEL CENTRO STUDI OPERA OMNIA LUIGI BOCCHERINI
LUCCA

# Geographies of Sound

## Sounding and Listening to the Urban Space of Early Modern Italy with a Contemporary Perspective

Edited by

Luigi Collarile and Maria Rosa De Luca

BREPOLS
TURNHOUT
MMXXIII

*The present volume has been made possibile by the friendly support of the*

 **DI**PARTIMENTO DI SCIENZE **UM**ANISTICHE (DISUM)

© BREPOLS 2023

All rights reserved. No part of this publication may be reproduced,
stored in a retrieval system, or transmitted, in any form or by any means,
electronic, mechanical, photocopying, recording, or otherwise, without
the prior permission of the publisher.

D/2023/0095/151

ISBN 978-2-503-60676-7

Printed in Italy

# Contents

**Luigi Collarile & Maria Rosa De Luca**
Preface — vii

**Valeria De Lucca**
Regulating Sound and Noise
in Seventeenth-Century Rome — 1

**Luigi Collarile**
*Ephemerides Itineris Romani*:
Experiencing the Sound of Italy in Two Swiss
Travel Diaries of the Seventeenth Century — 23

**Umberto Cecchinato**
Suoni pericolosi. Musica sacra, emozioni
e disciplinamento dell'ambiente sonoro
nelle chiese venete della prima età moderna — 59

**Angela Fiore**
Suoni, spazi, identità della Modena estense — 89

**Giovanni Florio**
Celebrating the Prince from Afar:
Echoes from the Jubilant Dominions in the Orations
to the Newly Elected Doges (XVI-XVII Century) — 107

**Nicola Usula**
Traditional Music in Seventeenth-Century Operas
'alla Veneziana': Intersections in the Italian Soundscape — 145

ELIA PIVETTA
Forms of Circulation of Musical Knowledge
in Eighteenth-Century Italy: Giambattista Martini's
*Risposta* to «abate Pavona friulano»                                    181

ANGELA FIORE
Urban Spaces and Musical Practices
of Neapolitan Female Monasteries
between the Seventeenth and Eighteenth Centuries                          209

MARIA ROSA DE LUCA
Ritualising a Resilient City:
Soundscape, Collective Performances
and Construction of Urban Imaginary                                       229

GIUSEPPINA LA FACE
La musica come persecuzione.
L'inquinamento musicale nelle città odierne                               257


ABSTRACTS AND BIOGRAPHIES                                                 269

INDEX                                                                     275

# PREFACE

SOUND IS AN ESSENTIAL ELEMENT of human experience. It is part of the complex semiotic system that enables human communities to orient themselves in time and space, to be informed, to participate in social life as conscious listeners, capable of deciphering and giving meaning to the collective action of the urban space in which they live. Deeper sound horizons reverberate at different levels in the sonic dimension of reality, contributing to a more complex semantic process of collective civic rituality and the construction of institutional and individual sound identities. In order to investigate the urban soundscape, it is important to define the nature of the sound phenomenon to be examined, but also the dynamics concerning its perception as part of complex anthropological processes. These perspectives can be considered through a historical point of view.

The studies collected in this volume aim to investigate sound as an element of urban space in early modern Italy. They consider different phenomenologies, investigated with innovative methodological perspectives. Particular importance is given to the sound of urban rituality, to its declinations and local connotations, to its ability to interact with public and private dimensions, to the social and aesthetic dynamics that regulate it, to the definition of the sonic identity of early modern urban space.

The publication of this volume concludes a research pathway initiated by the session 'Sound Geographies: Sound as Element of the Urban Space in Modern Italy', promoted by Luigi Collarile and Maria Rosa De Luca and included in the programme of the international conference *The Global City: The Urban Condition as a Pervasive Phenomenon*, organised by the Associazione Italiana di Storia Urbana in Bologna from 11 to 14 September 2019[1]. A short collective article, published in the volume of the conference proceedings, offered a first report of the session[2]. Extensively elaborated and revised, some papers have now become chapters of this volume, which aims to offer new perspectives on rethinking the soundscape of urban space in early modern Italian cities in a complex and articulate manner.

The structure of the book follows an itinerary through early modern Italy, in which the sound of urban life is explored by adopting different methodologies and a variety of approaches.

---

[1]. International conference *The Global City: The Urban Condition as a Pervasive Phenomenon*, University of Bologna, 11-14 September 2019, <https://aisuinternational.org/bologna-2019/>, accessed March 2023.

[2]. COLLARILE ET AL. 2020, pp. 3-18.

# Preface

In the first chapter Valeria De Lucca focuses on the question of how urban noise was regulated in early modern Rome. Based on an extensive documentary survey of proclamations and edicts of the time and the analysis of some precious testimonies, including in particular Grazioso Uberti's *Il contrasto musico* (1630), this study aims to investigate how noise was regulated in the urban life of a city like Rome and how the processes of regulating the civic soundscape impacted on its social, political and devotional identity. In the subsequent chapter, Luigi Collarile enriches this perspective through the testimonies of some foreign travellers. During their stay in Rome, they progressively discovered the sound dimension of the urban ceremonial. This process must be considered in the light of the cultural and social identity of the listeners and the dynamics involved in their interaction with the soundscape of the city.

The sound regulation of liturgical ritual was the main purpose of a wide reforming action promoted by the Council of Trent. In his essay, Umberto Cecchinato investigates the declinations of this powerful disciplinary action in the territories of the Republic of Venice. Giovanni Florio's study also considers this geographical and social context, investigating the sounding of the tributes with which the main cities of the Venetian territories honoured the election of a new doge. The embassies sent to Venice interacted in a complex manner with the city's urban ceremonial, amplifying in time and space the echoes of celebrations for the new doge.

After 1598, Modena became the principal seat of the Dukes of Este. Their arrival in the city entailed a series of important changes in the urban and architectural plan, as well as from a ritual point of view. Angela Fiore reconsiders this process from the perspective of the sound of the urban space. The dukes' interest in music favoured the development of many activities, contributing to the creation of a new sonic identity for the city.

The discovery of references to popular music (nursery rhymes, songs and dances) in operas 'alla venetiana' led Nicola Usula to explore the question of cross-fertilisation between art and traditional music in a genre that during the seventeenth century had a wide dissemination throughout the Italian peninsula and beyond the Alps. Traditional sound elements belonging to the Venetian soundscape became part of a pan-Italian musical tradition, in which the dichotomy between high and low, artistic and popular seems to have pursued the same dramaturgical aim as in the spoken theatre: the comic and realistic effect.

The correspondence between the Bolognese Padre Giambattista Martini, one of the greatest scholars of musical culture of his time, and a Friulian musician, Pietro Alessandro Pavona, provides an interesting case study to investigate the circulation of musical knowledge in the late eighteenth century. As Elia Pivetta has pointed out, the discussion focused on the content of an early choir book preserved in Cividale del Friuli, an emblematic memory of the ancient splendours of the local musical chapel. The interpretation of a work transmitted in that source, a *Kyrie* by the French composer Claudin de Sermisy, became the occasion for a reflection on the evolution of musical language.

# PREFACE

Another essay by Angela Fiore adds a new chapter to her investigations into the musical activities within the female monasteries of Naples. The perspective adopted is a sort of kaleidoscope through which to observe the complex devotional rituality of the city. The female monasteries, in fact, were responsible for a rich musical production that profoundly marked the soundscape of early modern Naples. Maria Rosa De Luca's essay investigates the ceremonial of some religious festivities in eighteenth-century Catania, in particular that for the patron of the city, Saint Agatha, in search of the multiple semantic planes involved in the representation of the festive city. The sounding of spaces and rituals amplified the collective action and the image of a resilient city, regenerated like a phoenix through an impressive work of urban, social and cultural reconstruction.

Giuseppina La Face's essay takes up the issue of urban noise regulation, reconsidered from a contemporary perspective. Today, music can become a polluting factor, catastrophically aggravated by the sound reproduction and amplification systems employed in modern music consumption. This study provides an overview of some issues related to the problem of sound pollution and emphasises the necessity of promoting new educational paths for a new culture of listening to and consuming music.

This book was published thanks to the financial support of the Department of Humanities of the University of Catania. We would like to express our gratitude to its director, Marina Paino. Our thanks also go to Roberto Illiano, Fulvia Morabito and Massimiliano Sala for having accepted our publishing project in the series 'Studies on Italian Music History', the staff of the Centro Studi Opera Omnia Luigi Boccherini, who took great care in the publication of this volume, and Brepols Publishers.

Many research paths explored in the studies collected here have a treasured source of inspiration: Lorenzo Bianconi. We dedicate this volume to him, with esteem and gratitude.

*Luigi Collarile & Maria Rosa De Luca*
Christmas 2022, between Catania and Basel

## BIBLIOGRAPHY

COLLARILE *ET AL.* 2020
COLLARILE, Luigi – DE LUCA, Maria Rosa – BRYANT, David – CECCHINATO, Umberto – DE LUCCA, Valeria – FILIPPI, Daniele V. – FIORE, Angela – FIORIO, Giovanni – LA FACE BIANCONI, Giuseppina – QUARANTA, Elena – RIEDO, Christoph 2020. 'Geografie sonore. Il suono come elemento dello spazio urbano nell'Italia dell'età moderna', in: *La città globale. La condizione urbana come fenomeno pervasivo*, 7 vols., edited by Marco Pretelli, Rosa Tamborrino and Ines Tolis, vol. VII (G), Turin, AISU, 2020, pp. 3-18; online: <https://aisuinternational.org/citta-e-ambiente-nellera-dellantropocene-e-della-globalizzazione-city-and-environment-in-the-era-of-anthropocene-and-globalization/>, accessed March 2023.

# Regulating Sound and Noise
# in Seventeenth-Century Rome*

*Valeria De Lucca*
(University of Southampton)

> *Our science has always desired to monitor, measure, abstract, and castrate meaning, forgetting that life is full of noise and that death alone is silent: work noise, noise of man, and noise of beast. Noise bought, sold, or prohibited. Nothing essential happens in the absence of noise*[1].

THIS CHAPTER INVESTIGATES the regulation of noise in the urban soundscape of seventeenth-century Rome. Most of the sounds that are the object of this study were considered out of place, disturbances, nuisances, or even crimes, and were therefore subject to bans, prohibited and punished by the governing authorities[2]. The main source of information for my study are contemporary edicts and bans, official documents that tell us about how, when and why those in power felt the need to curb and regulate what they perceived as noise. The element of individual perception is, of course, key to our understanding of noise as a cultural construct: ultimately, except for the disquisitions of contemporary physicists who tried to theorise and categorise the differences between sound and noise on the basis of scientific observation, seventeenth-century listeners were aware that these were relative concepts that

---

[*]. A version of this work was presented at the International Workshop *Noise, Silence, Privacy* (Copenhagen, 15-16 September 2022) organised by Christine Jeanneret, Principal Investigator of *SOUND: Soundscapes of Rosenborg*, a research grant funded by the Danske Frie Forskningsfond Project 2. I am very grateful to Christine Jeanneret and all the participants for their feedback. I am also grateful to Margaret Murata for her insightful comments on this text.

[1]. ATTALI 1985, p. 3.

[2]. BAILEY 1998, p. 195 and BAILEY 2004, after Mary Douglas' definition of dirt as «matter out of place». See DOUGLAS 1966 and PICKERING – RICE 2017.

depended on the perception of individuals or groups at any given moment[3]. As we will see, screaming and crying that could start a riot or cause disturbance to public order were curbed and prohibited, but enthusiastic shouts and cheering in support of political or religious figures were never banned in the documents under examination.

The idea of noise in the English-speaking world is so strictly connected to that of an individual physical reaction that its etymology from the Latin 'nausea' suggests a feeling of malady and sickness that derives from an unusual movement of our bodies, often brought on by external causes, such as in seasickness. An unusual sound, out of context, then, but also a «sound we are subjected to» without a chance to escape and that can cause discomfort[4]. In seventeenth-century Italian the term 'rumore' was used more broadly and mainly with two meanings. A first definition indicated a fabricated story or gossip, often meant to criticise or denigrate the object of the story (from Lat. 'rumor', as in the English 'rumour'). In its second meaning, it was a sound «disordinato e incomposto», or «out of order and disorganised»[5]. In the present study I am mostly concerned with the latter definition of noise, but, as we will see, at times the distinction between noise and murmuring, gossiping, or even chanting and insulting is quite blurred in bans and edicts.

Not all noise, of course, was curbed, prohibited or considered unwelcome. In his 1630 treatise titled *Il contrasto musico*, Grazioso Uberti, Roman jurist and musician, argues just the opposite[6]. The work is constructed as a discussion between two characters, Severo (literally 'Severe') and Giocondo ('Joyful'), as they walk around Rome and reflect on their ways of hearing the city. As their names give away, while Severo finds the city an unpleasant place full of loud noise and discordant sounds, Giocondo argues that much of the noise Severo hears is instrumental not only to people's wellbeing but also to the pursuit of harmony and pleasure. They hear noise in proximity to a school of music, for example, where Giocondo argues that the unpleasant sounds produced by the students are necessary practice towards their improvement. Even more important is the discordant sound of bells, which is essential not only to mark the time of everyday activities but also to save lives in case of alarm or to signal extraordinary times of celebration or mourning[7]. According to Giocondo, some noise was therefore to be tolerated, especially when it arose from actions that led to improvement or useful outcomes[8].

---

[3]. See, for example, MENGOLI 1670, in which the author speculates on definitions of sound and noise based on sound frequency and vibrations. For definitions of noise see NOVAK 2015.

[4]. See HEGARTY 2010, p. 4, also discussed in BOUR 2016.

[5]. See 'Romore', in: CRUSCA 1686 and 'Romore', in: PERGAMINO 1602.

[6]. UBERTI 1630.

[7]. Uberti's treatise has been discussed extensively in MURATA 2005, DELL'ANTONIO 2011, CARTER 2018, DE LUCCA – JEANNERET 2019. See also the modern edition with extensive introduction in ROSTIROLLA 1991.

[8]. See CARTER 2018 for a discussion of Uberti's treatise in the context of an overview on listening practices in early modern Italy and an account on the main methodological and disciplinary approaches to historical listening and acoustemology. See also GIBSON – BIDDLE 2017.

# Regulating Sound and Noise in Seventeenth-Century Rome

With this in mind, my investigation aims to explore definitions of sound and noise in early modern Rome and discuss how, why and to what ends government authorities tried to control and regulate certain types of noise. In order to achieve this, I examined around twenty years of edicts and bans that concern the production of sounds and noise in Rome between 1645 and 1691[9]. The purpose of this study is therefore not to provide an exhaustive survey of all the types of urban noise, nor to discuss prohibitions on music and organised sounds, but to present a cultural microhistory of listening habits and of the noise that was specifically targeted by bans and regulations written by elite and governing classes[10]. As will be apparent, these quite prosaic legal documents, each published several times over the years with very little change, present us with rare insights into the anxieties, fears, habits and aspirations as they were expressed by those who produced the noise as well as those who attempted to curb it[11]. Indeed, edicts and bans not only open a window on strata of Roman early modern society that are often neglected by macrohistory, revealing aspects of the soundscape of street sellers, prostitutes, military, charlatans, beggars, and the homeless who were often the objects of these bans and prohibitions. But they also tell us about the ways in which civic and religious authorities attempted to shape the sounds of individuals, groups of people, and specific areas, squares, and streets, inflecting the sonic identity of the city itself[12].

## Everyday Noise

Busy early modern cities burst with noise that resulted from human activities as well as by the presence of large animals in some of the squares and streets they shared with people. Reading edicts and bans, one gets the impression that the people of early modern Rome had a very high tolerance towards this kind of noise, which — given the average low decibel of the urban soundscape at the time — must have been, at least in some cases, perceived as very loud[13]. In fact, some of these activities required authorities to control and regulate sound, noise, and silence to guarantee both the safety of their citizens and an orderly unfolding and occurrence of everyday events.

---

[9]. For an overview on the justice system in early modern Rome see Fosi 2007. I scrutinised the printed bans and edicts held at the Biblioteca Apostolica Vaticana.

[10]. I have not taken into consideration, for example, police reports, which could expand the scope of this study. Picker 2003 offers an insightful analytical model of the implications of the prohibitions of street music in Victorian London.

[11]. See Sizer 2015 for a discussion of the social dynamics behind the documents describing, banning and regulating noise in medieval Europe. Some bans and edicts were published every year using the same formulaic text. When referring to a ban or edict below, therefore, I reference one instance of its appearance, even though the same document might have been published in previous or following years without any major changes.

[12]. On the soundscape of early modern cities, see Knighton – Mazuela-Anguita 2018.

[13]. Smith 1999.

The official bans concern mostly noise that is described as almost unbearable and that for its loudness could cause actions that might harm people and goods. Carriages, carts, horses and other large cattle were the common culprit, and their noise had to be regularly curbed by specific regulations. The edicts explain the dangers connected to them, so we learn that «[...] charioteers, coachmen, and multitudes of horses and carriages cause such racket that people fleeing from such inconvenience, inevitably block the Corso», and also that animals should proceed through the streets and squares quietly, without running, and this was obviously particularly important for cows and oxen, which could cause the greatest damage to people and goods[14]. The noise produced by the wooden and metal wheels of carriages and carts on the cobbled or unpaved streets was considered so loud that according to many it could potentially penetrate inside buildings and damage goods that were found there[15]. For example, in many of the treatises outlining instructions to the *maestro di casa* for the smooth and proper running of aristocratic and wealthy households, noise from carts in the streets is often mentioned as potentially damaging for wine, and for this reason the treatises recommend that cellars should not be housed near busy streets. In fact, some of these booklets explain that the noise produced by carts on the unpaved or roughly paved streets of early modern cities was the result of strong vibrations that could cause wine barrels to quiver and that could spoil their contents[16].

Some work-related noise, and particularly that connected to the use of machines, was considered not only unsafe for people's ears but was also recognised as a danger that could impair their cognitive skills and drive them mad. Millers, for example, tended to become «deaf and wicked like asses» because of all the noise they were subjected to during their work, according to a treatise of the time[17]. In other cases, loud noise produced by humans was also the result of specific forms of labour, and even possibly a strategy of self-advertisement. Street sellers, for example, could use their traditional way of attracting buyers and advertising what they sold by screaming their characteristic cries, but they could not do so everywhere and always. For

---

[14]. «E perché l'esperienza ha mostrato che l'insolenza de' cocchieri, carrozzieri e la moltitudine de' cavalli e cocchi alle volte causano tali rumori, che le genti fuggendo da tale impedimento, forzatamente impediscono la strada del Corso». BANDO 1645, f. 47r. See also BANDO 1668A, f. 65r, and EDITTO 1672A, f. 52r, which regulate the behaviour of coachmen in minute detail.

[15]. The typical Roman cobblestones known as *sampietrini* were initially used to pave the area around Saint Peter under pope Sixtus V in 1585 and were covering most of the city, including the Corso, by the middle of the eighteenth century. CIBIN 2003, pp. 67-78.

[16]. EVITASCANDALO 1620, pp. 51-52. LIBERATI 1658, p. 157.

[17]. «Un altro diffetto ancora provano i miseri molinari, che per lo strepito, & il rumore, che tutta la notte, e il giorno fanno i molini, divengono sordi, & balordi come asini, & sempre hanno un certo tintinnamento nelle orecchie, che da per tutto dove vanno, portano la impressione de' lor molini di dentro, & nel più bello del dormire, vengono col boccone in bocca destati da quel suono importuno, e fastidioso, che gli priva d'ogni quiete & riposo d'animo, & di corpo». GARZONI 1586, p. 563.

example, as we will see, their activity was strictly regulated around schools, and they were also banned from going inside certain buildings to sell their goods.

One everyday activity that must have taken place in a variety of venues, indoors and outdoors, and that is repeatedly and in numerous sources singled out not only as extremely noisy, but also as immoral and antisocial, was that of gaming, which could be the indication of wild betting and gambling that could cause significant debt, and could attract crowds and lead to consequent fights[18]. Cards, wooden gaming tiles, and dice slapped on the wooden table produced, according to Giocondo and Severo, such racket that people were repelled by the noise:

> GIO. Does that slapping of tiles sound pleasant to you? that tossing of dice? that throwing of cards? Do you think that all those complaints of players against Fortune comfort the soul? Those arguments that arise from gaming[19]?

Certain categories of people and strata of society were often singled out for their production of their everyday noise and sounds, and were the preferred targets of special rules, stricter limitations, and tougher forms of punishment. Homeless people and beggars, for example, and those who lived off the charity of others were often allowed to ask for money only outside of churches, and at specific times of the religious calendar they had to stay at a certain specified distance from the door of churches and other places of devotion[20]. The noise and sounds they made when begging or wandering and the disruption to prayer and services they caused was often used as an excuse to keep them away from places where they could cause not only disturbances, but also pose a threat to public order. Women, and particularly those who practiced the profession of the *meretrice* or prostitute, were also subject to special edict and rules to control their behaviour. Noise was strictly regulated around, inside, and outside their houses, so that at special times in the religious calendar they could not host performances in their house, nor attract customers with music, sounds, or cries. But bans and edicts suggest that women were also the object of offences and insults. For this reason, regulations to protect them prohibited anyone from singing defamatory songs or shout dishonest and insulting words in front of the houses of women of any social standing and condition, including prostitutes, or to cry, shout, or throw stones on their roofs, through doors or windows[21].

---

[18].   BANDO 1675, f. 58r.

[19].   «Suono grato ti pare quello sbattere di tavole? quel tirare de dadi? quel gettare di carte? ti pare, che confortino l'animo quei lamenti de giuocatori contra la fortuna? quelle contese, che nascono nel giuoco?». UBERTI 1630, pp. 49-50.

[20].   EDITTO 1691, f. 22r.

[21].   «[...] tanto di giorno come di notte cantaranno cose brutte infamatorie, e disoneste inanzi l'abitazione delle donne di qualsivoglia condizione etiam publiche meretrici, o faranno vociferationi, gridi, strepiti, & urli in dispreggio di alcuna persona, o tiraranno sassi nelli tetti, porte o finestre». BANDO 1650, f. 74r. For a discussion of women's houses as a metaphor and extension of their bodies see COHEN – COHEN 2001-2002, particularly p. 64.

There were kinds of noise, however, that not only posed a serious threat to the people of the city, but that could also undermine the authority of those in power. Like stench or smells produced by poor urban hygiene, noise could be the symptom or indication of events that could endanger the people of the city and had to be regulated for their own good, as well as to keep any potentially subversive action under control[22]. Indeed, the bulk of edicts and bans suggests that sounds and noise were often perceived as the indication of a riot or a tumultuous gathering, could invite people to a rebellion, or scare people and cause them to flee in a panic and hurt themselves or those around them[23]. For this reason, the use and permission to carry any kinds of guns at night, after the ringing of the bell of the Ave Maria, or in specific areas of the city, was strictly regulated, consistently and constantly. In addition to weapons posing a threat to people's lives, the edicts refer specifically to loud sounds, like the shot of a gun, which could frighten the numerous animals that shared many squares and streets of the city frequented by people, and this could in turn be dangerous, particularly for children. Noise seemed to be one of a number of risks connected to the use of *archibugi* or arquebuses, for example. Unlike the use of edged weapons, which were probably considered a common sight in Rome and less dangerous than a firearm, the use of the arquebus was regulated not only because they were much more effective at causing harm to people and animals, but also because of the noise they could cause at night, which could disturb the quiet of the neighbourhood but also alarm humans and beasts, invite to a riot, create tumult and confusion.

## Festive Noise and Sound

Festive occasions and celebrations were times of heightened social interaction that, in the competitive Roman society of the early modern period, could lead to an increase in violent acts in public spaces. During the sixteenth century, Rome saw a sharp rise in the number of reported suspicious wounds and injuries during the carnival period, for example, a time when the streets and squares of the city became the background for celebrations, tricks, and mockery that, also thanks to the use of masks, could easily degenerate into violence[24]. At such times of potentially higher danger for public safety and threat to authority, edicts and bans regulating noise and any disturbance to silence and public order were promulgated with more frequency and outlined in more details.

The Roman carnival attracted visitors and travellers from all over Europe and marked a time of merrymaking and relaxation of moral behaviour following Christmas and before Lent. During the months of carnival, the pope could grant permission to stage plays and operas, and

---

22. On smells as well as noise in early modern England see Cockayne 2007.
23. For an investigation of noise and dissent see Sizer 2015.
24. Blastenbrei 2006, p. 71.

large parts of the city filled with locals and visitors attending parades of carnival floats, horse races, street plays, and music-making. Aristocrats attended many of the street celebrations from balconies built for the occasion, and some sponsored and paraded in their own lavish carnival floats[25]. To divert the attention of the people of the city from such potentially immoral festivities, churches intensified their devotional practices, with the display of the Quarant'Ore machines creating a quite theatrical counterpart to the events that were happening in the streets and squares just outside the churches[26]. All these events created opportunities for noisy activities and loud sounds that, in the eyes of the local authorities, had to be curbed to guarantee public safety. Bans attempted — probably not very successfully judging by the number of incidents and injuries reported at these times — to curb noise made with any kind of weapon and instrument. The punishment for those who committed these crimes during the carnival period increased and could entail physical torture, a fine between 25 and 200 gold *scudi*, or even life in prison. But since most of the crimes were committed by people wanting to disguise their identity in order to go unpunished, with the excuse of wearing carnival costumes, those who committed an offence while masked could risk the death penalty[27].

Special prohibitions on screaming, whistling, or producing any insulting sound were in effect, particularly when the objects of the offense were women, prostitutes, and Jews running the *corsa degli Ebrei*[28]. This extremely denigrating ritual that had been taking place in Rome since the fifteenth century, recurred every year during carnival and saw eight races of groups of people, including naked young, elderly, Jews and horses, in eight days. The race of the naked Jews took place on the first Monday of carnival and was one of the most popular entertainments of the season. It attracted large, anonymous crowds that cheered, whistled, offended, and insulted the people who took part in it, and while these races were permitted by the authorities, the bans that were in effect and that included curbs on sounds and noise, show an attempt to limit the public appetite for such humiliating display[29]. This activity acquired tones that were considered so insulting and racist for the Jews who participated that in 1668 under pope Clement IX Rospigliosi it was suppressed in exchange for an annual fee of 300 gold *scudi* that the Jewish community had to pay[30].

---

[25]. De Lucca 2009.

[26]. On the Quarant'Ore see Petersen 2012.

[27]. The prohibition to disguise or conceal one's identity is one of the most common acts prohibited by bans. See for example Bando 1650, ff. 68v-69r for the many instances in which a disguise or carrying bright lights that could make it difficult to be recognised were prohibited.

[28]. Bando 1661, f. 3r. See Bando 1647, f. 9r, and others prohibiting insulting and molesting Jews specifically during the carnival celebrations.

[29]. Foa 2014.

[30]. Caffiero 2011, p. 11.

The time of carnival was also the most intense time for performances of operas and plays. Much has been written about the prohibitions that often were imposed on theatre and opera specifically, but the regulations also concerned the noise around and within the sites that hosted performances, which reveal insights into audience behaviour inside and outside the theatre. As musicologist Margaret Murata argued, plays and operas were often considered occasions for dangerous and immoral activities not only for what happened on stage but also because the mingling of many aristocrats, diplomats, clergy, and the presence of actresses as well as prostitutes, who looked for wealthy clients, created opportunities for fights and disturbances[31].

That opera audiences were noisy and loud during the performance of operas in early modern Rome is clear if we read the numerous accounts that tell us of arguments, whistling and loud talking that took place[32]. Even more telling are those accounts that remind us that some members of the audience wished they could have silence to enjoy the spectacle and complained about the disruption caused by some of those present. In 1606 while attending a play at the French embassy, the French ambassador «begged everyone to be silent, in the end ordering them in the name of His Majesty» to no avail[33]. The situation was not any better when music was made in smaller gatherings and Uberti reminds us that some people disliked music performances because they had to be quiet and could not talk and express their opinions during the performance[34]. The prohibitions, therefore, had to be very explicit in this regard and concerned «screaming, making noise, whistling, and other indecent acts both in the venue of the performance, entering as well as upon leaving, and [it was prohibited] also to occupy the stage, or in any way disturbing the performers and the audience», with special mention of the disruption that could be caused by *meretrici*, who were not allowed in the theatre at all[35]. The punishment for such anti-social behaviour during a play or an opera was physical torture, at times even in public, and a fine, usually 25 gold *scudi*.

The carriages that circulated around the theatres or venues where the play or opera was taking place also had to be quiet and not cause any noise during or after the event, making sure to stay away from the main entrance and that the drivers did not get into loud arguments about questions of precedence, who should go first, who should keep the right and who the left. The quiet conduct of the coachmen was, of course, considered as an extension of the decorum and

---

[31]. Murata 2012.

[32]. For a history of changing listening habits of opera goers see Johnson 1995.

[33]. Murata 2012, p. 194.

[34]. See Carter 2018, p. 33.

[35]. «[...] il far strepito, rumore, fischiate, ò altri atti indecenti cosi nel luogo delle commedie, come nell'entrare, e uscire come anco in occupare il palco delle scene, o in qualsivoglia modo apportare disturbo a comici, o spettatori sotto pena di tre tratti di corda da darseli in publico, o altre pene pecuniarie, e corporali ad arbitrio di Sua Eminenza secondo la qualità delle persone. Et alle publiche meretrici l'andar al luogo di dette commedie sotto pena della frusta». Bando 1661, f. 3r.

restraint that were required of their aristocratic masters and a requisite to maintain a certain degree of control over the crowds that gathered around venues on the day of the performance. Coachmen driving carriages to the theatres were required to drive «said carriage quietly, without rushing through, giving time to others in front of them, without taking the space of others, and without any shouting, arrogance, violence, racket, verbal or physical confrontations», and should maintain order and peace throughout the performance, before and after[36].

To conclude this overview of regulations on festive noise, one cannot think of a louder event in Rome than the celebration of Saint Peter and Paul, on 29 June, when the city staged one of the most outlandish pyrotechnic shows, la *girandola*. Castel Sant'Angelo and the dome of Saint Peter were lit up by the fireworks, and this activity was not without its risks[37]. In fact, Castel Sant'Angelo was the venue *par excellence* for this kind of loud — and dangerous — form of display. And while the *girandole* were planned and carefully organised, there were also people who liked to shoot fireworks and 'rockets' or *razzi* themselves, causing not only unplanned and unauthorised sounds, but also a potential fire hazard, since Castel Sant'Angelo held large quantities of explosives and gun powder[38].

## REGULATING NOISE FOR A GREATER GOOD

Attempts to shape the soundscape of specific neighbourhoods, streets and squares, or around individual buildings, prohibiting noise and regulating sound production, were commonly ascribed to the greater good of the people of Rome and their common interests. Often these regulations were meant to safeguard people and activities that required 'the act' of silence as a condition for concentration or that deserved respect and decorum, and concerned sounds and noises that were mostly produced outside or around certain buildings, but that could cross that blurred boundary between outside and inside, the street and the home[39].

The emphasis that many of the documents place on the inside/outside dichotomy reminds us that sound insulation of buildings from the outside world at the time was very limited. Except for the churches that could afford it and the palaces of the wealthy few, during the seventeenth

---

[36].    «[...] Di più, per nova provisione vuole, & ordina à tutti, e singoli Cocchieri di qualsivoglia sorte, o condizione, ò altra persona che conduca, e guidi Carrozza alle dette cummedie [*sic*], ò luogo dove si recitano, che debbiano [*sic*] ivi in detto luogo condurre la detta Carrozza quietamente, senza farla correre, e dar tempo ad altre, che fussero avanti alla loro, e non levare il luogo ad altre, ne tentare di levarlo, o di far strepito, o forza, o violenza, o rissa, o contrasto, o di parole, o di fatti». BANDO 1661, f. 3r.

[37].    On the *girandola* at Saint Peter's and Castel Sant'Angelo see FAGIOLO DELL'ARCO 1997, p. 106, FAGIOLO DELL'ARCO – CARANDINI 1977-1978, vol. I, and FAGIOLO 1997, p. 83.

[38].    BANDO 1668B, f. 100r.

[39].    «Yet silence is not necessarily an absence of sounds, but rather an act». BAILEY 1998, p. 199.

century most Roman houses still did not have glazed windows, but used parchment paper and waxed cloths to create some level of isolation from the weather and indiscreet gazes[40]. Sixteenth-century treatises that explain how to treat parchment paper so as to make it look like glass were still published in the mid-seventeenth century, and so were treatises on how to insulate the windows of churches that did not have the means to commission glass[41]. It is not surprising, therefore, that street sounds and noise could easily penetrate inside buildings, and that sounds produced inside could overflow to the outside, especially given the low levels of ambient sound[42]. Many documents tell us of the voices of prisoners that could be heard outside of jails, and Uberti gives a few examples of sounds from a school of music or from a domestic quarrel spilling out into the streets, as well as of serenatas performed in the square and attracting people to come to their windows[43]. Whispers and quiet gossip from the streets could easily be heard from people hiding inside buildings, and spying to report potential crimes to the police was a common practice facilitated by the low level of ambient sound and the limited insulation[44].

Schools and churches were some of the places around and inside which noise was not tolerated so as not to disturb those for whom silence was a requirement to accomplish their activities. In Uberti's treatise, Giocondo highlights to Severo that noise, even when produced through an activity that is considered essential and important such as that of blacksmiths, had to be curbed when silence is required to study and around churches:

> Gio. Both the laws and the magistrates who cover any form of disturbance,
> do not consider the noise coming from schools of music worthy of notice. In fact,
> they only imposed some regulation over the noise of the hammers of blacksmiths,
> which are prohibited around churches [...] and at times in proximity to some famous
> scholar so as not to disturb their studies [...][45].

---

[40]. COHEN – COHEN 2001-2002, particularly p. 68. In its definition of 'window', CRUSCA 1612 does not mention glazed windows, but they are mentioned in CRUSCA 1623, confirming that the seventeenth century saw an increase in the use of this kind of window in Italy.

[41]. ROSSELLI 1644, one chapter is entirely devoted to «fare una finestra che parerà di vetro». A similar chapter can be found in BIRELLI 1601, chapter 260. See also CAVAGLIERI 1693 for instructions on alternatives to glass to insultate churches that could not afford glazed panes.

[42]. GARRIOCH 2003, p. 8.

[43]. UBERTI 1630, passim. FOSI 2007, p. 32.

[44]. FOSI 2007, pp. 71, 142.

[45]. «E le leggi e i magistrati, che provedono ad ogni inconveniente, non stimano rumore considerabile quello delle scole di musica. E solo al rumore de' martelli de' fabri hanno data qualche provisione, con prohibirli intorno alle chiese [...] e col levarli tal volta da canto a qualche famoso dottore, per non disturbare i suoi studij [...]». UBERTI 1630, p. 28.

## REGULATING SOUND AND NOISE IN SEVENTEENTH-CENTURY ROME

The frequency with which bans on noise in and around schools were published suggests that regulating disturbances must have been a challenging enterprise, as the rhetoric of the opening of one of the edicts shows:

> Even though other times and with other bans we have provided regulations on the disturbances that used to occur at the Studio di Roma because of people who were not behaving properly and who were accustomed to creating problems and cause noise that disturbed the readers, who could not read, which caused a damage to the reputation of such honoured place, as well as great disconcert in His Holiness, the Most Eminent Protectors, and also caused a damage to those who wanted to study. Therefore, considering that foreign scholars and new people come frequently, and so that the foreigners are fully aware and cannot in any way pretend not to be aware, and that those who already know can be subject to punishment [...][46].

What follows is a long and detailed list of all the actions that were prohibited because they could cause disturbances. In particular, people had to observe silence when walking near scholars and professors of medicine, «especially in the presence of a corpse»; students had to enter the building in religious silence and devote themselves entirely to their books and studies, not to chit-chatting at the doors, trying to avoid all kinds of jokes and tricks; their conduct, in which avoiding making noise and impudent sounds was essential, had to be maintained not only inside the school, but also outside when walking around Rome, where they represented the institution; and while street sellers of doughnuts, cheese, fruit, chestnuts, and other treats were not allowed to enter the schools and advertise their business through their characteristic cries, students should also make sure not to annoy them once outside. Finally, goliardic songs, cries, gestures and jokes were strictly forbidden, including throwing «oranges, lemons, onions, stones, mud, eggs, even if full of water, nor anything else, even if just as a joke». The punishment for such disobedience could be physical torture and 50 gold *scudi*[47].

Most Roman neighbourhoods, the *rioni*, had dozens of churches, convents and monasteries, oratorios, hospitals and other religious institutions around which people gravitated. Pilgrims came to the city and visited the sacred sites and were hosted by their community of reference near churches where some of the masses were celebrated in their

---

46. «Scolari della Sapienza. Ancorché altre volte per altri bandi sia stato sufficientemente provisto alli disordini, che solevano suscitarsi nello Studio di Roma a mal'avezzi, & habituati a far brighe, e rumori, quali impedivano li Signori Lettori, che non potevano leggere, con poca riputatione di sì honorato studio, con malissima sodisfattione di Sua Santià, dell'Eminentiss. Protettori, e danno di quelli, che vogliono studiare; Però considerando, che continuamente vengono scolari forastieri, e gente nova acciò i forastieri n'habbino piena notitia, e non possino in modo alcuno pretendere ignoranza, e quelli, che lo sanno, si possino in modo alcuno punire [...]». EDITTO 1655, f. 74r. See also BANDO 1672, f. 25r for the students of the Compagnia di Gesù.

47. EDITTO 1655, f. 74r.

11

languages, processions transited from one place of devotion to the next, church bells tolled incessantly, each with its distinctive rings, to mark the passing of time, celebrate, commemorate, alert[48]. These outdoor rituals and practices must have inflected the soundscape of entire areas of Rome in quite unique ways, as the specific edicts that were promulgated for each type of event show. For example, during processions nobody could light *zaganelle*, *razzi*, or any other form of firework; children should not accompany the procession, no performances should take place along the path, cattle and horses should not be made to pass near people, and coachmen and charioteers should not stand by the streets and squares where the procession had to transit. Grooms of those cardinals who were participating in such events should not salute them with gunshots, nor parade with weapons and drums, trying to avoid any «romore o strepito»[49].

Disturbances were also not tolerated around churches and other places of devotion, where ball games in particular — «palla, pallone, o vero altri giochi di strepito mentre si celebrano le messe, et altri divini offici» — were forbidden, as were games of dice and cards that could produce noise or loud screams. Playing games with balls or any other game as well as unregulated singing or yelling was also forbidden, not only outside but also inside the cloisters of convents and monasteries since this type of sound was considered as a disturbance but also a possible threat to the peace, morality, and activities of devotion carried out inside[50].

In fact, one gets the impression that silence was a much rarer occurrence than noise, even in churches. As we learn from Uberti, it was not unusual for people to bring their dogs inside the church or talk to their servants asking them to go fetch something for them, often disturbing others:

> Some go to church accompanied by their servant and their dog, with rosary and book of offices in their hand. And if they have a whim to ask for something, they do that light-heartedly. And if their dog runs here and there, they call it, pet it, and do not find it strange at all[51].

The regulations on sounds and noise inside churches corroborate Uberti's story. In fact, in the church nobody could provoke an argument or a tumult, cause noise, or attack anyone or do anything else that could, with words or actions, disturb the divine offices. It was also prohibited

---

[48].    See Uberti 1630. While Severo complains about loud and discordant church bells in Uberti's treatise, no prohibition or ban seems to concern the sound of bells, which was essential to the regular and efficient accomplishment of everyday activities, as well as to alert people of any extraordinary event or danger. On bells and their function and meaning see the pathbreaking and now classic Corbin 1998.

[49].    Editto 1668a, f. 86r, and Editto 1668b, f. 21r.

[50].    Bando 1650, f. 75r. See also Fosi 2007, pp. 69-70.

[51].    «Sono alcuni che vanno alla chiesa accompagnati dal servitore e dal bracco, con la corona e l'officio in mano. Se le viene in mente di ordinare qualche cosa, lo fanno volentieri. Se il cane corre qua e là, lo chiamano, l'accarezzano, non si scandalizano punto». Uberti 1630, pp. 92-93.

## REGULATING SOUND AND NOISE IN SEVENTEENTH-CENTURY ROME

to walk around during the celebrations, and no rumours or gossips or indecent talking was tolerated. Only beggars and the homeless had to stay outside and could not cross the church's entry door so as not to disturb the presumed quiet and silence of those inside[52].


## EXTRAORDINARY MEASURES FOR EXTRAORDINARY TIMES

Times of extraordinary religious importance were also often junctures of political tension and required extraordinary measures of heightened control over people's behaviour in public spaces so as to guard the social and political stability of the city. Extraordinary rules concerned venues where fights, drinking, and gambling could occur, such as inns and taverns which had to close earlier and for longer in case night curfew was enforced[53]. In those cases, as during the Holy Week of Holy Year 1675, no one could produce any «screams, noise, across streets nor squares, nor any other indecent act against the quiet, modesty and respect that are due at such time of devotion». The punishment for this kind of disturbance during the Holy Year was 100 *scudi*, of which half would go to religious institutions, a quarter would go to the person who denounced the fact, whose identity would remain secret, and the last quarter to the executor who would carry out the punishment, which could be torture[54]. This ban also explains that the punishment will be decided on the basis of the status of the perpetrator and that the punishment will be more serious for those of higher social standing, so as to serve as an example for others of lower social condition[55]. The carrying of all sorts of shotguns, rifles and other noisy weapons was, of course, prohibited. All types of amusement and entertainment were strictly prohibited, and so were also the kinds of noise that derived from them. These included all sorts of plays, with and without music, in private as well as public spaces, improvised or written, on stage, in the squares, and in the palaces[56].

---

[52].   EDITTO 1672B, f. 94r.

[53].   «Per levare occasione di scandali, e perché facilmente si attenda al raccoglimento dello spirito, osterie e alberghi chiusi dalle due hore di notte sono a sedici hore del giorno seguente». BANDO 1675, f. 58r.

[54].   This kind of division of the fine was not unusual. See FORNILI 1991, pp. 146-150.

[55].   «In tutte le notti della Settimana Santa, cominciando dalla Domenica delle Palme, e nelle tre notti della Santa Pasqua, per occasione di Processioni o sotto altro qualisisia colore, o pretesto, non ardisca, né presumi di far gridi, rumori, e strepiti per le strade, o piazze, né alcun'atto indecente, e contro la quiete, modestia, e rispetto, che si deve portare a tempo così devoto sotto pena di 100 scudi d'oro, d'applicarsi per la metà a luoghi pii, e per una quarta parte all'accusatore, il quale sarà tenuto segreto, e l'altra parte all'esecutore, et altre pene ancora corporali ad arbitrio Nostro, secondo la qualità delle persone, alle quali quanto più saranno nobili, e qualificate, tanto più s'aggraverà la pena, acciò diano esempio a gli altri di minor conditione». BANDO 1675, f. 58r.

[56].   «Proibisce a tutti di fare, ordinare, o ammettere che si faccin in pubblico o in privato, nelle case proprie, o d'altro, alcuna attione concernente li spassi, o divertimenti sudetti, & in ispecie i festini, balli, moresche, bagordi, maschere, o travestimenti con abiti impropri senza maschera, commedie, giudiare, burattini, o rappresentazioni di

The very tone of the edicts became more emphatic at such times, warning perpetrators not only of the punishment imposed by the law, but — unusually so — also of God's revenge. An edict from 1691 during the *Sede vacante*, the time of power vacancy that followed the death of a pope, in this case Alexander VIII, and ended with the election of the new one, is a case in point:

> At every time faithful Christians are called to make recourse to His Holy Majesty and attend the Holy Sacraments and visit the Churches, but particularly right now they have to make sure to do so, making recourse to God, since it is already evident that the Divine Justice holds in their hand the scourge to punish us, as it is clear from evident signs not too far from us, with frightening earthquakes, plague, the number of pernicious insects in the fields, and the conflicts among the Christian rulers, which benefits the common enemy. Therefore, so that [devotion] could be practiced with positive effects, and having furthermore noticed that His Holy Majesty is getting increasingly irritated by the lack of respect for the holy temples, which should be places of prayer and not of chit-chatting [...][57].

Special bans were published for the «quiete e pace» required during the Vacant See, but ultimately some sounds were the usual suspects when it came to prohibitions[58]. A curb on the production of noise and disturbances around churches was strictly enforced and beggars had to remain not only outside of the entrance of places of devotion, but at a specified distance of *dieci canne d'architetto*. The punishment for beggars who did not respect this rule was the confiscation of all their alms and exile from Rome[59]. Night-time surveillance was reintroduced, no betting, gambling, and gaming of any sort was allowed, and all licenses concerning the carrying of arms, and especially *archibugi*, were revoked[60]. In fact, those who provoked even just a fist fight but had an *archibugio* on them could incur the punishment of five years in jail. Detailed lists were published in 1691 so as not to leave any doubt to the types of gunshot-related

---

qualsivoglia sorte ancora spirituali, tanto in palchi che in carri, quanto a piede e tanto imparate a mente, quanto all'improvviso, & in qualsivoglia modo, e luogo, come anco d'intervenire o assitere ad alcuno delli suddetti trattenimenti [...]». EDITTO 1689, f. 8r.

[57]. «In ogni tempo sono li fedeli Christiani tenuti di ricorrere a S.D.M. frequentare li Santissimi Sagramenti, e le Chiese, ma particolarmente in hoggi devesi ciò procurare facendo ricorso a Dio già che si vede, che la Divina Giustitia tiene in mano il flagello per castigarci, come se ne vedono segni evidenti non molto lungi da noi, e con li Terremoti spaventevoli, e col contagio, e con la quantità di nocivi animali per le campagne, e con la disunione de Prencipi Christiani, che serve di vantaggio al comune inimico. Quindi è, che a fine possa ciò pratticarsi con profitto scorgendosi per lo più che Sua Divina Maestà si va irritando per la poca riverenza a Sagri Tempi, che devono essere casa d'oratione, e non di radunanza per li cicaleggi [...]». EDITTO 1691, f. 22r.

[58]. See HUNT 2016.

[59]. EDITTO 1691, f. 22r.

[60]. BANDO 1691A, f.40r, and BANDO 1691B, f. 41r.

14

noises that were prohibited during any holiday, procession and other religious function during the time of mourning, both because they caused noise but also because of the turmoil that that could cause among people. These included a prohibition of shooting or letting others shoot near churches, «bombarde, mortaletti, archibugi, o qualsivoglia altro instrumento da fuoco» at a time in which, more than ever, noise and disturbances had to be kept to a minimum to control the people at a time of potential political instability[61].

## CONCLUSION

Noise and its regulation to the point of the imposition of silence aimed to define and shape the identity of early modern Rome as much as organized sounds and music. Attempts to shape the soundscape of the city, of specific areas or certain groups of people, were motivated by factors that reveal a great deal about anxieties, social tensions, and fears that were profoundly rooted in contemporary society. Indeed, some types of noise were prohibited in certain contexts because they posed a concrete danger to the life of people, the regular carrying out of everyday activities, or of practices that were considered particularly useful. However, most bans were actually meant to enact the authorities' agenda and the priorities of those who had to guarantee the stability of the political *status quo* through strict social control on specific groups of society. As Peter Bailey argued, «Silence, we might say, is the sound of authority — generational, patriarchal and formidably inscribed in the regimes of church and state», as many of the examples discussed so far illustrate[62]. The dichotomy noise/silence, therefore, articulates social, gender, and racial differences and tensions. The poorer social strata, the beggars or the homeless, or those from marginalised groups, such as prostitutes or Jews, were often seen as the culprit of disturbances and noise that could pose a threat to public decorum and safety and were therefore the targets of special regulations to control their production of sounds and noise, curb sounds made in or around their homes, or, as in the case of Jews running the carnival races, prohibit noise that people made to insult and humiliate them without necessarily eliminating the institutional cause. Ultimately, this kind of study opens a window not only on a microhistory of sound, noise and silence, but gives us also insights into the lives of beggars, prostitutes, street sellers, and marginalised ethnic groups, such as the Jews of Rome, who are generally neglected by conventional historical narratives and too often fall through the cracks of discussions of

---

[61]. «[...] commandiamo a tutte, e singole persone ecclesiastiche tanto secolari, come regolari dell'uno, e l'altro sesso, che durante il tempo della presente sede vacante non ardischino o presumino per occasioni delle Feste, Processioni, o altre funtioni ecclesiastiche di sparare o far sparare attorno le Chiese Bombarde, Mortaletti, Archibugi, o qualsivoglia altro instrumento da fuoco». EDITTO 1691, f. 34r.

[62]. BAILEY 1998, p. 199.

elites, rulers, lawmakers and their soundscapes. Listening to what was considered as noise and therefore a nuisance or disturbance can lend us a revealing lens to reimagine the whole sonic identity of the early modern city.

## BANS AND EDICTS

BANDO 1645
*Bando circa il corso de palii.*

BANDO 1647
*Bando concernente il particolare delle maschere, con la confirmatione dell'altri bandi.*

BANDO 1650
*Bandi generali.*

BANDO 1661
*Sopra le Maschere, e Corso de Palij.*

BANDO 1668A
*Bando contro cocchieri, carrettieri, carrari vetturali, barilari, bufalari, & altri che conducano bestie per Roma.*

BANDO 1668B
*Bando contro quelli, che tirano razzi verso il Castel Sant'Angelo.*

BANDO 1672
*Contro chi disturba li scolari delle scuole della Compagnia di Giesù.*

BANDO 1675
*Bando per la settimana santa e feste di Pasqua e resurrezione.*

BANDO 1691A
*Bando contro giuocatori.*

BANDO 1691B
*Bando e provisioni da osservarsi per la quiete della Città nella presente Sede Vacante.*

EDITTO 1655
*Editto da osservarsi tanto dentro, quanto intorno allo Studio, e Sapienza di Roma da Scolari & altri che in quello praticano.*

EDITTO 1668A
*Editto per le processioni del Santissimo Sacramento.*

# Regulating Sound and Noise in Seventeenth-Century Rome

Editto 1668b
*Editto sopra le stazioni di preghiera.*

Editto 1672a
*Editto contro cocchieri e carrozzieri.*

Editto 1672b
*Editto per l'osservanza del Culto Divino e veneratione delle Chiese.*

Editto 1689
*Editto.*

Editto 1691
*Editto.*

## Bibliography

Attali 1985
Attali, Jacques. *Noise: The Political Economy of Music*, translated by Brian Massumi, Minneapolis-London, University of Minnesota Press, 1985 [first French edition published in 1977].

Bailey 1998
Bailey, Peter. *Popular Culture and Performance in the Victorian City*, Cambridge, Cambridge University Press, 1998.

Bailey 2004
Id. 'Breaking the Sound Barrier', in: *Hearing History: A Reader*, edited by Mark M. Smith, Athena (GA), University of Georgia Press, 2004, pp. 23-35.

Blastenbrei 2006
Blastenbrei, Peter. 'Violence, Arms and Criminal Justice in Papal Rome, 1560-1600', in: *Renaissance Studies*, xx/1 (2006), pp. 68-87.

Bour 2016
Bour, Isabelle. 'Foreword: Noise and Sound in the Eighteenth Century', in: *Études Épistémè*, no. 29 (2016), <http://journals.openedition.org/episteme/1136>, accessed 18 October 2022.

Birelli 1601
Birelli, Giovanni Battista. *Opere [...] Tomo primo. Nel qual si tratta dell'alchimia*, Florence, Marescotti, 1601.

CAFFIERO 2011
CAFFIERO, Marina. 'Spazi urbani e scene rituali dell'ebraismo romano in età moderna' in: *Judei de Urbe. Roma e i suoi ebrei: una storia secolare. Atti del Convegno (Archivio di Stato di Roma, 7-9 novembre 2005)*, edited by Maria Caffiero and Anna Esposito, Rome, Ministero per i Beni e le Attività Culturali, Direzione Generale per gli Archivi, 2011 (Pubblicazione degli archivi di Sato. Saggi, 106).

CARTER 2018
CARTER, Tim. 'Listening to Music in Early Modern Italy: Some Problems for the Urban Musicologist', in: KNIGHTON – MAZUELA-ANGUITA 2018, pp. 25-49.

CAVAGLIERI 1693
CAVAGLIERI, Marcello. *Rettore ecclesiastico*, Naples, Giovanni Battista e Girolamo Sassi, 1693.

CIBIN 2003
CIBIN, Ludovica. *Selciato romano: il sampietrino. Materiale, lavorazione, evoluzioine storica, tipologie, apparecchiature, posa in opera*, Rome, Gangemi, 2003.

COCKAYNE 2007
COCKAYNE, Emily. *Hubbub: Filth, Noise & Stench in England 1600-1770*, New Haven-London, Yale University Press, 2007.

COHEN – COHEN 2001-2002
COHEN Elizabeth S. – COHEN Thomas V. 'Open and Shut: The Social Meanings of the Cinquecento Roman House', in: *Studies in the Decorative Arts*, IX/1 (Fall-Winter 2001-2002), pp. 61-84.

CORBIN 1998
CORBIN, Alain. *Village Bells: Sound and Meaning in the 19$^{th}$-Century French Countryside*, New York, Columbia University Press, 1998 [first French edition published in 1994].

CRUSCA 1612
*Vocabolario degli Accademici della Crusca*, Venice, Giovanni Alberti, 1612.

CRUSCA 1623
*Vocabolario degli Accademici della Crusca*, Venice, Bastiano de Rossi, 1623.

CRUSCA 1686
*Vocabolario degli Accademici della Crusca*, Venice, Giovanni Giacomo Hertz, 1686.

DELL'ANTONIO 2011
DELL'ANTONIO, ANDREW. *Listening as Spiritual Practice in Early Modern Italy*, Berkeley (CA), University of California Press, 2011.

## REGULATING SOUND AND NOISE IN SEVENTEENTH-CENTURY ROME

DE LUCCA 2009
DE LUCCA, Valeria. '«Pallade al valor, Venere al volto»: Music, Theatricality, and Performance in Marie Mancini Colonna's Patronage', in: *«The Wandering Life I Led»: Essays on Hortense Mancini, Duchess Mazarin and Early Modern Women's Border-Crossings*, edited by Susan Shifrin, Cambridge, Cambridge Scholars Publishing, 2009, pp. 113-156.

DE LUCCA – JEANNERET 2019
EAD. – JEANNERET, Christine. 'Exploring the Soundscape of Early Modern Rome through Uberti's Contrasto musico', in: *The Grand Theatre of the World: Music, Space, and the Performance of Identity in Early Modern Rome*, edited by Valeria De Lucca and Christine Jeanneret, Abingdon-New York, Routledge, 2019, pp. 11-30.

DOUGLAS 1966
DOUGLAS, Mary. *Purity and Danger*, London-New York, Routledge, 1966.

EVITASCANDALO 1620
EVITASCANDALO, Cesare. *Il maestro di casa* (1598), Viterbo, Discepoli, 1620.

FAGIOLO 1997
*La Festa a Roma: dal Rinascimento al 1870*, edited by Marcello Fagiolo, 2 vols., Turin-Rome-Milan, Allemandi, 1997.

FAGIOLO DELL'ARCO 1997
FAGIOLO DELL'ARCO, Maurizio. *La festa barocca*, Rome, De Luca, 1997 (Corpus delle feste a Roma, 1).

FAGIOLO DELL'ARCO – CARANDINI 1977-1978
ID. – CARANDINI, Silvia. *L'effimero barocco. Struttura della festa nella Roma del Seicento*, 2 vols., Rome, Bulzoni, 1977-1978.

FOA 2014
FOA, Anna. *Ebrei in Europa. Dalla peste nera all'emancipazione XIV-XIX secolo*, Rome-Bari, Laterza, 2014 (Economica Laterza, 313) [first edition published in 1990].

FORNILI 1991
FORNILI, Carlo Cirillo. *Delinquenti e carcerati a Roma alla metà del '600: opera dei Papi nella riforma carceraria*, Rome, Editrice Pontificia Università Gregoriana, 1991 (Miscellanea historiae pontificiae, 59).

FOSI 2007
FOSI, IRENE. *La giustizia del papa: sudditi e tribunali nello Stato Pontificio in età moderna*, Rome-Bari, Laterza, 2007 (Biblioteca storica, 31).

GARRIOCH 2003
GARRIOCH, David. 'Sounds of the City: The Soundscape of Early Modern European Towns', in: *Urban History*, XXX/1 (2003), pp. 5-25.

GARZONI 1586
GARZONI, Tommaso. *La piazza universale di tutte le professioni del mondo*, Venice, Giovanni Battista Somasco, 1586.

GIBSON – BIDDLE 2017
*Cultural Histories of Noise, Sound and Listening in Europe, 1300-1918*, edited by Kirsten Gibson and Ian Biddle, Abingdon-New York, Routledge, 2017.

HEGARTY 2010
HEGARTY, Paul. *Noise/Music: A History*, New York-London, Continuum, 2010.

HUNT 2016
HUNT, John M. *The Vacant See in Early Modern Rome: A Social History of the Papal Interregnum*, Leiden-Boston, Brill, 2016.

JOHNSON 1995
JOHNSON, James H. *Listening in Paris: A Cultural History*, Berkeley (CA), University of California Press, 1995.

KNIGHTON – MAZUELA-ANGUITA 2018
*Hearing the City in Early Modern Europe*, edited by Tess Knighton and Ascensión Mazuela-Anguita, Turnhout, Brepols, 2018 (Epitome musical).

LIBERATI 1658
LIBERATI, FRANCESCO. *Perfetto maestro di casa*, Rome, Bernabò, 1658.

MENGOLI 1670
MENGOLI, Pietro. *Speculazioni di musica*, Bologna, Erede del Benacci, 1670.

MURATA 2005
MURATA, Margaret. 'Image and Eloquence: Secular Song', in: *The Cambridge History of Seventeenth-Century Music*, edited by Tim Carter and John Butt, Cambridge, Cambridge University Press, 2005, pp. 378-425.

MURATA 2012
EAD. '*Theatri intra theatrum*, or The Church and the Stage in 17th-Century Rome', in: *Sleuthing the Muse: Essays in Honor of William F. Prizer*, edited by Kristine K. Forney and Jeremy L. Smith, Hillsdale (NY), Pendragon, 2012, pp. 181-200.

NOVAK 2015
NOVAK, David. 'Noise' in: *Keywords in Sound: Towards a Conceptual Lexicon*, edited by David Novak and Matt Sakakeeny, Durham (NC), Duke University Press, 2015, pp. 125-138.

PERGAMINO 1602
PERGAMINO, Giacomo. *Il Memoriale della Lingua*, Venice, Ciotti, 1602.

## REGULATING SOUND AND NOISE IN SEVENTEENTH-CENTURY ROME

PETERSEN 2012
PETERSEN, Nils Holger. 'The Quarant'Ore: Early Modern Ritual and Performativity', in: *Performativity and Performance in Baroque Rome*, edited by Peter Gillgren and Mårten Snickare, Farnham, Ashgate, 2012, pp. 115-133.

PICKER 2003
PICKER, John M. 'The Soundproof Study: Victorian Professional Identity and Urban Noise', in: ID. *Victorian Soundscape*, Oxford-New York, Oxford University Press, 2003, pp. 41-81; online edn, Oxford Academic, 1 Septermber 2007, <https://academic.oup.com/book/36012>, accessed March 2023.

PICKERING – RICE 2017
PICKERING, Hugh – RICE Tom. 'Noise as «Sound Out of Place»: Investigating the Links between Mary Douglas' Work on Dirt and Sound Studies Research', 2017, <https://www.researchcatalogue.net/view/374514/374515/0/500>, accessed March 2023.

ROSSELLI 1644
ROSSELLI, Timoteo. *Della summa de' secreti universali*, Venice, Barezzi, 1644.

ROSTIROLLA 1991
UBERTI, Grazioso. *Contrasto musico: opera dilettevole*, (Rome 1630), modern edition by Giancarlo Rostirolla, Lucca, LIM, 1991 (Musurgiana, 5).

SIZER 2015
SIZER, Michael. 'Murmur, Clamor, and Tumult: The Soundscape of Revolt and Oral Culture in the Middle Ages', in: *Radical History Review*, no. 121 (2015), pp. 9-31.

SMITH 1999
SMITH, Bruce R. *The Acoustic World of Early Modern England: Attending to the O-Factor*, Chicago-London, The University of Chicago Press, 1999.

UBERTI 1630
UBERTI, Grazioso. *Contrasto musico*, Rome, Lodovico Grignani, 1630.

# *Ephemerides Itineris Romani*:
# Experiencing the Sound of Italy in Two Swiss Travel Diaries of the Seventeenth Century

*Luigi Collarile*
(Schola Cantorum Basiliensis FHNW)

### Introduction

In the imagery of travellers who crossed the Alps during the early modern era, Italy was an idyllic landscape in which an extraordinary past reverberated in a picturesque present, populated by scientists and artists, men of letters and charlatans: a unique country rich in flavours, fragrances and sounds of great beauty (Ill. 1, p. 24)[1]. This is gleaned from a vast quantity of testimonies, precious sources not only for reconstructing the personal vicissitudes of the numerous travellers who ploughed through Italy along the routes of the so-called Grand Tour, but also for capturing valuable fragments of the landscape that forms the backdrop to the narration of the extraordinary experience of the journey to Italy[2].

In the declination of itineraries, modalities and purposes of travel, it is possible to observe the complexity of a phenomenon destined to profoundly mark the cultural and aesthetic horizon of early modern European society. From the late sixteenth century onwards, the journey to Italy represented an indispensable experience for the young of noble lineage who aspired to a leading role in the society of the time. It was a fundamental stage of cultural education, a sort of initiation into the beauties of art and life in the broadest sense. The ideal focus of this veritable rite of cultural initiation was Rome, the Eternal City with its ancient and modern monuments,

---

[1]. All translations of the original German and Latin texts quoted in this study are by the author.

[2]. Among the many studies dedicated to the phenomenon of the European Grand Tour, it is worth mentioning: Brizzi 1976; Hibbert 1987; Brilli 1995; Black 2003; Babel – Paravicini 2005; Imorde – Pieper 2008; Brilli 2014; De Seta 2014; Zedler – Zedler 2019.

Ill. 1: *Italia nuovamente piu perfetta che mai per inanzi posta in luce*, Amsterdam, Hendrik Hondius, 1631. Florence, Biblioteca Nazionale Centrale.

the capital of culture and faith (Ill. 2, p. 25). In reality, however, it was a much more varied phenomenon than this stereotypical image might lead one to believe.

This article intends to consider two case studies concerning two still little-investigated typologies within the vast and varied set of journeys to Italy. The first case concerns the journey made by a Swiss nobleman, Johann Georg Wagner, who left for Rome in the spring of 1661 together with a delegation of patricians, travelling to plead for the translation of a relic. A journey made for devotional purposes could also offer an opportunity to visit the main cultural attractions of Italy. The second case concerns the stay in Italy of two young Swiss Benedictines, Father Kolumban Ochsner and Father Wolfgang Weishaupt, who studied in Rome between 1639 and 1641. Recent investigations have highlighted how the experience of travelling to Italy was not the exclusive prerogative of the lay nobility, but also involved the ecclesiastical elite, who were also called to seal their religious, cultural and personal formation in Italy[3]. The rediscovery

---

[3]. With regard to the travels of Swiss Benedictines to Italy, see ERHART 2008, ERHART – KURATLI-HÜEBLIN 2014; and ERHART – COLLARILE 2015-2016.

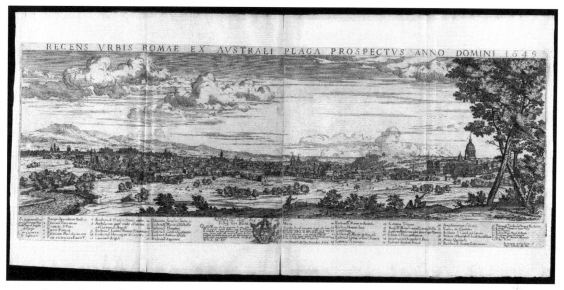

Ill. 2: Lieven Cruyl, Matteo Gregorio de Rossi, Giovanni Battista De Rossi, *Prospectus Locorum Urbis Romae*, Rome, 1666. Gent, Universiteitsbibliotheek.

of extensive documentation regarding the journeys to Italy of Benedictines from various Alpine monasteries has highlighted the extraordinary role that these experiences had in connecting the monastic environment with European culture, creating the premises for important phenomena of material and immaterial transfer of ideas, science and art[4].

These travel documents will be considered from a particular perspective: as sources for investigating the sound experience of the travellers[5]. The sound dimension is an essential part of the human experience. In travel diaries it is possible to find information about various situations connoted by sound. This is the case concerning the musical performances of religious ceremonies, but also the sound of bells marking the time or a dangerous situation, the roar of drums and cannons preluding a public event, improvised songs and dances in the street, the casual encounter of a musician in a tavern, or the noise of particular natural events[6]. The values of this varied series of sound experiences must be considered carefully, and not only with the aim of proving the documentary quality of the information transmitted in relation to the events described. If we consider the nature of testimonies — descriptions of ephemeral experiences fixed in written form after their unrepeatable acoustic manifestation —, it is evident how complicated is the question concerning the methodological approach to investigating the aural horizon of a journey: not only with regard to the identification of the events described, but

---

[4]. For investigations concerning the transfer of musical culture in Swiss monasteries see BACCIAGALUPPI 2010, CASTELLANI 2010, COLLARILE 2010; COLLARILE 2014; COLLARILE 2017.

[5]. See FABRIS 2015; FABRIS – MURATA 2015; CARTER 2018; FABRIS 2018.

[6]. See GARRIOCH 2003.

above all in defining the process by which a sound experience was converted into written form. Testimonies are never, nor can they be treated as aseptic reports of what a traveller has witnessed. The encounter with a particular event may have been fortuitous. Its recording in the travel diary, however, is the result of a deliberate selective process. The description of an experience involves the viewer's capacity of understanding of it and his ability to translate it into written form. This is a complex process, in which the cultural horizon, the personal sensibility and the aims of the writer play an essential role. In order to go beyond the mere extrapolation of a sequence of events connoted by sound, it is therefore necessary to observe these testimonies within a phenomenological perspective able to consider various aspects: the nature of the relationship between the traveller and the sound event; the cultural and aesthetic horizon of the person who listened to it and transformed it into a written report; and the purposes concerning the narration of a sound event in the perspective of the writer[7].

The two journeys examined here present interesting points of contact, but also substantial differences. Written in German, Johann Georg Wagner's travel diary is a later-elaborated memoir, printed a few years after the journey in order to celebrate the feat in which the author had taken part, alongside illustrious personalities of the Swiss Catholic patriciate. The diary written by Father Kolumban Ochsner, on the other hand, is a chronicle compiled to fulfil a specific task. Written primarily in Latin, this travel diary is a succinct description of the principal events occurring during a stay in Italy, delivered to the abbot after their return to the monastery together with other official travel documents. Preserved in the archives (not in the library), the travel diary was only accessible for reading to a few members of the monastery chapter.

In defining the social status of a traveller, his sound identity is a significant element. The departure of the delegation of Swiss noblemen was greeted solemnly. The public acknowledgements continued on the way to the Alps, only to cease later, making the identity of the travelling group of foreigners no longer recognisable. On the contrary, the journey of the two Benedictines was completely anonymous and silent. Identifiable by the monk's habit they wore, they crossed Italy mingled with other anonymous travellers in transit, sharing with them postal coaches, makeshift shelters, and meals in a tavern.

The routes followed by the two groups of travellers are similar. Both crossed the St Gotthard Pass and reached Rome after passing through Milan, Bologna and Florence. On the return journey, the delegation of Swiss patricians left Rome and crossed the Apennines to reach Venice; then, after travelling across the Po Valley to Milan, they continued on to the Alps. This was perhaps also the route followed by the two Benedictine monks, whose return journey to Switzerland is not reported in their travel diary.

In both cases, the travels to and from Rome lasted about a month. The time spent in Rome, however, was substantially different. The delegation of Swiss patricians stayed only a few

---

[7]. See PEROCCO 1997.

weeks. The two Benedictines lived in Rome for almost two years. The different length of stay substantially influenced the possibility of the foreigners to interact with the urban soundscape of the city.

Reporting in writing ephemeral sound experiences requires a complex elaboration process that must be considered from the perspective of the writer, considering his knowledge to understand what he heard, his ability to transform it into written form, and the aims he pursues in describing particular events of his journey, connoted by sound[8]. The sound dimension often emphasises the importance of certain events. This is the case of sumptuous performances during important ceremonies or particular festivities attended by the travellers. The evocation of the sonic dimension can also refer to an emotionally significant event: the sign of astonishment, which — like a sort of soundtrack — underlines something extraordinary experienced by a traveller during his journey.

## A Swiss Delegation in Rome in 1661

In the spring of 1661, Johann Georg Wagner (1624-1691) arrived in Rome together with a delegation of Swiss patricians to prepare the translation of an important relic, the body of St Remigius, for the church of Stans (Canton Nidwalden). Excavations carried out in the Roman catacombs from the late sixteenth century onwards had made available a harvest of relics, which fuelled a vast devotional trade. The recognition of a relic required a specific process, after which it could be assigned to a church. The modalities of its transfer then had to be agreed upon, including an appropriate festive programme[9].

The journey of the Swiss delegation is described in a small book compiled by Wagner and published in 1664 under the title *Italienische Sommer- oder Römer Reyss* (Ill. 3, p. 28)[10]. At the time of departure, Wagner was by no means the young scion of a patrician family leaving for an educational journey to Italy. Invested with the title of knight, he held the position of 'Stadtschreiber' of Solothurn and was a member of the city government. The patrician Johann Melchior Löuw was responsible for the translation of the relic. The delegation left Lucerne on 18 April 1661. After crossing the Canton Uri, they travelled over the St Gotthard Pass, then to Bellinzona, Como, and on 30 April to Milan. They then reached Piacenza, Parma, Modena, Bologna, Florence and Viterbo, arriving in Rome on 18 May. Here the Swiss patricians were welcomed by Cardinal Francesco Barberini, *Protector Helvetiae* and their main contact at the Roman curia[11].

---

[8]. See Agnew 2008.

[9]. For investigations regarding the phenomenon of relics in early modern Switzerland, see Achermann 1979.

[10]. Wagner 1664.

[11]. See *ibidem*, p. 49.

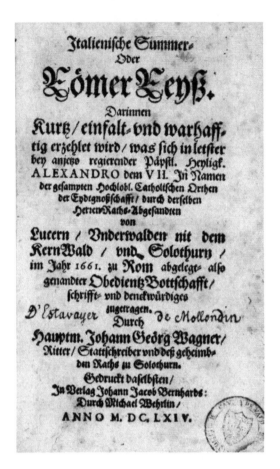

Ill. 3: Johann Georg Wagner, *Italienische Sommer- oder Römer Reyss*, Solothurn, Johann Jacob Bernhard, 1664: title page. Bern, Burgbibliothek.

During the two months spent in Rome, in addition to the audiences concerning the recognition process of the relic, Wagner and the other Swiss travellers visited the main churches and monuments of the city. At the beginning of July, they resumed the return journey. They did not, however, follow the same route they took on the outward journey. From Rome, they eaded to Terni, then passed through Spoleto, Foligno, Assisi, Tolentino, Recanati, Loreto, Fano, Rimini, and finally reached Venice (Ill. 4, p. 29). After a short stay, they resumed their journey to Padua, Vicenza, Verona, Brescia, Bergamo, Crema and Como. After crossing the St Gotthard Pass, they reached Lucerne. Johann Georg Wagner's travel ended with his arrival in Solothurn on 31 July 1661.

Events explicitly marked by sound are not numerous in the travel report published by Wagner three years later. In fact, the aural experience is a secondary aspect in the narration of the journey, emerging only in relation to particular events. It is interesting to observe, however, some of the dynamics that the sound dimension highlights.

Ill. 4: *Atlas curieux oder Neuer und Compendieuser Atlas*, Augsburg, Gabriel Bodenehr, 1704. Luzern, Zentral- und Hochschulbibliothek.

The departure of the delegation was celebrated solemnly, with trumpet blasts and festive bells. The public ceremony emphasised the official nature of the journey, requiring an appropriate public recognition. After leaving Lucerne, the delegation's passage was greeted on Swiss territory with public demonstrations marked by sound. Having crossed the Alps, they gradually became part of the indistinct stream of foreign travellers directed to Rome. The silencing of the public manifestations made the process of gradual anonymisation of journey of the Swiss delegation particularly tangible.

In the narration of the travel to Rome, events connoted by sound are almost completely absent. Except in rare cases, the noise of the landscape or urban life was not reported in the travel diaries. As ordinary events, they were not evoked within the reports, which generally refer only to extraordinary aspects of the travel experiences through the Belpaese. There is, however, also another aspect to be given due consideration. The relative rapidity with which travellers moved, indulging only in short stays in a city, prevented them in many cases from interacting with the local soundscape[12].

---

[12]. The relationship between travel time and sound perception was investigated in Collarile, *The Sound of the Venetian Terraferma* and Collarile, *Il suono di Milano*.

Concerning the perception of sound, the situation changes substantially in the time spent in Rome. The discovery of the rich urban ceremonial, closely linked to the liturgical and devotional calendar, leads travellers to gradually appreciate the sound dimension of the environment as well. This also happened to Wagner. Although the attention to the sonic dimension was not among his primary interests, his travel diary contains several reports concerning sound experiences.

One of the first sonically connoted events reported by Wagner in his travel diary was an exclusive ceremony in which the Swiss delegation — thanks to the recommendation of the captain of the Papal Guard — was able to participate. On 5 June 1661, Pentecost Sunday, Wagner and the other Swiss patricians attended a solemn mass celebrated at the Sistine Chapel in the presence of the Pope, Clement IX, and the college of Cardinals (ILL. 5, p. 31). In his diary, Wagner noted that he heard a «heroic choir composition performed by 15 or 16 of the best voices»[13]. He was impressed by the musical repertoire he listened to. The number of singers he saw on the choir loft, located in the middle of the nave, was accurately indicated. But it is not obvious what constituted the «heroic» aspect of the performance. According to the specific liturgical ceremonial, the Sistine Chapel, directed at that time by Mario Savioni, performed at the offertory the motet *Cum complerentur* by Giovanni Pierluigi da Palestrina, the main *auctoritas* of the specific repertoire of the papal chapel[14]. The expression used by Wagner could be an inexperienced attempt by a layman to describe the sophisticated music he listened to.

In the afternoon, together with Cardinal Pietro Vidoni, the Swiss delegation went to hear one of Rome's greatest musical attractions: the vespers at the church of Sant'Apollinare with music performed by the chapel of the Collegio Germanico, conducted at the time by the famous Jesuit Giacomo Carissimi[15]. Wagner could not fail to remark on the extraordinary performance he listened to: «But the musicians of Sant'Apollinare in Collegio Germano, where Cardinal

---

[13].    WAGNER 1664, p. 65: «Wüßten hierbey nit ob wir die Majestät Ihr Heyligt. oder die stattliche Ordnung aller anwesenden Cardinälen und derselben ansehenlichen Auffzug / oder aber das heroische choral Gesang von 15. oder 16. der allerbesten Stimmen mehrers verwunderen sollten?».

[14].    See ADAMI 1711, pp. 71-72: «La Mattina alla Messa. Cap. XXV. Non ha questa Funzione cosa di particolare osservazione, si che dee regolarsi come le altre Messe ordinarie. Celebra in questa Mattina un Cardinal Vescovo. Terminata l'Epistola il Signor Maestro farà dire con sollecitudine l'*Alleluia* con il primo Verso del Graduale, indi l'altro *Alleluia* da due Soprani nel tempo del quale il Papa scende dal Trono, e s'inginocchia avanti al Faldisotrio, e deposta la Mitra i due Soprani suddetti intonanto il Verso *Veni Sancte Spiritus*, il quale con la seguenza, e l'*Alleluia* dovrà durare sin tanto, che il Papa tornato al Soglio abbia letto l'Epistola, e l'Evangelio, e poi posto l'incenso nel Turibile, e che il Diacono abbia presa da Sua Santità la benedizione, e sia giunto al luogo dell'Evangelio. Il Mottetto all'Offertorio *Cum complerentur* è del Palestrina la libro 96. a carte 11. con la seconda parte, la quale si suol dire, e si termina al solito degli altri Mottetti, Se Sua Santità non assiste alla Messa tutta la Funzione si regola col Celebrante, il quale al Verso *Veni Sancte Spiritus* s'inginocchia avanti al Faldistorio, e la Funzione è tutta andante». The participation in the ceremonies at the Sistine Chapel during Holy Week was highly coveted by foreign travellers. On that occasion it was possible to hear the famous *Miserere* by Gregorio Allegri; see SCHILTZ 2016.

[15].    See CULLEY 1970.

Ill. 5: Giovanni Ambrogio Brambilla, *Speculum Romanae Magnificentiae*, 1582: Sistine Chapel. New York, The Metropolitan Museum of Art.

Vidone and we went to attend vespers, could be surpassed [in ability] for little or nothing in their kind»[16].

The following Sunday was the Feast of the Holy Trinity. Wagner attended the solemn celebrations held at the church of Ss. Trinità degli Spagnoli, where he could hear «beautiful music», performed not only in the church, but also outside the building where the Swiss delegation resided[17]. A week later, on 19 June, Wagner returned to the church of Sant'Apollinare to attend Sunday mass. On this occasion, he appreciated the performance of «stately music divided into three choirs»[18]. Again, Wagner probably listened to compositions by Carissimi or works belonging to the repertoire of the local chapel, performed under the direction of the celebrated Jesuit musician. Performances with three choirs were an usual practice at Sant'Apollinare in solemn ceremonies such as the one planned for the feast of Ss. Gervasio and Protasio, also explicitly mentioned in the main travel guides for foreigners[19]; but for a Swiss traveller such as Wagner, this particular kind of execution was a noteworthy episode. After the verspers at Sant'Apollinare, Wagner came across a procession in the parish of St Louis of the French, where he met two Cardinals: a symptomatic episode of the widespread presence of devotional celebrations that a foreigner could encounter in Rome[20].

A traveller who was in town at the end of June could not fail to attend the extraordinary celebrations for the feast of Ss. Peter and Paul. They began on the evening of 28 June, with solemn vespers celebrated at St Peter in the Vatican in the presence of the pope. The liturgical ceremony was concluded with the homage of a «chinea» by the Spanish ambassador, in the presence of a large number of knights who paraded in sumptuous uniforms through the streets of Rome. The «cavalcada Spagnola» and other rituals of the feast, culminating in the spectacular «girandola» of fireworks fired from Castel Sant'Angelo, are described in Wagner's diary (ILL. 6, p. 33)[21]. The music that the Swiss patrician heard at St Peter in the Vatican during the solemn vespers received a special mention: «In the evening, [we were] at St Peter's, where vespers and other religious services were celebrated with sweet music in a magnificent manner»[22].

---

16. WAGNER 1664, p. 65: «Denen aber die Musicanten bey St. Apollinare in Collegio Germano, darbey Herr Cardinal Vidone und wir zu der Vesper Zeit erschienen / in suo genere wenig oder gar nichts bevorgehen».

17. *Ibidem*, p. 70: «Ferners die stattliche Music bey den Spanischen Religiosen S.S. Trinitatis, an selbigen hochheyligen Fest nächst an unserem Pallast».

18. *Ibidem*, p. 72: «Da wir Sontags den 19. Dito nacher St. Appollinar den Gottsdienst und selbige stattliche zu 3. Choren abgetheylte Music abermahl anzuhören uns verfügt / haben wir die Procession der Französischen Kirchgenossen zu S. Luigi underwegs angetroffen».

19. See *GUIDA ANGELICA PERPETUA* 1634, p. 26: «19 [Giugno] ss. Gervasio, e Protasio mart[iri] festa alla chiesa delli Gesuiti [...]». About the performance of music in Roman churches around 1650 see BERGLUND 2012.

20. For the music in the church of St Louis of the French see CILIBERTI 2016.

21. See WAGNER 1664, pp. 86-87.

22. *Ibidem*, p. 89: «Auff den abend gen St. Peter allwo die Vesper mit lieblicher Music gehalten / und andere Kirchendienst stattlich versehen worden».

Ill. 6: *The Girandola at the Castel Sant'Angelo*. Rome, Matteo Gregorio Rossi, 1692. New York, The Metropolitan Museum of Art.

On 1 July 1661, Wagner attended the Litanies at the church of S. Maria Maggiore. Two aspects caught the attention of the Swiss traveller: the devotion of people present, both men and women, and the extraordinary beauty and power of the voice of a castrato of the local chapel, who sang in church («It was difficult to decide whether we should be more surprised by the devotion of the men and women present, or by a discantist who made his own voice and singing mastery heard in a powerful way»)[23].

It is not possible to determine whether Wagner's visit to these churches was the result of a casual or conscious choice. Information about the religious ceremonial of the city was provided in many travel guides for foreign travellers. They could 'pre-structure' the expectations of a visitor by providing information also about the music and other aspect of the local soundscape. It is likely that Wagner learnt from one of these guides that it was possible

---

[23]. *Ibidem*, p. 91: «köndten schwerlich entscheiden ob wir mehrers die Andacht desbeywesenden Mann- und Weibervolcks oder aber einen Discantisten / der sein Stimm und Singkunst gewaltig hören lassen / verwunderen solten».

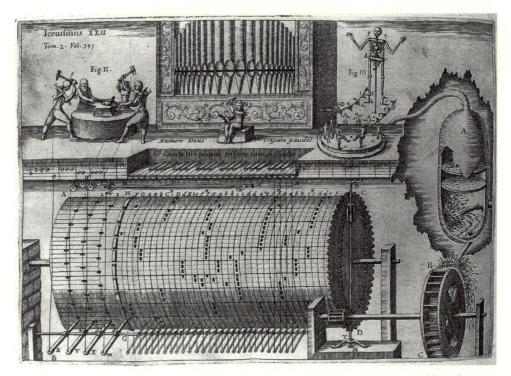

ILL. 7: Athanasius Kircher, *Musurgia universalis sive ars magna consoni et dissoni in x libros digesta*, Tomo II (Books VIII-X), Rome, Ludovico Grignani, 1650 p. 347: *Machinamentum IX*. Zürich, Zentralbibliothek.

to listen to beautiful music at the Chiesa Nuova: an experience, however, he was unable to enjoy himself[24]. When, on the morning of 7 June 1661, he visited the church officiated by the Philippines, no musical performance was scheduled. He himself reported this in his diary with disappointment, compensated by the following description of his visit to the Collegio Romano in the afternoon, when he met the «venerable, highly cultured and very famous mathematician» Athanasius Kircher and visited his celebrated «galeria» (ILL. 7)[25]. It was undoubtedly one of the most exclusive locations in Rome, as was the Villa Belvedere, in whose splendid gardens an extraordinary water organ could be admired and listened to: a great attraction for high-ranking tourists who — like Wagner and the other members of the Swiss delegation — were able to obtain access to the villa[26].

---

[24]. *Ibidem*, p. 69: «Erstlichen die schöne newe Kirchen S. Philippi Nerei, chiesa Noua genandt / auch desselben H. Capellen und Begräbnuß / allda etliche Musicanten sich treffenlich hören lassen».

[25]. *Ibidem*: «Disemnach deß Ehrwürdigen Hochgelehrten und weitberühmbten Mathematici R. P. Athanasij Kilchers Soc. Iesu. Kunstreiche und mit allerhand wunderliche sachen angefüllte galeria in Collegio Romano».

[26]. *Ibidem*, p. 82: «In einem Zimmer unfer von dannen der Heydnische Gott Apollo sampt den 9. Musis in Parnasso sizend deren jede ein besonderes Instrument in Handen haltend / sampt einer Orgel allein von dem Wasser und Wind angestim[m]et / zusamen spielen». The visit took place on 25 July 1661.

In Wagner's diary, there are episodes that diverge from a certain stereotypical narrative of the journey to Italy. One of these concerns the feast that the captain of the Papal Guard, Franz Pfyffer (a patrician from Lucerne), organised at his residence on the evening of 4 July to greet the Swiss delegation before starting the return journey. The private event was graced «by a magnific concert of instruments of all kinds»[27].

This scene is interesting also from another perspective. As soon as they arrived in Rome, Swiss travellers could find a first important reception point in the quarters of the Papal Guard. Here they could take care of some bureaucratic matters and plan their stay in the city. Later, thanks to the relationships that the Papal Guard enjoyed, they could obtain a privileged access to the Vatican palaces and participate at many important liturgical ceremonies, where access would otherwise have been very difficult.

The quarter of the Papal Guard was a strategic transit point not only for Swiss travellers, but also for goods to and from Switzerland. An emblematic case concerns a series of music editions by the famous virtuoso Girolamo Frescobaldi, the main organist at St Peter in the Vatican. In January 1647, Johann Rudolf Pfyffer (1611-1657), lieutenant of the Papal Guard in Rome, wrote to his cousin Alexander Pfyffer in Lucerne, announcing that he had successfully completed the purchase of «all the works by Girolamo Frescobaldi» («Tutte le opere del Girolamo Frescovaldi»), which he had required[28]. Pfyffer's letter is preserved in the archives of the Cistercian monastery of St Urban (Lucerne). It is there that the editions by Frescobaldi were deposited, as indicated in the inventory of the monastery's music collection, compiled in 1661[29]. Of particular interest is a paragraph of the letter, in which Pfyffer regretted not having sent the music editions to Lucerne sooner, entrusting them to the abbot of the monastery in Kempten, who was in Rome until a few days before. Pfyffer assured his cousin, promising that he would entrust the music books to the first person heading for Switzerland, perhaps to the captain of the Papal Guard himself, Nikolaus Fleckenstein, if he decided to return to Lucerne for a rest. Wagner's travel diary makes no mention of such missions. It is possible, however, that the Swiss delegation also had the unofficial task of carrying a few letters or some other goods: probably, a customary practice, although rarely documented because of its informal and often casual kind.

During the short time Wagner spent in Rome, besides the official meetings related to the practice for the translation of the relic, he attended religious ceremonies in various churches like any foreign tourist and visited the most important monuments of the city. However, considering the purpose of the journey of the Swiss delegation, the decision not to return to Switzerland by the shortest route, the one followed on the outward journey, but to make a long diversion to

---

[27]. *Ibidem*, p. 93: «in seinem Losament mit einem stattlichen Concert von allerhand Instrumenten».

[28]. See BACCIAGALUPPI – COLLARILE 2013.

[29]. For a critical edition of the inventory see BACCIAGALUPPI – COLLARILE 2010. Frescobaldi's editions are listed under nos. 053 and 063-067.

reach Venice, may seem surprising. In fact, even a journey with a specific devotional purpose could offer an opportunity to make a cultural trip through the beauties of Italy, along the usual routes taken at the time by numerous foreign tourists.

Wagner's report of the return journey is devoid of episodes connoted by sound, with one interesting exception. Considering the rich urban ceremonial of Venice and the numerous performances of music, it is not surprising that Wagner reported in his diary an episode connoted by sound. After going to the Benedictine monastery of St Giorgio Maggiore, the Swiss patricians visited a female monastery, where they listened to «beautiful music»[30]. Neither the location nor the day (shortly after mid-July) are specified in Wagner's diary. It was probably the monastery of St Roch and St Margherita. For the feast for St Margherita, scheduled for 20 July, the Augustinian nuns organised solemn ceremonies. As was usual in Venice, the feast for the patron saint included a rich musical programme. The Swiss travellers might have learnt about these ceremonies from a guidebook for foreigners, an essential tool for immediately connecting with the local urban and devotional ceremonial of Venice that was very rich in sound[31].

## TWO SWISS BENEDICTINES IN ROME BETWEEN 1639 AND 1641

On 1 October 1639, two young Benedictines, Father Kolumban Ochsner (ca. 1610-1658) and Father Wolfgang Weishaupt (ca. 1608-1676), left the monastery of Einsiedeln (Canton Schwyz) to travel to Rome[32]. Their journey had some precise purposes. In addition to deepening their Italian language skills and theological knowledge, they wished to study law at the *Studio della Sapienza* and undertake some diplomatic missions on behalf of the monastery[33]. The two Benedictines stayed in Italy for almost two years. The documentation relating to their travel to Italy includes the travel diary written by Father Ochsner, covering the first ten months of their journey (ILL. 8, p. 36)[34]; a letter to the Abbot of Einsiedeln, Father Plazidus Reimann (1594-1670), signed from Rome by both Benedictines on 6 July 1641; and a laissez-passer, granted to

---

[30]. WAGNER 1664, p. 115: «Disemnach besuchten wir eine auff Seiten der Statt gelegene schöne Kirchen S. Georgij und andere / höreten in einem Frawen Kloster ein stattliche Music». Concerning musical activity in the female monasteries of Venice see QUARANTA 1998 and GLIXON 2017.

[31]. Concerning musical performances in the urban ceremonial of Venice, see GLIXON 2003 and BRYANT – QUARANTA 2015.

[32]. For a portrait of the two Benedictines, see HENGGELER 1930, *ad nomen*.

[33]. See ADORNI – ONORI – VENZO 2017. On the specific case concerning the *cursus studiorum* followed in Rome by the Swiss Benedictines see ERHART 2008; ERHART – KURATLI-HÜEBLIN 2014; ERHART – COLLARILE 2015-2016.

[34]. Einsiedeln, Stiftsarchiv, A.PC.13 (d'ora in poi, OCHSNER, *Diary*). Unnumbered sheets.

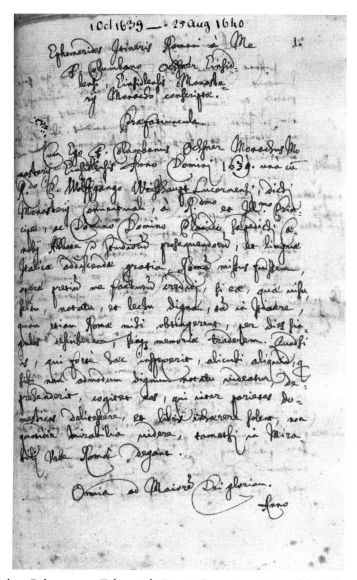

Ill. 8: Kolumban Ochsner osb, *Ephemerides Itineris Romani*, p. 1. Einsiedeln, Stiftsarchiv.

the two monks by Cardinal Francesco Barberini on 2 October 1641[35]. Unlike the journey of the Swiss delegation mentioned above, the travel diary of the two Benedictines was neither printed nor made public. Written in Latin (and then, in the final part, in Italian), it is part of the official documentation of their stay in Italy.

After leaving the monastery, the two Benedictines reached Lucerne, where they met the apostolic nuncio Girolamo Farnese. The next day they stayed overnight in Altdorf (Canton

---

[35]. Respectively, Einsiedeln, Stiftsarchiv, A.PC.15 and A.PC.14.

Uri). The following day, they crossed the St Gotthard Pass and reached Bellinzona, then Lugano, Mendrisio, arriving in Milan on 9 October. After a short visit to the tomb of St Carlo Borromeo, they resumed their journey to Piacenza, Bologna, Florence, Siena and Viterbo, reaching Rome on the evening of 25 October 1639.

Even in the case of Father Ochsner's diary, the narration of the travel to Rome is almost completely devoid of references to sound events. The only exception is the singing of a *Salve regina*, which the two Benedictines intoned as a sign of thanksgiving after reaching the St Gotthard Pass[36]. The most frequently expression used in the first part of the diary is «vidimus» («we have seen»), followed by succinct descriptions of the locations they visited. With the arrival in Rome, the narration progressively changes. The episodes connoted by sound become quantitatively more numerous.

In Father Ochsner's diary, the attention to the sound dimension is not a priority. However, the interest of the two Swiss Benedictines in sacred music performed in the churches of Rome is evident. Both monks probably had musical knowledge, music being an essential part of the cultural education promoted by the order. There is no information of their active participation in musical performances during their stay in Italy. But some situations, such as the private concert held by a theorbo virtuoso in their residence, highlight the quality of the contacts they had with the Roman musical environment, perhaps only partly documented in the travel diary.

Once in Rome, the two Benedictines reached the residence of the Papal Guard, where they spent the first night, after being welcomed by the captain, Nikolaus Fleckenstein, a member of another patrician family from Lucerne. The next day, they settled in the residence of the procurator of the Anglican Benedictine Congregation, Wilfrid Selby[37]. At that time, the English Benedictine held the position of procurator of the Swiss Benedictine Congregation in Rome[38]. As with other English religious, he probably resided at the Venerable English College, in the central Via di Monserrato. This is where the two Swiss Benedictines would have lived during the almost two years they spent in Rome.

After settling into their accommodation, the two Benedictines started to visit Rome. First they went to the sumptuous St Peter's Basilica in the Vatican, at that time a brand new monument of Catholicism (ILL. 9, p. 39). Here, on the evening of 27 October 1639, they attended vespers for the eve of the feast of the Holy Apostles Simon and Jude. Father Ochsner noted in his diary only a ritual peculiarity, which surprised the two Swiss monks. At the recitation of the verse

---

[36]. OCHSNER, *Diary*, 6 October 1639: «In monte Sancti Gothardi missae interfuimus, et unum Salve Regina decantavimus».

[37]. *Ibidem*, 26 October 1639: «Demum accessimus adhuc R. P. Ioannem Wilfridum Anglum, Congregationis Benedictinae Anglicanae Procuratorem qui benignè nos excipiens, et petitionibus nostris annuens, domum suam, imò omnia sua ad usum et comoditatem nostram nobis obtulit».

[38]. In this function, Father Selby oversaw the purchase of the main altarpiece for the church of the Benedictine Abbey of St Gallen (Switzerland) in 1644: see VOGLER 1979.

Ill. 9: Viviano Codazzi, *Basilica of St Peter in the Vatican*, 1630 *ca*. Madrid, Museo del Prado.

«Sit nomen Domini benedictum» from Psalm 113, the celebrants made the same reverence that was usually made at the «Gloria Patri»[39].

They returned to St Peter's Basilica three days later, where they attended another solemn vespers[40]. Evidently on both occasions the two Benedictines listened to the performances of the Cappella Giulia, at that time directed by Virgilio Mazzocchi, with the famous Girolamo Frescobaldi at the monumental organ of the basilica[41]. However, the attention of the two young Swiss monks was not yet focused on listening. It is a sensory awareness that gradually emerges in the succinct notes with which Father Ochsner described his experiences during the months spent in Rome. It progresses along with the discovery of the extraordinary urban ceremonial, consisting of a sumptuous programme of devotional celebrations and public and private events,

---

[39]. For investigations on the role of the Venerable English College within the framework of foreign religious institutions in early modern Rome, see Fosi 2021.

[40]. Ochsner, *Diary*, 30 June 1639: «[...] vespere Vesperis longe elegantissimis apud S. Petrum interfuimus».

[41]. See Rostirolla 2014, p. 300.

often marked by sound. Three weeks later, on 17 November, Father Ochsner noted in his diary that he had again attended vespers at St Peter's Basilica, where he could listen to beautiful music[42]. It was the discovery of a new sensory dimension. A month later, on 18 December, the Benedictine observed that the first and last verses of the hymn planned for Vespers were not played at the organ *alternatim*, as usual, but sung by the choir: it was a particular performance practice, which caught the attention of the Swiss monk[43].

During their stay in Rome, the two Swiss Benedictines had a privileged relationship with the Jesuit environment[44]. They attended various theological activities at the Collegio Germanico and participated in numerous devotional celebrations. It was a very important time for the Society of Jesus. On 27 September 1639, a solemn ceremony held in the Church of the Gesù, sumptuously embellished at the expense of Cardinal Antonio Barberini, nephew of Pope Urban VIII, opened the Jesuit Secular Year[45] (ILL. 10, p. 41). The two Swiss Benedictines witnessed several of the extraordinary celebrations organised between 1639 and 1640 to celebrate the centenary of the foundation of the Society of Jesus.

The two monks visited the Church of the Gesù for the first time on 16 November 1639. For them, it was the feast of St Othmar, illustrious abbot of the monastery of St Gallen[46]. They did not celebrate the occasion in a Benedictine church, but attended the solemn ceremonies scheduled for the first of three days during which the Jesuits celebrated the benefactors of the Society. For the occasion, a sumptuous catafalque was built in the church. Designed by Andrea Sacchi, it was «very high with four pyramids on the sides with many inscriptions, statues and figures representing dead bodies of bones, made of cardboard: and the whole church was adorned in black from the vault to the ground. But the cloths were not entirely black. The pillars remained white [...] so that the decoration would appear gloomy at once, and cheerful»[47]. The two Swiss monks went to the Gesù Church for three days to attend the celebrations. Father Ochsner was impressed by the pomp of the ceremonies, but made no mention of the musical performances in his diary. The first reference to musical performances heard in the Church

---

[42]. OCHSNER, *Diary*, 17 November 1639: «Sequenti die frequentavimus Vespera apud S. Petrum, eo quod fuerit dedicatio eius Ecclesiae. Fuit ivi praestantissima Musica».

[43]. *Ibidem*, 18 December 1639: «Fuimus et apud Sm. Petrum in vesperis, ubi notavimus primum et ultimum Hymni versum non ab Organo sea a choro decantari».

[44]. On the role of music making and singing in the Jesuit education see FILIPPI 2015 and FILIPPI 2017.

[45]. See FAGIOLO DELL'ARCO 1997, pp. 310-311. Regarding the musical activity in the Church of the Gesù see CULLEY 1970, DIXON 1980 and BASSANI 2012.

[46]. OCHSNER, *Diary*, 16 November 1639: «In festo S. Othmari frequentavimus solemne illud anniversarium, quod celebrarunt PP. Societatis Jesu in Domo professa à Giesù».

[47]. GIGLI 1994, vol. I (1608-1644), p. 323: «Et fecero un Catafalco altissimo con quattro piramidi nelle Cantonate con molte Scrittioni, et Statue, et figure rappresentanti corpi morti di ossa fatti di cartone: et tutta la Chiesa apparata di negro dalla volta sino a terra, ma però non erano i panni neri intieri, ma rimanevano i pilastri bianchi [...] acciò comparisse l'apparato mesto insieme, et allegro». See FAGIOLO DELL'ARCO 1997, pp. 311-312.

Ill. 10: Andrea Sacchi, Jan Miel, Filippo Gagliardi, *Urban VIII Visiting the Church of the Gesù during the Centenary Celebrations of the Jesuit Order*, 1639. Rome, Galleria Nazionale d'Arte Antica di Palazzo Barberini.

of the Gesù can be read in the description of the solemn vespers on the eve of the feast of St Francis Xavier, celebrated on 1 December 1639 on the 20th anniversary of the beatification of the Jesuit[48]. The music, performed with four choirs, was «so elegant», wrote the Benedictine in his diary, «that we will never hear the like again in our lifetime»[49].

Father Ochsner noted the magnificence of the celebrations at the Church of the Gesù also on another occasion. Between 17 and 19 February 1640, the church hosted a sumptuous *Teatro delle Quarant'Ore* designed by Niccolò Menghini (and maybe Gian Lorenzo Bernini), at the expense of the Congregation of the Blessed Virgin of the Assumption. The building was imposing: about 27 metres high, 16 metres wide and 13 metres deep, it could be moved by about forty people[50]. The two Swiss Benedictines first went to the adoration of the Blessed Sacrament at the Basilica of St Peter. Then they reached the Church of the Gesù. The comparison between the two ceremonies was merciless: «At St Peter's on the altar where the Blessed Sacrament was exposed, about 200 candles were burning; more than 3,000 at the Church of the Gesù»[51].

The regular attendance at theological activities promoted at the Collegio Germanico gave the two Benedictines the opportunity to hear several times the local music chapel, conducted by Giacomo Carissimi. They listened to it for the first time on 25 November 1639. It was the feast of St Catherine. As with other celebrations the two Benedictines attended during the first weeks after their arrival in Rome, Father Ochsner did not provide information about what he heard during the celebrations. He did so, in enthusiastic terms, a few weeks later. On Sunday 13 December 1639, during vespers for the feast of St Lucy, the Swiss monk wrote in his diary that he had heard «beautiful music» performed by the chapel of the Collegio Germanico (ILL. 11, p. 43)[52]. The two Swiss Benedictines returned to Sant'Apollinare on Sunday 15 January 1640. It was the feast of St Maurus Abbot, solemnly celebrated by the Benedictine order at the Abbey of St Paul Outside the Walls[53]. The two Benedictines, however, did not visit the great Benedictine basilica along the Via Ostiense. They tried, unsuccessfully, to celebrate a mass in honour of St Maurus at the Basilica of St John in Lateran. After lunch, they went to the Collegio

---

[48]. OCHSNER, *Diary*, 2 December 1639: «In festo S. Francisci Xaverii interfuimus Missae solemni et Vesperis in dictae domus professae PP. Soc. Jesu Ecclesia a Giesù».

[49]. *Ibidem*, 1 December 1639: «[...] in Vesperis in domo professa PP. Societatis Jesu, et ibi audivimus Musicam 4 Choris tam elegantem, qualem tota vita nostra nunquam audieramus». About the performance of polychoral music in the Church of the Gesù, see CULLEY 1970, DIXON 1980 and BASSANI 2012.

[50]. See FAGIOLO DELL'ARCO 1997, pp. 314-316.

[51]. OCHSNER, *Diary*, 19 February 1640: «[...] Apud S. Petrum in altari, in quo expositum erat *Sanctissimu*m Sacramentum, ardebant plus quam 200 luminaria. al Giesù vero plus quam 3000».

[52]. *Ibidem*, 13 December 1639: «In festo S. Luciae [...] interfuimus Vesperis in Collegio Germanico, ubi Musica praestantissima erat».

[53]. See *GUIDA ANGELICA PERPETUA* 1634, p. 5: «15 [gennaio] s. Mauro Abbate, festa a s. Paolo, e per tutto l'Ordine di s. Benedetto [...]».

Ill. 11: Giuseppe Vasi, *Delle Magnificenze di Roma antica e moderna*, Rome, s.n., ca. 1747: Sant'Apollinare's Church and Collegio Germanico. Luzern, Zentral- und Hochschulbibliothek.

Germanico. The Sunday Vespers at the church of Sant'Apollinare were a celebrated event for the quality of the performances of the local chapel. Father Ochsner wrote in his diary that the music was «most elegant». After the vespers, he attended the theological dissertation of an Alsatian student in the Collegio Germanico[54].

A few months later, on 23 July 1640, the Swiss Benedictines took part in the solemn celebrations for the feast of St Apollinaris, celebrated with great pomp in the Jesuit church dedicated to the saint. The reason they attended the service is mentioned in an emblematic note in Italian that Father Ochsner entered in his diary: «Fummo alla Musica all'Apollinare» («We were at the music at [the church of] Sant'Apollinare»)[55].

The last great celebration entered by Father Ochsner in his diary on 7 August 1640 was the solemn ceremony commemorating the first mass in the church of St Ignatius,

---

[54]. OCHSNER, *Diary*, 15 January 1640: «Post prandium interfuimus Vesperis in Collegio Germanico, ubi elegantissimam Musicam audivimus, et notavimus ad illum psal. 113 versum: Non nobis Domine, non nobis, sed nomini tua da gloriam, eandem reverentiam fieri quae fit ad Gloriam Patri. Post vesperas in aula eiusdem Collegii».

[55]. *Ibidem*, 23 July 1640.

sponsored by the prefect of Rome, Taddeo Barberini[56]. The Swiss monk reported that the mass, celebrated by the Father General of the Society of Jesus, was accompanied by «solemn music with four choirs»[57].

During the months spent in Rome, the two Benedictines visited many other churches, in several cases attending sumptuous musical performances. On 7 November 1639, they took part in a solemn celebration in honour of the dead of the French nation in the church of St Louis of the French. For this occasion, a sumptuous *castrum doloris* was erected in the church. The music performed during the ceremony was magnificent[58].

On Sunday 29 November, after celebrating mass in the chapel of their residence, the two Swiss went to the Collegio Romano to hear a theological disputation. Then, in the afternoon, they attended the vespers celebrated at the church of Sant'Andrea della Valle, officiated by the Theatine Fathers, where they listened to «beautiful music»[59]. On 17 January 1640, they participated in the ceremony for the feast of St Anthony Abbot, at the church dedicated to the saint, in the Esquilino. Here they assisted at the customary blessing of donkeys and horses. Then they went to the nearby basilica of Santa Maria Maggiore, where they heard «wonderful music» during vespers[60].

During Lent, the Swiss monks visited several churches for the adoration of the Quarant'Ore[61]. On 13 February 1640, they went to the church of St Francis Xavier, near the Collegio Romano. The devotional action was accompanied by «beautiful music and sermons»[62]. Good sermons and music could be heard also at St Maria in Vallicella, called Chiesa Nova, officiated by the Philippine Fathers. The two Benedictines visited the church for the first time on 12 March 1640, on the feast of St Gregory Pope: since 1628 the church hosted the head of the saint[63]. They returned there on the evening of Sunday 1 April 1640, «to hear the Music and

---

[56].    See FAGIOLO DELL'ARCO 1997, pp. 316-318.

[57].    OCHSNER, *Diary*, 7 August 1640: «In Ecclesia dei Giesuiti iam Missam celebravit eorum generalis. Postmodum fuit Missa solennis cum Musica 4. Chor. vespere». See DIXON 1980 and BASSANI 2012.

[58].    *Ibidem*, 7 November 1639: «Galli omnes, qui in Vrbe erant [...] in Ecclesia S. Ludovici Officio Defunctorum solemnissime decantato et erecto castro doloris magnificentissimo [...] fecerunt».

[59].    *Ibidem*, 29 November 1639: «Interfuimus et Vesperis apud S. Andream ad Theatinos, ubi pulcherrimam Musicam audivimus».

[60].    *Ibidem*, 17 January 1640: «[...] Interfuimus etiam Vesperis apud S. Mariam maiorem, ubi erat praestantissima Musica». For the music performances in the church of Santa Maria Maggiore see DELLA LIBERA 2000.

[61].    For the Quarantore see PETERSEN 2012.

[62].    OCHSNER, *Diary*, 13 February 1640: «Die et 2 sequentibus diebus fuit Oratio 40 horarum in Ecclesia S. Francisci Xaverii, prope collegium Romanum, cum Musica elegantissima et Concionibus».

[63].    See *GUIDA ANGELICA PERPETUA* 1634, pp. 13-14: «12 [marzo] s. Gregorio papa, confessore, e Dottore, festa [...] alla Chiesa nuoua, dou'è della sua Testa, postaui l'anno 1628».

*Ephemerides Itineris Romani*

the sermons, which were being given»[64]. On 9 April, they also heard sermons and music at the church of St Onofrio, officiated by the Franciscan order[65].

The ceremonies were sometimes attended by a large following of devotees. Some unforeseen events could also happen in the crowd. On 25 June 1640, the Swiss monks went to the church of St Eligio de' Ferrari, near St Giovanni Decollato, to take part in the annual feast organised by the ancient archconfraternity of blacksmiths. It attracted a large audience. Father Ochsner noted in his diary that the feast ended with spectacular fireworks. On that occasion, however, his coat and a shirt were stolen[66].

The two Swiss Benedictines attended some great ceremonies at the church of St Maria sopra Minerva, officiated by the Dominican order. On 7 March 1640, they participated in the «great feast for St Thomas of Aquinas»[67]. On Sunday, 22 July 1640, they took part in an extraordinary procession through the streets of Rome, starting from the Dominican church. They then attended the ceremonies in honour of St Dominic, solemnly celebrated on 3 and 4 August. On that occasion, they listened to music performed «in eight choirs»[68]. Father Ochsner's annotation is extremely concise. Exactly one year earlier, the Frenchman André Maugars (ca. 1580-1645) took part in the same ceremony, providing a detailed description of the musical performance in a volume published shortly after his return to Paris, entitled *Réponse faite à un curieux, sur le sentiment de la musique d'Italie*[69]:

> Pour vous faire mieux comprendre cet ordre, ie vous en donneray un exemple, en vous faisant une description du plus celebre & du plus excellent concert que i'aye ouy dans Rome, la veille & le iour St Dominique, en l'Eglise de la Minerue. Cette Eglise est assez longue & spacieuse, dans laquelle il y a deux grands Orgues esleuez des deux costez du maistre Autel, où l'on auoit mis deux chœurs de musique. Le long de la nef il y auoit huit autres chœurs, quatre d'un costé, & quatre de l'autre, éleuez sur des eschaffaux de huit à neuf pieds de haut, éloignez de pareille distance les uns des autres, & se regardans tous.

Maugars mentioned the case of the performances heard at the church of St Maria alla Minerva as an example of the extraordinary polychoral arrangements that could be heard in

---

[64]. OCHSNER, *Diary*, 1 April 1640: «Fuimus nocte in Chiesa nova per sentire la Musica e le prediche, che si facevano».

[65]. *Ibidem*, 9 April 1640: «[...] item fuimus apud S. Onophrium in Corso ubi fiebant Musicae et Sermones».

[66]. *Ibidem*, 25 June 1640: «Fabri ferrarii [...] celebrarunt festum S. Eligii. Fecero la sera fuochi artificiali. A me e stato rubbato uno capotto et una camicia».

[67]. *Ibidem*, 7 March 1640: «Fuimus alla Minerva dove si faceva grandissima festa per S. Thomaso d'Aquino».

[68]. *Ibidem*, 3 August 1640: «Fuimus apud Minervam al Vespro d'8 Chori». *Ibidem*, 4 August 1640: «Alla Minerva festa solennissima».

[69]. MAUGARS 1640, pp. 6-7.

Rome at that time[70]. According to Neil O'Regan, «this practice was probably not uncommon, so that other pieces which have come down to us with parts for three or four separate choirs might well have been performed with one or more of these choirs doubled up. [...] Since no music for more than six choirs survives in Roman sources — and very little for more than four — it is quite likely that descriptions of eight, ten and twelve choirs [...] meant in practice that the choirs were doubling up on music composed for four, five and six separate choirs»[71].

Alongside the descriptions of the many ceremonies with music heard in the churches of Rome, Father Ochsner's diary contains other typologies of events connoted by sound. One of these concerns graduation parties, organised at the end of a course of study. Due to the ephemeral nature of these events, information concerning these particular feasts is rare[72]. In some cases, these parties could include rich musical performances. The Swiss Benedictines took part in the graduation party of a student from Trentino, held on 5 December 1639 at the Collegio Romano[73]. During the sumptuous feast, which cost no less than 1,500 scudi, refined music for six choirs was performed[74]. During the months spent in Rome, the Benedictines attended several other graduation feasts, generally more sober than the party organised for the rich student from Trentino. One example was the doctoral feast for the Swiss Minorite Martinus Diener of Küssnacht and other clerics[75]. The graduation parties were not the only entertainment the students could indulge in. With surprise, Father Ochsner wrote in his diary that, on some days in April, he saw some students «dancing on the rope» in the courtyard of the Collegio Germanico[76].

Singing together was a widespread social practice. On 24 January 1640, on their return from a mass celebrated at the Capuchin church, the two Benedictines sang «Christmas songs in German and the litany of the Blessed Virgin Mary: Mr Fleckenstein conducted the music»[77]. It was only in appearance an occasion of light conviviality. The captain of the Papal Guard was ill. A few days earlier, he begged the two monks to pray for him during a visit to the Sistine Chapel

---

[70]. See Lionnet 1985; O'Regan 1995, pp. 113 and 137-138.

[71]. O'Regan 1995, p. 113.

[72]. On this topic see Allegri 2004; Pampalone 2014; Ciolfi 2018.

[73]. Father Ochsner did not know the name of the student.

[74]. Ochsner, *Diary*, 5 December 1639: «In Collegio Romano Tridentinus quidam [...] Doctor creatus fuit cum tanta pompa ut dicant ipsi Doctoratum 1500 Scutis constitisse. Et revera, si solam Musicam, quae [...] fuerit sane elegantissima, et 6. Choros».

[75]. *Ibidem*, 21 December 1639: «R.D. Martinus Diener ex Küssnacht, Helveticus Minorita defendit totam theologiam, sed non admodum docte».

[76]. *Ibidem*, 22-23 April 1640: «[...] vidimus in Schola ballare su la corda».

[77]. *Ibidem*, 24 January 1640: «[...] in reddituo cecinimus cantica natalitia germanica, et Lytanias de B. Virg. D.no Fleckenstein Musicam regente».

*Ephemerides Itineris Romani*

for the first vespers of Epiphany[78]. He died the following 8 March. His funeral was celebrated two days later in the chapel of the Swiss nation[79].

One of the most peculiar sound experiences noted in Father Ochsner's travel diary concerns a private concert. On 8 February 1640, at the residence of the procurator of the Anglican Benedictine Congregation where the two Benedictines were staying, they listened to a concert performed by a theorbo virtuoso (ILL. 12, p. 48). It was a very special event, as Father Ochsner's emotional description shows[80]:

> At the evening, in our home, a very skilled player of that instrument, commonly referred to by the name of theorbo, delighted us so sweetly that one could contemplate the joys of heaven and the heavenly harmonies.

The private concert performed by a famous theorbo player in the residence of the procurator of the Anglican Benedictine Congregation is certainly something worthy of note. The name of the musician is not mentioned in Father Ochsner's diary. It is possible, however, that the virtuoso was Giovanni Girolamo Kapsperger (ca. 1580-1651).

Founded in 1576, the Venerable English College was not distinguished, like other colleges in Rome, for its particular musical activities[81]. There is evidence of the presence of a chapel master, who was entrusted to organise the musical performances for about fifteen feasts a year, recruiting guest musicians. The episode described in Father Ochsner's diary shows, however, that the musical life of the college was richer than the official musical activity would lead one to believe.

During the time that the two Swiss Benedictines spent in Rome, the chapel of the Venerable English College was conducted by Virgilio Mazzocchi[82]. Like several other important musicians active in Rome at the time, including Stefano Landi and Giovanni Girolamo Kapsperger, Mazzocchi was in the service of the Barberini family. In 1640 he played a *cembalo triarmonico* in the performance of the dialogue/oratorio entitled *Esther*, composed by Pietro Della Valle. The vocal parts were entrusted to two famous singers: Bartolomeo Nicolini and Francesco Bianchi, a pupil of Kapsperger[83]. It is interesting to note that, at the time of the private concert described

---

[78]. *Ibidem*, 5 January 1640: «Fuimus in Vesperis Pontificis in Capella, ubi D. Capitaneus Fleckenstein 500 Vota [...] nobis impetraverat».

[79]. *Ibidem*, 8 and 10 March 1640.

[80]. «Die fui ego in Bibliotheca Angelica apud S. Augustinum. Vespere in domo nostra quidam praestantissimus Instrumentalista illo instrumento, quod vulgo Theorba vocant, adeo suaviter lusit, ut caeli gaudia angelicosque concentus facile quis meditari potuerit». *Ibidem*, 8 February 1640.

[81]. See DIXON 1994; GOSSETT 1973; FOSI 2021.

[82]. See FRANCHI 2008.

[83]. See KIRNBAUER 2013, pp. 130-132; DRAGOSITS 2021, p. 335.

Ill. 12: Antiveduto Grammatica, *Theorbo Player*, 1605 ca. Turin, Galleria Sabauda.

*Ephemerides Itineris Romani*

in Father Ochner's diary, Kapsperger lived in Via di Monserrato, near the Venerable English College[84]. In 1640, the famous theorbo player published his *Libro quarto d'intavolatura di chitarrone*. The content of the volume was copied by a certain Giuseppe Pozzobonelli, who acted as transcriber of pieces performed by Kapsperger on his instrument[85]. The «celestial music» that the Swiss Benedictines listened to during the private concert in their residence could be linked to the content of this collection, which was conceived in the context of performance activities related to a selected private patronage.

During the months spent in Rome, the two Swiss monks they had the opportunity to admire some prodigious sound machines: the hydraulic organs built in the gardens of some residences. On 6 November 1639, they listened to the organ placed in the gardens of the Villa Borghese[86]. On 23 January 1640, it was the turn of the organ built in the gardens of the residence of Cardinal Ippolito II d'Este in Tivoli[87]. The following 12 April, they listened to the hydraulic organ placed in the gardens of the Quirinale[88].

Father Ochsner described in his travel diary several events of the urban ceremonial of Rome. In February 1640, he witnessed the frenetic rituals of Carnival, which he reported in his diary not without some criticism[89]. Once the carnival was over, the urban scene changed rapidly[90]. Churches offered devotional celebrations featuring sermons on devotional themes, such as those the Swiss Benedictines attended at the Church of the Gesù[91]. Lent was a hard time, also marked by brutal rituals[92]. On 15 March 1640, the monks witnessed the execution of a witch, condemned to be dismembered in the square[93]. Four days later, after attending a mass

---

[84]. Kapsberger lived in Via di Monserrato 62. I thank Anne Marie Dragosits for this information.

[85]. See DRAGOSITS 2021, pp. 330-335.

[86]. OCHSNER, *Diary*, 6 November 1639: «[...] post prandium Villam Burghesiam perlustraremus [...] Vidimus et Organum mirabile, quod cantilenam quondam se solo carebat sono fidium, quam quinque imagunculae Musicoreum interea saltitantes, suis instrumentis ludere ludere putabantur».

[87]. *Ibidem*, 23 January 1639: «[...] vidimus locum illum, quo S. Gregorius Papatum fugiens se abdidit. [...] Porro civitas Tiburtina [...] fontes artificiosissimi plurimi, quorum unum organum mirabiliter pulsat. [...] In nemore dicti palatii aviculae suavissime cecinerunt, uti in Germania in mense Maio facere solent».

[88]. *Ibidem*, 12 April 1640: «Fuimus in Horto Papae nel monte Cavallo ubi vidimus [...] ad fontem opere musicae».

[89]. *Ibidem*, 11 February 1640: «Die Sabbato nimirum ante Sexagesimam Bachanalia incepta fuere, et omnes platae stultis repletae». *Ibidem*, 14 February 1640 «[...] spectavimus Bacchanalia». *Ibidem*, 21 February 1640 «Ultimo die Bacchanalium fuimus iterum in Cursu, ubi vidimus currere Equos, Barbaros, Asinos et Buvalos».

[90]. See FAGIOLO DELL'ARCO – CARANDINI 1978.

[91]. OCHSNER, *Diary*, 24 February 1640: «[...] interfuimus Concioni praestantissimo al Giesù». *Ibidem*, 29 February 1640: «[...] interfuimus Concioni al Giesù. Hic semel pro semper notandum, per totam Quadragesimam singulis diebus in plurimis Ecclesiis fieri Conciones et fere semper ab iisdem Concionatoribus».

[92]. See BOITEAUX 2008; BOITEAUX 2014; CAFFIERO 2012.

[93]. OCHSNER, *Diary*, 15 marzo 1640: «Strega segata in campo vaccino [in Foro romano]».

at the Pantheon, where they admired the beautiful paintings of the church, they came across the execution of four people, condemned to death by the Inquisition[94]. The next day it was the turn of the execution of a Jew, burnt alive in Campo de' Fiori[95]. In the pages of Father Ochsner's diary, entries concerning these tragic events are generally very concise. They were undoubtedly shocking experiences, also from a sonic point of view: the cries of the condemned, the noise of the crowd, the atrocious clatter of the execution machinery.

After the representation of death (virtual, such as in the rich ceremonials for Holy Week, and real, as in the executions carried out during Lent), the urban scene changed again. Public space was transformed into a symbolic location where the resurrection of the Son of God was staged. Solemnly celebrated during Easter ceremonies, the great mystery could also find its amplification in devotional performances, such as those attended by the two Benedictines on 15 April 1640, in Trastevere: «After lunch I attended a comedy in Trastevere at the Ponte Rotto. First scene: Angel and Death; second scene: Peace, Justice and Angel; third scene: St Peter; fourth scene: Devil and a little devil; fifth scene: Risen from the Dead and Death; sixth scene: Longinus and Angel; seventh scene: Mary and Choir of Angels at the Sepulchre»[96].

On a November day in 1639, Father Ochsner listened with pleasure to the performance of a street musician, who sang a beautiful song in Piazza Navona[97]. A few months later, on 16 August 1640, he admired the spectacle of the «barchette» (small boats) organised in Piazza Navona for the feast of St Roch.

Often, at the end of particular celebrations, it was possible to watch the firing of fireworks. Nothing, however, was comparable to what took place during the feast of St Peter and St Paul. On 28 June 1640, the two Benedictines attended the ceremony of the «Chinea, which was presented to the Pope» and they admired the fireworks and the «wine fountain»[98]. Father Ochsner wrote this entry in his travel diary in Italian. The use of the local language instead of Latin is a gradual process. It proves the progress he made in the written as well as the spoken Italian. The sound of the language of the environment thus fills the pages of his diary. But the landscape could also offer other surprising sonic phenomena. Fragrant thunder could pierce the sky of Rome even in December, as Father Ochsner reported[99].

---

[94].  *Ibidem*, 19 marzo 1640: «Celebravimus apud S. Mariam Rotundam [Pantheon] dove erano bellissimi quadri. Fuimus ad S. Petrum mentre si condemaronno 4 Condemnati dell'Inquisitione».

[95].  *Ibidem*, 20 marzo1640: «Unus ex dicti condemnatis Haebreus combustus est in Campo florae».

[96].  *Ibidem*, 15 April 1640: «Interfui post prandium Comediae in Trastevere al Ponte Rotto. Scena 1ma Angelus et Mors, 2da Pax, Justitia et Angelus. 3a S. Petrus. 4a diabolus et un diavoletto picciollo. 5a Mortuis resurgentes, et mors. 6ta Longinus, Angelus. 7ma Maria et Chorus Angelorum apud Sepulchrum».

[97].  *Ibidem*, 26 November 1639: «[...] in platea agonali valde mirabilem cantilenam quandam audivimus».

[98].  *Ibidem*, 28 june 1640: «Videmmo la Chinea, che si presentava al Papa e li fuochi artificiali, la fontana di vino».

[99].  *Ibidem*, 15 December 1639: «Sequens dies pluvius erat, et in eo tonitrua audiebantur».

## Ephemerides Itineris Romani

For reasons we do not know, the Benedictine did not continue writing his travel diary. There is no information about the period they spent in Rome between August 1640 and the autumn of 1641, nor about the itinerary followed by the two Benedictines to return to Switzerland. From a laissez-passer signed on 2 October 1641 by Cardinal Francesco Barberini, it is possible to establish that the two Benedictines left Rome in October 1641.

## Perspectives

The two study cases considered here show how complex was the phenomenon of the journey to Italy during the early modern age. It knew many different declinations, not always ascribable to some widespread typologies, such as that of the *grand tour* of a young nobleman. Within the numerous typologies of travels, the question concerning the sound experience has also known a wide range of possibilities. In the narration of the journey, sound perception is a progressive and surprising discovery of a new sensory dimension. It requires an adequate knowledge and interaction with the environment. Much more than other sensory aspects, it is closely linked to traveller's attention and interest in this kind of manifestation, to his ability to understand what he listened to and to describe it in writing. A guide for foreigners could help a traveller to better understand the rich urban ceremonial of a city like Rome or Venice, pre-structuring his expectations also from a sonic point of view. It is interesting to note, however, that — even in the face of identical manifestations — sound perception is an aspect intimately linked to the emotional sphere. The analysis of sound experience therefore requires a hermeneutic approach[100]. In many cases, rather than what the sources say, it is important to observe what they do not say, considering the voluntary or involuntary selective processes that guided the writer[101].

The journey to Italy was an extraordinary cultural and human experience for the travellers. This is true for both lay and religious. Many of the Benedictines, who studied in Rome, later obtained prominent positions within the monasteries of the order. Father Weishaupt, one of the two Benedictines who stayed in Rome between 1639 and 1641, thirty-five years later oversaw the purchase of a residence in Bellinzona (Tessin) acquired by the monastery of Einsiedeln. This house was fundamentally a pied-à-terre south of the Alps, thanks to which the Benedictine monastery strengthened relationships with Italy and Milan in particular. Along this axis, an intense process of cultural transfer took place until the beginning of the nineteenth century, involving also a large circulation of musical culture.

---

[100]. See Dompnier 2009.

[101]. See Carter 2002.

# Luigi Collarile

## Sources

Adami 1711
Adami, Andrea. *Osservazioni per ben regolare il coro de i cantori della Cappella Pontificia tanto nelle funzioni ordinarie, che straordinarie*, Rome, Antonio de' Rossi, 1711.

*Guida angelica perpetua* 1634
*Guida angelica perpetua* [...] *per visitare le chiese di Roma, e sapere le Feste che vi si celebrano*, Rome, Francesco Cavalli, 1634.

Maugars 1640
Maugars, André. *Réponse faite à un curieux, sur le sentiment de la musique d'Italie. Escrite à Rome le premier Octobre 1639*, Paris, s.n., [1640].

Ochsner *Diary*
Ochsner, Kolumban. *Ephemerides Itineris Romani à me F. Columbano Ochsner Einsiedlensi, Einsidlensis Monasterii Monacho conscriptae*, manuscript, Einsiedeln, Stiftsarchiv, A.PC.13.

Wagner 1664
Wagner, Johann Georg. *Italienische Summer-, oder, Römer Reyss: darinnen kurtz, einfalt- und warhafftig erzehlet wird, was sich in letzter bey anjetzo regierender Päpstl. Heyligk. Alexandro dem VII. In Namen der gesampten hochlobl. Catholischen Orthen der Eydtgnossschafft, durch derselben Herren Raths-Abgesandten von Lucern, Underwalden nit dem Kernwald, und Solothurn, im Jahr 1661. zu Rom abgelegt-, also genandter Obedientz Bottschafft, Schrifft-, und denckwürdiges zugetragen*, Solothurn, Johann Jacob Bernhard, 1664.

## Bibliography

Achermann 1979
Achermann, Hansjakob. *Die Katakombenheiligen und ihre Translationen in der Schweizerischen Quart des Bistums Konstanz*, Stans, Verlag Historischer Verein Nidwalden, 1979.

Adorni – Onori – Venzo 2017
Adorni, Giuliana – Onori, Teresa – Venzo, Manola Ida. 'Laurearsi a Roma *in utroque iure*. Forestieri e stranieri nei primi *Registra doctorum et decretorum*', in: *Venire a Roma, restare a Roma. Forestieri e stranieri fra Quattro e Settecento*, edited by Sara Cabibbo and Alessandro Serra, Rome, TrE-Press, 2017, pp. 101-118.

Agnew 2008
Agnew, Vanessa. *Enlightenment Orpheus: The Power of Music in Other Worlds*, Oxford, Oxford University Press, 2008.

Allegri 2004
Allegri, Domenico. *Music of an Academic Defense (Rome, 1617)*, edited by Anthony John with historical and textual commentary by Louise Rice and Clare Woods, Middleton (WI), A-R Editions, 2004 (Recent Researches in the Music of the Baroque Era, 134).

## Ephemerides Itineris Romani

Babel – Paravicini 2005
*Grand Tour. Adeliges Reisen und europäische Kultur vom 14. bis zum 18. Jahrhundert. Akten der Internationalen Kolloquien in der Villa Vigoni 1999 und im Deutschen Historischen Institut Paris 2000*, edited by Rainer Babel and Werner Paravicini, Ostfildern, Jan Thorbecke, 2005 (Beihefte der Francia, 60).

Bacciagaluppi 2010
Bacciagaluppi, Claudio. '«La musique prédomine trop dans nos abbaïes helvétiques». Einige Quellen zur Stellung der Figuralmusik in Schweizer Klöstern', in: Castellani 2010, pp. 139-176.

Bacciagaluppi – Collarile 2010
*The St Urban Inventory (1661)*, edited by Claudio Bacciagaluppi and Luigi Collarile in collaboration with Annaïck Bouquin, in: *Historical Music Inventories 1500-1800*, edited by Claudio Bacciagaluppi, Luigi Collarile, Laurent Pugin and Luca Zoppelli, <http://in-dev.rism.digital>, accessed February 2022.

Bacciagaluppi – Collarile 2013
Bacciagaluppi, Claudio – Collarile, Luigi. '«Tutte le opere del Girolamo Frescovaldi». 1647: Roma-Lucerna, solo andata', in: *A fresco. Hommage en l'honneur du professeur Etienne Darbellay*, edited by Brenno Boccadoro and Georges Starobinski, Bern, Peter Lang, 2013, pp. 69-88.

Bassani 2012
Bassani, Florian. 'Musiche policorali nella Chiesa del Gesù: aspetti di prassi esecutiva', in: *La musique à Rome au XVIIe siècle. Études et perspectives de recherche*, edited by Caroline Giron-Panel and Anne-Madeleine Goulet, Rome, École française de Rome, 2012 (Collection de l'École française de Rome, 466), pp. 357-377.

Berglund 2012
Berglund, Lars. 'Angels or Sirens? Questions of Reception and Performativity in Roman Church Music around 1650', in: *Performativity and Performance in Baroque Rome*, edited by Peter Gillgren and Mårten Snickare, Farnham, Ashgate, 2012 (Visual Culture in Early Modernity), pp. 99-114.

Black 2003
Black, Jeremy. *Italy and the Grand Tour*, New Haven (CT), Yale University Press, 2003.

Boiteaux 2008
Boiteaux, Martine. 'Violences rituelles: Juifs et Chrétiens dans la Rome pontificale', in *Le destin des rituels: faire corps dans l'espace urbain, Italie-France-Allemagne*, edited by Bertrand Gilles and Ilaria Taddei, Rome, École Française de Rome, 2008 (Collection de l'École Française de Rome, 404), pp. 191-207.

Boiteaux 2014
Ead. 'Preaching to the Jews in Early Modern Rome: Words and Images', in: *The Jewish-Christian Encounter in Medieval Preaching*, edited by Jonathan Adams and Jussi Hanska, Abingdon-New York, Routledge, 2014, pp. 296-322.

Brilli 1995
Brilli, Antonio. *Quando viaggiare era un'arte. Il romanzo del Grand Tour*, Bologna, il Mulino, 1995.

## BRILLI 2014
ID. *Il grande racconto del viaggio in Italia. Itinerari di ieri per viaggiatori di oggi*, Bologna, il Mulino, 2014.

## BRIZZI 1976
BRIZZI, Gian Paolo. 'La pratica del viaggio di istruzione in Italia nel Sei-Settecento', in: *Annali dell'Istituto Storico Italo-Germanico in Trento*, II (1976), pp. 203-291.

## BRYANT – QUARANTA 2015
BRYANT, David – QUARANTA, Elena. 'Music and Musicians in Late Seventeenth- and Early Eighteenth-Century Venice: A Guide for Foreigners', in: *Europäische Musiker in Venedig, Rom und Neapel (1650-1750) / Les musiciens européens à Venise, Rome et Naples (1650-1750) / Musicisti europei a Venezia, Roma e Napoli (1650-1750)*, edited by Anne-Madeleine Goulet and Gesa zur Nieden, Kassel, Bärenreiter, 2015 (Analecta Musicologica, 52), pp. 87-117.

## CAFFIERO 2012
CAFFIERO, Marina. *Legami pericolosi: ebrei e cristiani tra eresia, libri proibiti e stregoneria*, Turin, Einaudi, 2012.

## CARTER 2002
CARTER, Tim. 'The Sounds of Silence: Models for an Urban Musicology', in: *Urban History*, XXIX/1 (2002), pp. 8-18.

## CARTER 2018
ID. 'Hearing and Listening: Some Problems for the Urban Musicologist', in: *Hearing the City in Early Modern Europe*, edited by Tess Knighton and Ascensión Mazuela-Anguita, Turnhout, Brepols, 2018 (Epitome musical), pp. 25-52.

## CASTELLANI 2010
*Musik aus Klöstern des Alpenraums. Bericht über den Internationalen Kongress an der Universität Freiburg (Schweiz), 23. Bis 24. November 2007*, edited by Giuliano Castellani, Bern, Peter Lang, 2010 (Publikationen der Schweizerischen Musikforschenden Gesellschaft. Serie 2, 55).

## CILIBERTI 2016
CILIBERTI, Galliano. *«Qu'une plus belle nüit ne pouvoit précéder le beau iour». Musica e cerimonie nelle istituzioni religiose francesi a Roma nel Seiento*, Città di Castello, Aguaplano, 2016 (Studi, 12).

## CIOLFI 2018
CIOLFI, Simone. 'Music and Splendour in Roman Graduation Ceremonies', in: *Music and Power in the Baroque Era*, edited by Rudolf Rasch, Turnhout, Brepols, 2018 (Music, Criticism and Politics, 6), pp. 203-220.

## COLLARILE 2010
COLLARILE, Luigi. 'Milano-Einsiedeln via Bellinzona (1675-1852): circolazione e recezione di musica italiana nei monasteri benedettini della Svizzera interna', in: *Schweizer Jahrbuch für Musikwissenschaft*, n.s. 30 (2010), pp. 117-161.

*Ephemerides Itineris Romani*

COLLARILE 2014
ID. 'Musikalische Erlebnisse von St. Galler Benediktinern auf ihrer Grand Tour durch Italien (1699-1749)', in: ERHART – KURATLI-HÜEBLIN 2014, pp. 154-168.

COLLARILE 2017
ID. 'Paesaggi sonori nei diari di viaggio in Italia di benedettini svizzeri del primo Settecento', in: *Siculorum Gymnasium*, n.s. 3, LXX (2017), pp. 245-272.

COLLARILE, *Il suono di Milano*
ID. 'Il suono di Milano in alcuni diari di viaggio di benedettini svizzeri della prima età moderna', in: *Vita musicale nella «gran città» di Milano. Dagli Sforza all'età spagnola*, in preparation.

COLLARILE, *The Sound of the Venetian Terraferma*
ID. 'The Sound of the Venetian Terraferma in the Narration of the Grand Tour. Proposals for a Phenomenological Interpretation', in: *The Soundscape of Early Modern Venice and Venetian Terraferma*, edited by David Bryant and Luigi Collarile, in preparation.

CULLEY 1970
CULLEY, Thomas D. *Jesuits and Music: A Study of the Musicians Connected with the German College in Rome during the 17th Century and their Activities in Northern Europe*, Rome, Jesuit Historical Institute, 1970 (Sources and Studies of the History of the Jesuits, 2).

DELLA LIBERA 2000
DELLA LIBERA, Luca. 'Repertori ed organici vocali-strumentali nella basilica di Santa Maria Maggiore a Roma: 1557-1624', in: *Studi musicali*, XIX/1 (2000), pp. 3-57.

DE SETA 2014
DE SETA, Cesare. *L'Italia nello specchio del Grand Tour*, Milan, Rizzoli, 2014.

DIXON 1980
DIXON, Graham. 'Musical Activity in the Church of the Gesù in Rome during the Early Baroque', in: *Archivum Historicum Societatis Iesu*, XLIX (1980), pp. 323-337.

DIXON 1994
ID. 'Music in the Venerable English College in the Early Baroque', in: *La musica a Roma attraverso le fonti d'archivio*, edited by Bianca Maria Antolini, Arnaldo Morelli and Vera Vita Spagnuolo, Lucca, LIM, 1994 (Strumenti della ricerca musicale, 2), pp. 469-478.

DOMPNIER 2009
DOMPNIER, Bernard. 'Déchiffrer', in: *Les cérémonies extraordinaires du catholicisme baroque*, edited by Bernard Dompnier, Clermont-Ferrand, Presses Universitaires Blaise Pascal, 2009, pp. 11-16.

DRAGOSITS 2021
DRAGOSITS, Anne Marie. *Giovanni Girolamo Kapsperger: «ein ziemlich extravaganter Mann»*, Lucca, LIM, 2021 (Studi e Saggi, 35).

ERHART 2008

ERHART, Peter. 'Diarium Romani itineris. Die Grand Tour zweier St. Galler Mönche nach Rom und Neapel im Jubeljahr 1700', in: *Sankt Gallen und Italien / San Gallo e l'Italia*, edited by Renato Martinoni and Ernst Tremp, St. Gallen, Verlag am Klosterhof, 2008, pp. 87-123.

ERHART – COLLARILE 2015-2016

*Itinera Italica. Römische Tagebücher aus dem Kloster Sankt Gallen. Diari romani dal monastero di San Gallo*, edited by Peter Erhart and Luigi Collarile, 2 vols., St. Gallen, Stiftsarchiv; Bolzano-Vienna, Folio Verlag, 2015-2016.

ERHART – KURATLI-HÜEBLIN 2014

*Vedi Napoli e poi muori. Grand Tour der Mönche*, edited by Peter Erhart and Jakob Kuratli-Hüeblin, St. Gallen, Verlag am Klosterhof, 2014.

FABRIS 2015

FABRIS, Dinko. 'Italian Soundscapes: Souvenirs from the *Grand Tour*', in: FABRIS – MURATA 2015, pp. 23-32.

FABRIS 2018

ID. 'Urban Musicologies', in: *Hearing the City in Early Modern Europe, op. cit.*, pp. 53-68.

FABRIS – MURATA 2015

*Passaggio in Italia: Music on the Grand Tour in the Seventeenth Century*, edited by Dinko Fabris and Margaret Murata, Turnhout, Brepols, 2015 (Music History and Performance: Practices in Context, 1).

FAGIOLO DELL'ARCO 1997

FAGIOLO DELL'ARCO, Maurizio. *La festa barocca*, Rome, Edizioni De Luca, 1997 (Corpus delle feste a Roma, 1).

FAGIOLO DELL'ARCO – CARANDINI 1978

*L'effimero barocco: strutture della festa nella Roma del '600*, edited by Maurizio Fagiolo dell'Arco and Silvia Carandini, 2 vols., Rome, Bulzoni, 1977-1978 (Biblioteca di storia dell'arte, 10-11).

FILIPPI 2015

FILIPPI, Daniele V. 'A Sound Doctrine: Early Modern Jesuits and the Singing of the Catechism', in: *Early Music History*, XXXIV (2015), pp. 1-43.

FILIPPI 2017

ID. '«Catechismum modulans docebat». Teaching the Doctrine through Singing in Early Modern Catholicism', in: *Listening to Early Modern Catholicism: Perspectives from Musicology*, edited by Daniele V. Filippi and Michael Noone, Leiden, Boston, Brill, 2017, pp. 129-148.

FOSI 2021

FOSI, Irene. 'The Venerable English College between the Late 16th and 17th Centuries', in: *A Companion to Religious Minorities in Early Modern Rome*, edited by Matthew Coneys Wainwright and Emily Michelson, Leiden-Boston, Brill, 2021 (Brill's Companion to the Christian Tradition, 95), pp. 115-141.

## Ephemerides Itineris Romani

FRANCHI 2008

FRANCHI, Saverio. 'Mazzocchi, Domenico', in: *Dizionario Biografico degli Italiani. 72*, 2008, <https://www.treccani.it/enciclopedia/domenico-mazzocchi_(Dizionario-Biografico)>, accessed March 2023.

GARRIOCH 2003

GARRIOCH, David. 'Sounds of the City. The Soundscape of Early Modern European Towns', in: *Urban History*, XXX/1 (2003), pp. 5-25.

GIGLI 1994

GIGLI, Giacinto. *Diario di Roma*, edited by Manlio Barberito, 3 vols., Rome, Editore Carlo Colombo, 1994.

GLIXON 2003

GLIXON, Jonathan. *Honoring God and the City: Music at the Venetian Confraternities, 1260-1807*, Oxford-New York, Oxford University Press, 2003.

GLIXON 2017

ID. *Mirrors of Heaven or Wordly Theaters? Venetian Nunneries and Their Music*, Oxford-New York, Oxford University Press, 2017.

GOSSETT 1973

GOSSETT, Suzanne. 'Drama in the English College, Rome, 1591-1660', in: *English Literary Renaissance*, III/1 (1973), pp. 60-93.

HENGGELER 1930

HENGGELER, Rudolf. *Professbuch der fürstlichen Benediktinerabtei der Heiligen Gallus und Otmar zu St. Gallen*, Zug, Eberhard Kalt-Zehnder, 1930 (Monasticon-Benedictinum Helvetiae).

HIBBERT 1987

HIBBERT, Christopher. *The Grand Tour*, London, Thames Methuen, 1987.

IMORDE – PIEPER 2008

*Die Grand Tour in Moderne und Nachmoderne*, edited by Joseph Imorde and Jan Pieper, Tübingen, Walther de Gruyter, 2008.

KIRNBAUER 2013

KIRNBAUER, Martin. *Vieltönige Musik. Spielarten chromatischer und enharmonischer Musik in Rom in der ersten Hälfte des 17. Jahrhunderts*, Basel, Schwabe, 2013 (Schola Cantorum Basiliensis Scripta, 3).

LIONNET 1985

LIONNET, Jean. 'André Maugars: Risposta data a un curioso sul sentimento della musica d'Italia', in: *Nuova rivista musicale italiana*, XIX/4 (1985), pp. 681-707.

O'REGAN 1995
O'REGAN, Neil. 'The Performance of Roman Sacred Polyphonic Music in the Late Sixteenth and Early Seventeenth Centuries: Evidence from Archival Sources', in: *Performance Practice Review*, VIII/2 (1995), pp. 107-146.

PAMPALONE 2014
PAMPALONE, Antonella. *Cerimonie di laurea nella Roma barocca: Pietro da Cortona e i frontespizi ermetici di tesi*, Rome, Gangemi, 2014.

PEROCCO 1997
PEROCCO, Daria. *Viaggiare e raccontare. Narrazione di viaggio e esperienze di racconto tra Cinque e Seicento*, Alessandria, Edizioni dell'Orso, 1997.

PETERSEN 2012
PETERSEN, Nils Holger. 'The Quarant'Ore: Early Modern Ritual and Performativity', in: *Performativity and Performance in Baroque Rome, op. cit.*, pp. 115-133.

QUARANTA 1998
QUARANTA, Elena. *Oltre San Marco. Organizzazione e prassi della musica nelle chiese di Venezia nel Rinascimento*, Florence, Olschki, 1998 (Studi di musica veneta, 26).

ROSTIROLLA 2014
ROSTIROLLA, Giancarlo. *Musica e musicisti nella Basilica di San Pietro. Cinque secoli di storia della Cappella Giulia*, Città del Vaticano, Edizioni Capitolo Vaticano, 2014.

SCHILTZ 2016
SCHILTZ, Katelijne. 'Gregorio Allegris *Miserere* im Reiseberichten des 18. und 19. Jahrhunderts', in: *Prinzenrollen 1715/16. Wittelsbacher in Rom und Regensburg*, edited by Andrea Zedler and Jörg Zedler, Munich, Herbert Utz Verlag, 2016, pp. 223-256.

VOGLER 1979
VOGLER, Werner. 'Das Hochaltarbild der St.-Galler Stiftskirche. Ein Werk von Giovanni Francesco Romanelli', in: *Zeitschrift für schweizerische Archäologie und Kunstgeschichte*, XXXVI/4 (1979), pp. 248-258.

ZEDLER – ZEDLER 2019
*Giro d'Italia. Die Reiseberichte des bayerischen Kurprinzen Karl Albrecht (1715/16). Eine historisch-kritische Edition*, edited by Andrea Zedler and Jörg Zedler, Vienna, Böhlau, 2019.

# Suoni pericolosi.
## Musica sacra, emozioni e disciplinamento dell'ambiente sonoro nelle chiese venete della prima età moderna

*Umberto Cecchinato*
(Università di Trento)

### Introduzione

Il 20 giugno 1528 il patriarca Geronimo Querini emana un ordine diretto a tutto il clero veneziano: una «prava corruptela» era diffusa durante le celebrazioni liturgiche. Trombe, flauti, cornetti, salterii, chitarre e canti lascivi stridevano e riecheggiavano nelle chiese cittadine, facendo somigliare gli uffici divini a commedie e balli. L'atmosfera musicale attirava giovani libidinosi che, fomentati dal suono, confluivano nelle chiese con mire poco devote: proferivano parole inoneste e disturbavano i rituali con schiamazzi e risa, portavano armi e si scontravano con i propri rivali. Le chiese, afferma il patriarca, non erano più luoghi di devozione, ma «meretricum scholae». Per purgare le messe da questi comportamenti, Querini vieta perentoriamente di assoldare strumentisti e impone ai cantori e agli organisti un canto «modesto et congruo», adatto alla lode divina[1].

La regolamentazione della musica sacra e la condanna di alcuni strumenti musicali da parte dei religiosi più intransigenti sono da tempo argomento di studio. Le ricerche si sono concentrate soprattutto sul Concilio di Trento e hanno dato vita a un duraturo dibattito, imperniato sostanzialmente su due temi: la depurazione degli elementi profani dalla musica sacra e la repressione della polifonia. Le contaminazioni profane sono spesso ridotte alla prassi di intrecciare le sezioni della messa polifonica con una melodia o un'intera composizione profana, come nelle messe 'della caccia et la battaglia'; la messa al bando della polifonia è fatta

---

[1]. Trascritto interamente da Quaranta 1998, pp. 410-411 e da Glixon 2017, p. 288.

corrispondere a un cambiamento di estetica dettato dalla cultura umanistica[2]. Di conseguenza, la normativa riguardante la musica è intepretata come il tentativo di risoluzione di un problema di forma musicale. Per esempio, il significato della parola *lascivus* — che dal famoso canone tridentino contro gli elementi profani[3] compare quasi sempre nella normativa ecclesiastica — è stato inteso come veicolante «a sense of immoderation, empty virtuosity, lacking the restraint and sobriety proper to worship» trascurando il significato morale che il termine aveva nella cultura ecclesiastica dell'epoca[4].

Decreti come quello del patriarca Querini si prestano a interpretazioni che vanno al di là degli aspetti stilistici o estetici. Il documento lascia trapelare preoccupazioni etiche e morali profondamente connesse alla realtà sociale. Gli strumenti vietati — «buccinis, tibiis, cornibus, psalteriis, cytharis» — non producevano solamente dei richiami per attirare la folla: secondo Querini, i loro suoni erano in grado di sedurre e spingere le persone ad agire peccaminosamente. Il testo dichiara apertamente che i giovani agivano lascivamente perché sedotti dai loro incitamenti — «iis incitamentis allecti». Il patriarca sostiene dunque che le persone si comportavano come se fossero alle feste pubbliche a causa dell'ambiente sonoro 'mondano' che gli strumenti musicali contribuivano a creare nelle chiese veneziane.

Querini non era ovviamente l'unico a pensarla in questo modo. Il già citato canone tridentino fornì alle autorità ecclesiastiche una cornice normativa per regolamentare la musica da chiesa. Come è noto, l'azione di riforma fu delegata ai *sinoda* vescovili[5], ma manca ancora una lettura sistematica e d'insieme dei decreti sinodali in prospettiva sociale e culturale, e le ricerche riguardanti alle azioni di riforma delle singole diocesi sono poche[6]. La vasta storiografia sui sensi, sulle emozioni e sull'ambiente sonoro del Rinascimento invitano a rileggere i decreti come quello di Querini alla luce dei saperi medici e morali, guardando anche a ciò che succedeva realmente nelle chiese dell'epoca[7].

---

[2]. Un recente saggio di Cesarino Ruini si impernia su questi punti: *cfr*. RUINI 2015, p. 103.

[3]. CT, vol. VIII, p. 936: «Ab ecclesiis vero musicas eas, ubi sive organo sive cantu lascivum aut impurum aliquid miscetur, item saeculares omnes actiones, vana atque adeo profana colloquia, deambulationes, strepitus, clamores arceant, ut domus Dei vere domus orationis esse videatur ac dici possit».

[4]. L'interpretazione è di David Crook ed è citata da O'REGAN 2013, p. 340. Del termine *impurus* non è suggerita una traduzione, ma richiama chiaramente al concetto di contaminazione teorizzato nel classico di DOUGLAS 2014. L'anomalia è notata anche da BERTOGLIO 2017, pp. 337-338. Condivido con Bertoglio molti punti di vista: purtroppo sono venuto a conoscenza del suo studio solo tardivamente e in questa sede non ho potuto fare piena giustizia al suo importante contributo.

[5]. MONSON 2002, p. 3; BERTOGLIO 2017, p. 314.

[6]. Le analisi generali offrono per lo più dei repertori di fonti: si veda per esempio FABBRI 1993. Ricerche sulle azioni di riforma nelle diocesi di Milano e Bologna sono state pubblicate dallo stesso MONSON 2006. Una prima analisi della normativa veneziana si deve a COLLARILE 2010, pp. 127-132.

[7]. Sul rapporto tra rituali religiosi e sensi nell'ambito della Riforma/Controriforma DE BOER 2013 e DE BOER – GÖTTLER 2013. Per un'introduzione alla storia delle emozioni si vedano PLAMPER 2015 e ROSENWEIN –

# SUONI PERICOLOSI

## LA LASCIVIA IN CHIESA

I comportamenti di cui si lamenta Querini erano ampiamente diffusi nelle chiese dell'epoca. La musica polifonica era suonata consuetudinariamente in tutta la Penisola in occasione di feste patronali, celebrazioni solenni, processioni e cicli festivi legati al calendario rituale della chiesa di Roma[8]. A Venezia come altrove, la musica era un importante elemento catalizzatore: più persone partecipavano, più le celebrazioni erano onorate e solenni. In quelle occasioni, le chiese erano ornate con mascheroni argentei, festoni colorati, piante, fiori. Talvolta, per attirare più persone, l'evento era annunciato per le vie cittadine da una processione musicale e mascherata[9].

Tra le folle che entravano in chiesa però, molte persone non avevano scopi devozionali. Alcuni, come il medico e letterato trevigiano Bartolomeo Burchelati, vi si recavano per dilettarsi ascoltando le «musiche esquisite», «sì per consolatione dell'anima christiana, come per consolatione di questi duoi sensi, udire et vedere, ministri, et satelliti anzi spaciose finestre di quella»: la pratica era considerata una nobile e pia «ricreatione»[10]. Altri ancora andavano in chiesa per corteggiare.

I corteggiamenti erano talmente diffusi e appariscenti che i viaggiatori stranieri li consideravano una sorta di spettacolo. Saint-Didier nella guida *La ville et la Republique de Venise* (1680) dedica un intero capitolo alle «festes particulieres» che si tenevano nelle chiese lagunari, celebrate «avec solemnité, et qu'une belle musique» e richiamavano «un grand concours de monde». Le feste in chiesa offrivano ampia soddisfazione a coloro «qui ne cherchent qu'à se divertir, ou qui aiment la musique»: ma a chi conosceva bene tali divertimenti era forse più interessante «observer dans se rencontres les divers personnages des amans, leurs regards, leurs gestes, et toutes les manieres differentes, avec lesquelles ils assurent les dames qu'ils servent de l'excez de leur passion»[11].

Nell'anno in cui fu pubblicata la guida di Saint-Didier, un agente degli Inquisitori di Stato, Domenico Pavani, fu incaricato di recarsi nelle chiese di Venezia nei giorni di festa per vigilare sugli scandali che avvenivano durante la messa. Tra il giugno del 1680 e il settembre del

---

CRISTIANI 2018. Le analisi che incrociano sensi, emozioni, l'amministrazione del potere da parte delle autorità e la vita sociale sono ancora poche. Recentemente Manuel Bertolini ha analizzato il disciplinamento dell'ambiente sonoro delle chiese di area riformata: BERTOLINI 2019 e BERTOLINI 2018. ROMBOUGH 2019 analizza la repressione dei suoni profani nei luoghi sacri alla luce della tradizione medica del tempo.

[8]. Un punto di partenza è fornito dagli studi di BRYANT – QUARANTA 2006, GLIXON 2003 e QUARANTA 1998.

[9]. QUARANTA 1998, pp. 189-226.

[10]. BURCHELATI 1596, c. 1v.

[11]. SAINT-DIDIER 1680, pp. 445-448.

1681, Pavani spedì alla magistratura ventinove relazioni, contenenti dettagli interessanti sulle dinamiche di corteggiamento[12].

Uomini e donne occupavano spesso aree separate. Gli uomini si riunivano in «bozzoli» a confabulare tra loro, mentre le donne sedevano al centro della chiesa o nelle vicinanze degli altari. Il 20 giugno 1680, per esempio, in occasione delle celebrazioni che si tenevano per il Corpus Domini nell'omonima chiesa, le nobildonne «erano tutte insieme sopra una lunga banca, e li nobil huomeni vi stavano in faccia tra loro discorendo»[13]. Anche se separati, i due gruppi comunicavano con occhiate, ammiccamenti, risatine e riverenze: nella chiesa dei Carmini il 26 dicembre 1680, vi fu «grande concorso de nobili et nobildone, le quali erano tutte ingenochiate all'altar di San Nicola, e li nobilhuomeni erano pocco discosti dalle medeme, li quali tra loro discorrevano, e quando si partivano le nobil done li medemi gli facevano riverenza con qualche riso»[14]. Nella stessa chiesa, il successivo 6 gennaio, Pavani vede

> [...] molti nobili et gentildone, le quali udivano le messe all'altar della Beata Vergine; et osservando diligentemente vidi che li nobili stavano in piedi imbozzolati in quatro o cinque tra loro discorendo, parte nel mezo della chiesa e parte vicino alle collone adirimpetto al detto altar, e risguardavano le dette, le quali gli davano certe cignate d'occhio e loro ridevano insieme, et anco le medesime; e quando si partirono si hanno fatto riverenza scambievolmente[15].

Queste relazioni permettono di comprendere fino a che punto i corteggiamenti fossero tollerati dai devoti presenti alla messa e dalle autorità. Le occhiate e i cenni che intercorrevano tra i due gruppi, sebbene registrate da Pavani, non erano considerate scandalose. L'11 agosto 1680 l'agente entrò nella chiesa della Salute, dove, scrisse «non ho veduto scandoli, perché le nobildonne vanno sopra le banche all'altar grande et molte all'altar di Sant'Antonio, e li nobilhuomeni stano giù discosti tra loro discorendo in molti bozzoli; vero è che ridono, et tra loro alcune volte si bacciono in fronte, e molti stano fuori di chiesa spacizando sopra li scalini alle porte, e quando vegono venir o uscir le nobildonne di chiesa gli fanno riverenza cortegiandole»[16]. Lo stesso accadde il 26 novembre successivo, quando nella chiesa vi fu grande concorso di nobildonne e nobiluomini, le prime «tutte erano ingenochiate sopra le banche grande, tra loro discorendo», mentre i secondi «alcuni spasizavano et alcuni erano in bozzolo che discorevano, risguardando le medesime con qualche riso»[17].

---

12. Ringrazio Federico Barbierato per avermi segnalato la fonte.

13. ASVe, Inquisitori di Stato, b. 622, fasc. *Pavani Domenico 1681*, rel. 3 luglio 1680.

14. ASVe, Inquisitori di Stato, b. 622, fasc. *Pavani Domenico 1681*, rel. 2 gennaio 1680.

15. ASVe, Inquisitori di Stato, b. 622, fasc. *Pavani Domenico 1681*, rel. 14 gennaio 1680 m.v.

16. ASVe, Inquisitori di Stato, b. 622, fasc. *Pavani Domenico 1681*, rel. 26 agosto 1680.

17. ASVe, Inquisitori di Stato, b. 622, fasc. *Pavani Domenico 1681*, rel. 26 novembre 1680.

# SUONI PERICOLOSI

Il corteggiamento diventava scandaloso, e quindi riferibile «con giustificatione» agli Inquisitori, quando tra i due gruppi avvenivano contatti verbali e fisici. Per esempio il 2 giugno 1680, durante una festa per la consacrazione di una monaca nella chiesa di San Zaccaria, Pavani coglie in fallo «molti che rendevano scandolo», fra i quali identifica tre nobili: Piero Donà, che stava «sentato sopra una cariega in mezo molte gentildone, et discoreva con le medesime con grande riso, togliendogli la ventola hor ad una hor all'altra fuori di mano facendosi fresco, facendo ridere altri nobili che vi erano vicino», Geronimo Pisani dal Banco «il qual discoreva con una gentildona et insieme ridevano, et era voltato con la schena verso l'altare maggiore, non ostante il monsignor Illustrissimo Patriarca faceva la levatione del santissimo» e Andrea Bon, il quale, posizionato «dietro una colona, e faceva ridere le gentildone togliendogli la ventola di mano, facendosi fresco che causava che altri nobili ridevano»[18]. Pochi giorni dopo, il 13 giugno, Pavani è ai Frari, dove nota un nobile «appoggiato al banco del Nome di Dio, il qual discoreva secretamente con quatro gentildone che erano sentate sopra il medesimo, et questo faceva chiasso e riso, et causava che le medesime ridevano non ostante che si celebrava la messa al detto altare attacato al detto banco»[19]. Ancora, Pavani nota un molestatore 'seriale' che si recava in chiesa con l'unico scopo di corteggiare le donne presenti: un certo Stefano Civran «turco fatto cristian» che faceva «atti di scandolo» a «tutte le donne che passano per chiesa inanzi et indietro, et anco a quelle ingenochiate», parlando loro da vicino («si approssima vicino a faccia a faccia et gli mottiva parole») e andando continuamente alla ricerca di nuove vittime, inseguendole in diverse chiese («mai sta fermo in un solo locco, ma va sempre a caminando per chiesa, et quando non vede done di sua satisfattione si trasporta da una chiesa all'altra»)[20].

I corteggiamenti potevano stimolare rancore in alcuni presenti. Alla Salute, nel novembre 1680, mentre alcuni aristocratici facevano «gran chiasso e riso» sotto l'altare maggiore «bacciandosi uno con l'altro», Pavani sentì un uomo affermare «se fossimo noi altri [popolani] che facessimo tanto bacane e chiasso, ne condurerebbero in galia». Un giudizio del genere è però lontano dalla condanna morale e sembra indicare che i corteggiamenti apparissero normali agli occhi della popolazione.

## UN CASO DI CONTAMINAZIONE LASCIVA DELLA MUSICA SACRA

La musica polifonica non fungeva solamente da richiamo e da sottofondo sonoro a questi atti. Talvolta, giocava un ruolo più attivo, servendo da mezzo di comunicazione tra amanti. Un esempio è fornito dal caso di Francesco Dei, un prete processato nel secondo decennio del

---

[18]. ASVe, Inquisitori di Stato, b. 622, fasc. *Pavani Domenico 1681*, rel. 10 giugno 1680.

[19]. ASVe, Inquisitori di Stato, b. 622, fasc. *Pavani Domenico 1681*, rel. 14 giugno 1680.

[20]. ASVe, Inquisitori di Stato, b. 622, fasc. *Pavani Domenico 1681*, rel. 9 aprile 1681.

Seicento a causa di una relazione amorosa con Barbarella, monaca conversa del monastero di San Daniele di Venezia. Francesco officiava nella chiesa della monaca in qualità di mansionario, soprattutto nelle occasioni di messa solenne, durante le quali cantava insieme ad altri quattro preti[21]. Probabilmente proprio grazie a questo incarico ebbe un primo contatto con Barbarella. A breve, l'intesa tra i due parve evidente alle monache del monastero e ai religiosi che vi si recavano a dire messa. Un prete, Vincenzo da San Domenico, rivelò che spesso i due si incontravano in sagrestia e che la lunga durata dei loro incontri scandalizzava tutti «perché i rasona delle volte forte, et i ride, et quelli che è in giesia sente, et se scandaliza»[22]. La loro relazione era nota anche ai nobiluomini che frequentavano la chiesa: un Nicolò Da Mosto aveva sentito dire che Francesco aveva «interesse di amori» nel monastero, mentre un Domenico Da Mosto raccontò di aver visto Francesco ragionare in parlatorio con una monaca che, gli era stato detto, «era sua morosa»[23].

La relazione tra i due si manifestava particolarmente in tempo di festa, quando Francesco cantava la messa. Fu questo a muovere una denuncia anonima ai Provveditori sopra i monasteri, il 9 dicembre 1617. Francesco, vi si legge, era entrato in chiesa alla festa dell'Avvento «facendo atti con il fazoleto», mentre il giorno dei morti la conversa era apparsa «alla porta [del parlatorio] con una filza de bozolai» preparati per l'amante[24]. Oltre a ciò, mentre cantava la messa accompagnato dall'organo, il prete lanciava i propri strali amorosi camuffandoli nel testo di un mottetto del noto compositore Lodovico Viadana:

> [...] il va in organo come si canta mese, et canta "veni domine in cor meum, ostende amorem tuum ut posim te amare, quia amore langueo, alleluia, alleluia" et lui non sa cantar, el falla, e qua tutte ride con un chiaso che par si fazi comedie; et va ancho come si mete fuora il Santissimo a Sant'Anna con il ferariol, si in zanochia all'altar e canta "quis dabit capiti meo" et infin "et mente totus ardeo" et qua tutti ride che è una gran vergogna[25].

Dopo la denuncia Francesco, probabilmente avvertito del fatto che i Provveditori avevano avviato un'inchiesta nei suoi confronti, cercò di calmare le acque evitando il monastero per un po' di tempo. Ciò nonostante, continuò a intrattenere rapporti epistolari con Barbarella,

---

[21]. Dei quali anche un altro, Battistin da Castello, fu processato dai Provveditori per la frequentazione assidua delle monache di San Daniele: purtroppo degli atti pare essere rimasta solamente la copia di un costituto, inserito nel processo a Dei. ASVe, Provveditori Monasteri, b. 265, fasc. *1617 febb* (A), c. 4v.

[22]. ASVe, Provveditori Monasteri, b. 265, fasc. *1617 febb* (A), c. 3v.

[23]. ASVe, Provveditori Monasteri, b. 265, fasc. *1617 febb* (A), c. 11r e c. 12v.

[24]. Secondo un testimone quel giorno presente in coro insieme a Francesco, la porta in questione era una finestra della grata posta «dove se facevano le esequie» e la monaca era «vestita lasciva»: *cfr.* ASVe, Provveditori Monasteri, b. 265, fasc. *1617 febb* (A), c. 11v. Il regalo di dolci era un atto di corteggiamento codificato.

[25]. ASVe, Provveditori Monasteri, b. 265, fasc. *1617 febb* (A), c. 9r.

# SUONI PERICOLOSI

provati da due lettere firmate da quest'ultima. La tregua amorosa durò un paio di mesi: in una delle lettere, la monaca aveva dato appuntamento 'visivo' al suo amato: «mo luni [lunedì] si canta messa per Sant'Agata, et mercore [mercoledì] per la sagra: a rivedersi da lontano»[26].

L'appuntamento ebbe effettivamente luogo e gli atti amorosi tra i due ripresero: l'evento mosse un'altra denuncia, questa volta firmata dalla priora del monastero, presentata pochi giorni dopo la festa in questione, il 9 febbraio 1618. Nella querela si affermava che Francesco Dei

> [...] il giorno di Sant'Agata [...] il cantò evangelio, et finite che fu le mese grande, el s'aconziò sopra i scalini del altar del sagramento, e lì faceva moti con il fazoletto, con suspiri che si sentiva fin in choro da noi, senza timor di Dio né di chi era presente, con tanto scandolo che molte de choro si partì per non veder tal cosa". La priora incitava i Provveditori a punire la sfacciatezza del prete, minacciandoli che in caso contrario "mi risolverò renonciar il priorado[27].

Dopo questa seconda sollecitazione, i Provveditori fecero arrestare Francesco, lo processarono e condannarono il 19 giugno 1618 a un anno di prigione serrata alla luce e gli proibirono di parlare alle monache — anche parenti — per il resto della sua vita[28]. Dal processo emergono ulteriori aspetti sulla tolleranza del pubblico verso i corteggiamenti in chiesa. Nella prima denuncia si parla di risa stimolate dalle parole del prete e dal modo in cui erano cantate: per le querelanti l'ilarità suscitata rendeva dissacrante e sacrilega l'azione del religioso («par si fazi comedie»)[29]. Coloro che frequentavano la chiesa erano al corrente della relazione amorosa e comprendevano il messaggio nascosto veicolato dalle parole cantate dal prete, le quali prese in sé non avevano nulla di sbagliato, come afferma anche un giudice nel corso degli interrogatori[30]. Si può anche pensare che gli 'errori' commessi dal prete nelle vocalizzazioni («lui non sa cantar, el falla») fossero frutto dell'adozione di un atteggiamento buffonesco finalizzato a comunicare più nettamente le proprie reali intenzioni. Ad ogni modo il pubblico sembra reagire con complicità ai gesti di Dei. Solamente i religiosi appaiono scandalizzati: nella prima denuncia, le monache sollecitano i Provveditori ad intervenire perché «tutto il intero

---

[26]. ASVe, Provveditori Monasteri, b. 265, fasc. *1617 febb* (A), lettera *A*.

[27]. ASVe, Provveditori Monasteri, b. 265, fasc. *1617 febb* (A), c. 14r.

[28]. Il caso è citato anche da GLIXON 2017, pp. 65-67, ma senza mettere in evidenza le intenzioni di Francesco Dei.

[29]. Sul potere dissacrante del riso si veda MINOIS 2004.

[30]. Le parole, anzi, richiamano un passo del Cantico dei cantici. «Cantavi "Veni domine in cor meum, ostende amore tuum ut possim te amari, quia amore langueo" parole che se ben buone in se stesse, essendo ditte in contemplacione di chi non dovevi, erano mal intese». ASVe, Provveditori Monasteri, b. 265, fasc. *1617 febb* (A), c. 22v.

convento ne haverà allegreza che si leva ste bufonarie»[31]; nella seconda si parla di «scandolo» che costringe alcune religiose ad allontanarsi dal coro. Il tenore degli interrogatori dei testimoni segnalati nelle denunce tradisce l'indifferenza — se non la simpatia — provata dai laici nei confronti del prete: i due nobili Da Mosto, per esempio, non appaiono stupiti dalla relazione amorosa di cui sono a conoscenza[32]. Anche la ritrosia delle autorità a intervenire, dimostrata dal tono più risoluto della seconda denuncia — dove la priora minaccia anche di dimettersi — sembra indicare che queste manifestazioni fossero all'ordine del giorno: delle trasgressioni operate da molti.

## Il disciplinamento comportamentale nelle chiese

Sin dagli inizi del Cinquecento e soprattutto dopo il Concilio di Trento, i vescovi riformatori lottarono su più piani per estirpare questi comportamenti — anche se con poco successo, come dimostrano le fonti seicentesche appena viste.

In primo luogo, si cercò di inculcare una diversa sensibilità verso gli spazi sacri. La socialità festiva, considerata peccaminosa dai moralisti, fu combattuta ed espulsa dalle vicinanze delle chiese e dagli annessi di queste ultime. I banchi dei *scaleteri* e dei *festari* — presso i quali i corteggiatori potevano trovare i dolci da regalare alle proprie amanti — furono banditi dai sagrati e dai cimiteri. Questi ultimi furono chiusi con mura e cancelli per tenere distante qualsiasi pratica profana[33].

Gli sforzi dei riformatori riguardarono anche il portamento, i gesti e le espressioni di coloro che celebravano la messa: imposero loro imposto di presentarsi nell'area del coro con le vesti in ordine e l'aspetto curato, e di adottare un atteggiamento austero che ispirasse devozione. Anche i non religiosi che aiutavano gli officianti furono sottoposti alle stesse regole: i cantori e gli strumentisti laici furono obbligati a vestire le «cottole» in modo da non differenziarsi dagli ecclesiastici e ad adottare gli stessi atteggiamenti austeri e devoti[34].

Alcuni provvedimenti colpivano anche i comportamenti del pubblico: molti vescovi proibirono alle persone di passeggiare per la chiesa durante gli uffici liturgici e di compiere gli atti di corteggiamento. Visitando la Prepositura di Asolo nel 1578, il vescovo di Treviso Francesco Corner raccomandò ai parroci di esortare i fedeli a «star divotamente alle messe in genochioni con tutti doi li genochi sino alla benedition del sacerdote», quindi per tutta la durata delle

---

31.  ASVe, Provveditori Monasteri, b. 265, fasc. *1617 febb* (A), c. 14r.

32.  ASVe, Provveditori Monasteri, b. 265, fasc. *1617 febb* (A), c. 11r. e 12v.

33.  Per una prima mappatura dei proclami contro le attività festive nei luoghi sacri e nel territorio cittadino si veda Bryant – Cecchinato 2016.

34.  Per le «cottole» si veda Quaranta 1998, pp. 168-175. Per un quadro dello stato del clero nell'Italia prima del Concilio di Trento, De Boer 2004, pp. 9-45.

## Suoni pericolosi

liturgie, «eccettuando però mentre se dirà l'Evangelio, nel qual tempo debba ogn'uno star rito in piedi». Durante la stessa visita il prelato, giunto nella parrocchia di Santa Maria di Zianigo, proibì totalmente i «parlamenti che intendiamo farsi nella giesia, così al tempo della messa come avanti et doppoi»[35].

Poiché nella chiesa si doveva stare con «humiltà et riverenza» i vestiti dai colori sgargianti e le armi solitamente indossate dai corteggiatori furono colpiti con leggi suntuarie e divieti. Carlo Borromeo, nelle *Avvertenze* pubblicate nel 1574, raccomandò ai confessori della sua arcidiocesi di vietare questi «superflui adornamenti»: a essere colpiti erano abiti e gioielli che potessero in qualsiasi modo spingere a una condotta peccaminosa e destare pensieri lascivi per ragioni intrinseche o agli occhi del pubblico, indossati «con intentione di mostrare varii affetti d'amore inhonesto, et dar segno d'essi con vestire varii colori o in altro modo»[36]. Le armi portate dagli uomini a scopo di difesa o per essere esibite durante il corteggiamento furono bandite: nella visita del 1578, il vescovo di Treviso Francesco Corner comanda ai parroci di varie chiese della diocesi di sospendere le celebrazioni qualora qualcuno fosse entrato in chiesa armato, e di non riprendere fino a che le armi non fossero state riposte all'esterno dell'edificio sacro[37].

La socialità peccaminosa fu combattuta anche ristrutturando architettonicamente l'area del coro e le navate. Alcuni provvedimenti mettevano ordine alla confusione promiscua creata dalla folla festiva. Il coro e l'altare furono delimitati da colonnette che dovevano scongiurare le incursioni dei laici nelle vicinanze del sacro desco. L'ingresso all'area del coro fu riservato unicamente agli ufficianti e a coloro che erano autorizzati ad aiutarli nello svolgimento dei rituali liturgici. La promiscuità che vigeva tra le navate fu combattuta con la costruzione di paratie e tramezzi che impedivano i contatti visivi e orali tra le persone di sesso opposto. In alcuni casi, a donne e uomini fu imposto di accedere alle chiese da porte differenti[38].

Questi provvedimenti dimostrano la volontà di eliminare il contagio sensoriale alla quale erano esposti coloro che si recavano in chiesa in queste occasioni: per i moralisti le tentazioni del demonio si trasmettevano — come le malattie — attraverso i sensi[39]. È possibile reinterpretare in tal modo anche la regolamentazione dell'ambiente sonoro: mezzo potente e temuto, la musica era considerata infatti un pericoloso agente contaminante[40].

---

[35]. Citt. in ADTv, Visite pastorali antiche, b. 7, fasc. I, c. 158r e fasc. III, c. 35r-36v.

[36]. Sui vestiti si veda quanto scritto da De Boer 2004, pp. 70-73. La citazione si legge a p. 72.

[37]. ADTv, Visite pastorali antiche, b. 7, fasc. III, cc. 11r e 149v.

[38]. Tutti questi provvedimenti sono riscontrabili nelle visite pastorali trevigiane condotte da Giorgio e da Francesco Corner rispettivamente nel 1566 e nel 1578 per le quali si veda ADTv, Visite pastorali antiche, b. 6, fascc. II-III e b. 7, fascc. I-III.

[39]. De Boer 2004, pp. 70-76.

[40]. La bibliografia sul potere della musica è vasta. Per una bibliografia ragionata sull'argomento si veda Chemotti 2022.

# Umberto Cecchinato

## Suoni pericolosi: musica, corpo, emozioni e comportamento

La tradizione galenica concepiva il corpo umano come un organismo poroso, un 'contenitore' semimpermeabile dove circolavano quattro umori: il sangue, la flemma, la bile gialla o collera, la bile nera o melancolia. I fluidi umorali svolgevano due importanti funzioni: nutrire il corpo e regolare il temperamento delle persone. Il temperamento, basato su quattro qualità — caldo, freddo, umido, secco — determinava lo stato di salute dell'individuo. Il suo equilibrio, insieme a quello dei quattro umori, era responsabile delle disposizioni fisiologiche e psicologiche. Il corpo poroso era esposto all'influenza degli agenti esterni: odori, suoni e qualsiasi cosa viaggiasse nell'aria, oltre a tutto ciò che il corpo assorbiva tramite il tatto. Questi agenti agivano costantemente sull'equilibrio umorale interno provocando il suo continuo mutamento. Lo squilibrio del temperamento e degli umori determinava lo stato di infermità fisica o psicologica: per far tornare alla salute il malato, il medico doveva riequilibrarne gli umori e, in tal modo, il temperamento[41].

L'udito era particolarmente esposto all'azione di questi agenti: ciò che si udiva era incontrollabile, a meno che non si sopprimesse radicalmente la fonte sonora. Nella concezione medica del tempo, il suono aveva caratteristiche fisiche e si muoveva insieme all'aria. Secondo Giuseppe Rosaccio l'orecchio aveva forma di chiocciola per due ragioni. Questa forma permetteva di raccogliere «l'aere et il suono»: «l'aria sonora» così raccolta riempiva il timpano — «osso poroso e secco» che si trovava in fondo all'orecchio — ed era da quest'ultimo trasmessa al «senso commune» attraverso il nervo che collegava le due parti, con un'azione «a guisa di mantice». La forma a spirale dell'orecchio proteggeva anche il senso comune dai suoni forti e dagli strepiti: in caso contrario la creatura sarebbe diventata sorda[42]. Il «senso commune» era un senso interiore, proprio dell'anima, e permetteva a quest'ultima di svolgere l'attività intellettiva e razionale, ovvero di processare le informazioni derivate dai cinque sensi esterni. Il contatto diretto tra il suono e il senso comune rendeva l'udito una via di comunicazione privilegiata dell'anima con il mondo esterno e le sue influenze. Anche per questo all'udito, nella tradizione medievale, era attribuita grande importanza rispetto agli altri sensi[43]. I moralisti ritenevano impossibile non rimanere contagiati dal suono prodotto durante le feste: il predicatore duecentesco Guillaume Peyraut riserva uno spazio di riguardo alle parole cantate nella lista di peccati inseriti nella sua *Summa de vitiis* e le definisce «sagitta diaboli inevitabilis»[44].

---

[41].    Siraisi 1990, pp. 78-114; Paster 1993, pp. 1-11 e Paster 2004, pp. 1-24.

[42].    Rosaccio 1602, p. 44.

[43].    Si veda Ginzburg 1986, p. 152. Ficino assegnava poteri magici maggiori alle melodie e alle parole rispetto alle immagini: su questo e sulla gerarchia dei due sensi Tomlinson 1993, pp. 101-144.

[44].    Arcangeli 2000, p. 76.

SUONI PERICOLOSI

Oltre ad avere un accesso all'anima privilegiato rispetto a ciò che agiva sugli altri sensi, la musica aveva effetti sulle passioni e sui comportamenti delle persone e degli animali. Fin dall'Antichità, i suoni prodotti dall'uomo erano investiti di particolari poteri: nella cosmologia pitagorica, i pianeti e il mondo ultraterreno risuonavano armonicamente secondo precise misure e proporzioni; le stesse misure erano presenti nel corpo umano e potevano essere riprodotte musicalmente attraverso gli strumenti o il canto[45].

Alcuni umanisti rinascimentali spiegavano gli effetti della musica accostando i modi musicali degli antichi — dorico, frigio, lidio e misolidio — alla teoria umorale. Il matematico e teorico musicale spagnolo Bartolomeo Ramos de Pareja (1440-1522), per esempio, nel trattato *Musica Practica*, stampato a Bologna nel 1482, riprende la suddivisione boeziana, e stabilisce le connessioni esistenti tra le tre tipologie di musica. I tre ambiti — umano, mondano e strumentale — sono rappresentati rispettivamente dagli umori, dalle sfere celesti e dai modi musicali. Ramos stabilisce la connessione tra questi tre ambiti: egli afferma che la *musica instrumentalis* aveva conformità e similitudine con la *musica humana*, poiché i modi musicali influivano sui quattro temperamenti dell'uomo, aumentandoli o diminuendoli. Il modo dorico dominava la flemma, il frigio agiva sulla bile gialla, il lidio regolava l'umore sanguigno, mentre il misolidio più lento e tranquillo, influenzava la bile nera. Ognuno dei quattro modi plagali (Hypodorico, Hypofrigio, Hypolidio e Hypomesolidio) derivati dai modi autentici agiva sugli stessi fluidi umorali ma in modo opposto. Ramos procede in seguito a connettere i quattro modi alle sfere celesti che secondo gli astrologi influivano sul mondo sublunare: i quattro elementi, gli umori, i caratteri morali, i colori, le stagioni, ecc.[46].

L'azione sui fluidi umorali si ripercuoteva sulle emozioni che questi ultimi veicolavano, dunque una musica ben modulata aveva la capacità di muovere negli ascoltatori diverse passioni. Inoltre, secondo il sapere medico del tempo, gli stati psicologici e fisiologici erano strettamente connessi: i comportamenti erano considerati un'espressione dell'interazione delle quattro qualità del temperamento. Agendo sull'equilibrio umorale, la musica, oltre a stimolare certi stati emotivi, induceva gli ascoltatori ad agire in determinati modi: a peccare o a divenire più devota; a infuriarsi o a calmarsi.

I modi armonici non erano le uniche componenti musicali a interagire con organi e fluidi corporali: anche i ritmi e gli accenti pulsavano attraverso l'orecchio e colpivano il corpo, stimolando moti e passioni. In modo simile a Ramos, Nicolas Bergier, nel trattato *De la musique speculative* (ca. 1608), crea un sistema di correlazioni tra i ritmi musicali — spondaico, pirrico, dattilo, ecc. — e le rispettive risposte corporee emotive e comportamentali. I modi ritmici influenzano le passioni al pari di quelli armonici: Bergier, suonando il proprio flauto un ritmo

---

[45]. Sulla corrispondenza tra le misure armoniche universali e quelle del corpo umano si veda VAN ORDEN 2005, pp. 54-62.

[46]. Tutti questi aspetti in TOMLINSON 1993, pp. 78-84.

spondaico, afferma di essere riuscito a calmare un uomo ebbro che avanzava furioso mulinando la propria spada. Al contrario, il ritmo pirrico era utilizzato in battaglia, perché rendeva gli uomini belligeranti e stimolava la rabbia[47].

## La lotta alla musica lasciva

Se i moralisti definivano *lascivus* o *impurus* un brano musicale non era solamente perché quest'ultimo appariva loro contaminato da elementi profani, ma perché credevano veicolasse una corruttela sensoriale concreta. La musica lasciva aveva un impatto morale, effeminava gli animi e degradava la mascolinità[48].

Regolando lo spazio sonoro liturgico, le autorità ecclesiastiche miravano a disciplinare i comportamenti che avevano luogo durante la messa, usando consapevolmente le influenze che la musica aveva sulla psicologia umana — e di conseguenza sulle emozioni e sulle azioni delle persone. Gli intellettuali dell'epoca, come nota Gail Kern Paster, dubitavano fortemente che la forza della ragione potesse limitare o regolare le emozioni o le loro influenze comportamentali, specialmente se si trattava di popolani o persone non istruite[49]. Molti erano convinti che la musica fosse in grado di stimolare negli ascoltatori diverse emozioni: per queste persone, ottenere il controllo delle fonti sonore equivaleva a controllare il comportamento di coloro che le ascoltavano. Alcuni, come il patriarca Querini, credevano che la gente si corteggiasse in chiesa perché spinta dalle canzoni lascive e dal timbro prodotto dagli strumenti musicali usati durante il ballo.

Le istanze di 'riforma' della musica sacra possono essere rilette in questa prospettiva. Per esempio, la famosa lettera inviata da Bernardino Cirillo Franco a Ugolino Gualteruzzi il 16 febbraio 1549, spesso citata dai musicologi e considerata un attacco alla polifonia da chiesa e un'espressione della riforma musicale voluta dai padri conciliaristi[50]. Le intenzioni espresse dal vescovo palesano chiaramente la credenza dei poteri della musica. Secondo Cirillo Franco, la musica degli Antichi aveva «maggiori effetti che noi non facciamo hora né con la retorica, né con l'oratoria, nel moderare le passioni et effetti dell'animo». Il prelato auspicava dunque una riscoperta dei modi musicali antichi, i quali, usati sapientemente, avrebbero permesso di ispirare negli ascoltatori i comportamenti convenienti durante le messe. La musica a lui contemporanea

---

47.   Il trattato di Bergier è analizzato da Van Orden 2005, pp. 84-86.

48.   Bertoglio 2017, pp. 125-127.

49.   Si vedano Paster 2004, pp. 19-20 e Rowe 2004, p. 172. Anche l'azione riformatrice di Carlo Borromeo si basava sulla sfiducia nel libero arbitrio: De Boer 2004, pp. 74-76. Più recentemente, De Boer ha invitato a studiare le implicazioni etiche della cultura sui sensi, e i modi in cui la percezione sensoriale era considerata come fonte di comportamenti appropriati e inappropriati. De Boer 2013, pp. 249.

50.   Così, per esempio, la interpreta Mischiati 1995. Per tutte le citazioni, *cfr*. Cirillo 1567, *passim*.

mancava del necessario sapere teorico ed era improntata quasi esclusivamente all'uso pratico: pertanto essa era usata impropriamente e istigava gli ascoltatori ad agire male. Le melodie usate durante i riti liturgici fornivano una chiara testimonianza: nell'accompagnamento del Kyrie, per esempio, si sarebbe dovuto usare il modo misolidio, «che havrebbe pesto, nonché contrito, il cuore e l'animo, et mossa, se non a pianto, almeno ad affetto pietoso ogni mente indurata», in conformità con i contenuti del testo sacro, invocante la misericordia divina. Al contrario, Cirillo Franco nota che ai suoi tempi si «cantano tutte simil cose in genere promiscuo et incerto» provocando negli ascoltatori non pietà e devozione, bensì sentimenti profani: «dicono alle volte "che bella messa è stata cantata in cappella!" E quale per tua fe? Risponde o "L'ombre armato", o "Hercules Dux Ferrariae", o "La Filomena". Che diavolo ha da far la messa con l'huomo armato, né con Filomena, né col duca di Ferrara?». Cirillo qui si riferisce alla contaminazione tra generi sacri e profani diffusissima sin dal Quattrocento nella musica da chiesa; i titoli citati sono canzoni da ballo pubblico molto famose all'epoca, e fanno pensare che la contaminazione si spingesse ben oltre le tradizioni delle messe da battaglia o dei *contrafacta* studiate dai musicologi[51]. Questa contaminazione era considerata pericolosa perché la musica profana muoveva istinti lontani dalla devozione; inoltre, al contrario della musica sacra, la musica profana aveva effetti assicurati: secondo Cirillo il suono delle danze — «la pavana e la gagliarda» — attirava le «buone donne da San Rocco e da piazza Lombarda», le quali subito «si pongono sul lor moto, e par che sentano il dittirambo dionisiaco». Cirillo suggeriva che la musica fosse adattata alla situazione sociale nella quale era eseguita: quella da chiesa muova a pietà, quella da ballo spinga al movimento sfrenato. Ogni situazione vuole dei comportamenti diversi, pertanto la musica deve ispirarli in modo conveniente.

> Io vorrei, in somma, che quando havesse a cantare una messa in chiesa, secondo la suggetta sostanza delle parole constasse la musica di certi concenti, e numeri atti a movere a religione e pietà gli affetti nostri, e così ne' salmi et himni, et altre laudi che si porgono a Dio; e che su la pavana e la gagliarda, se non bastano su li numeri e cadentie che vi sono, vi se n'aggiungessino degli altri, sin che facessino ballar sino le banche di casa; e che ciascun modo s'adattasse al suggetto suo.

Componendo le messe secondo un uso sapiente dei modi antichi vi era dunque la speranza di «bandir di chiesa certe corruttele che vi sono, et introdurvi qualche armonia affetuosa, atta a movere a religione e pietà, et inclinare a devotione».

L'azione di disciplinamento dello spazio sonoro delle chiese era dunque auspicata da moralisti convinti che grazie ai poteri della musica fosse possibile correggere i comportamenti delle persone in chiesa. Questa convinzione era diffusa anche in altre regioni europee, dove

---

[51]. Per esempio, WILSON 2009. Anche BERTOGLIO 2017, pp. 145-151 ha ridiscusso questa interpretazione, fornendone una simile a quella espressa nelle prossime pagine.

alcune accademie furono ufficializzate con l'esplicita intenzione di combattere la depravazione morale derivante dalla musica sregolata e di usare la musica come un mezzo di controllo sociale. La patente con cui Carlo IX ufficializzava l'*Académie de poésie et de musique* nel 1570 — periodo particolarmente cruento di scontri tra ugonotti e cattolici — dichiara che «la musica attualmente suonata nel paese dovrebbe essere regolata da leggi specifiche, perché la mente e il comportamento di molti uomini sono condizionati dalle sue qualità, cosicché se la musica è disordinata, la morale è depravata, mentre quando la musica è ordinata, anche gli uomini sono moralmente disciplinati»[52].

La purificazione della musica da chiesa dagli elementi profani non fu attuata in modo unitario e sistematico. Sensibilità e zelo diversi muovevano i vescovi riformatori; oltre a ciò, l'azione di disciplinamento si scontrava con le tradizioni musicali in vigore nelle chiese delle diocesi. Questa divergenza di opinioni e visioni si tradusse in un'azione frammentaria, ricostruibile in primo luogo sui decreti pubblicati in seguito ai sinodi diocesani tenuti dai vescovi dopo la fine del Concilio di Trento, in secondo luogo sull'effettiva azione di riforma attuata nelle diocesi, ricostruibile con lo studio delle visite pastorali.

## Le azioni di riforma

Come dimostra l'ordine del patriarca Querini, già prima del Concilio di Trento i moralisti tentavano di regolare l'ambiente sonoro delle chiese. Giovanni Morone bandisce la musica polifonica dalla cattedrale di Modena nel 1537. Girolamo Seripando segue il suo esempio nel 1540, vietandone l'esecuzione presso le monache agostiniane di Santa Monica di Roma[53]. Nelle *Constitutiones* di Matteo Giberti, edite nel 1542, il vescovo raccomanda ai chierici di salmodiare con gravità e modestia, per dare sollievo alle orecchie degli ascoltatori ed eccitarli alla devozione, affinché gli uffici liturgici non siano occasioni per udire «publicae cantilenae et lascivae»[54]. Tuttavia questi interventi appaiono isolati e senza seguito.

Durante il Concilio di Trento, il problema dell'uso della musica nelle liturgie è un elemento secondario all'interno del più ampio contesto degli abusi della messa, ed è discusso nella ventiduesima sessione tenuta nel settembre 1562[55]. Le proposte avanzate dalla commissione — l'eliminazione degli elementi profani, l'abolizione della polifonia, l'esclusione degli strumenti musicali diversi dall'organo — sono via via attenuate durante i dibattiti, e riassunte nel generico canone approvato al termine della sessione:

---

52. Citato da Gouk 2013. Traduzione dell'autore.
53. Poco si sa dei divieti emanati da Moroni e Seripando. Si veda Monson 2002, p. 5.
54. Constitutiones 1542, c. 16v.
55. Monson 2002, p. 11 e Bertoglio 2017, pp. 313-348.

## Suoni pericolosi

[...] ab ecclesiis vero musicas eas, ubi sive organo sive cantu lascivum aut impurum aliquid miscetur, item saeculares omnes actiones, vana atque adeo profana colloquia, deambulationes, strepitus, clamores arceant, ut domus Dei vere domus orationis esse videatur ac dici possit[56].

L'ambiguità del decreto permetteva implicitamente l'esecuzione di musiche polifoniche e l'uso dell'organo durante le messe, mentre proibiva esplicitamente solo gli elementi profani; non vi si fanno riferimenti riguardo alla questione dell'intelligibilità delle parole[57]. Come si nota, l'accenno alla musica rientrava in una più ampia condanna dei comportamenti solitamente tenuti dalla folla: deambulare nella chiesa, conversare con i propri amanti, fare chiasso ecc. Il problema dell'impurità della musica sacra era dunque associato, dai padri conciliari, a quello dei comportamenti festivi visti in precedenza.

Il problema è ripreso nella ventiquattresima sessione, tenutasi tra il settembre e il novembre 1563, alla quale partecipano come legati papali prelati già impegnati nella riforma dei propri territori, come Giovanni Morone e Bernardo Navagero. Importante apporto è dato dalla partecipazione di Gabriele Paleotti, molto probabilmente anch'egli interessato a definire delle regole più chiare sull'uso della musica liturgica[58]. Il canone XII, non meno ambiguo del precedente, fu approvato in seguito a scritture, discussioni e riscritture: le messe avrebbero dovuto essere cantate con decoro, «congrua canendi seu modulandi ratione», lasciando però ai sinodi regionali il compito di impartire le istruzioni al clero sulla base degli usi locali[59].

Entrambi i canoni lasciavano dunque ampia libertà di applicazione ai vescovi e miravano a fornire un *framework* su cui basare le azioni di riforma: quando e come applicarli dipendeva dalla volontà e dalla sensibilità dei vescovi e va pertanto verificata per ogni singola diocesi. L'intento dei riformatori di estirpare le parti lascive della musica si può seguire attraverso l'analisi dei decreti e delle costituzioni sinodali pubblicati negli anni immediatamente seguenti il Concilio: emerge un quadro frammentario, con diversi gradi di intervento, legati all'importanza che i vari prelati davano alla musica sacra e alla necessità di adattarsi alle tradizioni delle singole parrocchie[60]. Per esempio, il riformatore convinto Giovanni Morone, nelle *Constitutiones in synodo Mutinensi* stampate nel 1565, non proibisce la polifonia come aveva fatto precedentemente, ma si limita a ripetere letteralmente il canone tridentino XI, vietando, si noti bene, i canti lascivi e impuri, e a proibire l'intervento dei *tibicines* durante l'elevazione e la celebrazione delle *missae novae*, che pure si dovevano celebrare solo con il consenso del vescovo; era invece permesso il canto delle

---

56. CT, vol. VIII, p. 963.
57. MONSON 2002, pp. 11-13.
58. *Ibidem*, p. 13.
59. *Ibidem*, p. 18, n. 50. Trascrizione in CT, vol. IX, pp. 983-984. Tralascio in questa sede il tentativo di riforma della musica nei monasteri femminili, per il quale si veda MONSON 2002, pp. 19-22.
60. L'analisi che segue è basata prevalentemente sull'elenco fornito da FABBRI 1993, pp. 18-19.

«orationes vel laudes ad hoc sacrificium tantum pertinentes» accompagnato dall'organo[61]. Nemmeno nelle *Constitutiones* del vescovo di Luni e Sarzana si accenna alla polifonia, mentre si vietano i flauti, i suoni profani e le *modulationes* del canto, tutti elementi introdotti per stimolare i sentimenti carnali piuttosto che la pietà[62]. Lo stesso comanda il vescovo di Piacenza nelle *Constitutiones* del 1570: si escludono dalla messa i flauti e le *tibiae*, strumenti usati solitamente nelle danze e in altri spettacoli[63]. Nelle costituzioni sinodali di Parma, stampate nel 1576, le prescrizioni sulla musica si limitano al suono dell'organo: si raccomanda di non suonare né accompagnare melodie e canti lascivi o inonesti[64]. Più ambigue le costituzioni di Rossano in Calabria, dove si raccomanda unicamente di cantare le messe solenni con devozione, in modo distinto e con voce intellegibile[65]. Il sinodo di Salerno del 1579 rilascia solamente alcune istruzioni all'organista, raccomandando di suonare il proprio strumento «temporum ratione servata» e proibendo sotto pena di un carlino di suonare melodie profane[66].

Altre *Constitutiones* contengono elementi che testimoniano una sensibilità e un'attenzione diversa nei confronti della musica sacra e della sua funzione nell'ambito liturgico. Quelle pubblicate nel 1566 sotto Carlo Borromeo, per esempio, bandiscono dalle chiese i canti e i suoni profani, le «molles flexiones» che caratterizzavano i canti sacri e qualsiasi influenza lasciva. Come ha notato Chiara Bertoglio, i riformatori intransigenti pensavano che la *musica mollis* corrompesse l'animo dell'ascoltatore, stimolando negli uomini qualità all'epoca considerate femminili[67]. I canti e suoni dovevano essere gravi, pii e distinti, affinché le parole fossero comprensibili e la musica eccitasse gli animi alla devozione («ut simul et verba intelligantur et ad pietatem auditores excitentur»). Riguardo agli strumenti, Borromeo bandisce dalla chiesa «tibiae, cornuae et reliqua musica instrumenta» e accetta solamente l'organo, a patto che le parole di inni, salmi e cantici eseguiti con l'accompagnamento di quest'ultimo strumento fossero pronunciate distintamente[68]. Un altro riformatore convinto, Giulio Feltrio Della Rovere, nel sinodo tenuto a Ravenna nel 1568 compie la riorganizzazione della cappella musicale della cattedrale: istituisce un maestro di coro con il compito di dirigere i cantori, impartisce norme

---

[61]. L'ambiguità può indicare la volontà di rispettare i diversi costumi sonori delle parrocchie della diocesi. Per gli ordini, CONSTITUTIONES 1565, rispettivamente pp. 75 e 80-81.

[62]. CONSTITUTIONES 1568, p. 13: «Non admittantur in missa tubicines, aut profanorum sonorum, et cantuum modulationes, potius ad aures carnales demulcendas, quam ad pietatem inducendam inventae».

[63]. CONSTITUTIONES 1570, p. 53: «Tubarum, tibiarum[q]ue soni, aliaque musica instrumenta, quae in saltationibus, choreis, aliisque prophanarum rerum actionibus, aut spectaculis, adhiberi solent, ab ecclesia cum in omni missae parte excludantur, tum maxi me, cum Iesu Christi, Domini corpus sustollitur».

[64]. CONSTITUTIONES 1576, c. 20r: «In organo nihil lascive, atque inhoneste canatur, pulseturque».

[65]. CONSTITUTIONES 1579, pp. 34 e 38.

[66]. CONSTITUTIONES 1580A, p. 56: «Caveat autem omnino ne profanos cantus organo referat: si in praedictorum aliquo secus fecerit, singulis vicibus unius caroleni poenam subeat».

[67]. BERTOGLIO 2017, pp. 125-126.

[68]. Trascrizione fornita da FABBRI 1993, p. 20.

di condotta a questi ultimi, assume un maestro di musica che avrebbe insegnato al seminario il canto ecclesiastico, affinché i preti non offendano le orecchie degli ascoltatori con dissonanze ed errori. Per il prelato, il canto deve ispirare la devozione al popolo: si raccomanda dunque l'intelligibilità e il canto piano, ma si lascia la libertà ai cantori di aggiungere consonanze a piacere, purché non si muti il carattere originale del canto («liberum tamen sit cantoribus consonantias aliquas adiungere, non mutata cantus origine»). Della Rovere appare preoccupato dal carattere di suoni e canzoni: nelle disposizioni per l'organista si vieta di suonare melodie lascive e impure, affinché lo strumento possa ispirare pietà e devozione; sono vietati altri generi di strumenti musicali[69]. Le stesse preoccupazioni emergono dalle costituzioni rilasciate dal successivo sinodo di Ravenna (1580), contenenti nutrite disposizioni disciplinari riguardanti i cantori del coro e un unico riferimento alla natura della musica suonata che riprende, traducendolo, il precetto di Della Rovere riguardo ai suoni dell'organo[70]. Il sinodo di Reggio Emilia del 1581 raccomanda ai chierici di cantare le messe in modo che gli astanti comprendessero le parole: il canto piano e grave eccitava gli animi alla devozione, mentre il bando di canti e suoni d'organo lascivi doveva rendere le chiese veri luoghi di orazione[71]. Anche nella *Synodus Cassinensis*, i cui decreti sono dati alle stampe nel 1592, si sottolinea l'importanza della musica nello stimolare la devozione nel cuore dei fedeli («quantam vero inter alia pietatis exercitia, et incitamenta religionis efficaciam non modo ad Deum laudandum, sed etiam ad nostra devotionem excitandam ecclesiastici cantus habeant, nemo ignorat»): il canto rapisce l'animo, alletta ed eleva lo spirito alla contemplazione divina («sensus namque mentis nostrae organa sunt, quos cum sonora harmoniae modulatio suapte natura demulceat, ea ratione in sublime rapiatur animus et ad Divinam contemplandam, laudandamque Maiestatem elevatur»). È pertanto raccomandato di non suonare melodie lascive o impudiche con l'organo durante le messe solenni; ai cantori si impone un canto atto a stimolare la devozione negli ascoltatori[72]. Ancora, nelle *Constitutiones* di Castellaneta del 1595 vi è una parte dedicata all'organo e alla musica (*De organo et musica*) in cui si raccomanda di abbandonare le lascivie e di accomodare i suoni in modo da incitare gli astanti alla pietà («sitque organorum sonus et vocum in illis modulatio eiusmodi, quae ad pietatem et religionem audientes excitet»); gli strumenti differenti dall'organo sono ammessi nelle chiese solo dietro licenza espressa del vescovo. Si raccomanda di cantare le liturgie «omnes recte et

---

[69].   Trascrizione fornita da *ibidem*, pp. 20-22.

[70].   Constitutiones 1580b, c. 58r: «Che nell'organo non si possano sonare cose lascive, o impure conforme al decreto del Concilio di Trento».

[71].   Constitutiones 1582, pp. 47-48: «Ut in divinae laudis officiis, quae debitae servitutis obsequio exhibentur, cunctorum mens vigilet, et fidelium devotio excitetur, ac psallentes placita gravique modulatione decantent. Ab ecclesiis musica omnia, in quibus sive organo sive cantu lascivum, aut impurum, aliquid admistum sit, omnino arceantur, ut domus Dei, vere domus orationis esse videatur, ac dici possit. Si quis vero contra fecerit, ab officio per octo dies suspendetur, aliaque pęna arbitrio nustro plectetur».

[72].   Synodus 1592b, pp. 28 e 33-36.

secure [...] cum musica et cantu plano, ne dissonantia cum irreverentia divinorum officiorum audiatur»: errori e dissonanze sono considerati offensivi e i sacerdoti ignoranti di musica non sono ammessi. Si impone un canto grave e distinto, senza melodie o testi profani: sono proibite le improvvisazioni e i cantori devono seguire i testi appositi, senza aggiungere modulazioni[73].

L'area veneta presenta la stessa varietà di approcci. A Venezia, i successori di Geronimo Querini rivolgono diversi gradi di attenzione al problema della musica sacra. Giovanni Trevisan raccoglie una serie di decreti nelle *Constitutiones* dirette al clero veneziano, date alle stampe nel 1587, nei quali il patriarca dimostra una certa sensibilità: nel cap. III della prima parte, *De celebratione missarum, de divinis officiis ac de residentia*, si parla di «abhominabiles insolentias, terribiles sclopos vel strepitus, aut sonos periculosos» praticati nelle chiese particolarmente nella notte di Natale, i quali «devotio fidelium diminuitur et cultus divinus contemni videtur»[74]. Il cap. VI impone il silenzio nelle chiese, massime durante gli uffici divini e la recitazione dei salmi, agli ecclesiastici e ai laici di sesso femminile e maschile; i trasgressori saranno ripresi dai sacerdoti e puniti acerbamente, i bambini castigati dai parenti e dai maestri[75]. Il cap. VIII vieta ai sacerdoti di cantare le melodie e cantilene che abbellivano epistole, vangeli e prefazioni, delle quali si dice che «intellectum audientium impediant vel perturbent, et per hoc mentibus fidelium devotio minuatur»[76]. Il cap. X impone ai sacerdoti di cantare le messe solenni nel modo istituito dai santi padri: si vieta di cantare i mottetti «nisi sint ad laudem Dei et beatae Virginis Mariae aut aliorum sanctorum»[77]. Ma già pochi anni dopo il successore Lorenzo Priuli dimostra un'attenzione del tutto diversa nei confronti della musica, limitandosi a espellere dalle messe e dagli altri uffici liturgici «cantus inusitati et musica instrumenta, quae profanis actionibus adhiberi solent», a raccomandare di solennizzare le celebrazioni con «modesta psallentium gravitas» e con «placida modulatione»[78].

Anche nella Terraferma si registrano tendenze disparate. A Verona il problema dell'uso della musica sacra è affrontato prima del Concilio di Trento dal riformatore dei costumi ecclesiastici Matteo Giberti. I precetti inseriti nelle sue *Constitutiones* raccomandano ai chierici di cantare con «modesta honestaque psallendi gravitate, placidaque et grata modulatione» in modo da attirare gli ascoltatori e provocare ed eccitare nei loro animi la devozione e non la lascivia[79]. Questi decreti saranno ripresi letteralmente dopo il Concilio tridentino da Bernardo Navagero e dal suo successore Agostino Valier nelle *Constitutiones* pubblicate rispettivamente

---

73. SYNODUS 1595, pp. 201-203.
74. CONSTITUTIONES 1587, c. 4v.
75. *Ibidem*, c. 5r
76. *Ibidem*, 5v.
77. *Ibidem*, 6r.
78. SYNODUS 1592A, pp. 26-27.
79. CONSTITUTIONES 1542, c. 16v.

## SUONI PERICOLOSI

nel 1563 e nel 1589[80]. A Brescia, il vescovo Bollani dedica una breve raccomandazione ai cantori ecclesiastici, ovvero di togliere dal suono dell'organo le «modulationes profanas» e di cantare in modo grave e distinto in modo che si comprendano le parole e che gli animi degli ascoltatori siano mossi a pietà e alla meditazione delle cose celesti[81]. A Vicenza, al contrario, non vi è alcun accenno alla musica sacra[82]. A Treviso, l'unico riferimento al modo di cantare è nelle *Costitutioni* di Giorgio Corner del 1565, nelle quali si vietano «li suoni et li canti lascivi et immoderati» durante le *missae novae*, e nei decreti sinodali emanati dal suo successore Francesco Corner, il quale proibisce l'uso di qualunque tipo di strumento musicale nella celebrazione dei matrimoni[83]. A Rovigo, lo stesso[84]. Le *Constitutiones* pubblicate per la diocesi di Concordia (oggi, Concordia Saggittaria), nel capitolo *De divinorum officiorum celebratione et recitatione* sono inserite minuziosamente le indicazioni da seguire nella pratica rituale, ma non compaiono riferimenti precisi alla musica. Nel capitolo *De chori, seu caerimoniarum magistro* si ordina al maestro di vigilare affinché i canti siano eseguiti secondo lo stile romano: «omnia canenda, ut more Romano canantur, invigilet»[85]. A Padova il problema è affrontato in modo ambiguo, sebbene il sinodo sia stato voluto da un convinto riformatore, Federico Corner: si raccomanda che la musica sia eseguita senza *modulationes* lascive e suoni che macchino la dignità dei divini uffici[86].

Queste fonti normative indica chiaramente che le preoccupazioni dei vescovi che applicano la riforma tridentina si concentrano sugli elementi profani e lascivi dalla musica da chiesa in generale. Ogni azione era legata al contesto e alla diversa sensibilità dei riformatori: alcuni appaiono più preoccupati a ridare dignità al rito liturgico, imponendo un canto piano

---

[80]. CONSTITUTIONES 1563, cc. 20v-21r. CONSTITUTIONES 1589, p. 63.

[81]. CONSTITUTIONES 1575, pp. 93-94: «Cantus vero nullos edat, nisi graves, distinctosque, ut et quae canuntur clarius percipiantur, et audientium animi ad pietatem, rerumque coelestium meditationem inducantur. Et ab organo modulationes profanas omnes amovendas studeat».

[82]. Consultate nella riedizione seicentesca voluta da Dionisio Dolfin, con aggiunta di decreti sinodali del 1623. CONSTITUTIONES 1623.

[83]. *Cfr.* rispettivamente COSTITUTIONI 1565, p. 14 e CONSTITUTIONES 1581, p. 153. L'attenzione dei vescovi trevigiani sembra concentrarsi nella lotta contro il ballo, che viene colpito con numerosi decreti, piuttosto che negli abusi della musica sacra. Oltre alle costituzioni dei Corner, si vedano anche DECRETA 1604A, DECRETA 1604B.

[84]. DECRETA 1594.

[85]. Per esempio, all'organista è raccomandato di suonare dal momento in cui il vescovo si palesava alla porta fino a quando non si fosse seduto al proprio luogo, e di fare lo stesso al termine degli uffici mentre il prelato usciva; o ancora, si impone a tutti i coristi di cantare a voce alternata in modo devoto: *cfr.* SYNODI 1587, pp. 45-48.

[86]. CONSTITUTIONES 1580c, c. 64r: «Quibus diebus musica erit adhibenda magistrum capellae, atque organistam moneant, ut praesto sint atque illud inspiciant, ne divina eloquia lascivis modulationibus committantur, ne ve alienis, et ab ecclesiastica gravitate abhorrentibus sonis rerum sacrarum dignitas dehonestetur». Per Corner si veda GULLINO 1983.

improntato sulla spiritualità e sulla devozione; altri invece colpiscono le parti profane e lascive delle melodie — quei «sonos periculosos» di cui parlano le costituzioni del patriarca veneziano Giovanni Trevisan — che allontanavano gli ascoltatori dalla devozione, ispiravano pensieri lascivi o impuri e corrompevano gli animi.

Particolare attenzione è rivolta agli strumenti musicali: se l'organo è generalmente accettato, tutti gli strumenti che sono utilizzati nelle «congregationes illicitas» — commedie e balli — paragonati agli strumenti delle feste pagane[87], sono banditi dalle chiese. Ciò dimostra che a preoccupare era un determinato tipo di suono, non solamente le parole che veicolavano la lascivia, che pure fu oggetto di riflessione approfondita di teorici e musicisti dell'epoca[88]. Si voleva agire sull'ambiente sonoro delle chiese, distinguendolo nettamente da quello delle feste mondane.

## Effetti concreti della riforma

L'esistenza di leggi non implica la loro effettiva applicazione né dimostra, nei casi in cui fossero applicate, la loro reale efficacia. La situazione andrebbe verificata diocesi per diocesi, con uno studio approfondito dei ricchi fondi archivistici delle visite pastorali: allo stato attuale della ricerca — in questo campo ancora *in fieri* — si possono trarre alcune considerazioni su due diocesi, quella di Treviso e quella di Ceneda.

A Treviso la riforma fu applicata subito dopo la fine del Concilio di Trento dal vescovo Giorgio Corner. Insediatosi nella diocesi nel 1564, il prelato iniziò fin da subito la sua azione di riforma, sfruttando l'esperienza maturata nella sua partecipazione diretta alle ultime sedute del concilio. Durante il suo vescovado egli indice ben tre sinodi sindodali, pubblica delle costituzioni contenenti anche provvedimenti per la disciplina del clero, fonda il seminario: era dunque un riformatore convinto, tanto da essere accostato da alcuni storici a Carlo Borromeo[89]. Sul versante della musica, il vescovo pubblicò il decreto, già citato in precedenza, che bandiva «li suoni et li canti lascivi et immoderati» dalle celebrazioni in occasione delle prime messe dei parroci. Come si nota, sebbene il decreto riprendesse esplicitamente i dettami tridentini, era limitato alle sole *missae novae* e non faceva alcun riferimento alla pratica polifonica[90]. È invece

---

[87]. Certi strumenti erano osteggiati sin dai Padri della Chiesa e questa avversione ebbe durata secolare. Si veda Romita 1936.

[88]. L'idea che i rinascimentali assegnassero potere magico alle parole piuttosto che ai suoni della musica deriva dal classico studio di Walker 2002 ed è stata successivamente accolta da molti. Ma anche Tomlinson ha notato che, a supporto di tale argomentazione, Walker non cita i testi di Ficino: si veda Tomlinson 1993, pp. 101-105. Per un esempio di riflessione sul potere del canto, si veda Collarile 2022, pp. 66-68.

[89]. Riguardo al Corner si veda Gullino 1983.

[90]. Il decreto sembra mescolare le istanze contenute nei già citati canoni tridentini sulla musica sacra e nel seguente canone sulla celebrazione delle prime messe dei parroci. CT, vol. VIII, p. 918: «item abusus videtur, quod

## SUONI PERICOLOSI

risaputo che il vescovo manteneva nella cappella musicale del duomo di Treviso un nutrito *ensemble* che comprendeva anche alcuni strumentisti[91].

Un'attenzione particolare rivolta agli strumenti musicali emerge in un ordine destinato ai monasteri femminili della diocesi. La questione dell'uso della musica nelle chiese di competenza di istituzioni religiose femminili era stata toccata durante il Concilio di Trento, dove i riformatori più rigorosi avevano proposto di vietare l'ingaggio di musici esterni e il canto figurato o accompagnato da strumenti musicali. Al termine del Concilio, però, il decreto fu edulcorato lasciando ai vescovi locali il potere decisionale a riguardo[92]. Nel 1575 Giorgio Corner, accogliendo parte delle posizioni più intransigenti, imponeva che le feste solenni delle monache dovessero essere «soltanto di voci, senza concerto e suoni di qualsivoglia strumento, da corda o di fiato, eccetto che possano suonare il loro organo, e invitar soltanto i cantori del duomo». In seguito il decreto fu ripreso nel 1587 dal successivo vescovo Francesco Corner[93]. Il divieto degli strumenti e la limitazione nella scelta dei musici possono essere visti come un tentativo di difendere l'integrità dei monasteri femminili dalle insidie tese da possibili corteggiatori con doti musicali, come il già citato Francesco Dei, il cui caso sarà ripreso tra poco. Ma le paure dei due vescovi — e dei conciliaristi più intransigenti — si comprendono più profondamente tenendo presenti le credenze legate agli strumenti musicali e al loro potere: l'allontanamento dalle chiese delle monache di strumenti da ballo avrebbe preservato queste ultime da suoni insidiosi, veicolanti la lascivia anche solamente tramite il timbro. Ad ogni modo, l'ordine suscitò le proteste dei principali monasteri femminili cittadini. Nonostante la perentorietà del divieto, infatti, in un dispaccio risalente al 1588 il vicario Biagio Guilermo informava le monache dei monasteri di San Paolo, Ognissanti, San Teonisto e San Biagio che il vescovo Francesco Corner, più permissivo del suo predecessore, «desidera in le cose ragionevoli condiscender et compiacer» le monache a seguito della richiesta pervenutagli riguardo «il cantar nelle feste»: il prelato permetteva loro di trattare con il maestro di cappella del duomo per ingaggiarne gli strumentisti salariati, a patto però che le monache non ingaggiassero musici estranei alla cappella vescovile e che non «adoperino altri instrumenti che li due tromboni rispetto del basso et l'organo». Inoltre il vicario raccomandava di evitare i contatti tra i musici e le monache, vietando a queste ultime di regalare ai primi «né buzzolai, né malvasia, né vino, né altro eccetto che li denari»[94].

Se ci si sposta nella confinante diocesi di Ceneda si nota che il primo vescovo post-tridentino a emanare provvedimenti riguardanti la musica nelle chiese è Leonardo Mocenigo, insediatosi

---

in celebratione novarum missarum fiant convivia sumptuosa et tripudia et alia, ex quibus saepe magna proveniunt scandala».

[91].  Sulla cappella musicale del duomo di Treviso si veda D'ALESSI 1954.

[92].  MONSON 2002, pp. 16-18.

[93].  Cit. in BRYANT – POZZOBON 1995, p. 6.

[94].  Per l'originale si veda ASTv, CRS, San Paolo di Treviso, b. 14, cc. 35r-36r.

nel 1599[95]. Dai documenti raccolti Mocenigo non appare un riformatore particolarmente sensibile al problema del controllo dello spazio sonoro: nel 1605 vieta ai laici l'accesso all'area del coro e impone, sotto pena di scomunica, che «mentre se canta la messa o il vespero, non possi alcuno de quelli che cantano in fuori [...] star in coro»[96]. Con questo ordine, un po' oscuro, il prelato sembra voler escludere i musici laici dalle celebrazioni liturgiche: coloro che «cantano in fuori» potrebbero essere identificati con i musici da festa, cantanti o strumentisti che sovente erano ingaggiati per solennizzare le feste di chiese parrocchiali e conventuali ma anche per i balli che spesso si tenevano all'esterno di esse. Ad ogni modo era un provvedimento piuttosto blando: e infatti le feste in musica polifonica con intervento di cantori e strumentisti furono continuamente organizzate nelle istituzioni ecclesiastiche della sua diocesi per tutta la durata del suo vescovado[97]. A queste feste partecipavano anche le alte gerarchie ecclesiastiche: nel novembre del 1608 e del 1609 un vicario foraneo è ospitato insieme al suo seguito presso il convento di Santi Martino e Rosa di Conegliano, dove poté godere delle musiche eseguite in onore di San Martino, santo patrono dell'istituzione. In entrambe le occasioni suonò una compagnia di strumentisti e cantori di cui facevano parte un violino e un cornetto[98].

I due brevi esempi confermano che l'azione nei confronti della musica cambiava di diocesi in diocesi e che era condotta con modalità diverse a seconda della sensibilità dei vescovi che vi si insediavano. Inoltre, anche i riformatori più convinti adottavano, nei confronti della musica suonata in chiesa, un atteggiamento permissivo: ciò doveva avvenire necessariamente, perché tali pratiche erano profondamente radicate nelle consuetudini rituali locali ed erano appoggiate e partecipate dagli stessi prelati.

## CONCLUSIONI

Per tutto il Cinquecento, i moralisti riformatori cercarono di inculcare nei fedeli un comportamento devoto durante le messe e una sensibilità diversa degli spazi sacri. Questi tentativi interessarono anche l'ambiente sonoro che caratterizzava le chiese in tempo di messa. I moralisti avversavano la socialità festiva che aveva luogo durante le liturgie solenni. Essi cercarono a più riprese, attraverso ordini e decreti, di disciplinare il comportamento nelle chiese.

I decreti sinodali colpiscono generalmente gli elementi profani e lascivi della musica sacra. Le preoccupazioni riguardo alla corruttela non si riferivano solo ad aspetti formali — come

---

[95]. Nelle visite pastorali dei vescovi precedenti non compaiono accenni alla musica. Gli atti sono raccolti in ADDV, bb. 33-34.

[96]. ADVV, b. 33, fasc. VI, n. 26bis, cc. 1r-3v.

[97]. *Cfr.* CECCHINATO 2013.

[98]. ASTv, CRS, Santi Martino e Rosa di Conegliano, b. 16, reg. *Giornale 1608-1610*, cc. 18r e 49r.

## SUONI PERICOLOSI

l'inserimento di melodie profane o l'esecuzione di polifonia — ma riguardavano problemi morali più profondi. La musica era considerata un potente mezzo di influenza etica e comportamentale. Avendo un accesso privilegiato all'anima, essa influiva sulle emozioni, corrompeva gli animi degli ascoltatori e li spingeva a comportarsi in diversi modi. Già prima del Concilio di Trento alcuni vescovi riformatori — come Giberti, Morone e Seripando — emanarono ordini per regolare le pratiche musicali. Il Concilio di Trento fornì invece un *framework* normativo da applicare su più larga scala, ma non fissò uno standard, delegando l'azione di riforma alle autorità locali.

L'applicazione del canone tridentino era quindi legata alle diverse sensibilità dei prelati e appare frammentaria e diversificata in tutto il territorio italiano. Alcuni mirano a imporre il canto piano improntato sulla spiritualità e sulla devozione per ridare dignità al rito liturgico. Altri colpiscono esplicitamente i «sonos periculosos», quelle influenze lascive che allontanavano gli ascoltatori dalla devozione, ispirando loro pensieri lascivi o impuri. Infine, l'azione di riforma interessò in particolar modo gli strumenti musicali: se l'organo è generalmente accettato, si vogliono bandire tutti gli strumenti solitamente utilizzati nelle feste. In questi provvedimenti è possibile scorgere la volontà di agire sull'ambiente sonoro in generale, non solamente sul canto o sulla musica polifonica. Controllando l'ambiente sonoro, alcuni riformisti miravano a cambiare anche i comportamenti di chi partecipava alla messa.

### ABBREVIAZIONI

ADVV = Vittorio Veneto, Archivio Diocesano
ADTv = Treviso, Archivio Diocesano
ASTv = Treviso, Archivio di Stato
ASTv, CRS = Treviso, Archivio di Stato, Corporazioni Religiose Soppresse
ASVe = Venezia, Archivio di Stato
ASVe, Provveditori Monasteri = Venezia, Archivio di Stato, Provveditori sopra i monasteri, Atti.
BCTv = Treviso, Biblioteca Civica
c./cc. = carta/carte
CT = *Concilium Tridentinum: diariorum, actorum, epistolarum, tractatuum, nova collectio*, edited by Societas Goerresiana, Freiburg i.B., Herder, 1950
DSI = *Dizionario Storico dell'Inquisizione*, diretto da Adriano Prosperi, con la collaborazione di Vincenzo Lavenia e John Tedeschi, 4 voll., Pisa, Scuola Normale Superiore, 2010.
TML = *Thesaurus Musicarum Latinarum*. Online: <http://www.chmtl.indiana.edu/tml/start.html>.

### FONTI MANOSCRITTE E EDIZIONI ANTICHE

BURCHELATI 1596
BURCHELATI, Bartolomeo. *Gli intretenimenti christiani*, Treviso, Biblioteca Civica, ms. 1046, II 1.3 (1596).

# Umberto Cecchinato

### Cirillo 1567
Cirillo, Franco. *Delle lettere volgari di diversi nobilissimi huomini et eccellentissimi ingegni, scritte in diverse materie. Libro terzo, nuovamente mandato in luce. Con privilegio della Illustrissima Signoria di Venetia. In Venetia, MDLXVII.*

### Constitutiones 1542
*Constitutiones editae per reverendiss. in Christo patrem dominum Io. Matthaeum Gibertum, episcopum Veronensis, ac in civitate et dioc. veronen. legatum apostolicum, ex sanctorum patrum dictis et canonicis institutis ac variis negociis quotidie occurrentibus et longo rerum usu collectae et in unum redactae. Veronae, apud Antonium Putelle tum MDXLII.*

### Constitutiones 1563
*Constitutiones editae per reverendiss. in Christo Patrem d. Io. Matthęum Gibertum, episcopum Veronen. ac in civitate et dioc. Veron. legatum apostolicum, ex sanctorum patrum dictis, et canonicis institutis, ac variis negotiis quotidie occurrentibus et longo rerum usu collectae, et in unum redactae. Venetiis, apud Franciscum Rampazetum. M D LXIII.*

### Constitutiones 1565
*Constitutiones in synodo Mutinensi sub illustrissimo et reverendissimo in Christo Patre Domino Ioanne, Miseratione divina Episcopo Portuensi, Sanctaque Romanae Ecclesiae Cardinale Morono nuncupato, et Ecclesiae Mutinensis perpetuo administratore, ediatae et publicatae. Mutinae, apud Haeredes Cornelii Gadaldini. M D L XV.*

### Constitutiones 1568
*Constitutiones et decreta condita in diocesana sinodo Lunensi et Sarzanensi sub illustrissimo et reverendissimo domino domino Benedicto Lomellino, miseratione divina S.R.E. Tit. S. Sabinae presbitero, Cardinali Lunensi et Sarzanensi, Episcopo et Comite, Genuae, apud Antonium Bellonum, M. D. L. XVIII.*

### Constitutiones 1570
*Constitutiones editae, et promulgatae in Synodo Dioecesana Placentina; quam illustrissimus et reuerendissimus D.D. Paulus de Aretio S.R.E. presbyter cardinalis, Dei, et Apostolicae sedis gratia episcopus Placentiae, et comes, habuit anno 1570 die 27 Augusti. Additis praeterea summorum Pontificum constitutionibus, et decretis Tridentini Concilij, vulgari sermone expressis, quae promulgari iussum est, Placentiae apud Franciscum Comitem 1570.*

### Constitutiones 1575
*Constitutiones reverendissimi d. d. Dominici Bollani, Brixiae episcopi, in dioecesana synodo promulgatae, anno Domini M D LXXIIII, die IIII mensis novembris. Adiectis ad extremum edictis, quae, ex earundem constitutionum praescripto, certis per annum temporibus, sunt in ecclesiis populo enuncianda. Brixiae, apud Vincentium Sabbium M D LXXV.*

### Constitutiones 1576
*Constitutiones a synodo dioecesana Parmen. anno 1575 editae. Parmae, ex typographia Seth Vioti. M D L XXVI.*

## SUONI PERICOLOSI

### CONSTITUTIONES 1579

*Constitutiones editae in synodo dioecesana Rossanensi. Quam reverendissimus P. D. Lancilotus, Archiepiscopus habuit Anno Domini* M. D. L. XXIIII *Cal. Iunii. Addita sunt quędam decreta Tridentini Concilii et Constitutiones summorum Pontificum quarum cognitio necessaria erat. Romae, apud Hęredes Antonii Bladii impressores camerales, Anno Domini* M D L XXIX.

### CONSTITUTIONES 1580A

*Constitutiones editae, a M. Antonio Marsilio Columna archiepiscopo Salernitano, in dioecesana synodo. celebrata Salerni Non. Maij. 1579. Adiectis praeterea summorum pontificum constitutionibus, & Concilij Tridentini decretis, quae cum clero tum populo sunt enuncianda. His, praeter statuta Ecclesiae Salernitanae, Ritus Curiae archiepiscopalis, ac alia plura, quae appositus index demonstrabit, adiunctus est libellus De vita, & gestis B. Matthaei Apostoli, & Euangelistae, eiusque gloriosi corporis in Salernitam urbem translatione, ab eodem archepiscopo ad augendam populi pietatem conscriptus. Neapoli, ex officina Salviana.* M D L XXX.

### CONSTITUTIONES 1580B

*Constitutiones, et decreta condita in synodo dioecesana Rauennatensi, quam illustrissimus, & reuerendissimus dominus d. Christophorus Boncompagnus Dei, & apostolicae sedis gratia archiepiscopus Rauennae habuit. Anno Domini 1580 die quinta Maij. Additis praeterea quibusdam summorum pontificum constitutionibus, quas certis diebus promulgari iussum est. Ravennae. Apud Franciscum Thebaldinum impress. Archiepisc.* M D L XXX.

### CONSTITUTIONES 1580C

*Constitutiones et decreta illustrissimo et reverendissimo domino domino Federici Cornelii Patavii Episcopi, comitisque Saccensis. In Dioecesana Synodo promulgatae die xxx aprilis, prima et secunda maii, anno Domini* M. D. L. XXIX. *Adiectis in fine, quae a Confessariis et concionatoribus urbis et dioeceis maxime sunt animadvertenda. Patavii. Ex officina Laurentii Pasquati,* M. D. L XXX.

### CONSTITUTIONES 1581

*Illustrissimi ac reverendissimi Francisci Cornelii Tarvisii episcopi constitutiones. Ex sacri Concilii Tridentini praescripto Diocesanae Synodo nuper celebratae quo perpetuo serventur traditae, apud Guerraeos fratres, Venetiae.*

### CONSTITUTIONES 1582

*Constitutiones Reverendissimi in Christo patris, et D. D. Benedicti Manzoli episcopi Regiensis, et Principis in Synodo Dioecesana editę.* MDLXXXI. *Bononiae, Apud Io. Rossium.* MDLXXXII, *Curiae Episc. et S. Inquisit. concessu.*

### CONSTITUTIONES 1587

*Constitutiones et privilegia patriarchatus et cleri Venetiarum. Illustrissimi ac Reverendissimi D.D. Ioannis Trivisani iuris utriusque doct. Patriarchae Venetiae Dalmatiaeque Primatis etc., Venetiis, ex bibliotheca Aldina,* MDLXXXVII.

### CONSTITUTIONES 1589

*Constitutiones editae per reverendiss. in Christo Patrem d. Io. Matthaeum Gibertum, episcopum Veronae, ac in civitate et dioecesi Veronen. legatum apostolicum. Ex sanctorum patrum dictis, et canonicis institutis, ac variis negotiis quotidie occurrentibus, et longo rerum usu collectae et in unum redactae. Ab illustrissimo ac reverendiss. d. d. Augustino Valerio S. R. E. tit. S. Marci presbytero Card. ac Veronae item episcopo recognitae, notationibus illustratae,*

# Umberto Cecchinato

*atque ad Concilii Tridentini decreta revocatae. Quibus adiectus est eiusdem Cardinalis libellus, cur non ediderit constitutiones. Veronae, apud Hieronymum Discipulum impressorem episcopalem. M D LXXXIX.*

### Constitutiones 1623
*Constitutiones et decreta alias promulgata in synodo diœcesana sub Illustriss. et Reverendiss. D. Michaele Priolo, episcopo Vicentino anno Domini 1583. Quibus illustriss. et reverendiss. D. D. Dionisius Delphiny episcopus pariter Vicentinus, dux, comes et marchio. In hac nova editione etc. Vicentiae, apud Franciscum Grossum Impressorem Episcopale. M. DC. XXV.*

### Decreta 1594
*Decreta condita et publicata in synodo diocesana Adriae, in cathedrali ecclesia celebrata die 17 septembris 1592. Sub reverendiss. in Christo P. et D. D. F. Laurentio Laureto, eiusdem ecclesiae Adriensis episcopo. Adiunctę sunt pręterea aliquot constitutiones pontificię quarum mentio fit in his decretis. Ravennae, apud Petrum et Camill. frat. de Ioannellis. M D XC IIII.*

### Decreta 1604a
*Decreta Synodalia ecclesiae Tarvisinae usque ad annum MDCI, apud Evangelistam Deuchinum, Tarvisii.*

### Decreta 1604b
*Decreta edita in synodo diocesana Tarvisina Tertia, quam Aloysius archiepiscopus Molinus episcopus Tarvisinus habuit. Anno Domini MDCIV Clemente VIII summo pont., apud Evangelistam Deuchinum, Tarvisii.*

### Rosaccio 1602
ROSACCIO, Giuseppe. *Il microcosmo del dottore in filosofia et medicina Gioseppe Rosaccio cosmografo. Nel quale si tratta brevemente dell'anima vegetabile, sensibile et rationale. Dell'huomo sua complessione et fisionomia. Delle infirmità che nascono in tutte le parti del corpo, et loro cura. In Verona, per Francesco dalle Donne. Con licenza de' superiori, 1602.*

### Saint-Didier 1680
SAINT-DIDIER, Alexandre Touissant de Limojon. *La ville et la Republique de Venise*, Parigi, chez Guillaume de Luyne libraire Juré, au Palais dans la Salle des Merciers à la Justice, 1680.

### Synodi 1587
*Synodi Dioecesis Concordiensis. Constitutiones et decreta per illustriss. et reverendissimum D. D. Mattheum Sanutum, Concordiae episcopum, ducem, marchionem et comitem. Die octava, nona, et decima aprilis 1587. Promulgata Xisto Quinto pontifice maximo. Venetiis, apud Ioan. Baptistam ab Hostio. 1587.*

### Synodus 1592a
*Synodus Veneta ab illustr. et reueren. D.D. Laurentio Priolo patriarcha Venetiarum, Dalmatiaeque primate, secundo anno sui patriarchatus celebrata, diebus 9. 10. & 11. Septembris M D XC II. Sanctis D. N. Clemente Octavo pontifice maximo sedente. Cum privilegio. Venetiis, apud Franciscum de Patrianis. M D X CII. Super pontem Rivoalti, ad insigna Erculis.*

### Synodus 1592b
*Synodus Cassinensis. Romae A. D. M. D. XCII.*

84

# SUONI PERICOLOSI

SYNODUS 1595
*Synodus dioecesana Castellanetensis quam Bernardus Benedictus Nicosiensis, episcopus Castellanetensis habuit, anno salutis 1595.*

## BIBLIOGRAFIA

ARCANGELI 2000
ARCANGELI, Alessandro. *Davide o Salomè? Il dibattito europeo sulla danza nella prima età moderna,* Treviso-Roma, Fondazione Benetton studi e ricerche-Viella, 2000 (Ludica, 5).

BERTOGLIO 2017
BERTOGLIO, Chiara. *Reforming Music: Music and the Religious Reformations of the Sixteenth Century,* Berlino, De Gruyter, 2017.

BERTOLINI 2018
BERTOLINI, Manuel. 'Governare lo spazio sonoro nella prima età moderna: l'esempio di Ginevra e Milano', in: *Società e Storia,* n. 159 (2018), pp. 35-52.

BERTOLINI 2019
ID. *Un ambiguo sodalizio. Percorsi di musica e storia religiosa nella prima età moderna,* Milano, Unicopli, 2019.

BRYANT – CECCHINATO 2016
BRYANT, David – CECCHINATO, Umberto. 'Venice, City of Music. Festivities and Entertainment in Early Modern Age', in: *Musik und Vergnügen am Hohen Ufer. Fest- und Kulturtransfer zwischen Hannover und Venedig in der Frühen Neuzeit,* a cura di Sabine Meine, Nicole K. Strohmann e Thomas Weißmann, Regensburg, Schnell und Steiner, 2016, pp. 35-48.

BRYANT – POZZOBON 1995
ID. – POZZOBON, Michele. *Musica devozione città. La Scuola di Santa Maria dei Battuti (e un suo manoscritto musicale) nella Treviso del Rinascimento,* Treviso, Canova, 1995 (Memorie, 4).

BRYANT – QUARANTA 2006
ID. – QUARANTA, Elena. *Produzione, circolazione e consumo. Consuetudine e quotidianità della polifonia sacra nelle chiese monastiche e parrocchiali dal tardo Medioevo alla fine degli antichi regimi,* Bologna, il Mulino, 2006 (Quaderni di Musica e Storia, 5).

CECCHINATO 2013
CECCHINATO, Umberto. 'Rito e consuetudine nelle feste patronali del Trevigiano tra Cinque e Seicento: le pratiche musicali sacre e profane', in: *Ateneo Veneto,* XII/2 (2013), pp. 127-153.

CHEMOTTI 2022
CHEMOTTI, Antonio. 'Musica ed emozioni nelle processioni funebri in Italia nel lungo Rinascimento', in: *Sensibilità moderne. Storie di affetti, passioni e sensi (secoli XV-XVIII),* a cura di Tiziana Plebani e Alessandro Arcangeli, Roma, Carocci, 2023 (Studi storici, 399), pp. 53-66.

COLLARILE 2010
COLLARILE, Luigi. *Sacri concerti. Studi sul mottetto a Venezia nel secondo Seicento*, tesi di dottorato, Friburgo, Université de Fribourg, 2010.

COLLARILE 2022
ID. 'Tra Pesaro, Padova e Venezia. Intorno a due mottetti ritrovati di Bartolomeo Barbarino', in: *Studi Musicali*, n.s. XIII/1 (2022), pp. 43-100.

D'ALESSI 1954
D'ALESSI, Giovanni. *La cappella musicale del duomo di Treviso (1300-1633)*, Vedelago (Treviso), Tipografia Ars et Religio, 1954.

DE BOER 2004
DE BOER, Wietse. *La conquista dell'anima. Fede, disciplina e ordine pubblico nella Milano della Controriforma*, Torino, Einaudi, 2004 (Biblioteca di cultura storica, 249).

DE BOER 2013
ID. 'The Counter-Reformation of the Senses', in: *Ashgate Research Companion to the Counter-Reformation*, a cura di Alexandra Bamji, Geert H. Janssen e Mary Laven, Farnham, Ashgate, 2013, pp. 243-260.

DE BOER – GÖTTLER 2013
DE BOER, Wietse – GÖTTLER, Christine. *Religion and the Senses in Early Modern Europe*, Leida-Boston, Brill, 2012.

DOUGLAS 2014
DOUGLAS, Mary. *Purezza e pericolo. Un'analisi dei concetti di contaminazione e tabù*, Bologna, il Mulino, 2014 (Incontri, 8).

FABBRI 1993
FABBRI, Paolo. 'La normativa istituzionale', in: *La cappella musicale nell'Italia della controriforma. Atti del convegno internazionale di studi (Cento, 13-15 ottobre 1989)*, a cura di Oscar Mischiati e Paolo Russo, Firenze, Olschki, 1993 (Quaderni della Rivista Italiana di Musicologia, 27), pp. 17-38.

GINZBURG 1986
GINZBURG, Carlo. *Miti, emblemi, spie. Morfologia e storia*, Torino, Einaudi, 1986 (PBE, 567).

GLIXON 2003
GLIXON, Jonathan. *Honoring God and the City: Music at the Venetian Confraternities 1260-1807*, Oxford-New York, Oxford University Press, 2003.

GLIXON 2017
ID. *Mirrors of Heaven or Worldly Theaters? Venetian Nunneries and Their Music*, Oxford-New York, Oxford University Press, 2017.

## Suoni pericolosi

GOUK 2013
GOUK, Penelope. 'Music as a Means of Social Control: Some Examples of Practice and Theory in Early Modern Europe', in: *The Emotional Power of Music: Multidisciplinary Perspectives on Musical Arousal, Expression, and Social Control*, a cura di Tom Cochrane, Bernardino Fantini e Klaus R. Scherer, Oxford, Oxford University Press, 2013, pp. 434-444.

GULLINO 1983
GULLINO, Giuseppe. 'Corner, Federico', in: *Dizionario Biografico degli Italiani. 29*, Roma, Istituto della Enciclopedia Italiana, 1983, <https://www.treccani.it/enciclopedia/federico-corner_res-44ddc14e-87eb-11dc-8e9d-0016357eee51_(Dizionario-Biografico)/>, consultato a marzo 2023.

MINOIS 2004
MINOIS, Georges. *Storia del riso e della derisione*, Bari, Dedalo, 2004.

MISCHIATI 1995
MISCHIATI, Oscar. 'Il Concilio di Trento e la polifonia. Una diversa proposta di lettura e di prospettiva storiografica', in: *Musica e liturgia nella riforma tridentina. Trento, Castello del Buonconsiglio, 23 settembre-26 novembre 1995*, a cura di Danilo Curti e Marco Gozzi, Trento, Provincia Autonoma, 1995, pp. 19-29.

MONSON 2002
MONSON, Craig A. 'The Council of Trent Revisited', in: *Journal of the American Musicological Society*, LV/1 (2002), pp. 1-37.

MONSON 2006
ID. 'Renewal, Reform, and Reaction in Catholic Music', in: *European Music, 1520-1640*, a cura di James Haar, Woodbridge, Boydell, 2006 (Studies in Medieval and Renaissance Music, 5), pp. 401-421.

O'REGAN 2013
O'REGAN, Neal. 'Music and the Counter-Reformation', in: *Ashgate Research Companion to the Counter-Reformation, op. cit.*, pp. 337-354.

PASTER 1993
PASTER, Gail Kern. *The Body Embarrassed: Drama and the Disciplines of Shame in Early Modern England*, Ithaca-New York, Cornell University, 1993.

PASTER 2004
EAD. *Humoring the Body: Emotions and the Shakespearean Stage*, Chicago-Londra, The University of Chicago Press, 2004.

PLAMPER 2015
PLAMPER, Jan. *The History of Emotions: An Introduction*, Oxford, Oxford University Press, 2015.

QUARANTA 1998
QUARANTA, Elena. *Oltre San Marco. Organizzazione e prassi della musica nelle chiese di Venezia nel Rinascimento*, Firenze, Olschki, 1998 (Studi di musica veneta, 26).

ROMBOUGH 2019
ROMBOUGH, Julia. 'Noisy Soundscapes and Women's Institutions in Early Modern Florence', in: *The Sixteenth Century Journal*, L/2 (2019), pp. 449-469.

ROMITA 1936
ROMITA, Fiorenzo. *Ius musicae liturgicae. Dissertatio historico-iuridica*, Torino, Ex Officina Libraria Marietti, 1936.

ROSENWEIN – CRISTIANI 2018
ROSENWEIN, Barbara H. – CRISTIANI, Riccardo. *What is the History of Emotions*, Cambridge, Polity Press, 2018.

ROWE 2004
ROWE, Katherine. 'Humoral Knowledge and Liberal Cognition in Davenant's *Machbeth*', in: *Reading the Early Modern Passions: Essays in the Cultural History of Emotion*, a cura di Gail Kern Paster, Katherine Rowe e Mary Floyd-Wilson, Philadelphia, University of Pennsylvania Press, 2004, pp. 169-191.

RUINI 2015
RUINI, Cesarino. 'Le disposizioni conciliari concernenti la musica liturgica: il ruolo del cardinale Gabriele Paleotti', in: *Il Concilio di Trento e le arti 1563-2013*, a cura di Marinella Pigozzi, Bologna, Bononia University Press, 2015, pp. 101-108.

SIRAISI 1990
SIRAISI, Nancy G. *Medieval and Early Renaissance Medicine: An Introduction to Knowledge and Practice*, Chicago-Londra, The University of Chicago Press, 1990.

TOMLINSON 1993
TOMLINSON, Gary. *Music in Renaissance Magic: Toward a Historiography of Others*, Chicago-Londra, The University of Chicago Press, 1993.

VAN ORDEN 2005
VAN ORDEN, Kate. *Music, Discipline, and Arms in Early Modern France*, Chicago-Londra, The University of Chicago Press, 2005.

WALKER 2002
WALKER, D. P. *Magia spirituale e magia demoniaca da Ficino a Campanella*, Torino, Aragno, 2002 (Biblioteca Aragno).

WILSON 2009
WILSON, Blake. *Singing Poetry in Renaissance Florence: The Cantasi Come Tradition (1350-1550)*, Firenze, Olschki, 2009 (Italian Medieval and Renaissance Studies, 9).

# Suoni, spazi, identità della Modena estense

*Angela Fiore*
(Università di Messina)

## Introduzione

La storia musicale della città di Modena è essenzialmente legata all'interesse per la musica esercitato nel corso dei secoli dagli Este, duchi di Ferrara Modena e Reggio Emilia. Affidata alla dinastia degli Este a fine XIII secolo, Modena diverrà solo a fine Cinquecento capitale dello Stato Estense[1]. Difatti, nel 1598, a seguito delle convenzioni faentine, gli Este furono costretti a trasferirsi rapidamente da Ferrara a Modena, all'epoca seconda città del ducato[2]. Sorse così una nuova capitale, dove l'intero patrimonio culturale estense, fatto di codici miniati, preziose cinquecentine, oggetti d'arte, strumenti e manoscritti musicali, venne frettolosamente trasportato nei drammatici giorni del trasferimento della corte. Il passaggio tra XVI e XVII secolo rappresentò per gli Este e per Modena un momento di profonda trasformazione. Dopo il trasferimento e il nuovo assetto della corte, si cercò di ripristinare nella nuova sede lo splendore artistico e musicale che aveva caratterizzato Ferrara. Il lungo ducato di Cesare I d'Este, primo reggente modenese, fu infatti sostanzialmente incentrato sull'assestamento nella nuova capitale: un processo durato circa dieci anni. Seppur in maniera

---

[1]. Entrata ufficialmente nel ducato estense nel 1452, Modena tornò nel 1510 a far parte per un breve periodo dello Stato della Chiesa. Successivamente, negli anni Trenta del XVI secolo, la città ritornò progressivamente sotto il controllo di Ferrara.

[2]. L'episodio è noto come 'devoluzione di Ferrara', attraverso la quale lo Stato Pontificio retto da Clemente VIII, entrò in possesso di Ferrara. Alla morte del duca Alfonso II, non essendoci alcun erede diretto, il Papa non rinnovò agli estensi l'investitura del feudo di Ferrara, che pertanto ritornò allo Stato della Chiesa. Il passaggio della corte, guidata dal novello duca Cesare, avvenne nella notte tra 29 e 30 gennaio 1598. Documentazione d'archivio e cronache coeve testimoniano la drammaticità di tali eventi. Alcuni passaggi relativi al trasferimento della corte si possono leggere nelle cronache di Giovanni Battista Spaccini: Spaccini 1993, p. 98.

progressiva, il destino e lo *status* della città cambiarono inevitabilmente: furono decenni segnati dalla necessità di dare a Modena la nuova veste di capitale, dalla volontà di affermare il prestigio della casata e rivendicare i propri interessi presso le corti italiane ed europee.

La città di Modena divenne nel corso del Seicento il contesto territoriale di riferimento dei fenomeni culturali che la animarono. Modena, a differenza di altre città italiane, era sede di un ducato. Furono dunque i duchi d'Este a gestire non solo le relazioni politiche tra le istituzioni, ma anche quelle culturali. Non esisteva attività che non richiedesse l'assenso della corte. Probabilmente, l'esistenza di una corte contribuì a migliorare la qualità della vita e favorire la creazione di un ambiente culturale e musicale vivace, in grado di dialogare con le più prestigiose corti europee.

## La corte e la città

Le attività musicali già presenti a Modena tra fine Cinquecento e inizio XVII secolo erano per lo più legate alla Cattedrale cittadina. Fu grazie alla collaborazione con alcuni musicisti della Cattedrale quali Geminiano Capilupi Giovanni Battista Stefanini e il più celebre Orazio Vecchi, che la corte riuscì gradualmente a ripristinare il suo prestigio musicale. Questa osmosi tra corte e chiesa stimolò la creazione di gruppi di musicisti legati alla corte che favorirono nel tempo la costituzione di una compagine ducale[3]. Cesare d'Este organizzò inizialmente un ensemble strumentale di cinque musicisti locali chiamato 'Compagnia dei Violini', attivo a partire dal 1610 circa. Questo gruppo di musicisti era incaricato di suonare in alcune occasioni a corte, ma soprattutto al di fuori della stessa, nelle piazze e nelle strade. La corte controllava le attività di questi musicisti rilasciando licenze occasionali.

Una vera cappella ducale fu definitivamente istituita nel 1629 all'inizio del regno di Francesco I. Il 'concerto degli stromenti' a Modena divenne uno dei migliori in Italia, grazie alla presenza di musicisti come Marco Uccellini che ottenne l'incarico di 'Capo degli istrumentisti del serenissimo duca di Modena'[4]. La Cappella Ducale fornì un ambiente eccezionale per lo sviluppo di forme strumentali, contribuendo ad istituire una tradizione locale di strumenti ad arco. Le fonti archivistiche testimoniano la vivacità di questo periodo e la circolazione di musicisti sia all'interno che all'esterno della corte. La Cappella Ducale interveniva non solo in buona parte delle occasioni festive dinastiche, ma anche nella solennizzazione di liturgie in alcune chiese cittadine, prendeva parte alle occasioni mondane

---

[3]. Sulle consuetudini musicali della Modena cinquecentesca si rimanda a Taddei – Chiarelli 2007.

[4]. La definizione è rintracciabile in alcune raccolte di sonate di Uccellini quali Op. IV del 1645, Op. V del 1649, Op. VIII del 1669.

organizzate presso dimore e palazzi nobiliari, alle rappresentazioni teatrali, agli spettacoli e feste di piazza[5].

Francesco I fu molto probabilmente il duca più intraprendente che ebbe Modena. Grande mecenate e collezionista, in carica dal 1629 al 1658, Francesco I diede l'impulso alla trasformazione di Modena in una città di stampo moderno, il cui emblema era rappresentato dall'imponente Palazzo Ducale. Gli anni della reggenza di Francesco I furono infatti caratterizzati dalla crescita fisica della città: sorsero nuove chiese, conventi, nonché palazzi nobiliari e teatri. Questa fioritura architettonica corrispose anche ad uno sviluppo culturale: Modena divenne depositaria delle innovazioni e delle tendenze artistiche patrocinate da una corte illuminata, sorprendentemente sensibile al fermento musicale del periodo barocco.

È però durante i due decenni del regno di Francesco II d'Este il periodo di massimo splendore musicale della città[6]. Francesco II, decimo duca di Modena e Reggio dal 1674 alla morte, che lo colse nel 1694 all'età di soli trentaquattro anni, fu un raffinato intenditore dell'arte musicale. Era egli stesso un musicista e la maggioranza delle sue energie e delle sue finanze le spese proprio in musica. Poco interessato ai compiti di Stato che amava definire 'noiosissime occupationi', Francesco II fu soprattutto promotore di un'intensa attività culturale della città, tra cui il rinnovo dell'Università, le attività delle accademie letterarie, la prosecuzione di opere artistiche e architettoniche di Palazzo Ducale e il riordino della Biblioteca Estense[7]. Francesco II comprese la necessità di ingrandire e in qualche modo stabilizzare la Cappella Ducale e fornì anche molte più occasioni per fare musica grazie alla sinergia con alcune istituzioni cittadine: l'Oratorio di San Carlo Rotondo, luogo deputato all'esecuzioni di oratori durante il periodo di Quaresima; l'attività di alcuni teatri presenti nella città; l'Accademia de' Dissonanti. Inoltre, durante il Seicento, gli spazi della città furono spesso palcoscenico di eventi spettacolari con il coinvolgimento di differenti istituzioni civili e religiose e il supporto di musica e musicisti rinomati. La corte estense si configurò come un polo di attrazione per musicisti e maestranze artistiche provenienti sia dalle zone vicine che da altre parti d'Italia. La città divenne così ben presto un ambiente promettente per la circolazione di musica e musicisti, per la produzione e la pratica performativa. I luoghi fisici della città furono partecipi dell'evoluzione stessa del linguaggio musicale, influenzando le modalità di produzione di fruizione e di ascolto della musica.

---

[5]. Relativamente alla storia della Cappella ducale durante il ducato di Francesco II si veda CROWTHER 1990.

[6]. A Francesco I seguì Alfonso IV. Nel 1662, alla morte di Alfonso IV, l'erede al trono Francesco II aveva solo due anni e il governo del ducato venne così assunto dalla vedova di Alfonso IV, Laura Martinozzi. Il regno di Laura Martinozzi si concluse nel 1674, quando il figlio Francesco II si riappropriò del potere congiurando contro la madre.

[7]. Archivio di Stato di Modena (ASMO), Archivio segreto Estense, *Cancelleria - Sezione estero*, b. 1639/1. Si rimanda anche a CONT 2009.

# Angela Fiore

## *En plein air*

Le piazze e le strade modenesi furono spesso proscenio per la celebrazione di eventi straordinari organizzati dalla corte. Piazza Grande antistante il Duomo, l'odierna piazza Roma avanti Palazzo Ducale, il Largo Sant'Agostino, il Giardino Ducale furono i luoghi maggiormente utilizzati in occasioni di feste e cerimonie. Gli eventi spettacolari esterni prevedevano un accompagnamento musicale affidato soprattutto a strumentisti a fiato e a percussione come trombe, pifferi e tamburi. Essi avevano il compito di sonorizzare strade e piazze, di precedere un corteo, di enfatizzare ogni rituale e coinvolgere il tessuto cittadino. Il carattere 'colloquiale' degli eventi spettacolari esterni permetteva al meglio di creare specifiche forme di interazione tra diverse tipologie di sorgenti sonore: i suoni della strada, il vocio delle persone si fondevano ai suoni delle performance, consensualmente prodotti e condivisi da gruppi sociali differenti.

Già a fine Cinquecento, negli spazi aperti cittadini, si assisteva a mascherate e quintane con carri allegorici e rappresentazioni teatrali. In questo tipo di eventi, in cui aspetti dotti si fondevano a quelli popolari, prendevano vita macchine effimere e palcoscenici itineranti. A seguito della devoluzione, con l'inizio del ducato di Cesare d'Este, vi fu un sostanziale incremento di rappresentazioni in spazi esterni[8]. Piazza Grande, era stata per tutto il Cinquecento un punto nevralgico della città. Ai lati della piazza si ergevano infatti i principali edifici del potere civico e religioso: la Cattedrale con la sua torre campanaria detta 'Ghirlandina', il Palazzo Comunale, il Palazzo della Ragione. Anche durante il XVII secolo in questa piazza ebbero luogo le principali cerimonie religiose, in particolare liturgie legate all'anno liturgico, alla Cattedrale e i riti di San Geminiano patrono di Modena.

Piazza Grande fu anche teatro di spettacoli organizzati in occasione di genetliaci, visite illustri o eventi politici, il cui fine era anche quello di esaltare la magnificenza della dinastia estense. Le cronache di Giovanni Battista Spaccini restituiscono alcune informazioni sullo svolgersi di questi eventi, testimoniando il fasto e il coinvolgimento cittadino[9]. Per il Carnevale del 1604, il cronista racconta, ad esempio, di una mascherata avvenuta in Piazza Grande. Ad essa avevano preso parte diversi nobili modenesi, era stato organizzato un «giocondissimo spettacolo» con «balletti alla francese, con una dolcissima e piena musica»

---

[8]. Sulle feste di piazza durante il ducato di Cesare d'Este si veda Calore 1983; Martinelli Braglia 2007.

[9]. La cronaca di Giovanni Battista Spaccini è un resoconto prezioso, che offre un quadro vivo degli avvenimenti più importanti della città di Modena. Spaccini produsse ben nove volumi di cronache: i primi due sono un rifacimento dei diari di Iacopino e Tommasino Lancellotti, mentre i restanti riportano gli episodi di cui Spaccini fu testimone tra il 1588 e il 1636. Spaccini 1993. Modena conserva oggi un ricco patrimonio cronachistico. Attualmente è in corso un progetto di digitalizzazione ed indicizzazione delle cronache modenesi presso il Centro interdipartimentale di ricerca sulle Digital Humanities. Il progetto curato dallo storico Carlo Baja Guarienti prevede l'elaborazione di un modello per l'edizione digitale delle cronache della prima età moderna.

proseguita fino a notte fonda. La musica era stata «concertata dal signor Orazio Vecchi». La mascherata, secondo quanto racconta Spaccini, aveva attraversato le strade della città, preceduta da «molti suonatori de diversi istromenti, vestiti di colori lievi et festeggianti per iscacciare la Malinconia»[10].

Nel 1654 Francesco I sposò Lucrezia Barberini. Il matrimonio venne celebrato per procura presso la Casa Santa di Loreto il 15 aprile 1654, seguirono i festeggiamenti a Modena organizzati in grande pompa: luminarie, musiche, tornei e carri allegorici. L'ingresso a Modena della terza sposa di Francesco I avvenne nella notte del 24 aprile 1654, salutato «con suoni di campane, e con tutto quello applauso che si puoté maggiore». L'erudito Leone Allacci descrive accuratamente i festeggiamenti che animarono la città per alcuni giorni con il coinvolgimento di più spazi cittadini[11]. Presso Piazza Grande venne costruito dall'architetto ducale Gaspare Vigarani «un amenosissimo Teatro, di forma ovata» con palchi per gli spettatori e spazi destinati ai musicisti:

> Fuori dalla circonferenza del Teatro [...] che pareva essere un viale d'un Giardino, nasceva con maggiore altezza del sudetto recinto, una spalliera coperta di Cedri, Aranzi, Pomigranati, Gelsomini & altri fiori, quale serviva per parapetto alli palchi de Musici, e d'altre genti, e dietro ad essi Palchi erano posti altissimi Alberi, si che pareva, che in detto sito fioresse un bellissimo Giardino[12].

Carri allegorici raffiguranti le allegorie della Primavera, di Bacco e Apollo, di Flora dea dei Giardini ed Ebe dea della gioventù, si muovevano al «suono di pifferi & al concento di trombe» e «un'Armonia di circa quaranta instrumenti musicali che da varie parti furono raccolti» legava le differenti componenti della performance teatrale. Giochi ed effetti di luce, con torce e lumi perimetravano la Cattedrale con le sue torri e gli edifici limitrofi quali il Palazzo della Ragione e la torre dell'orologio, in modo tale che «pareva essersi mutata la notte in chiarissimo giorno». Poco distante da Piazza Grande, nella piazza del Vescovato, si ergeva infine una imponente «colonna, che attorniata di maschere e fiori, sosteneva un'infinità di lumi»[13].

Francesco I fece edificare Palazzo Ducale nel 1634, uno dei più imponenti palazzi principeschi del XVII secolo. Il cortile interno di Palazzo Ducale e la piazza antistante furono i luoghi utilizzati per tornei e mascherate a cavallo con effetti pirotecnici, grandiosi allestimenti, caroselli equestri, armeggiamenti, balli. Gli spettacoli con giochi d'arme erano soprattutto legati a ricorrenze del casato e a visite illustri, spesso corredati di un sontuoso teatro effimero innalzato

---

10. *Ibidem*, pp. 105-106.
11. ALLACCI 1654.
12. *Ibidem*, p. 81.
13. *Ibidem*, p. 83.

Ill. 1: Guglielmo Silvester [Sivestri], *Incisioni di vedute della città di Modena: Piazza Grande* 1789.

per l'occasione. Le fonti superstiti contengono descrizioni e testi, apparati iconografici, ma esigue sono le indicazioni relative alla musica, genericamente attribuita al maestro di cappella. L'evento probabilmente più celebre ambientato in questo sito fu la sontuosa cerimonia organizzata per la nascita di Francesco II nel 1660, una 'festa d'armi' sul tema della vittoria della virtù sul vizio, indetta nello stesso giorno del battesimo del nuovo erede del casato, il 12 giugno. Girolamo Graziani fu autore dei versi, Gaspare Vigarani curò l'allestimento scenografico, mentre il maestro di cappella Benedetto Ferrari ebbe l'incarico della composizione della musica ad oggi perduta[14]. La «più qualificata nobiltà» aveva preso parte alla cerimonia e il sostegno musicale dell'evento aveva visto «più chori di esquisiti musici, secondati dal rimbombo strepitoso de bronzi tonanti e dalle acclamationi festose del popolo»[15]. La Biblioteca Estense conserva oggi il

---

[14]. Graziani, urbinate di nascita ma modenese d'adozione, coniugava la vena poetica con l'arte diplomatica: dal 1637 al 1660 compose tutti i libretti dei tornei celebrativi indetti a corte. Benedetto Ferrari (1597-1681) era detto anche Benedetto della Tiorba, in quanto eccellente tiorbista. Nato a Reggio Emilia, lavorò a Roma, Parma, Venezia, dedicandosi soprattutto alla composizione di melodrammi. Fu a Modena dal 1623 al 1637, e una seconda volta a partire dal 1653, dopo aver ricevuto l'incarico di maestro della cappella ducale da Francesco I d'Este. Gaspare Vigarani (1588-1663) è stato un architetto attivo presso casa d'Este a partire dal 1631, anno in cui venne nominato da Francesco I 'Ingegnere e Soprintendente generale delle fabbriche e delle feste'. Vigarani si dedicò molto all'allestimento delle macchine effimere per spettacoli e feste di piazza e alla progettazione di teatri e sale da spettacolo.

[15]. Graziani 1660, c. 7. Il pregiato manoscritto si conserva in I-Moe Gamma. B.1.17.

pregiato manoscritto che descrive nei dettagli il torneo e i suoi apparati, i costumi e il progetto per il teatro costruito in occasione della cerimonia:

> Era il Teatro si vago nella dipositione, si attrativo nel colorito, e si pellegrino nell'ordine, che esso solo havrebbe potuto servire di sufficiente spettacolo, per appagare il gusto, e sodisfare la curiosità de riguardanti. Sorgenao d'og'intorno comodi scalini, che rappresentavano finissimo marmo, e che venivano con bella proportione interrotti da sei porte di eguale grandezza e distanza ne lati del teatro [...] Quattro delle sei porte sudette finivano in alte Torri adorne di varie colonne sparse di vene d'oro e d'argento, e che su la cima sostenevano ciascuna di loro due grandi Aquile Estensi [...]. Sopra gli scalini sorgeva all'intorno del Teatro un bell'ordine di Palchi, che havevano per base un gran cornicione di finto marmo, su cui posavano vaghissime balaustre [...][16].

La descrizione sottolinea il fasto, la grandiosità dell'architettura effimera, dei giochi di luce organizzati per l'occasione. Spettacolari furono anche i costumi dei fanti «guerniti di armi forbite, e di ricche bande, e di gran pennacchi» e le coreografie a cavallo, le cui movenze erano scandite dallo «strepito de risuonanti Tamburi»[17]. Grazie alla compartecipazione degli artisti di corte Graziani e Vigarani, il *Trionfo della virtù* rappresentò molto probabilmente uno degli esempi più esuberanti e magnificenti delle feste di piazza modenesi, per drammaturgia e risorse scenografiche.

Di qualche anno più tardi, 1718, è la testimonianza del genetliaco del principe Rinaldo I d'Este, per il quale venne organizzato un sonoro carosello. Un documento d'archivio contenente la descrizione della prova generale del carosello fornisce alcune informazioni a riguardo, descrivendo la giostra e il suo sviluppo[18]. Quattro le macchine effimere predisposte per l'occasione: la prima rappresentante la Discordia prevedeva «4 trombetti con timbali e 4 oboe tutti a cavallo vestiti all'eroica e dietro à se 18 huomini vestiti pure alla medesima guisa, un musico»; la seconda rappresentava la Guerra trainata da quattro cavalli bianchi e «accompagnata come la prima». La terza macchina rappresentava il fiume modenese Panaro e il combattimento tra Orazi e Curiazi. Il cronista conclude sottolineando che le movenze degli attori erano scandite al suono di «timbali, trombe et oboe» e che ogni spazio cittadino in quel giorno «risuonava di stromenti musicali»[19].

Queste occasioni non erano intese solo come un mezzo per festeggiare una ricorrenza, intrattenere la corte e il popolo o per fare cultura, esse costituivano delle eccellenti possibilità per un duca di dimostrare la magnificenza della corte. La musica a Modena a fine Seicento

---

16. *Ibidem*, c. 6.
17. *Ibidem*.
18. ASMO, Archivio per Materie, Spettacoli, 9/A.
19. *Ibidem*.

## Chiesa e corte

Luogo simbolo per la spettacolarità modenese e per la storia estense furono la chiesa di Sant'Agostino e il largo ad essa adiacente. Sant'Agostino è probabilmente l'edificio religioso maggiormente emblematico e in grado di narrare la magnificenza della casata. Le vicende storiche della chiesa sono strettamente legate alle tradizioni funerarie estensi: la sua posizione strategica nella topografia urbana, la spazialità interna e le caratteristiche architettoniche dell'edificio ben si prestavano infatti ad ospitare celebrazioni imponenti e soprattutto decorazioni effimere. Il Largo fungeva da cornice alle celebrazioni liturgiche che avevano luogo nella chiesa, ospitando cortei e processioni. La chiesa fu fondata dagli Eremitani di regola agostiniana nel 1338 e rinnovata tra il 1662 e il 1663 per volontà della duchessa reggente Laura Martinozzi, che ne patrocinò la trasformazione proprio per celebrarvi i funerali del marito Alfonso IV.

Le celebrazioni più sontuose organizzate in Sant'Agostino furono quelle del 2 aprile 1659 per le esequie di Francesco I d'Este. Per tale occasione, vennero progettati apparati effimeri destinati al decoro della piazza, della facciata della chiesa e della navata interna. L'imponente processione funebre attraversava punti nevralgici della città: partiva da Palazzo Ducale e, attraversando tutta la via Emilia, arrivava a porta Sant'Agostino. Il corteo era scandito da una coreografia precisa, testimoniata da documentazione dell'Archivio segreto estense che descrive minuziosamente la successione delle varie componenti, le movenze e l'abbigliamento. Anche i musici di corte ne prendevano parte, ma al fine di garantire un adeguato sostegno sonoro adatto alla solennità di esequie ducali, per l'occasione erano stati chiamati in aggiunta musici e strumentisti dalle attigue città:

> Nello stato di Sua Altezza Serenissima non vi sono altre voci di concerto, che quelle del Signore Daino, e Signore Marzio, onde sarà necessario chiamare le altre da Bologna, Ferrara, e Parma escludendo però tutti li Musici de Prencipi, e si figura, che il numero di Musici, et Instromenti forestieri possa ascendere a venti persone incirca[20].

Memoria dei solenni funerali si trova descritta e illustrata nell'*Idea di un prencipe et eroe christiano*, opera monumentale composta del padre Domenico Gamberti, commissionata dal

---

[20]. Si tratta della relazione sul corteo funebre in occasione delle esequie di Francesco I. ASMO, Casa e Stato, b. 345, fasc. 2, «Funerale». Sugli apparati effimeri dei funerali estensi durante il ducato di Francesco I si rimanda a SIROCCHI 2020.

## SUONI, SPAZI, IDENTITÀ DELLA MODENA ESTENSE

duca Alfonso IV. Gamberti descrive le varie componenti del «funeral teatro» con i decori provvisori per la facciata e per la navata. Non mancano le descrizioni degli spazi riservati ai musici e al corredo sonoro dell'evento:

> La musica, divisa in quattro gran Cori, fu piena, e nobilissima, non solo per l'ingegnosa, e bene concertata composizione del sig. Benedetto Ferrari, Mastro della Cappella Ducale, ma ancora per l'eccellenza, e squisitezza de' Musici, sì della Città, e di S.A. Serenissima, sì anche Forestieri; e per la scelta copia degli stromenti di corde, e di fiato, havuti da molti luoghi più celebri d'Italia[21].

Come parte essenziale della vita di corte, la musica accompagnava la quotidianità devozionale del duca così come le cerimonie straordinarie o dinastiche, organizzate spesso nelle chiese della città. Come precedentemente detto, già a inizio Seicento, poco dopo il trasferimento della corte nella nuova capitale del ducato, la presenza a corte di membri della cappella della cattedrale, costituisce una prova del legame fra corte e chiesa. Gli stessi eventi dinastici furono spesso corredati da musiche che risuonavano nelle chiese cittadine. Nel corso del Seicento, gli Este interagirono con diverse istituzioni ecclesiastiche cittadine inviando periodicamente musicisti di corte per solennizzare le celebrazioni liturgiche patrocinate dagli Este e puntualmente attestate dai rendiconti di spesa. L'Archivio di Stato di Modena conserva una buona documentazione della cappella ducale relativa all'ingaggio e ai pagamenti dei musicisti di corte inviati dallo stesso duca d'Este in alcune chiese monasteri o congregazioni cittadine in determinate festività. Si tratta molto spesso di ricevute sottoscritte dagli stessi musicisti. Nell'esempio seguente si riporta ad esempio la lista delle funzioni religiose a cui aveva preso parte Simone Ascani, tiorbista della cappella ducale. Dal documento si evince la partecipazione di Ascani ad una serie di celebrazioni del 1699 fatte per servizio del duca Rinaldo e svoltesi presso diverse istituzioni della città: «Primo vespro e messa» presso le monache di Santa Teresa; «L'ottavario di S. Contardo» presso la chiesa della Madonna del Parto; una non specificata novena presso la chiesa di San Vincenzo, mentre per tutti i venerdì di Quaresima era previsto «il miserere ai P. Gesuiti».

Alcune celebrazioni riguardano anche avvenimenti della corte, ad esempio la «Messa solenne in S. Domenico per il parto della M. della Regina de Romani» ovvero Carlotta Felicita di Brunswick-Lüneburg, sposa di Rinaldo d'Este. Nel febbraio 1700 si fa invece cenno alla «fonzione del Batesmo in Domo» probabilmente di Gianfederico d'Este nato nel settembre 1700; presso la chiesa di San Bartolomeo era invece celebrato «Il giorno della Nassita» del duca (ILL. 2, p. 98).

La comparazione di questo tipo di documentazione permette di acquisire una copiosa serie di dati relativi all'attività musicale delle singole chiese, agli organici utilizzati in occasione

---

[21]. GAMBERTI 1659, p. 568.

ILL. 2: ASMO - Archivio per Materie, Musica e musicisti, b. 3.

di una festività, oltre a conoscere il nome degli interpreti e aggiungere tasselli alla storia della compagine ducale.

Tra le chiese maggiormente rappresentative, di cui spesso si trova traccia nella documentazione archivistica estense, vi è la chiesa del Voto che sorse per l'adempimento del

# Suoni, spazi, identità della Modena estense

voto fatto dai modenesi alla Madonna della Ghiara, affinché facesse cessare la terribile peste del 1630; la chiesa di San Vincenzo edificata dai teatini nel 1617, sul corso Canalgrande, una delle strade più importanti della città[22]. Inoltre, anche alcune comunità monastiche cittadine, intrattennero rapporti con la corte tramite la musica. Tra le istituzioni sacre, è doveroso citare l'oratorio di San Carlo, un vero centro di produzione musicale cittadino. Luogo di culto della congregazione teatina di San Carlo, l'oratorio venne edificato nel 1634. L'appellativo 'rotondo' deriva dalla forma ottagonale della struttura[23]. L'oratorio venne scelto da Francesco II come luogo per ospitare l'esecuzione di oratori in musica durante il periodo quaresimale. Modena è stata infatti un centro importante per la diffusione e lo sviluppo di questo genere. Francesco II collezionò e commissionò oratori di compositori di corte ma anche esterni: affiancano le composizioni di Pier Simone Agostini, Benedetto Ferrari, Domenico Gabrielli, Antonio Giannettini, gli oratori di Alessandro Scarlatti e Alessandro Stradella. Molte delle partiture basate su testi di poeti e letterati locali in contatto con la corte sono oggi rintracciabili nella collezione della Biblioteca Estense[24]. Alcuni oratori alludono ai fasti della casata raccontando le storie di Santi della dinastia[25], altri hanno soggetti marcatamente politici o rimandano a personaggi biblici. L'oratorio consentiva di evidenziare le salde virtù cristiane, la fede e la devozione della casata e permetteva anche di essere strumento di propaganda politica. La fulgida produzione oratoriale della corte organizzata presso San Carlo Rotondo permise infatti di rinsaldare il legame con la potente congregazione teatina di San Carlo, tramite la quale si realizzerà buona parte del programma politico culturale estense[26].

## Tra pubblico e privato

Anche l'attività teatrale di Modena avviatasi a fine XVII secolo, sebbene legata in massima parte a spazi interni, prese parte al *soundscape* cittadino. Grazie all'operato della corte i teatri diedero vita ad una numerosa serie di opportunità di consumo spettacolare e musicale.

---

[22]. San Vincenzo era considerata una chiesa 'estense' grazie al coinvolgimento di Francesco I alla realizzazione del tempio.

[23]. Modena fu uno dei centri di maggiore interesse e rilievo per la storia dell'oratorio musicale nel Seicento. In merito si veda Crowther 1992.

[24]. Tra gli autori dei testi si ricorda Giovanni Battista Giardini, segretario di lettere di Francesco II e Giovanni Battista Rosselli Genesini.

[25]. Ad esempio, l'oratorio *San Contardo d'Este* composto da Antonio Ferrari su libretto di Giulio Giuseppe Manzini, oppure il più celebre *Santa Beatrice d'Este* messo in musica da Giovanni Lorenzo Lulier con sinfonia introduttiva di Arcangelo Corelli.

[26]. La congregazione teatina di S. Carlo era impegnata nell'educazione dei rampolli della classe dominante presso il Collegio dei Nobili, era attiva nella pratica musicale, nell'insegnamento della musica e nelle attività musicali che avevano luogo nella piccola cappella della congregazione pure controllata dal duca. Sulle pratiche musicali del collegio di San Carlo si trovano indicazioni in Chiarelli 1991 e Lorenzetti 1997.

La dimensione sonora dell'esperienza teatrale ha così influito largamente nel processo di costruzione identitaria della città. A partire dalla metà del XVII secolo diversi teatri cittadini si aprirono al melodramma grazie al sostegno dei diversi duchi[27].

Esigenza imprescindibile per la vita sociale di una città sede di corte era però la presenza di un teatro ducale. La prima attività teatrale cittadina venne svolta presso il Teatro della Spelta, costruito per volontà del duca Francesco I, desideroso di fornire alla nuova capitale del ducato un teatro all'altezza delle esigenze di corte. La realizzazione della sala, all'interno delle mura del Palazzo Comunale fu affidata a Gaspare Vigarani. Il primo teatro di corte, ospitato all'interno del Palazzo Ducale, si fa invece risalire al 1669. Si trattava di un teatrino da stanza, di ridotte dimensioni, destinato soltanto all'uso privato della corte.

Ma l'attività teatrale più interessante, in grado di coniugare le esigenze della corte con quelle cittadine, è senza dubbio rintracciabile nella storia del Teatro Valentini divenuto poi Teatro Fontanelli. La sua posizione nella geografia urbana risultava strategica: il teatro era situato tra la via Emilia e la Rua Grande (attuale via Farini) e direttamente connesso al Palazzo Ducale. La sua ubicazione resta oggi visibile in alcune piante storiche della città di Modena. Il Teatro Valentini era una sorta di camerone 'da spettacolo' presente all'interno di un palazzo nobiliare chiamato Palazzo Valentini e edificato intorno al 1542 da Giovanni Andrea Valentini. Il Valentini era conosciuto per essere 'il teatro pubblico delle commedie' perché inizialmente adibito alle recite dei comici al servizio della corte. Probabilmente la sua realizzazione venne affidata sempre a Vigarani. Nel 1681 il Valentini fu interamente distrutto da un incendio. Ritornerà in attività qualche anno più tardi, nel 1685 grazie al marchese Decio Fontanelli che lo rilevò e gli donò nuova vita consacrandolo al melodramma. Il teatro, ribattezzato col nome di Teatro Fontanelli, fu infatti scelto da Francesco II come luogo dove ospitare le rappresentazioni teatrali patrocinate dalla corte ma aperte ad un pubblico pagante e divenne in breve tempo il teatro più importante degli Stati estensi, direttamente legato alla politica culturale del duca[28]. Durante il ducato di Francesco II, il teatro ospitò le rappresentazioni di diversi compositori afferenti alla corte come Domenico Gabrielli, Carlo Pallavicini, Antonio Giannettini, affiancate da riprese di spettacoli veneziani. Il Fontanelli diventerà un centro nevralgico di produzione musicale cittadina. Nel 1705 il Teatro venne ceduto da Giulio Fontanelli, figlio del marchese Decio, al conte Teodoro Rangoni che a sua volta ne cambierà il nome in Teatro Rangoni. Nell'Ottocento l'edificio subì vari ampliamenti per assumere dal 1816 il nome di Teatro Comunale della via Emilia[29].

---

[27]. Sull'attività teatrale modenese si rimanda a FABBRI 1985; MARTINELLI BRAGLIA 2007; MARTINELLI BRAGLIA 2016; MARTINELLI BRAGLIA 2019.

[28]. Sul Teatro Fontanelli e la ricostruzione della sua attività si veda MARTINELLI BRAGLIA 1985.

[29]. Durante il XVIII secolo sorsero nuovi teatri a Modena: il teatro Molza in attività tra 1713 e 1764, inaugurato nel 1713 con l'opera *La fede tradita e vendicata*, su musica di Francesco Gasparini; il Teatro San Carlo, inaugurato

## SUONI, SPAZI, IDENTITÀ DELLA MODENA ESTENSE

La Biblioteca Estense custodisce oggi oltre ad alcune partiture di melodrammi eseguiti al Fontanelli, anche la collezione di libretti della famiglia Fontanelli[30]. Molti di essi sono relativi ad esecuzioni modenesi di drammi per musica avvenute proprio presso il Fontanelli durante il ducato di Francesco II. La presenza e la corrispondenza di documentazione d'archivio, fonti librettistiche e fonti musicali permette di ricostruire l'intero processo produttivo di alcuni allestimenti del Fontanelli, fornendo una copiosa serie di dati sulle rappresentazioni, sui cast impiegati e le maestranze[31].

Le differenti occasioni di musica presenti nella città ducale determinarono nel corso del tempo, un paesaggio sonoro variegato, costituito sia da aspetti appariscenti ma anche da una pratica musicale più intima e riservata alla quotidianità della corte. Ad una cerchia maggiormente ristretta si legano invece le attività musicali afferenti al Palazzo Ducale e ai suoi ambienti interni. Francesco II fu un avido fruitore di musica: il duca sentiva l'esigenza di collezionare e commissionare musica strumentale per il proprio svago ed esercizio e per l'intrattenimento a corte. Quello della 'camera' del duca era uno spazio sonoro raffinato, orientato verso un ascolto competente destinato ad estimatori, cultori, cortigiani che spesso figurano essere non solo fruitori ma anche esecutori. A questi luoghi si riferisce anche l'attività musicale svolta dall'Accademia de' Dissonanti, fondata nel 1683 come centro di scambi culturali per artisti, musicisti e poeti[32]. Sebbene controverso sia il ruolo svolto da Francesco II nella sua creazione, di certo il duca ne incrementò l'attività artistica[33]. Il repertorio dedicato a questa istituzione era per lo più composto da cantate o accademie per voci soliste e basso continuo o con uno o più strumenti obbligati. I testi poetici scritti spesso dagli stessi nobili, appartenevano alla poesia accademica volta alla glorificazione del prestigio estense. Molte di queste cantate furono composte per occasioni specifiche legate al duca o alla corte. Francesco II fu probabilmente ossessionato da questo genere musicale, dato l'ingente numero di antologie di cantate presenti nella collezione estense in rapporto sproporzionato agli altri generi presenti. L'esecuzione delle cantate avveniva con molta probabilità all'interno delle mura stesse di Palazzo Ducale, come si evince dalle sue leggi costitutive:

---

nel 1753 e legato alle attività culturali del Collegio dei Nobili; il Teatro di San Rocco, attivo dal 1791 al 1835; e infine a partire dal 1841 l'attuale Teatro Comunale che oggi reca intitolazione a Luciano Pavarotti.

[30]. Si tratta di un migliaio di libretti per musica datati da inizio Seicento a circa il 1760, collezione acquistata dalla Biblioteca Estense al tempo di Girolamo Tiraboschi. Nella collezione figurano libretti di drammi per musica ma anche oratori e azioni drammatiche.

[31]. Si rimanda al saggio di CHIARELLI 2009.

[32]. Prima del 1682 l'Accademia molto probabilmente esisteva con la semplice denominazione di Accademia di Modena. In seguito, vennero avanzate alcune proposte per cambiarne il nome. Fra le varie possibilità fu presentata anche quella di dotare l'Accademia di un simbolo che rappresentasse l'armonia nella varietà degli accordi. Perciò gli accademici di Modena furono detti 'Dissonanti' con il motto 'Digerit in numerum dissonantes'.

[33]. Si veda JANDER 1975, in particolare p. 525.

## ANGELA FIORE

> Il Duca protegge questa di Modena, e ne onora colla sovrana sue Presenza le
> Funzioni; ma queste vuole ancora, che si facciono nella stessa sua Corte con invito
> della Nobiltà, con apparato del Luogo, con accompagnamento d'Orchestra, e di
> musica, e con quella pompa in fine, che alla grandezza di tal Principe corrisponda[34].

La cantata da camera era infatti una forma musicale particolarmente adatta ad essere
praticata negli spazi interni nei palazzi nobiliari.

### DIGITAL HUMANITIES PER LO STUDIO DEL PAESAGGIO SONORO STORICO

L'analisi dei differenti contesti produttivi di Modena porta a comprendere quanto gli
spazi cittadini non possano essere considerati solo dei semplici luoghi: essi permettono di
identificare tempi, cerimonie, cultura performativa e dell'ascolto.

Modena è una città straordinariamente ricca di testimonianze musicali e archivistiche[35].
In particolare, la sua storia musicale è ben rappresentata dalla collezione musicale estense,
considerata oggi come una delle più prestigiose raccolte dinastiche europee. La collezione estense
rappresenta una risorsa indispensabile per lo studio di alcuni generi musicali. Sebbene in molti
casi le fonti modenesi siano riflesso del collezionismo musicale, spesso raccontano anche delle
attività di produzione, esecuzione e committenza musicale della corte. Come si è visto nelle
pagine precedenti, la raccolta fornisce indicazioni anche su come la corte abbia interagito con la
città attraverso la musica e attraverso le arti in generale. Affiancando alla lettura di manoscritti
musicali, fonti come libretti, documentazione d'archivio, cronache, testimonianze storiche, è
possibile decodificare il paesaggio musicale diffuso della città, il suo quotidiano, le implicazioni
funzionali dell'attività sonora delle istituzioni che le davano forma.

Il significato identitario della città può essere però pienamente compreso solo adottando
un punto di vista multidisciplinare. Essenziale è quindi lo studio comparato di fonti storico-
musicali con quelle cartografiche: Modena possiede infatti anche una ricca serie di carte
geografiche antiche, rintracciabili presso la Biblioteca Estense, l'Archivio di Stato e l'Archivio
Comunale che consentono di seguire l'evoluzione urbana del luogo. Tale comparazione offre
numerosi dettagli sulle tradizioni locali e sulle complesse relazioni tra suono e spazio all'interno
del contesto cittadino, mostrando chiavi di lettura alternative delle stesse fonti musicali come

---

[34]. *Leggi / dell'Accademia / de' Dissonanti / di Modena, pubblicate / Sotto gli Auspizi di S. A. Serenissima / Con Licenza de' Superiori* [colophon] In Modena, 1731, Per Bartolomeo Soliani.

[35]. Modena beneficia inoltre di un buon numero di studi che nel corso degli anni hanno contribuito a delineare il profilo di una città che ha tutte le caratteristiche per definirsi un centro musicale sia nel contesto italiano che europeo. Si rimanda ai contributi già precedentemente citati di Owen Jander e Victor Crowther, Graziella Martinelli Braglia, Alessandra Chiarelli, Carolyn Gianturco.

prodotto della quotidianità sonora e spettacolare della città. Il contesto urbano consente al contempo di identificare i centri di produzione e consumo musicale; di mappare la presenza di musica e musicisti; di considerare la musica come attività sociale, politica e non meramente artistica.

Nella diversità dei dati desunti da questa tipologia di analisi, gli strumenti digitali sono fondamentali per creare reti relazioni e visualizzazioni significative che non potrebbero essere evidenziate altrimenti. Nasce così l'idea del progetto digitale *Este Soundscape* dedicato ai risultati ottenuti dallo studio del patrimonio musicale e cartografico della Modena estense. Basato sulla costruzione di una piattaforma digitale, il progetto nasce nell'ambito del programma *Digital Humanities – per la ricerca e la valorizzazione del patrimonio storico documentario-estense* all'interno del quale sono stati condotti due progetti di ricerca, dedicati rispettivamente allo studio e alla catalogazione dei fondi musicale e cartografico posseduti dalla Biblioteca Estense Universitaria[36].

Il progetto *Este soundscape* intende far conoscere ed esplorare i luoghi, gli eventi, le persone che hanno contribuito alla costruzione del paesaggio sonoro della città di Modena, sfruttando le potenzialità delle *digital humanities*[37]. Cuore del progetto è una mappa virtuale navigabile, sottesa da una banca dati, che permetterà di ottenere varie forme di interrogazione sulla città, sulle istituzioni, sulle persone e sulla musica in essa prodotta. La cartografia digitale, con il supporto dei più recenti software, e in particolare grazie alla tecnologia GIS (Geographic Information System), offre infatti la possibilità di osservare i cambiamenti del territorio, sovrapponendo ad esempio mappe storiche ad immagini satellitari e permettendo di evidenziare i cambiamenti del territorio[38]. Ai fini della ricerca musicologica, la cartografia è molto utile non

---

[36]. Tra 2018 e 2020 Gallerie Estensi e l'Università di Modena e Reggio Emilia, con il sostegno della Fondazione di Modena, hanno portato avanti un importante progetto di digitalizzazione di parte del patrimonio documentario della Biblioteca Estense Universitaria. Nello specifico, i fondi interessati dal progetto sono stati la collezione di carte geografiche (affidato a Sara Belotti), la collezione musicale (Angela Fiore) e l'archivio Muratoriano (Andrea Lazzarini). La biblioteca digitale estense è oggi consultabile in rete e consente di accedere ad un'importante risorsa documentaria. <https://edl.beniculturali.it/home/cover>, visitato a marzo 2023.

[37]. Il progetto *Este Soundscape* nasce assieme alla geografa Sara Belotti. La piattaforma web è stata ideata inizialmente progettata presso il Centro interdipartimentale di ricerca sulle Digital Humanities DHMoRe dell'Università di Modena e Reggio Emilia, con la collaborazione di Lorenzo Baraldi, ingegnere dell'AImageLab-Dipartimento di Ingegneria 'Enzo Ferrari' dell'Università di Modena e Reggio Emilia. Attualmente le autrici proseguono il progetto e lo sviluppo della piattaforma in maniera indipendente. Si rimanda anche a: FIORE – BELOTTI 2020.

[38]. Tra gli strumenti digitali, anche i supporti cartografici possono contribuire a nuove visualizzazioni dei dati, grazie allo sviluppo di numerosi *tools* di *mapping* e, in particolare, dei GIS (*Geographical Information Systems*), ossia sistemi informativi territoriali che consentono di acquisire, immagazzinare, organizzare, catalogare, modificare, rielaborare, integrare, restituire dati riguardanti fenomeni che si svolgono sul territorio. La struttura di tali sistemi si basa su di un archivio digitale (*database*) a cui sono associate le informazioni geografiche (coordinate) per la

solo per localizzare i centri di produzione musicale, ma anche per indagare gli spazi, le modalità di produzione della musica e soprattutto comprendere in quali modi territorio ed espressione musicale hanno interagito e si sono vicendevolmente influenzati[39].

La piattaforma web fornirà l'accesso alle fonti musicali relative al ducato estense già digitalizzate e presenti nella *Estense Digital Library*, ma sarà possibile anche 'leggerle' avendo immediati riferimenti al loro contesto di produzione. Difatti, l'interazione tra le parti costitutive della piattaforma consentirà di passare liberamente dalla visualizzazione spaziale alle schede di approfondimento, ottenendo informazioni su opere, documenti, persone ed eventi spettacolari[40].

Ricostruire e mappare l'attività musicale delle varie istituzioni presenti a Modena porterà a comprendere quanto la musica abbia influito nello sviluppo del paesaggio urbano e nella storia culturale della città. Il progetto, grazie al contributo della tecnologia digitale, si prefigge di proporre un modello collaborativo e multidisciplinare per la ricerca storica e fornire nuove idee per la valorizzazione del patrimonio culturale e, più in generale, della città.

## BIBLIOGRAFIA

ALLACCI 1654
ALLACCI, Leone. *Del viaggio della Signora D. Lucretia Barberini Duchessa di Modena da Roma a Modena. Lettere di Leone Allacci. All'ill.mo Sig.r il Sig.r Marcantonio Spinola*, Genova, s.n., 1654.

CALORE 1983
CALORE, Marina. *Spettacoli a Modena tra '500 e '600. Dalla città alla capitale*, Modena, Aedes Muratoriana, 1983.

---

georeferenziazione dei dati stessi. Un GIS utilizza un modello logico che suddivide gli elementi in strati sovrapposti (*layers*), con numerosi benefici tecnici e di gestione dei dati, permettendo interrogazioni simultanee sui vari livelli informativi ed estrazione di informazioni in base al loro posizionamento.

[39]. Per la creazione della mappa digitale è stata scelta come base la mappa di Modena opera del cartografo Domenico Vandelli appartenente alla collezione della Biblioteca Estense e relativa alla Modena di fine Seicento.

[40]. La mappa interattiva è stata attualmente realizzata in una versione Beta, che prevede l'uso di una sola carta storica riferita al periodo di riferimento del progetto, ma la flessibilità del GIS consentirà, nel futuro, l'inserimento di altre mappe, anche prodotte in periodi diversi, che, sovrapponendosi, permetteranno di apprezzare le modifiche subite dalla struttura urbana della città. Nel tempo, infatti la città e le sue istituzioni hanno cambiato volto, talvolta posizione, denominazione o addirittura lo stesso significato. Al contempo, l'arco cronologico scelto per l'avvio del progetto, attualmente focalizzato sul Seicento, potrebbe essere esteso per mostrare l'evoluzione culturale della città su di una scala temporale più ampia. A ciò si aggiunge la possibilità di inserire, accanto alle informazioni sulla produzione musicale modenese, altri dati di carattere storico, artistico, iconografico riguardanti i luoghi della città presi in analisi, consentendo di ampliare le applicazioni, al fine di restituire l'identità storica locale nella sua complessità e ricchezza.

# Suoni, spazi, identità della Modena estense

Chiarelli 1991
Chiarelli, Alessandra. 'La Musica', in: *La Chiesa e il Collegio di S. Carlo a Modena*, a cura di Daniele Benati, Lucia Peruzzi e Vincenzo Vandelli, Modena, Banca Popolare dell'Emilia-Artioli, 1991, pp. 249-255.

Chiarelli 2009
Ead. 'Teatro e collezionismo in un fondo di libretti e in alcuni documenti del Sei, Sette e primo Ottocento', in: *Quaderni Estensi,* no. 1 (2009), pp. 191-207.

Cont 2009
Cont, Alessandro. '«Sono nato principe libero, tale voglio conservarmi»: Francesco II d'Este (1660-1694)', in: *Memorie Scientifiche, Giuridiche, Letterarie, Accademia Nazionale di Scienze Lettere e Arti di Modena*, s. VIII, XII/2 (2009), pp. 407-459.

Crowther 1990
Crowther, Victor. 'A Case-Study in the Power of the Purse: The Management of the Ducal 'Cappella' in Modena in the Reign of Francesco II d'Este', in: *Journal of the Royal Musical Association*, CXV/2 (1990), pp. 207-219.

Crowther 1992
Id. *The Oratorio in Modena*, Oxford, Clarendon Press, 1992.

Fabbri 1985
Fabbri, Paolo. 'Il municipio e la corte: il teatro per musica tra Reggio e Modena nel secondo Seicento', in: *Alessandro Stradella e Modena. Atti del Convegno internazionale di Studi, Modena, 15-17 dicembre 1983*, a cura di Carolyn Gianturco, Modena, Teatro Comunale di Modena-Coptip, 1985, pp. 160-186.

Fiore – Belotti 2020
Fiore, Angela – Belotti, Sara. 'Merging music and landscape: un approccio digitale per lo studio dell'identità culturale della Modena estense', in: *Magazén: International Journal for Digital and Public Humanities,* I/1 (2020), pp. 75-100.

Gamberti 1659
Gamberti, Domenico. *L'idea di un prencipe et eroe christiano in Francesco I. d'Este [...] effigiata co profili della virtu di prencipe suoi maggiori ereditate,* Modena, Soliani, 1659.

Graziani 1660
Graziani, Girolamo. *Trionfo della Virtù. Festa d'armi a cavallo rappresentata nella nascita del Sereniss. Sig. Prencipe di Modona l'anno MDCLX*, Modena, Soliani, 1660.

Jander 1975
Jander, Owen. 'The Cantata in Accademia: Music for the Accademia de' Dissonanti and Their Duke, Francesco II d'Este', in: *Rivista Italiana di Musicologia*, X (1975), pp. 519-544.

LORENZETTI 1997
LORENZETTI, Stefano. '«Per animare agli esercizi nobili». Esperienza musicale e identità nobiliare nei collegi di educazione', in: *Quaderni Storici: Storia e musica*, XXXII/95/2 (1997), pp. 435-460.

MARTINELLI BRAGLIA 1985
MARTINELLI BRAGLIA, Graziella. 'Il Teatro Fontanelli: note su impresari ed artisti nella Modena di Francesco II e Rinaldo', in: *Alessandro Stradella e Modena, op. cit.*, pp. 138-159.

MARTINELLI BRAGLIA 2007
EAD. 'Luoghi e artefici dello spettacolo nella Modena di Orazio Vecchi', in: TADDEI – CHIARELLI 2007, pp. 17-50.

MARTINELLI BRAGLIA 2016
EAD. 'Il teatro di Francesco II d'Este nel palazzo ducale di Modena (1686)', in: *Memorie scientifiche, giuridiche, letterarie / Accademia nazionale di scienze, lettere e arti di Modena,* s. VIII, XIX/1 (2016), pp. 159-177.

MARTINELLI BRAGLIA 2019
EAD. 'Il Teatro ducale grande di Modena: «drammi in musica» e impresari all'epoca di Francesco I e Francesco II d'Este', in: *Memorie scientifiche, giuridiche, letterarie / Accademia nazionale di scienze, lettere e arti di Modena,* s. IX, III (2019), pp. 31-62.

SIROCCHI 2020
SIROCCHI, Simone. 'Haec potest ars doloris. I funerali estensi di secondo Seicento', in: *Studi Secenteschi,* LXI (2020), pp. 151-175.

SPACCINI 1993
SPACCINI, Giovanni Battista. *Cronaca di Modena, Anni 1588-1602*, a cura di Albano Biondi, Rolando Bussi e Carlo Giovannini, Modena, Panini, 1993.

TADDEI – CHIARELLI 2007
*Il Theatro dell'udito: società, Musica, Storia e Cultura nell'epoca di Orazio Vecchi. Conferenze tenute durante le celebrazioni del IV centenario della morte di Orazio Vecchi*, a cura di Ferdinando Taddei e Alessandra Chiarelli, Modena, Mucchi, 2007.

# Celebrating the Prince from Afar:
# Echoes from the Jubilant Dominions in the Orations to the Newly Elected Doges (XVI-XVII Century)[*]

*Giovanni Florio*
(Università di Padova)

In 1562 the Roman-born polygraph Francesco Sansovino[1] published his anthology *Delle orationi recitate a Principi di Venetia nella loro creatione da gli ambasciadori di diverse città*[2]. As overtly suggested by its title, the book consists of a reasoned selection of encomiastic speeches delivered before the newly-elected doges by various illustrious representatives hailing from cities — and *almost cities* — subdued to the Republic of Venice[3]. According to Sansovino, the anthology's main value lay in offering the reader the opportunity to compare the ingenuity of various rhetors dealing with the same topic: the praise of the doge[4], the «paradoxical Prince» of the Most Serene Republic[5]. Although marginal, the anthology should be considered as an integral part of Sansovino's ambitious editorial project aiming, on the one hand, to dignify renaissance vernacular rhetoric, and on the other hand, to present the praise of Venice and its Prince as an autonomous encomiastic subgenre[6].

---

[*]. This article is part of a project that has received funding from the European Research Council (ERC) under the European Union's Horizon 2020 Research and Innovation programme (G.A. 758450 – ERC-StG2017 'Republics on the Stage of Kings: Representing Republican State Power in the Europe of Absolute Monarchies, late 16th – early 18th century').

[1]. For a detailed biography, see Bonora 1994.

[2]. Sansovino 1562.

[3]. Despite its title, the anthology also included several orations delivered by rhetors on their own behalfs, one speech delivered by Bernardino Tomitano on behalf of the University of Padua (1553), another one made by Francesco Baraterio on behalf of Orazio Farnese (1559) and, finally an oration offered to the Venetian Senate by the ambassador of Bergamo Paolo Zanco (*ibidem*).

[4]. «Orationi [...] nelle quali con grandissimo utile de' lettori si vede la forza dell'eloquenza di molti huomini illustri in una materia sola». *Ibidem*, cover.

[5]. Muir 1977, pp. 251-298. On the institutional and ceremonial features of the Venetian doge, see also Cecchetti 1864; Benzoni 1982; Ravegnani 2013, as well as the introductory chapter of Da Mosto 1960.

[6]. See Bolzoni 1984, pp. 1057-1060; Bonora 1994; Panzera 2012a Panzera 2012b, as well as De Vivo 2007, pp. 21-22.

# Giovanni Florio

The statement of Venice's radical uniqueness went hand in hand with a claim of full literary dignity of its vernacular rhetoric: Sansovino's anthology matched the main editorial lines he was carrying out in those years, on the long wave of the Italian 'question of the language'. In this regard, opening the anthology with a mention of Pietro Bembo[7] and re-publishing Gian Giorgio Trissino's vernacular oration to Doge Andrea Gritti (1523)[8] were rather programmatic editorial choices, fulfilling both literary and explanatory needs. Sansovino leveraged Trissino's words to provide the reader with an extremely accurate definition of the ceremonial occasion in which such encomiastic speeches were meant to be delivered. According to Trissino, the congratulatory embassy — the convention of electing an ambassador, sending him to Venice and appointing him to pay homage to the newly-elected doge with a congratulatory oration[9] — should be primarily considered as a «nice and honourable custom» common to all Venetian subject cities[10]. Upon his reception in the Venetian Palazzo Ducale and in the Collegio hall, the ambassador of Vicenza chose a legal definition to accredit himself before the new doge enthroned among the *Serenissima Signoria* and the *Consulta dei Savi*[11]. By defining the congratulatory embassy as a *consuetudine*[12], Trissino consciously demonstrated his awareness that no written law approved by the Venetian government actually forced the Venetian subject cities to pay homage to the newly elected doge in this way: looking at the legislative repertories collected, through the centuries, by the chancelleries of the main Venetian subject cities[13], we have to go back to 1476 to find a Maggior Consiglio's act that refers explicitly to the congratulatory embassy; and furthermore,

---

[7]. See 'Francesco Sansovino ai lettori', introductory chapter of Sansovino 1562.

[8]. Sansovino 1562, fols. 1r-4r (first edition: Trissino 1524). This episode was also reported in Sanudo [ed. 1892], pp. 398-399 and 475-482. For a brief introduction on Gian Giorgio Trissino, see D'Achille 2011 as well as the thorough bibliography published in Corrieri 2012.

[9]. On this topic, see Florio 2019.

[10]. «Bella et honorevole consuetudine è questa [...] che dopo la creatione di ciascun Duce tutte le città suggette a questo felicissimo stato mandano i loro ambasciadori a sua Serenità». Sansovino 1562, fol. 1r.

[11]. For a general introduction to the institutional composition and constitutional attribution of the Pien Collegio, see Ferro 1845-1847, vol. II, pp. [4]37-439. With reference to the communicative and diplomatic functions of the Pien Collegio, see De Vivo 2012, pp. 138-152; more specifically, on the Pien Collegio as recipient of the congratulatory embassies hailing from the dominions, see Sinding-Larsen 1974, pp. 134-135. For an analysis of the decorative programme of the Pien Collegio hall, see *ibidem*, *passim*, and Wolters 1987, pp. 246-255.

[12]. Sansovino rather prefers to define it as a «honorevole usanza» (Sansovino 1562, fol. 1r). The juridical, cultural and anthropological relevance of the *consuetudine* within the Venetian political context has been a topic frequently raised by Claudio Povolo, of whom I shall limit myself to mention: Povolo 2008; Povolo 2006a; Povolo 2006b.

[13]. For instance, Archivio di Stato di Verona, Archivio antico del Comune, Processi, b. 59, file 1360, or Biblioteca Civica Bertoliana di Vicenza, Archivio Torre, b. 676. See also Pinetti 1929.

## Celebrating the Prince from Afar

it is an act that only prevents the neo-elected doge from receiving delegations composed of more than twenty members[14].

This original lack of normative sources[15] could only partially explain the lack of historiographical interest in this peculiar diplomatic ceremony[16]; the widespread inclination to consider the ducal ceremonial as an urban phenomenon has not helped to shed any light on the involvement of the Venetian dominions in the ducal election and in its celebration[17]. Nevertheless, this lack of both primary and secondary sources could be partially addressed by considering anthologies like that of Sansovino and, more generally, the texts of the congratulatory orations delivered before the newly-elected doges by the representatives of the various Venetian dominions and subject cities[18]. Widely circulating between the sixteenth and the first half of the seventeenth century[19], the printed editions of these encomiastic speeches represent a huge — and largely unexplored — *corpus* of sources[20]. Reconsidering this encomiastic subgenre and its rhetorical *topoi* from an historical perspective could help us appreciate the involvement of the Venetian dominions in shaping the ceremonial landscape — and soundscape — of the ducal election.

---

[14]. See *ibidem*, file 1, f. not numbered, dated 27 February 1475 *more veneto*, as well as Archivio di Stato di Verona, Archivio antico del Comune, Processi, b. 59, file 1360, not numbered, dated 27 February 1475 *more veneto*. On this act, see also Musatti 1888, pp. 114-115 and Cecchetti 1864, pp. 204-205. Until the early seventeenth century, this act was periodically reiterated but without substantial changes. The most relevant legislative interventions concerned the enforcement of the surveillance on its violation. Nevertheless, such attempts to tighten this prohibition up are the clearest evidence of its lack of efficacy. See Bistort 1912, pp. 242-245 and *Parte presa* [1615]. For a complete overview on the evolution of this norm, see *Promissio* [1675], chapter XXIII.

[15]. This was the result of a survey within the Venetian central archives promoted by several Venetian subject cities at the beginning of March 1675. See Biblioteca Civica Bertoliana di Vicenza, Archivio Torre, b. 1439, 9 March 1675, as well as Archivio di Stato di Padova, Archivio Civico Antico, Nunzi e Ambasciatori, b. 101, 5 March 1675.

[16]. Paradigmatically, Andrea Da Mosto dismissed the Venetian congratulatory embassies as an empty ritual or, at least, as an annoying ceremonial duty poorly tolerated by the Venetian doges. Da Mosto 1960, p. xxvi.

[17]. On the Venetian ducal and civic ritual, see Muir 1977; Howard 1993-1994; Casini 1996; Urban 1998; Fenlon 2007; Hopkins 2013; Viallon 2008. On the popular participation in the political and ceremonial rituality of the Venetian ducal election, see Van Gelder 2018; Van Gelder 2019. On the popular involvement in shaping the Venetian civic ritual, see also Judde de Larivière 2015.

[18]. For a thorough description of the historical and institutional evolution of the diplomatic *apparati* of the Venetian subject cities, see Morpurgo 1878; Borgherini Scarabellin 1911; Pinetti 1929; Fasolo 1935; Scroccaro 1986; Varanini 1992; Florio 2017b.

[19]. Despite the absence of complete and definitive statistics, the extent of the phenomenon still can be deduced from the huge number of titles recorded in Cicogna 1847, pp. 319-349, Da Mosto 1960, pp. 558-598, and partially in Griffante 2003-2006.

[20]. See Sinding-Larsen 1974, pp. 134-149; Doglio 1983; Špoljarić 2018; O'Connell 2016a; O'Connell 2016b; Florio 2019.

# Giovanni Florio

Orations like this one, composed by the ambassador of Lendinara Orazio Toscanella on the occasion of Girolamo Priuli's ducal election (1559), offer us a suggestive glimpse of the reaction that an almost-city of the Venetian *Terraferma* could have had in receiving the news of a ducal enthronement:

> As soon as the news of the creation [of the new doge] was heard in Lendinara, a thousand fires were suddenly lit and a rejoicing second to none, [accompanied by] the sound of bells and voices which smote the stars, was heard[21].

The rejoicing of Capodistria for Francesco Donà's election (1545) was depicted more soberly — but not less incisively — by Francesco Grisonio:

> [...] with standards and emblems fluttering in the air; with fires and flames arising from everywhere to the sky; with lanterns and torches hence the earth seemed to be a new starry sky; with drums, noises and the rumble of martial instruments; with voices, jubilations and applause of a consoled heart[22].

Around the 1545, Francesco Grisonio depicted more soberly — but not less incisively — the rejoicing of Capodistria for Francesco Donà's election:

> Your most faithful City of Capodistria, with sounds, fireworks, salvoes, living voices, celebrations, solemnities and in every possible way, has shown from afar such joy which, rooted in the heart, is spreading through all its parts[23].

Almost sixty-one years later, Nicolò Manzuoli rather preferred to focus on the «solemn musics» coming from the local churches in order to describe to Leonardo Donà how Capodistria had welcomed the news of his ducal election:

---

21. «Subito che in Lendinara s'udì novelle della sua creazione, furono accesi a un tratto mille fuochi, et con suono di campane et di voci che ferivano le stelle, si sentì un giubilo a niuno alt[r]o secondo». Sansovino 1562, fol. 74v.

22. «[...] con vesilli et insegne all'aria sparte, con fuochi e fiamme sorgenti in ogni parte al Cielo, con faci e lumiere, onde nuovo stellato Ciel parea la Terra, con tamburri, strepiti e rimbombi di guerrieri stromenti, con voci, giubili et applausi de consolati cuori». Michele 1596, p. 25; see also the edition of the same oration published in Consalvi 1597, pp. 115-126.

23. «La fedelissima vostra Città di Capodistria con suoni, fuochi, artigliarie, vive voci, feste, solennità et tutti gli altri a lei possibili modi ha dimostrato absente quella tanta allegrezza che radicata nel cuore per tutte le sue parti si diffonde». Sansovino 1562, fol. 10r.

# Celebrating the Prince from Afar

> That most devoted people [of Capodistria], [...] made merry and rejoiced
> with unusual displays, also giving due thanks to His Divine Majesty within the Holy
> Temples by means of solemn musics and devoted orisons[24].

Apart from rhetorical stereotypes, such redundant statements offer us a vivid description of the spreading of the ducal election's soundscape from Venice throughout the Venetian dominions. The civic celebration of the republican Prince, the tolling of Venice's bells, the acclamation of the Venetian people and the sound of the solemn mass performed in St. Mark's basilica did not end in Venice but echoed throughout all the lands controlled by the Most Serene Republic. A myriad of 'other' ducal celebrations, performed by each Venetian subject city, ran parallel to the historiographically far better-known one performed in the city of Venice[25]. As lamented by the Paduan orator Ottonello Descalzo before Doge Pasquale Cicogna in 1585, it was a pity that the new Prince would only be able to attend the «glorious triumphs» in his honour performed in Venice, without having the opportunity to enjoy the resounding jubilation displayed by the Paduans. According to Descalzo, the news of Cicogna's election, just arrived from Venice, had spread spontaneously, uncontrollably and noisily through the population. As asserted by the orator, the collective euphoria had been irrepressible: people had immediately and chaotically begun to meet each other in the streets and in the squares of Padua. Even faces had become a medium spreading the joyous news coming from Venice: people realized that the new Prince had been elected simply by looking at each other's happy appearance. In a short while everyone began to loudly bless and glorify the name of the new doge and the wisdom of the ducal electors. At the apex of the frenzy, an even more noisy disturbance of the Paduan 'ordinary' soundscape made the news official: all at once, drums started rolling, «bombards thundering, towers flamings, fields burning, trumpets ringings [and] bells tolling». The effect was amazing: according to Descalzo, it seemed as if thunder, lightning and rain were falling down in unison from the sky. Nevertheless, even in the middle of such chaos, «blurred voices» praising the doge could still be heard: people's shouts — Descalzo said — were loud enough to reach the stars[26].

---

[24]. «Quel popolo devotissimo [...] con insolite dimostrazioni fece festa et allegrezza, rendendo anco ne sacri Tempii, con solenni musiche et con devote orationi, i debiti ringratiamenti a sua divina Maestà». Manzuoli 1606. On Nicolò Manzuoli and its oration, see Florio 2017a.

[25]. For a detailed description of the Venetian ducal election and its civic celebration, see Muir 1977, pp. 277-289 and Casini 1996. See also the bibliography mentioned *supra*, at fn. 17.

[26]. «Deh, perché non fu lecito che Vostra Serenità dopo i glori[o]si trionfi di questa alma Città per lo novello suo prencipato havesse potuto mirare il gaudio, il giubilo, il contento da noi dimostrato per tal cagione; corre alla gente non capendo per l'allegrezza in se stessa benedicendo, et insieme essaltando il lodatissimo nome suo, et il giudicio intiero di chi la elesse, s'incontrava l'un l'altro, et con lieti sembianti communicavano l'essaltatatione sua

In 1554, the same ascending — and resounding — climax had been chosen by Giovan Domenico Roncale to describe to Doge Francesco Venier how the city of Rovigo welcomed the news of his ducal election[27]. In Roncale's rhetorical depiction, the announcement of Venier's enthronement was spread through the «universe» directly by the «voice of God»: once arrived in Rovigo, the news first reached the city's ears and then penetrated its heart[28]. This inner and quiet joy progressively exploded into a noisy, chaotic, collective and — above all — public rejoicing: pious voices began to thank God for the doge's election, first within the monasteries, then in the private houses and, finally, in the squares and in the streets, the quintessential public — and publication — spaces[29]. As in Descalzo's oration, the swell of sounds and noise marks the progressive escalation of the celebration from an intimate matter to a public dimension. «Most pious voices» and «most devout orisons» started «rending the air» together with «children's shouts» and «the people's voice»; finally, «endless sounds, noises, fireworks, public parties and celebrations» joined the cacophonic concert dedicated to the new Prince[30]. This transition from *private* to *public* spaces[31] — and from *private* to *public* sounds — are assumed here — and in other similar orations[32] — as an incisive synthesis of the whole process of publication of the doge's election throughout the Venetian *Terraferma*: trumpets, drums, fireworks, peals and cannon salvoes coming from public buildings — notably city halls, squares, churches and civic towers — dominates the subject city's soundscape as depicted by the ambassadors appointed to pay homage to the new

---

al prencipato come proprio lor bene. S'udi in un punto toccar tamburi, tuonar bombarde, fiammeggiar torri, arder campi, dar segno trombe, suonar campane, come suole avvenire nel cielo alle volte che tuona, et balena, et piove insieme abondevolmente con maraviglia et con gaudio di ciascuno, et fra questi rumori certe voci confuse s'udivano inalzare alle stelle le lodi Vostre». MICHELE 1587, p. not numbered.

[27]. For a brief biography, see LUCIOLI 2017.

[28]. «La [...] felicissima nova, altissimo Prencipe, dalla voce di Dio subito per lo universo spargendosi, è pervenuta a gli orecchi della vostra fidelissima città di Rovigo, et indi penetratale al core». SANSOVINO 1562, fol. 48v (first edition: RONCALE 1554).

[29]. On this topic, see the exhaustive bibliography offered by NEVOLA 2013. With particular reference to early modern Venice, see MUIR – WEISSMAN 1977; INFELISE 1997; FENLON 2009; COWAN 2008; JUDDE DE LARIVIÈRE 2011; DE VIVO 2012; DE VIVO 2016; ROSPOCHER – SALZBERG 2013; ROSPOCHER 2013; SALZBERG 2013.

[30]. «[Rovigo], non contenta de i voti, de i sacrifici e de i dolci conce[r]ti da pietosissime voci formati ne monasteri, nelle case e nelle piazze, che percotendo l'aria devotissime orationi al gran motor de i cieli, ringratiandolo hanno offerte, n[é] bastandole i gridi de fanciulli, la voce del popolo, gli infiniti suoni, strepiti, fuochi, feste et solennità publiche da lei in ciascun luoco fatte [...]». SANSOVINO 1562, fols. 48v-49r.

[31]. On the hermeneutic values of this spatial dichotomy, see RAU 2019, p. 93.

[32]. See, for instance, the oration delivered by Orazio Toscanella to Doge Girolamo Priuli. SANSOVINO 1562, fols. 74r-76v.

doge. In their rhetorical reconstructions of such festive events, the icastic sound of the exulting city echoes in its countryside and, in so doing, contributes to spreading beyond the city walls not only the news of the ducal election, but also the praise of the new Prince. In the oration he delivered on behalf of the Paduan *Universitas Artistarum*, Bernardino Tomitano cast a glance to the soundscape surrounding Padua immediately after Marcantonio Trevisan's ducal election (1553)[33]: all «the neighbouring cities give signs of happiness by burning fires, playing trumpets and tolling bells». Tomitano was particularly inclined to interpret such joyous outbursts as communicative acts: as he said, the subject cities used to welcome ducal elections with such resounding celebrations in order to «show to the World the inner affection by which people's souls feel encumbered»[34].

Shaped by the rhetorical ingenuity of the orator, the static landscape surrounding the subject city, once stimulated by the vibration of the urban rejoicing, becomes a dynamic soundscape, actively participating in the ovation offered to the new doge. «Not only the city [of Belluno] is happy», said the ambassador Paolo Novello to Doge Marcantonio Trevisan,

> but even everything all around [...]. Even those shady valleys resound of a certain something new; those rivers murmur much more sweetly, and those horrible mountains seem to rise more strongly [...] in order to revere You [...]. All the things of which that land is full — animate or inanimate — [...] exulted, and by exulting they celebrate You, and by celebrating You they honour You[35].

Through the emission of sounds, the subject city and its district could finally participate in the doge's celebration and — albeit metaphorically — in his election. «You were enthroned», said the ambassador of Chioggia to the neo-elected Leonardo Donà (1606), «by the voice of all the human beings by means of a public and universal applause». A few

---

33.    For a detailed biography, see DAVI 1995 and GIRARDI 1995.

34.    «[...] le città vicine fanno segno d'allegria ardendo fuochi, sonando trombe, toccando squille e molt'altri segni facendo, onde l'interno affetto, dal qual si sentono ingombrar gli animi de i popoli, possano far manifesto al mondo». SANSOVINO 1562, fol. 22r; see also the first edition of the oration in TOMITANO 1554. More directly, in 1606 the ambassador Agostino Del Bene said to Doge Leonardo Donà that the city of Verona «through very evident signs and clear evidence of ineffable joy had published to the world the huge rejoicing which [...] it was feeling inside itself» («con apertissimi segni et chiari dimostramenti di letitia ineffabile publicò al mondo l'immenso giubilo che in se stessa [...] provava»). DEL BENE 1606. On the meanings of the words (and of the practice of) *pubblicare* and *comunicare* in the early modern Venetian context, see DE VIVO 2012.

35.    «Né pur sol la città sola è lieta, ma etiandio il tutto d'ogn'intorno [...]. In fin quelle ombrose valli, non so che più nuovo risuonano; quei fiumi più soavemente assai mormorano, et quegli horridi monti par che a forza più si ergano mostrando i gioghi loro infin qui per vedervi, per reverirvi, per honorarvi [...]. Tutte le cose di che quel paese è ripieno, animate et inanimate, a tutta prova essultano, et essultando vi celebrano, et celebrando vi honorano». SANSOVINO 1562, fol. 29r.

113

lines later, such collective «voice» was better defined as a «scream» or, to be more specific, as «a public noise of joy and immense delight which fills all these lucky surroundings»[36]. If we are to trust Giovanni Vida, something similar happened in Capodistria immediately before Sebastiano Venier's election (1577): «in the manner of an echo, *Veniero, Veniero* was heard repeated» everywhere. As explained by the ambassador, in this way the whole district of Capodistria was prophetically predicting Venier's enthronement[37].

Taking into account the countryside's reactions was an obligation for ambassadors representing regional bodies politic. In 1606, while praising Doge Leonardo Donà on behalf of the *Patria del Friuli*, Massimiliano Montegnacco chose to give a bird's eye description of the Friulian soundscape[38]: «as soon as it heard the most appreciated and craved news» of Donà's ducal election, the whole Patria del Friuli started «singing with clear signs of happiness». The result was «a very sweet concert of very happy voices» praising God and the doge «accompanied by the sound of all the bells, the din of the artilleries, of the trumpets and of the drums»: finally, «the whole Friuli was heard resounding, from the mountains to the sea»[39]. In this as in other congratulatory speeches devoted to the newly elected doges, the wide arc of territories extending beyond and in front of the Venetian lagoon acts as a sort of sounding board amplifying and propagating the new doge's urban celebration. Such a *physical* reaction to the vibrations emitted by the city of Venice[40] — and even by the very

---

[36]. «Comunemente foste voi dalle voci de gl'huomini tutti intronizato a questa suprema dignità con publico, et universale applauso». «A questo grido [...], et a questo publico romore di gaudio et di letitia immensa [...]». Di MARANGONI 1606.

[37]. «Né fin'hora per tutta quella Città si è sentito altro che rissonare di ogni intorno il chiaro et glorioso nome di Vostra Sublimità non solamente dopoi che si è intesa la desideratissima novella di così degna elettione, ma anco inanzi ella a guisa di echo replicar si udiva, Veniero, Veniero, come presaga, e certa, che dovesse succedere un tanto bene». VIDA 1577.

[38]. For a brief biography of Massimiliano Montegnacco, see CAVAZZA 2012.

[39]. «[La Patria del Friuli] tantosto che sentì la gratissima et bramata nova [...] piena di maravigliosa letitia, d'ineffabile contento et di suprema consolatione, d'interno affetto tutta si commosse, et intonando con chiarissimi segni d'allegrezza, e con un soavissimo concerto di lietissime voci, et amplissime laudi a Iddio, et alla Serenità Vostra, accompagnate dal sono di tutte le campane, dal strepito delle artigliarie, delle trombe et de i tamburi si sentì risonar tutto'l Friuli da i monti sino al mare». MONTEGNACCO 1606.

[40]. In 1606, the ambassador appointed to praise Doge Leonardo Donà on behalf of Cavarzere refer to the news of the ducal election as a «sounding trumpet» which had «reached the ear» and «pierced the heart» of the subject town («La sonora tromba della qual creatione mirabile pervenuta alle orecchie, anzi trapassata al cuore della fidelissima Terra Vostra di Cavarzere»). DALLA PORTA 1606. Similarly, for the anonymous ambassadors sent to Venice by Pirano on the occasion of Marcantonio Trevisan's enthronement (1553), the «welcome and awaited rumor» of the ducal election was comparable with a «the great thunder» («si udì il gran tuono della grata et aspettata voce della sua [...] creatione»). SANSOVINO 1562, fol. 39v; see also the two editions of the same oration printed in 1553: *ORATIONE* 1553A and *ORATIONE* 1553B.

sound of the doge's name — was assumed as *natural* in the strictest sense of the word. The already-mentioned Giovan Domenico Roncale, for instance, founded the entire argument of his congratulation to Doge Francesco Venier on a definition of sound as the most natural and instinctive means to display an irrepressible inner joy:

> Every living being of all kinds [...] naturally forces itself to express [...] the joy it has conceived inside itself by means of different voices, noises, gestures, and other infinite signs[41].

The use of acoustic images to describe the dominions celebrating the newly elected doge represents a distinctive topos of the encomiastic subgenre we are considering. Bowed before Doge Leonardo Donà (1606), Santo di Marangoni defined the people of Chioggia as a «hoarse and disordered flock of simple seabirds»: «celebrat[ing] and solemnis[ing]» the doge's «name» «by flapping their wings» and by emitting «shrill voices of confused happiness». The overlapping of a wide range of inarticulate sounds and noises was once again defined as the most natural reaction to the ducal election. The task of imposing order and meaning to this chaos weighed heavily on the orator's shoulders. As explained by Santo di Marangoni to Leonardo Donà, the seagull's calls emitted by Chioggia «expresses with natural roughness the efficacy and the reverence of its affection» towards the new Prince[42]. In praising the same doge, Pietro Geslino explained that the «noises of drums, and trumpets, the sounds of bells, games, fires and celebrations» which had been heard in Feltre «for many continuous days, denote both the infinite love [...] and the contentment» of the subject city towards its new Prince[43]. Humbly bowed before the doge, the orator invokes all the performative efficacy of his eloquence in order to give meaning to the joyful chaos coming from the dominions[44]: in 1556, the orator of Crema said to Lorenzo Priuli that it was «easy to show such happiness, after it has already been outwardly manifested»; nevertheless, to explain the «reasons» of such feeling would be «really difficult [...] for

---

[41]. «Naturalmente [...] ciascun animante di qualunque sorte con varie voci, strepiti, noti et altri infiniti segni si sforza a tutto suo potere mostrar fuori quale allegrezza intrinsicamente habbi concetta». SANSOVINO 1562, fol. 48r.

[42]. «Quel populo tutto, quasi roco et incomposto stuolo di semplici uccelli marini, dibattendo l'ali con stridule voci di confusa allegrezza, festeggia et solenniza il nome di Vostra Serenità, et esprime con la rozezza naturale l'efficacia, et la riverenza dell'affetto suo». DI MARANGONI 1606.

[43]. «Per molti giorni continovi non si sono uditi se non strepiti di tamburi e di trombe, suoni di campane, giochi, fuochi, feste, cose tutte denotanti e l'amor infinito che noi vostri fedelissimi sudditi vi portiamo, et il contento che sentimo della vostra grandezza». GESLINO 1606.

[44]. On the concept of performative utterance, see the pivotal AUSTIN 1962.

# GIOVANNI FLORIO

any eloquent tongue»[45]. Three years later, the orator of Chioggia Giuliano Scarpa said to the newly elected Girolamo Priuli that his diplomatic task was «to show the very true reasons for which your very devoted people resound with happy voices and rejoicings» and to «make it known and clear also with words»[46]. Through the power of his words, the orator strives to transform an incoherent mass of auditory stimuli into a symphony or — to use a recurring expression from the texts we are considering — into a *concert* in honour of the new republican Prince. In 1545, Francesco Grisonio put the sound produced by the name of the new doge at the heart of his speech, assuming it to be a sort of ordering and harmonising principle:

> [...] a concert of peoples moved to speech by such suave and powerful harmony of many virtues was heard continuously clamoring 'Donato, Donato' not only within the city [of Capodistria], but also everywhere[47].

«The people's voice — concluded Grisonio — is [...] the voice of God»: the echo of the doge's name, infinitely repeated by the inhabitants of Capodistria, indicated to everyone the joyous news coming from Venice[48]. Once distilled by the orator, the noisy chaos characterising the ducal celebration turns into a well-ordered multi-voice chorus, a polyphonic symphony within which every social body, class or context — as well as every age group or gender — can find its own place. In the idyllic soundscape evoked by the orators, everyone, be they citizen or commoner, city or country dweller, lay or cleric, rich or poor, old or young, male or female,

---

45. «[...] sia però facile quest'allegrezza dimostrare poscia ch'ella già fuori si manifesta, ma le cagioni di questa, e tante e sì alte, ben difficile sarà ad ogni faconda lingua et a questa debil mia quasi impossibile». Giacomo Gennaro edited in FINO 1572, fol. 16v.

46. «[...] per dimostrare le verissime cause onde l'affettionatissimo popol suo di liete voci e giubili risuoni, ardino allegri fuochi per la città, facilmente noi tutti siamo condotti in questo honoratissimo luoco per far ciò anco palese e chiaro con le parole». SANSOVINO 1562, fol. 66r (first edition: SCARPA [1559]).

47. «Non in questa Città solo, ma per tutto s'udiva un concerto de popoli messi in voce da quella sì soave e potente harmonia di tante virtù che risonava sempre Donato, Donato. Et pur (come si dice) la voce del Popolo è ella voce di Dio, che tanta felicità a dito ci mostrava». SANSOVINO 1562, fol. 11r. A very similar argument could be found in the anthology of orations to Marino Grimani edited by Antonio Maria Consalvi in 1597. The rhetor Sallustio Lucillo identified three different socio-political categories exulting for the doge's election: «the City» of Venice, «the subject» living in the dominions, and the Venetian patriciate (identified in its political expression: «the Senate» together with «the Republic»). In Lucillo's rhetoric construction, each of these categories was pushed to celebrate the doge not only by his republican virtues, but also by a specific sound: the «subjects» and the Republic were both invited to celebrate «by the very noble shout» of Grimani's «very famous name», while the City of Venice by «the unstoppable trumpet of [His] Serenity's fame». CONSALVI 1597, p. 141. For more, in general, on the performative representation of the doge as a harmonising principle, see CUMMING 1992.

48. SANSOVINO 1562, fol. 11r.

# CELEBRATING THE PRINCE FROM AFAR

is equally involved in praising the new republican Prince. According to Orazio Toscanella, in 1559, when the news of Girolamo Priuli's ducal election reached Lendinara,

> [...] every person, of any age, gender [and] status gave sign of infinite happiness. The river, the squares, every public and private place suddenly resounded to Your Serenity's highest name[49].

Giorgio Piloni, used a very similar image to describe to Marino Grimani how the city of Belluno had reacted to his enthronement:

> [...] the souls of all the inhabitants of Belluno were [so] filled with joy, happiness and extraordinary solace that suddenly [...] the whole city was seen admirably rejoicing and becoming exceedingly glad and entirely light-hearted: somebody, by running to the Holy Temples and thanking God, prayed for [the doge's] highest felicity; others wished him a prosperous future by celebrating his virtues with very loud voices. [People of] every gender, every age, every status [...] performed joyous concerts in his honour with chants, sounds, celebrations and fires[50].

Re-semanticised by the orator, the cacophonic soundscape of the jubilant subject city turns into a coherent political expression, although limited to a mere display of monolithic consensus towards the new Prince and, through him, towards the Republic. Having described the soundscape generated by the election of Marcantonio Trevisan (1553), the ambassador of Chioggia exclaimed:

> It seems to me I hear not only the voices of the people of Venice, but also those of all the cities subjected to Your Serenity exclaiming with happy rejoicings: There, Lord God has given us not just a very fair Prince, but [also] a very caring and compassionate Father[51].

---

[49]. «Ogni persona, d'ogni età, d'ogni sesso, d'ogni conditione mostrò segno d'infinita allegrezza. Il fiume, le piazze, tutti i luoghi publici et privati a un tratto risonarono dell'altissimo nome di Vostra Serenità». SANSOVINO 1562, fols. 74v-75r.

[50]. «[...] si riempirno in modo gli animi de tutti i Bellunesi di giubilo, d'allegreza e di straordinaria consolatione che in un subito tutta quella sua Città si vide mirabilmente a gioire e divenir sopra modo tutta lieta e tutta gioconda: chi a sacri tempi correndo e Dio ringratiando gli pregava somma felicità; chi con altissime voci celebrando le sue virtù gli augurava prosperi avvenimenti; et ogni sesso, ogni età, ogni conditione da eccessivo gaudio sopraffatti con canti, suoni, feste e fuochi facevan in suo honor lietissimi concerti». MICHELE 1596, p. 69; see also the edition of the same oration published in CONSALVI 1597, p. 86.

[51]. «Parmi di sentir le voci del popolo, non solo di Venetia, ma di tutte le città suddite alla Vostra Serenità esclamar con lieti giubili: Ecco che'l Signor Dio ci ha dato non pure un Principe giustissimo et santissimo, ma un padre amorevolissimo et pietosissimo». SILLA 1553.

Dissent and its soundscape struggle to find a place within an encomiastic subgenre — and ritual — overtly aiming to performatively reproduce, through its celebration, the sovereignty of the Most Serene Republic upon the Venetian dominions[52]. Giving to the new doge a vivid testimony of uniform and incorruptible devotion was the main rhetorical — and diplomatic — task which local ambassadors were supposed to accomplish[53]; in this respect, the subject city's festive soundscape offered them an intuitive — but not less performatively efficient — image.

At the same time, the redundant insistence on the acoustic elements of the dominions' ducal celebration allowed the local ambassadors to meet a more urgent and empirical communicative demand. Beyond the rhetorical stereotype, such emphatic statements hide a deep institutional awareness which can be better appreciated by shifting the focus of the analysis from the oration's sender to its receiver or, to be less cryptic, from the orator to the object of his encomiastic argument: the Venetian doge, the elective head of the Most Serene Republic. It is certainly true that the *Promissione Ducale* — the «ducal oath» that regulated the constitutional and ceremonial duties of the doge — presents only a few references to the congratulatory embassy[54]: nevertheless, this 'constitutional' text played a significant role not only in giving rise to the embassy of obedience, but also in shaping a specific rhetorical style in praising the Venetian Prince. Since the early sixteenth century, for instance, the *Promissione* was amended in order to tighten up the orders which prohibited the doge from leaving the city of Venice or passing the lagoon's border without an expressed authorisation by both the Minor and the Maggior Consiglio[55]. However indirectly, the civic sensibility of the Venetian republicanism put a physical — even before political, anthropological or social — distance between the

---

[52].    See FLORIO 2019; FLORIO 2017A; FLORIO 2014, as well as DE VIVO 2012, p. 305. Regarding the presence of expressions of dissent — or, at least, «tensions» — within the *orationes in creatione ducis* and other similar encomiastic texts, see ŠPOLJARIĆ 2018 and O'CONNELL 2016A.

[53].    According to Gian Giorgio Trissino, the «nice and honourable custom» of greeting the ducal election with a congratulatory embassy was mainly a «sign of obedience and love» («segno di ubidientia e di amore») displayed by the Venetian subject cities. SANSOVINO 1562, fol. 1r. In Orazio Toscanella's opinion, to pay homage to the new doge through an embassy «it really was a blessed order [...] established by the ancients [...] because in this way the subjects could preserve/keep and increase their Prince's love, and because it is wholesome that the servants recognise their Lord» («Fu veramente santissimo ordine quello che instituirono gli antichi di rallegrarsi nelle novelle creationi de Prencipi et di mandar loro oratori a questo fine. [...] Perché a questo modo i sudditi si conservano et accrescono l'amor del suo Prencipe, perché è honesto che i servi riconoscano il suo Signore»). *Ibidem*, fol. 74v.

[54].    MUSATTI 1888.

[55].    *Ibidem*, pp. 122-123. On similar prohibitions, see GIRGENSOHN 2004, p. 103. More in general, on the effect of the republican discourse on the Venetian institutional framework and, specifically, on the limitations of the ducal prerogatives, see CONTI 2002.

## CELEBRATING THE PRINCE FROM AFAR

Venetian Prince and his subjects living in the dominions[56]. This radical separation became rather evident on the occasion of the doge's election and public celebration: by preventing the Prince from leaving Venice even on the occasion of his coronation, the *Promissione* made it impossible to display, in the Venetian dominions, princely ritual that were common in other European political contexts, such as joyous entries, ritual journeys or triumphs[57]. The Venetian republican Prince had to remain confined in Venice as did the ceremonial rituality which characterised the celebration of his — residual — princely authority. If hosting a ducal entry was an impracticable option for the Venetian subject cities, entering Venice to praise the new doge could still be a difficult task to achieve: since 1476 the *Promissione Ducale* was integrated with the already-mentioned Maggior Consiglio's act that prevented the new doge from receiving congratulatory delegations composed of more than twenty members[58]. Aiming to scale down the residual princely feature of the doge, the Maggior Consiglio exploited the same act in order to shorten even the duration of the ducal audience: on the occasion of the congratulatory embassy, the doge was prohibited from listening to orations which were excessively long. Nevertheless, the recurring legislative efforts made by the Senate and by the Maggior Consiglio to tighten this prohibition up proves its lack of efficacy[59]. Paradoxically, the embassy of obedience — the custom of paying homage to the new doge by sending a ceremonial embassy to Venice — seems to have found its own *raison d'être* precisely in such vigorous attempts to limit the contacts between the doge and the representatives of the Venetian dominions: the very existence of a political and ceremonial diaphragm between the Prince and his subjects was assumed by the political authorities of the main Venetian subject cities as a sufficient legal justification for sending a congratulatory embassy to Venice and to accredit it to the new doge. A similar political and legal awareness is clearly identifiable, for

---

[56]. The legal and political separateness between Venice and its Dominions is a topic frequently raised, among others, by Claudio Povolo. See, for instance, POVOLO 1994; POVOLO 1997; POVOLO 2006B. On the constitutional, institutional and social framework of the Venetian *Stato da Terra*, see also the pivotal COZZI 1982 and COZZI 1997. On the lack of integration of the Venetian dominions in the republican government and decision-making process, see BERENGO 1956 and VENTURA 1993. For a more nuanced view on the same topic, see MUIR 2000. Finally, particularly useful are the historiographic overviews KNAPTON 1998 and VARANINI 2011.

[57]. Of the massive bibliography on this topic, see GRAHAM – MCALLISTER JOHNSON 1979; BOUTIER – DEWERPE – NORDMAN 1984; BRYANT 1986; BRYANT 2010; KIPLING 1998; HILL COLE 1999; BERTELLI 2001, pp. 36-38; VISCEGLIA 2001; MULRYNE – WATANABE-O'KELLY – SHEWRING 2004; BREEN 2004; FOSI 2004; WINTROUB 2006; DAMEN 2007; RUSSELL – VISENTIN 2007; CANOVA-GREEN – ANDREWS – WAGNER 2013; CHECA CREMADES – FERNÁNDEZ-GONZÁLEZ 2015; MULRYNE – ALIVERTI – TESTAVERDE 2015; MURPHY 2016; RODRÍGUEZ MOYA – MÍNGUEZ CORNELLES 2016; MULRYNE – DE JONGE – MORRIS – MARTENS 2019.

[58]. MUSATTI 1888, pp. 114-115.

[59]. See *supra*, fn. 14.

# GIOVANNI FLORIO

instance, in the letters of credence which the city council of Brescia issued on 23 May 1606 in order to accredit the ambassador Lodovico Federici — and his colleagues — to the newly-elected Leonardo Donà:

> The endless and inestimable joy that this most loyal and devoted city has felt and feels for the deserved election of Your Serenity would have required and needed that all of us, its Citizens, came together to take comfort at the feet of Your Excellency [...]. Nevertheless, as this is impossible to do — or, being it possible, it is prohibited to us by the laws of Yours Sublimity —, we send at Your feet the Magnificent D. Ludovico di Federici and D. Giovan Battista Savallo [...] our ambassadors to this end, to whom You may deign to give the same trust that You would give us[60].

The oration delivered by Federici on 29 May 1606 perfectly reflected this legal argument: indeed, the heart of his encomiastic speech was an accurate rhetorical transposition of the letter of credence released by the civic chancellery of Brescia. «I would to God», lamented the rhetor, «that we, by means of our tongues, could represent to Your Serenity the happiness shown by the whole city [of Brescia]»: «all the people of every rank and status, and nearly the very walls of the houses gave sign of wanting to come [to Venice] in order to bow before such a glorious Prince and such Most Serene Republic». Nevertheless, considering that «there is no greater sign of reverence [...] than the obedience», that such obedience «had been ordered [...] by a ducal [letter]» and, finally, having been urged by the local Venetian governors (the *rettori*), Brescia decided to limit its embassy to only a few representatives[61].

---

60. «L'infinita et inestimabile alegrezza che ha sentuto et sente questa sua fidelissima et devotissima città per la meritissima elettione di Vostra Serenità haverebbe voluto, et ricercava, che tutti noi suoi cittadini unitamente venissimo a consolarsi a piedi di Vostra Celsitudine [...]. Ma ciò non potendosi fare, o quando si potesse essendoci vietato dalle leggi di Vostra Sublimità, mandiamo i Magnifici D. Ludovico di Federici et D. Giovan Battista Savallo [...] nostri oratori a piedi di quella per questo effetto, a quali Ella si degnarà prestar quella credenza che farebbe a noi stessi». Archivio Storico Civico del Comune di Brescia, Lettere pubbliche, reg. 31, fol. 99v, dated 23 May 1606. Between the 1675 and the 1676, both the city chancelleries of Padua and Verona used a very similar formula to accredit their congratulatory embassies before Doge Nicolò Sagredo. See ALMERIGHI 1676, p. 34; BON [1675], pp. 43-44. I would like to thank Cristina Setti for having helped me in collecting this last source.

61. «O volesse Dio che noi co'l ministerio delle nostre lingue potessimo rappresentare alla Serenità Vostra l'allegrezza mostrata da tutta Brescia nel partir nostro; poiché tutte le persone d'ogni grado e qualità, et quasi le mura istesse delle case mostravano segno di voler venire a inchinarsi a tanto glorioso Principe, et a tanta Serenissima Repubblica. Et se non fosse che non v'è maggior segno di riverenza verso al suo Signore che l'obedienza, et che con diploma Ducale non ci fosse stata comandata et dalli Illustrissimi Signori Rettori persuasa la modesta limitatione della nostra Ambasceria, la Città nostra, come altre volte ha fatto et saputo fare, haverebbe con infinita copia de Cittadini, et con assai maggior pompa, mostrato l'intima consolatione che ha sentito, et sente per veder nel capo di Vostra Serenità questo glorioso, et ammirando diadema». FEDERICI 1606.

## CELEBRATING THE PRINCE FROM AFAR

The diplomatic task matches the encomiastic needs in the oration's paragraphs used by the rhetors to declare their diplomatic duties and, above all, to justify the absolute necessity of their appearance in the Ducal Palace. In 1554, after having portrayed the festive soundscape of Rovigo in all its detail, Giovan Domenico Roncale explained to Doge Francesco Venier that his city, «as not being allowed (as it wished)» to move entirely to Venice, had been necessarily forced to «send» some ambassadors «on its behalf» in order to «partially vent the incredible overabundance of its heart»[62]. In 1577, The Capodistrian Giovanni Vida exploited a very similar argument in order to justify to Sebastiano Venier the necessity of his embassy[63] and Curzio Clavello, ambassador of Crema, did the same in 1570 on the occasion of Alvise Mocenigo's ducal election: his «homeland» was completely aware that the Venetian Prince could neither spiritually nor physically enjoy «the incredible happiness, the extreme joy and the infinite content» felt by its inhabitants; considering this, Crema had decided to send an embassy to Venice in order to «make manifest» to the doge — «through the living voice of its ambassadors» — that «the souls of its citizens are endlessly rejoicing and glad»[64]. Venetian law and magistrates could only put up a poor barrier to such a natural, enthusiastic and gushing display of loyalty and consensus. Or, at least, that was the conclusion of the oration which Bartolomeo Malmignatti, as ambassador of Lendinara, tributed to Francesco Venier in 1554: as he explained, the «authority» of the local *rettore* had been surely able to «hold the bodies of those subjects» but not «their souls and hearts». The few representatives physically sent to Venice had to be seen as a vivid representation of the whole population of Lendinara: as stated by Malmignatti, all the inhabitants were — at least symbolically — there, in the Pien Collegio hall, praising the new Prince together with their ambassadors[65]. In 1618, Giacomo Siega chose a little variation of the same argument in order to rhetorically justify his weakness in praising Doge Antonio Priuli: «if only you», said the

---

[62]. «[Rovigo] è stata sforzata, per isfogare in parte la incredibile sovrabondanza del cor suo (non potendo come desiava tutta insieme essa venire), a mandar in sua vece a piedi della Sublimità Vostra noi». SANSOVINO 1562, fol. 49r.

[63]. «Poi ché non può quella città [di Capodistria] insieme venire dinanzi il Serenissimo cospetto vostro, né ad altri che al Sommo Dio è permesso di mirare l'intimo de' cuori, ha voluto almeno mandare noi duo suoi cittadini». VIDA 1577.

[64]. «Non potendo la Serenità vostra [...] penetrare nella profonda parte de' nostri cuori, né mirando scoprire l'incredibile allegrezza, l'estremo giubilo et l'infinito contento qual'hora sente la fedelissima Patria nostra di Crema per la sua meritevole elettione al Principato, non contenta essa del suo secreto piacere ha voluto con la viva voce de' suoi ambasciatori far a voi noto che [...] gli animi de' suoi cittadini senza fine gioiscono et lieti sono». FINO 1572, fol. 32r.

[65]. «Et non creda Vostra Sublimità che si si habbiano contentati mandare a questa congratulatione noi pochi, li quali corporalmente vede, perché ha ben potuto l'autorità del Clarissimo nostro Rettore ritenere li corpi di quei sudditi, ma non già gli animi et i cuori loro, che non habbiano voluto venir tutti in compagnia nostra a far riverenza a questa Maestà et rallegrarsi delle glorie et trionfi suoi». SANSOVINO 1562, fol. 56r (first edition: MALMIGNATTI 1554).

# GIOVANNI FLORIO

ambassador addressing the city of Verona, «could have come before the presence of this Most August [Prince], [...] you would have entirely come and you [would have] spoken with words more limited but no less affectionate [than mine]»[66].

Despite the legal and communicative limits imposed on the embassies, Verona, as well as the other Venetian subject cities, clearly perceived and rhetorically presented its ambassador's *living voice* as the only possible way to make its jubilations resound inside the Ducal Palace: in this respect, to evoke the local festive soundscape within the Pien Collegio hall seemed to be a valid option to bridge the distance to Venice and to allow the new Prince to enjoy the celebrations in his honour performed in — and by — each Venetian dominion. The ambassadors that the Istrian city of Pirano sent to Doge Marcantonio Trevisan in 1553 were completely aware of the crucial diplomatic and communicative task they were entrusted[67]: officially, their main assignment was to — symbolically — renew the *pact of submission*[68] to Venice signed by their ancestors; nevertheless there was also «another [...] reason for their appearance» before the newly elected doge. As they admitted, they had been sent to Venice in order to make manifest to the new doge — «by means of [their] tongues and living voices» — the «huge happiness» felt by the inhabitants of Pirano once they had been reached by «the great thunder» generated by the «welcome and awaited rumour» of the ducal election[69]. The same necessity was expressed by Giorgio Piloni in 1585: after having welcomed the news of the election of Pasquale Cicogna with a resounding exultation, Belluno decided to send a delegation to Venice in order to «make manifest» to the new doge its «marvellous solace». Here again, the declared task assumed by the local representatives was to «uncover with [their] living voices the cause of [...] such happiness»[70]. To «depict» to the new doge the «true reasons of» its «happiness» was also the main diplomatic task which the city of Verona assigned to the ambassador Agostino

---

66.    «Son sicuro, Patria mia, che se voi stessa havesti potuto venire alla presentia di questo Augustissimo, confesso tutta saresti venuta, e con parole più limite diresti, e non meno affettuose». SIEGA 1618.

67.    SANSOVINO 1562, fol. 39r-v.

68.    Of the huge bibliography on the Venetian *patti di dedizione* (and in addition to the contributions already mentioned at footnote 56), I shall limit myself to mention MENNITI IPPOLITO 1986, and the more recent ORTALLI 2002. On the idea of the 'voluntary submission' to Venice and on its rhetoric transposition, see O'CONNELL 2016B.

69.    «L'altra veramente cagion del comparir nostro [...] fu accioché con lo strumento delle lingue et vive voci nostre, verace testimonio de cuori nostri, gli potessimo far manifesta quella immensa allegrezza che senza termine di tempo o misura di quantità si diffuse per gli penetrali de nostri petti, tosto che s'udì il gran tuono della grata, et aspettata voce della sua [...] creatione». SANSOVINO 1562, fol. 39v. In 1606, Daniele Dalla Porta depicted the news of Leonardo Donà's election as a 'sounding trumpet' which first «reached the ears» and then «pierced the heart» of Cavarzere. DALLA PORTA 1606.

70.    «Onde desiderando la Patria nostra che questa sua meravigliosa consolatione fosse ancora alla Sublimità vostra manifestata, ha inviato noi, acciocché prestandole la debita obedienza, scuopriamo con vive voci la causa di tanta nostra contentezza». MICHELE 1596, pp. 69-70; see also the edition of the same oration published in CONSALVI 1597, pp. 8-87.

## CELEBRATING THE PRINCE FROM AFAR

Del Bene in 1606: after having honoured Leonardo Donà with «most evident signs and clear evidence of ineffable joy», Verona considered it appropriate to «revere [him] in person». In this regard, to send a congratulatory embassy to Venice seemed to be the only reasonable — if not obligatory — choice[71]. Analogously, in 1585 Ottonello Descalzo justified his insistence in describing the Paduan festive soundscape to Doge Pasquale Cicogna as fulfilling an explicit diplomatic duty: to «depict» to the new Prince the rejoicing of Padua was a declared task assigned by the Paduan citizens to their representatives in Venice. As asserted by Descalzo, by entrusting their message to the «living voices of their orators», the citizens of Padua were trying to bridge the impossibility of bringing their «immeasurable happiness» to Venice and to celebrate the doge in his presence[72]. Bowed before the same doge, the ambassador hailing from Bergamo admitted sadly that «fireworks, sounds, gestures and voices» were only poor media, useful only to show happiness «from afar». Nevertheless, the congratulatory embassy could offer a valid solution: here again the orator presented himself and the sound of his voice as an efficient means to bring the festive soundscape of the mainland as near as possible to the doge's ears. In this respect, the congratulatory oration could not limit itself to describe the sound of the jubilant dominion but, in a certain sense, it had to simulate it: as admitted by the ambassador of Bergamo, fireworks, sounds, gestures and voices had to be faithfully «represented by the fire of devoted sentences, by the sounds of a well-ordered speech, by gestures of delightful [rhetorical] action and by voices of a befitting pronunciation»[73].

However indirectly, the restrictions imposed upon the doge's mobility — and, therefore, the absolute necessity of bringing to him a sample of the local celebration in order to enable

---

[71]. «Essa Città, d'insolita et non più sentita allegrezza ripiena, et in pubblico et in privato con apertissimi segni et chiari dimostramenti di letitia ineffabile publicò al mondo l'immenso giubilo che in se stessa perciò provava: così hora ci ha mandati a i piedi vostri, sì per inchinarvi et riverirvi presentialmente come suo Principe naturale, et sì per offerirvi et consacrarvi il cor suo». DEL BENE 1606. On the embassy of Agostino Del Bene to Leonardo Donà, see POLA 1614 and FLORIO 2014, pp. 140-141. For a brief biography of Agostino del Bene, see SARPI 2001, pp. 494-496.

[72]. «[...] i cittadini [di Padova] più maturi et antichi [...], per tentare in quanto per noi si può adempire ogni ufficio, hanno voluto in vece di trionfi e trofei, con la viva voce de' suoi oratori ritrarvi in parte sì smisurata allegrezza». MICHELE 1587, p. not numbered.

[73]. «[...] dimostrava all'hora da lontano questa sua interiore allegrezza con esteriori segni di fuochi, di suoni, di gesti et di voci, et questa io vorrei hora d'appresso a Vostra Sublimità rappresentare con fuoco d'affettuosi concetti, con suono di numerosa locutione, con gesti di lieta attione et con voci d'accomodata pronuntia». MICHELE 1587, p. not numbered. Ten years later, a very similar expression was used by the paduan ambassador Francesco Centon in order to praise Doge Marino Grimani. MICHELE 1596, pp. 7-8 and CONSALVI 1597, pp. 45-46. The unsuitability of fireworks and, consequently, the absolute necessity to send an embassy at the doge's feet is a recurrent rhetoric topos in the orations delivered by the representatives of Chioggia, despite the proximity between their city and Venice. See, for instance, FALCONETTO 1568, as well as SANSOVINO 1562, fol. 66r.

# GIOVANNI FLORIO

him to enjoy it — forced the ambassador to embody the subject city rather than represent it. This process of identification between the representative (the ambassador) and the represented (the subject city) was well highlighted, for instance, by the jurist Ettore Ferramosca, sent to Venice in 1606 «on behalf of the most loyal [...] city of Vicenza»: once arrived in front of Leonardo Donà, he explained that his city, «being not allowed to entirely appear» in the Pien Collegio hall, had decided to «gather the joy of all» its inhabitants within the ambassadors and to «appoint them to represent it at [the doge's] feet»[74]. The representation by mandate ratified by the letters of credence acquired a much more extensive, empirical and tangible meaning once reshaped by the rhetorical ingenuity of the local representative[75]. According to Cornelio Frangipane[76] and his oration for Francesco Donà's election (1545), the local ambassador had to lend his voice and body to the subject city or — to quote him directly — to «show in the face, in the words and in the gestures the unbelievable happiness» felt by the subject city. In a certain sense, the ambassador couldn't limit himself to reporting to the new Prince the celebrations in his honour performed in — and by — the subject city, but, using the performative efficacy of his words, he had to make himself into a living and tangible representation of the whole subject city exulting for the new Prince[77]. The ambassador *was* the city, as pointed out by the Paduan rhetor Giovan Battista Selvatico in 1606: «Here is [the City of Padua]», he said indicating himself to Doge Leonardo Donà, «which, without distinction of rank, class, status, age (I would also say gender, if feminine modesty and the respect for this place allowed it), gathers all humble and reverent people in Your presence»[78]. Similarly, «Most Serene Prince, here is your most loyal city of Verona» said Giacomo Siega presenting himself to Antonio Priuli in 1618[79]. The concept

---

74. «Noi sudditi devotissimi veniamo a nome di fidelissima sua Città [di Vicenza], che non potendo qua tutta comparire, raccolta di tutti l'allegrezza in noi soli, che a piedi della Serenità Vostra rappresentarla deviamo ci commette». FERRAMOSCA 1606.

75. For an exhaustive conceptualisation of the idea of representation see the fundamental PITKIN 1967 and, in an historical perspective, HOFMANN 2003. In this regard, the introductory chapter of BURKE 1992 is also particularly useful. More specifically, on the 'representation as embodiment' see the recent HAYAT – PÉNEAU – SINTOMER 2018. Coming back to the topic of this article, the ambiguity of the early modern concept of 'representation as authorisation' (or 'delegation') has been convincingly highlighted in DELLA MISERICORDIA 2010. Finally, a fruitful approach on early modern representation of representativeness — or, to be more precise, on the problem of the representativeness' reification through rhetoric — has been provided in NEU 2010.

76. For a brief biography, see CAVAZZA 1998 and CAVAZZA 2009.

77. «[...] noi, da vera interna letitia sospinti, siam venuti a rallegrarci con voi, altissimo Signore, et a dimostrare ne'l volto, ne le parole et ne gesti la incredibile allegrezza che sentiamo de la vostra maggioranza». SANSOVINO 1562, fol. 7v (first edition: FRANGIPANE 1545).

78. «Eccola, invitissimo Prencipe, che senza alcuna distintione di grado, di ordine, di stato, di età (direi di sesso ancora, quando la pudicitia femminile, et la riverenza del luogo lo comportasse) tutta humile, et riverente comparisce al cospetto vostro». SELVATICO 1606.

79. «Eccovi, Prencipe Serenissimo, la vostra fedelissima Città di Verona». SIEGA 1618.

## CELEBRATING THE PRINCE FROM AFAR

was redundantly repeated by the ambassador: «Here is your daughter, here is your servant», he insistently explained by making himself a living representation of his homeland[80]. In 1613, Doge Marcantonio Memmo heard a very similar statement pronounced by Ottonello Belli, an illustrious jurist hailing from Capodistria. «For Your Serenity it is easy», argued the rhetor, «to imagine [the whole City of Capodistria] in this small number of citizens»[81]:

> [...] the eye [...] has already remained satisfied to see, even if through our presence only, the City of Capodistria reverently presenting at Your feet the ancient tribute of [its] voluntary submission[82].

Even the poor liveries worn by the Capodistrian representatives should be considered an integral part of the *mimesis'* process evoked by Belli: such shabby clothing, he said, «explains very well [...] the appearance of our city»[83]. As he rhetorically admitted, it was not so «easy [...] to present a City» only «by the means of a little voice»: the sound, indeed, should be considered just one of the many communicative codes that cooperated in shaping the congratulatory ritual. The increasing relevance accorded to the body language by early modern diplomacy appears quite self evident within the text of the orations we are considering[84]. The already-mentioned Cornelio Frangipane, for instance, concluded his praise of Francesco Donà with a perfect identification between the bow he was performing before the new Prince and the bow ideally tributed to him by the entire territory of the Patria del Friuli:

> Meanwhile my Homeland, by lowering the high hills and stopping the flowing rivers, bows all humbly and reverently and it obediently offers itself [as] a maidservant of Your Serenity[85].

Being embodied by an ambassador, the Venetian dominion could reach Venice, enter into the Ducal Palace and celebrate the doge in his presence; by borrowing the physical body

---

[80]. «Eccovi la vostra figlia, eccovi la vostra serva». *Ibidem.*

[81]. «È facile alla Serenità Vostra [...] figurarla in questo poco numero di Cittadini». BELLI 1613.

[82]. «L'occhio è di già rimasto in lei appagato nel qui vedere alla sola nostra presenza la Città di Capodistria riverente a suoi piedi prestarle il debito antico tributo di volontaria soggettione». *Ibidem.*

[83]. «Questo tacito nostro comparire, positivo [...], senza pompa, esplica assai bene per se stesso lo aspetto della Città nostra». *Ibidem.*

[84]. See LAZZARINI 2009 and LAZZARINI 2015, pp. 146-166 and 197-202. More in general, on early modern culture of gestures, see BREMMER – ROODENBURG 1993 (especially BURKE 1993); KNOX 1990B; KNOX 1990A, as well as NICCOLI 2007. For a special focus on the Venetian cultural context, see KNOX 1993, and FAGGION 2019. For a long term perspectives, see the fundamental BERTELLI – CENTANNI 1995, as well as BRADDICK 2009.

[85]. «Intanto la mia patria abbassando gli alti colli et arrestando i correnti fiumi, tutta humile et riverente si inchina et si dona ubidientente ancella de la vostra Serenità». SANSOVINO 1562, fol. 9v.

of its representative, the local body politic could not only make its voice audible in Venice, but also bow at the doge's feet, performing, in this way, the most recognisable representation of its submission. Nevertheless, even in displaying such an extreme act of humiliation, the local representatives were completely aware of the republican feature of the Prince they were praising. Cornelio Frangipane and his colleagues were completely aware of the gap existing between the symbolic dimension of the dogeship and the constitutional reality of the Venetian Republic. Orators knew that by bowing at the doge's feet they were recognizing a sovereignty which actually rested in the Venetian patriciate and in the Republican magistratures as its political emanation[86].

The congratulatory orations dedicated to the Venetian doges rested on a complex system of representations and embodiments: if the subject city needed the ambassador's physical body to revere the Republic, the Republic needed to be embodied by the doge in order to receive such reverence. The congratulatory embassy, indeed, partook of a pervasive system of political communication which rested on both the symbolic overlapping of the doge's natural body with the Republic's political one[87], and the artificial attribution to the doge of an effective personal power, an actual decision-making autonomy and, in other words, of a fictitious monarchical feature. Early modern political treatise writers were perfectly aware of this[88] as well as the authors of the orations we are considering. As stated to Leonardo Donà by the already-mentioned Santo di Marangoni, the Venetian doge existed only because of the necessity «to visibly represent the majesty» of the Republic. The doge, he said, was only the «head» of the Venetian Republic, as it was established by ancestors «by means of an ancient and necessary decree». The doge — he continued — was the «vertex» of a «well founded pyramid», the point of convergence of all the «lines» — or «orders» — which composed the republican political architecture[89]. Such a vertex had an empirical representation in the Pien Collegio, commonly recognised as the «main seat of the Republic», «the brightest throne of the public majesty» or, in other words, as the purest synthesis of the Venetian

---

86. For a updated consideration on the Venetian republican system and its constitution, see VIGGIANO 2013 as well as CONTI 2002.

87. On the sovereign's two bodies, see KANTOROWICZ 1957 as well as BERTELLI 2001. For a special focus on the Venetian doge, see MUIR 1977, pp. 251-298.

88. See, for instance, the paradigmatic GIANNOTTI 1540, fols. 74v-75r and BOTERO 1605, fols. 38r-v. See also FERRO 1845-1847, vol. I, p. 628.

89. «Tra le molte cose [...] che rendono straordinariamente contenti i sudditi di questa Eccelsa Republica una è veramente singolare, et maravigliosa; e questa è, che havendosi a rappresentare visibile la maestà di così fatto Imperio, per antico et necessario decreto fu determinato di constituire un capo, nel quale concorrendo, et conterminandosi tutti gli ordini, et le proportioni del governo, quasi linee di ben fondata piramide in quella sommità a punto». DI MARANGONI 1606.

126

# CELEBRATING THE PRINCE FROM AFAR

political system[90]. That was the Prince whom the Venetian dominions praise by the means of their congratulatory embassies: the doge who appeared to the local representatives was a *primus inter pares*, seated perfectly at the center of the Pien Collegio hall as the head of a magistrature — the Pien Collegio itself — composed by the executive body of the Senate (*Consulta dei Savi*) and that of the Maggior Consiglio (*Serenissima Signoria*)[91]. As reminded by Nicolò Manzuoli to Leonardo Donà (1606), the doge was a Prince, but his crown — the source and the seat of the republican sovereignty — was composed of senators and patricians[92], as overtly suggested by his collocation in the Collegio hall.

The congratulatory embassy made a meeting possible between the embodiment of the Venetian Republic — the doge — and those of the subject communities — the orators. In this respect, the Venetian Prince and the local ambassador, through the meeting of their bodies natural within the Pien Collegio hall, operated in order to bridge the gap between two abstract and distant — if not separated — bodies politic: the Venetian city-republic and its dominions. During the congratulatory embassy, such embodiments provided the dialogue between ruler and ruled with an all the more empiric — and audible — dimension: through the bodies natural of the doge and of the ambassador, the bodies politic of the Republic and of the subject dominion could bow and stand, rejoice and triumph, produce sounds and hear them. The recurring acoustic imagery which characterised the orations in praise of the newly elected doges met encomiastic needs, but in so doing it also fulfilled the subjects' atavic aspiration to a direct — if not personal — connection with the Prince. Such need was all the more felt in a context such as the Venetian one, characterized by a structural separateness between Venice and its dominions[93].

---

[90]. «Il Pien Collegio [...] si può a ragione chiamare la sede principale della repubblica, ed il trono più luminoso della pubblica maestà». FERRO 1845-1847, vol. II, p. [4]37. For a similar definition, see also ARGELATI 1737, p. 97.

[91]. See MARANINI 1931, especially pp. 297-383, and BESTA 1899, especially pp. 142-143 and 177-190, SINDING-LARSEN 1974, especially pp. 141-142.

[92]. See SINDING-LARSEN 1974, p. 134.

[93]. See NUBOLA 2001; DELLA MISERICORDIA 2004; DELLA MISERICORDIA 2010; ÁLVAREZ-OSSORIO ALVARIÑO 1997; IRACE 2007; FLORIO 2017A.

# GIOVANNI FLORIO

## SOURCES

ALMERIGHI 1676
ALMERIGHI, Francesco. *Relazione della Ambasciata di Padova al Serenissimo Nicolò Sagredo e di quanto s'è fatto di più nell'assonzione di Sua Serenità al Principato di Venezia*, Padua, Pietro Maria Frambotto, 1676.

ARGELATI 1737
ARGELATI, Francesco. *Pratica del Foro Veneto*, Venice, Agostino Savioli a San Salvator, 1737.

BELLI 1613
BELLI, Ottonello. *Oratione al Serenissimo M. Antonio Memmo per la essaltatione sua al Principato di Venetia*, Venice, Giovanni Alberti, 1613.

BON [1675]
[BON, Domenico]. *L'Ambascieria di Verona in congratulatione al Serenissimo Nicolò Sagredo*, Verona, Gio. Battista Merlo, [1675].

BOTERO 1605
BOTERO, Giovanni. *Relatione della Republica Venetiana*, Venice, Giorgio Varisco, 1605.

CONSALVI 1597
CONSALVI, Antonio Maria. *Orationi fatte al Serenissimo Prencipe di Venetia Marino Grimani nella sua assontione al Prencipato*, Venice, Presso il Muschio, 1597.

DALLA PORTA 1606
DALLA PORTA, Daniele. *Oratione della Terra di Cavarzere nella creatione del Serenissimo Prencipe D. D. Leonardo Donato*, Venice, Roberto Meglieti, 1606.

DEL BENE 1606
DEL BENE, Agostino. *Oratione di Agostino Del Bene giurisconsulto, ambasciatore della Città di Verona al Serenissimo Leonardo Donato*, Venice, Gio. Antonio Rampazzetto, [1606].

DI MARANGONI 1606
DI MARANGONI, Santo. *Oratione della Città di Chioggia nella creatione del Serenissimo Prencipe D. D. Lionardo Donato*, Venice, Roberto Meglieti, 1606 [first edition: Venice, Gio. Antonio Rampazetto, 1606].

FALCONETTO 1568
FALCONETTO, Domenico. *Oratione dell'Eccellente M. Dominico Falconetto, ambasciatore della Città di Chioggia. Nella creatione del Serenissimo Principe M. Pietro Loredano*, Venice, Si vendono alla libraria dalla Stella, 1568.

FEDERICI 1606
FEDERICI, Lodovico. *Oratione al Serenissimo Prencipe D. D. Leonardo Donato*, Venice, Roberto Meglieti, 1606.

# Celebrating the Prince from Afar

FERRAMOSCA 1606
FERRAMOSCA, Ettore. *Oratione di Hettore Ferramosca Dottore et Cavaliere dell'Eccell. Senato Veneto, et Ambasciatore della Città di Vicenza*, Venice, Roberto Meglieti, 1606.

FINO 1572
FINO, Alemanio. *Oratione del Cavellier Michele Benvenuto recitata nel Duomo di Crema a XVI Settembre MDXLIX, correndo l'anno centesimo, dopo che Cremaschi si diedero a Signori Venetiani. Con altre orationi recitate d'Ambasciatori Cremaschi, nella creatione de' Principi di Venetia*, Venice, Domenico Nicolino, 1572.

FRANGIPANE 1545
FRANGIPANE, Cornelio. *Oratione di m. Cornelio Frangepane da Castello, ambasciatore della patria del Friuli, nella creatione del Serenissimo Principe Donato*, Venice, Vincenzo Vaugris, al segno d'Erasmo, in merceria, presso l'horologio di San Marco, 1545.

GESLINO 1606
GESLINO, Pietro. *Oratione di Pietro Geslino Iure Consulto Ambasciatore per la Città di Feltre per la Creatione del Serenissimo Leonardo Donato Prencipe di Venetia*, Venice, Roberto Meietti, 1606.

GIANNOTTI 1540
GIANNOTTI, Donato. *Libro de la Republica di vinitiani*, Rome, Antonio Blado d'Asola, 1540.

MALMIGNATTI 1554
MALMIGNATTI, Bartolomeo. *Oratione di M. Bartholomeo Malmignatti, oratore della Magnifica Communità di Lendenara nella congratulatione del Serenissimo Prencipe Veniero*, Venice, Giovan Griffio, 1554.

MANZUOLI 1606
MANZUOLI, Nicolò. *Oratione di Nicolo Manzuoli, Dottore di leggi, ambasciatore della Città di Capo d'Istria al Serenissimo Prencipe Leonardo Donato, nella sua creatione*, Venice, Roberto Meglieti, 1606.

MICHELE 1587
MICHELE, Agostino. *Scielta delle orationi fatte nella creatione del Serenissimo Prencipe di Vinegia Pasqual Cicogna*, Venice, Giov. Antonio Rampazetto, 1587.

MICHELE 1596
ID. *Le glorie immortali del Serenissimo Prencipe di Vinegia Marino Grimani descritte in dodici singolarissime orationi*, Venice, Francesco Bariletti, 1596.

MONTEGNACCO 1606
MONTEGNACCO, Massimiliano. *Oratione dell'Illustre et Eccellentissimo Signor Massimiliano Montegnaco, ambasciatore della Patria al Serenissimo Principe Leonardo Donato*, Venice, Bartolomeo degli Alberti, 1606.

ORATIONE 1553A
*Oratione delli oratori della fidelissima Communità di Pirano al Serenissimo Prencipe Trevisano nella sua felice creatione*, Venice, s.n., 1553.

129

# GIOVANNI FLORIO

*ORATIONE* 1553B
*Oratione delli oratori della fidelissima Communità di Pirano al Serenissimo Prencipe Trevisano nella sua felice creatione*, Venice, Curtio Troiano de Navo, 1553.

*PARTE PRESA* [1615]
*Parte presa nell'Eccellentissimo Maggior Consiglio. Vacante Ducatu. In materia de Ambasciatori, che saranno mandati dalle Città a rallegrarsi nella creatione del Serenissimo Prencipe*, Venice, Roberto Meietti et Evangelista Deuchino Compagni, [1615].

POLA 1614
POLA, Francesco. *Elogium Augustini Delbenii V. CL. et alia de eodem scripta*, Verona, Tamianis, 1614.

*PROMISSIO* [1675]
*Promissio Serenissimi Venetiarum Ducis Serenissimo Nicolao Sagredo*, [Venice, s.n., 1675].

RONCALE 1554
RONCALE, Giovanni Domenico. *L'Oratione del cavalliero Giovandomenico Roncale ambasciatore di Rovigo al serenissimo prencipe Veniero nella sua creatione*, Venice, s.n., 1554.

SANUDO [ed. 1892]
SANUDO, Marino. *I Diarii di Marino Sanuto. 34*, edited by Federico Stefani, Guglielmo Berchet and Nicolò Barozzi, Venice, A spese degli editori, 1892.

SANSOVINO 1562
SANSOVINO, Francesco. *Delle orationi recitate a Principi di Venetia nella loro creatione da gli ambasciadori di diverse città. Libro primo*, Venice, [Francesco Sansovino], 1562.

SCARPA [1559]
SCARPA, Giuliano. *Oratione di M. Giuliano Scarpa ambasciatore della Città di Chioggia, nella creatione del Serenissimo Prencipe M. Girolamo Priuli*, Venice, Al segno del Pozzo, [1559].

SELVATICO 1606
SELVATICO, Giovan Battista. *Oratione del Molto Illustre Sig. Gio. Battista Salvatico di legge Dottore, et Cavaliere, uno degl'Ambasciadori della Città di Padova, da lui recitata l'anno 1606 di XII d'Aprile. Nella creatione del Serenissimo Leonardo Donato Prencipe di Venetia. Revista, et Ristampata*, Venice, Stampata per Gio. Antonio Rampazetto, et Ristampata per Roberto Meglieti, 1606.

SIEGA 1618
SIEGA, Giacomo. *Riverente officio di congratulatione fatto dall'Eccellente Signor Giacomo Siega, Ambasciator di Verona a piedi del Serenissimo Antonio Priuli per la sua felicissima essaltatione al Principato di Venetia*, Venice, Antonio Pinelli, 1618.

SILLA 1553
SILLA, Gasparo. *Oratione di M. Gasparo Silla ambasciatore di Chioggia. Al Serenissimo Principe Trivisano nella sua creatione*, Venice, Francesco Rocca a San Polo, 1553.

# Celebrating the Prince from Afar

### Trissino 1524
Trissino, Giangiorgio. *Oratione del Trissino al Serenissimo Principe di Venetia*, Rome, Lodovico degli Arrighi vicentino, e Lautitio, 1524.

### Tomitano 1554
Tomitano, Bernardino. *Oratione di M. Bernardin Tomitano, recitata per nome de lo Studio de le Arti padovano, ne la creatione del Serenissimo Principe di Vinetia M. Marcantonio Trivisano*, Venice, Giovanni Griffio, 1554.

### Vida 1577
Vida, Giovanni. *Oratione di Giovanni Vida dottor di leggi, ambasciator della città di Capodistria, nella creatione del Serenissimo Prencipe di Vinegia, Sebastiano Veniero*, s.l., s.n., [1577].

## Bibliography

### Álvarez-Ossorio Alvariño 1997
Álvarez-Ossorio Alvariño, Antonio. '«Pervenire alle orecchie della Maestà»: el agente lombardo en la corte madrilena', in: *Annali di storia moderna e contemporanea*, III (1997), pp. 173-223.

### Austin 1962
Austin, John L. *How to do Things with Words*, Oxford, Clarendon, 1962.

### Benzoni 1982
*I dogi*, edited by Gino Benzoni, Milan, Electa, 1982.

### Berengo 1956
Berengo, Marino. *La società veneta alla fine del Settecento*, Florence, Sansoni, 1956.

### Bertelli 2001
Bertelli, Sergio. *The King's Body: Sacred Rituals of Power in Medieval and Early Modern Europe*, University Park (PA), The Pennsylvania State University Press, 2001.

### Bertelli – Centanni 1995
*Il gesto: nel rito e nel cerimoniale dal mondo antico ad oggi*, edited by Sergio Bertelli and Monica Centanni, Florence, Ponte delle Grazie, 1995 (Laboratorio di Storia, 9).

### Besta 1899
Besta, Enrico. *Il Senato veneziano (origine, costituzione, attribuzione e riti)*, Venice, Deputazione di Storia Patria, 1899.

### Bistort 1912
Bistort, Giulio. *Il magistrato alle pompe nella Republica di Venezia: studio storico*, Venice, A spese della Società, 1912.

# Giovanni Florio

Bolzoni 1984

Bolzoni, Lina. 'Oratoria e prediche', in: *Letteratura Italiana. III/3: Le forme del testo. La prosa*, edited by Alberto Asor Rosa, Turin, Einaudi, 1984, pp. 1041-1074.

Bonora 1994

Bonora, Elena. *Ricerche su Sansovino: impreditore, librario e letterato*, Venice, Istituto Veneto di Scienze, Lettere ed Arti, 1994.

Borgherini Scarabellin 1911

Borgherini Scarabellin, Maria. 'Il nunzio rappresentante di Padova in Venezia durante il dominio della Repubblica con speciale riguardo al '700', in: *Nuovo Archivio Veneto*, n.s. XXII/1 (1911), pp. 365-412.

Boutier – Dewerpe – Nordman 1984

Boutier, Jean – Dewerpe, Alain – Nordman, Daniel. *Un tour de France royal. Le voyage de Charles IX (1564-1566)*, Paris, Aubier, 1984.

Braddick 2009

*The Politics of Gesture: Historical Perspectives*, edited by Michael J. Braddick, *Past and Present*, CCIII/issue supplement 4 (2009).

Breen 2004

Breen, Michael P. 'Addressing La Ville des Dieux: Entry Ceremonies and Urban Audiences in Seventeenth-Century Dijon', in: *Journal of Social History*, XXXVIII/2 (2004), pp. 341-364.

Bremmer – Roodenburg 1993

*A Cultural History of Gesture: from Antiquity to the Present Day*, edited by Jan N. Bremmer and Herman Roodenburg, Cambridge, Polity Press, 1993.

Bryant 1986

Bryant, Lawrence M. *The King and the City in the Parisian Royal Entry Ceremony: Politics, Ritual, and Art in the Renaissance*, Geneva, Droz, 1986.

Bryant 2010

Id. *Ritual, Ceremony and the Changing Monarchy in France, 1350-1789*, Farnham-Burlington, Ashgate, 2010 (Collected Studies, 937).

Burke 1992

Burke, Peter. *The Fabrication of Louis XIV*, New Haven-London, Yale University Press, 1992.

Burke 1993

Id. 'The Language of Gesture in Early Modern Italy', in: Bremmer – Roodenburg 1993, pp. 71-83.

Canova-Green – Andrews – Wagner 2013

*Writing Royal Entries in Early Modern Europe*, edited by Marie-Claude Canova-Green, Jean Andrews and Marie-France Wagner, Turnhout, Brepols, 2013 (Early European Research, 3).

# CELEBRATING THE PRINCE FROM AFAR

CASINI 1996

CASINI, Matteo. *I gesti del principe. La festa politica a Firenze e Venezia in età rinascimentale*, Venice, Marsilio, 1996.

CAVAZZA 1998

CAVAZZA, Silvano. 'Frangipane, Cornelio', in: *Dizionario Biografico degli Italiani. 50*, Rome, Istituto della Enciclopedia Italiana, 1998, <https://www.treccani.it/enciclopedia/cornelio-frangipane_(Dizionario-Biografico)/> accessed March 2023.

CAVAZZA 2009

ID. 'Frangipane Cornelio', in: *Nuovo Liruti. Dizionario biografico dei friulani. 2: L'età veneta*, edited by Cesare Scalon, Claudio Griggio and Ugo Rozzo, Udine, Forum, 2009.

CAVAZZA 2012

ID. 'Montegnacco, Girolamo', in: *Dizionario Biografico degli Italiani. 76*, Rome, Istituto della Enciclopedia Italiana, 2012, <https://www.treccani.it/enciclopedia/girolamo-montegnacco_(Dizionario-Biografico)>, accessed March 2023.

CECCHETTI 1864

CECCHETTI, Bartolomeo. *Il doge di Venezia*, Venice, Naratovich, 1864.

CHECA CREMADES – FERNÁNDEZ-GONZÁLEZ 2015

*Festival Culture in the World of the Spanish Habsburgs*, edited by Fernando Checa Cremades and Laura Fernández-González, Farnham-Burlington, Ashgate, 2015.

CICOGNA 1847

CICOGNA, Emmanuele Antonio. *Saggio di bibliografia veneziana*, Venice, Tipografia di G. B. Merlo, 1847.

CONTI 2002

CONTI, Vittorio. 'The Mechanisation of Virtue: Republican Rituals in Italian Political Thought in the Sixteenth and Seventeenth Centuries', in: *Republicanism: A Shared European Heritage. 2: The Values of Republicanism in Early Modern*, edited by Martin van Gelderen and Quentin Skinner, Cambridge, Cambridge University Press, 2002, pp. 77-83.

CORRIERI 2012

CORRIERI, Alessandro, 'Giangiorgio Trissino', in: *Cinquecento plurale. La cultura non ortodossa nell'Italia del XVI secolo: letteratura, arte, religione*, Rome, Dipartimento di Studi Umanistici, Università di Roma Tre, <http://dsu.uniroma3.it/cinquecentoplurale/bibliografie/giangiorgio-trissino/>, accessed March 2023.

COWAN 2008

COWAN, Alexander. 'Gossip and Street Culture in Early Modern Venice', in: *Journal of Early Modern History*, XII/3-4 (2008), pp. 313-333.

## Giovanni Florio

COZZI 1982
COZZI, Gaetano. *Repubblica di Venezia e Stati italiani. Politica e giustizia dal secolo XVI al secolo XVIII*, Turin, Einaudi, 1982.

COZZI 1997
ID. *Ambiente veneziano, ambiente veneto. Saggi su politica, società, cultura nella Repubblica di Venezia in età moderna*, Venice, Fondazione Giorgio Cini, 1997.

CUMMING 1992
CUMMING, Julie E. 'Music for the Doge in Early Renaissance Venice', in: *Speculum*, LXVII/2 (1992), pp. 324-364.

D'ACHILLE 2011
D'ACHILLE, Paolo. 'Trissino, Gian Giorgio', in: *Enciclopedia dell'Italiano. 2*, edited by Raffaele Simone, Rome, Istituto della Enciclopedia italiana, 2011, pp. 1522-1524.

DAMEN 2007
DAMEN, Mario. 'Princely Entries and Gift Exchange in the Burgundian Low Countries: a Crucial Link in Late Medieval Political Culture', in: *Journal of Medieval History*, XXXIII/3 (2007), pp. 233-249.

DA MOSTO 1960
DA MOSTO, Andrea. *I dogi di Venezia nella vita pubblica e privata*, Florence, Martello-Giunti, 1977.

DAVI 1995
DAVI, Maria Rosa. *Bernardino Tomitano filosofo, medico e letterato (1517-1576). Profilo biografico e critico*, Trieste, Lint, 1995 (Contributi alla storia dell'Università di Padova, 28).

DELLA MISERICORDIA 2004
DELLA MISERICORDIA, Massimo. '«Per non privarci de nostre raxone, li siamo stati desobidienti». Patto, giustizia e resistenza nella cultura politica delle comunità alpine nello stato di Milano (XV secolo)', in: *Forme della comunicazione politica in Europa nei secoli XV-XVIII. Suppliche, gravamina, lettere*, edited by Cecilia Nubola and Andreas Würgler, Bologna, il Mulino; Berlin, Duncker & Humblot, 2004, pp. 147-215.

DELLA MISERICORDIA 2010
ID. «Como se tuta questa universitade parlasse». La rappresentanza politica delle comunità nello stato di Milano (*XV secolo*), 2010, <http://www.adfontes.it/biblioteca/scaffale/mdm-mixv/indice.html>, accessed March 2023.

DE VIVO 2007
DE VIVO, Filippo. *Information and Communication in Venice: Rethinking Early Modern Politics*, Oxford, Oxford University Press, 2007.

DE VIVO 2012
ID. *Patrizi, informatori, barbieri. Politica e comunicazione a Venezia nella prima età moderna*, Milan, Feltrinelli, 2012.

## CELEBRATING THE PRINCE FROM AFAR

DE VIVO 2016
ID. 'Walking in Sixteenth-Century Venice: Mobilizing the Early Modern City', in: *I Tatti Studies in the Italian Renaissance*, XIX/1 (2016), pp. 115-141.

DOGLIO 1983
DOGLIO, Maria Luisa. 'La letteratura ufficiale e l'oratoria celebrativa', in: *Storia della Cultura Veneta. IV/1: Il Seicento*, edited by Girolamo Arnaldi and Manlio Pastore Stocchi, Vicenza, Neri Pozza, 1983, pp. 163-187.

FAGGION 2019
FAGGION, Lucien. 'L'éloquence muette ou le langage du corps: l'Arte de' cenni de Giovanni Bonifacio (1616)', in: *«Arcana imperii». Gouverner par le secret à l'époque moderne (France, Espagne, Italie)*, edited by Sylvain Andrè, Philippe Castejón and Sébastien Malaprade, Paris, Les Indes Savantes, 2019, pp. 123-139.

FASOLO 1935
FASOLO, Giulio. 'Il nunzio permanente di Vicenza a Venezia nel secolo XVI', in: *Archivio Veneto*, s. V, LXV/33-34 (1935), pp. 90-178.

FENLON 2007
FENLON, Iain. *The Ceremonial City: History, Memory and Myth in Renaissance Venice*, New Haven-London, Yale University Press, 2007.

FENLON 2009
ID. *Piazza San Marco*, Cambridge (MA), Harvard University Press, 2009.

FERRO 1845-1847
FERRO, Marco. *Dizionario del Diritto Comune e Veneto*, (1778-1781), 2 vols., Venice, Santini, 1845-1847.

FLORIO 2014
FLORIO, Giovanni. 'Venezia e le Comunità di Terraferma di fronte all'Interdetto (1606-1607). Protagonisti e forme di un dialogo asimmetrico sul tema della sovranità', in: *Ateneo Veneto*, s. III, XIII/2 (2014), pp. 119-144.

FLORIO 2017A
ID. 'La formalizzazione di una funzione informale. La rappresentanza politica dei corpi sudditi nella Venezia della prima età moderna', in: *Imperial. Il ruolo della rappresentanza politica informale nella costruzione e nello sviluppo delle entità statuali (XV-XXI secolo)*, edited by Giuseppe Ambrosino and Loris De Nardi, Verona, Quiedit, 2017, pp. 19-38.

FLORIO 2017B
ID. 'Un contributo involontario alla «guerra delle scritture»: Nicolò Manzuoli e la sua orazione al doge Leonardo Donà (1606)', in: *Momiano e L'Istria: una comunità e una regione dell'Alto Adriatico (Storia, Arte, Diritto, Antropologia). Atti del Convegno internazionale di studi Momjan (Momiano 14-16 VI 2013)*, edited by Lorella Limoncin Toth, Buje/Buie, Università Popolare Aperta di Buie, 2017 (Acta Bullearum, 3), pp. 225-236.

# GIOVANNI FLORIO

FLORIO 2019

ID. 'S'incliner devant au Prince républicain. Images de la souveraineté et de l'assujettissement dans les ambassades d'obéissance aux doges de Venise', in: *L'humiliation. Droit, récits et représentations (XIIᵉ-XXIᵉ siècles)*, edited by Lucien Faggion, Christophe Regina and Alexandra Roger, Paris, Classiques Garnier, 2019 (POLEN – Pouvoirs, lettres, normes, 15), pp. 221-240.

FOSI 2004

FOSI, Irene. 'Court and City in the Ceremony of the Possesso in the Sixteenth Century', in: *Court and Politics in Papal Rome, 1492-1700*, edited by Gianvittorio Signorotto and Maria Antonietta Visceglia, Cambridge, Cambridge University Press, 2004.

GIRARDI 1995

GIRARDI, Maria Teresa. *Il sapere e le lettere in Bernardino Tomitano*, Milan, Vita e Pensiero, 1995 (Bibliotheca erudita. Studi e documenti di storia e filologia, 9).

GIRGENSOHN 2004

GIRGENSOHN, Dieter. *Francesco Foscari. Promissione Ducale 1423*, Venice, La Malcontenta, 2004.

GRAHAM – MCALLISTER JOHNSON 1979

GRAHAM, Victor E. – MCALLISTER JOHNSON, William. *The Royal Tour of France by Charles IX and Catherine de' Medici: Festivals and Entries, 1564-6*, Toronto, University of Toronto Press, 1979.

GRIFFANTE 2003-2006

GRIFFANTE, Caterina. *Le edizioni veneziane del Seicento: censimento*, 2 vols., Milan, Bibliografica, 2003-2006.

HAYAT – PÉNEAU – SINTOMER 2018

*La représentation-incarnation*, edited by Samuel Hayat, Corinne Péneau and Yves Sintomer, Paris, Presses de Sciences Po, 2018 (Raisons Politiques, 72.4).

HILL COLE 1999

HILL COLE, Mary. *The Portable Queen: Elizabeth I and the Politics of Ceremony*, Amherst, University of Massachusetts Press, 1999.

HOFMANN 2003

HOFMANN, Hasso. *Repräsentation. Studien zur Wort und Begriffsgeschichte von der Antike bis ins 19. Jahrhundert*, Berlin, Duncker & Humblot, 2003.

HOPKINS 2013

HOPKINS, Andrew. 'Symbol of Venice: The Doge in Ritual', in: *Late Medieval and Early Modern Ritual: Studies in Italian Urban Culture*, edited by Samuel Cohn, Marcello Fantoni, Franco Franceschi and Fabrizio Ricciardelli, Turnhout, Brepols, 2013 (Europa Sacra, 7), pp. 227-239.

HOWARD 1993-1994

HOWARD, Deborah. 'Ritual space in Renaissance Venice', in: *Scroope*, no. 5 (1993-1994), pp. 4-11.

## Celebrating the Prince from Afar

INFELISE 1997

INFELISE, Mario. 'Professione reportista. Copisti e gazzettieri nella Venezia del '600', in: *Venezia. Itinerari per la storia della città*, edited by Stefano Gasparri, Giovanni Levi and Pierandrea Moro, Bologna, il Mulino, 1997, pp. 183-209.

IRACE 2007

IRACE, Erminia. 'Una voce poco fa. Note sulle difficili pratiche della comunicazione tra il centro e le periferie dello Stato Ecclesiastico (Perugia, metà XVI - metà XVII secolo)', in: *Offices, écrit et papauté (XIIIᵉ-XVIIᵉ siècle)*, edited by Armand Jamme and Olivier Poncet Olivier, Rome, École Française de Rome, 2007, pp. 273-299.

JUDDE DE LARIVIÈRE 2011

JUDDE DE LARIVIÈRE, Claire. 'Du Broglio à Rialto: cris et chuchotements dans l'espace public à Venise, au XVIᵉ siècle', in: *L'espace public au Moyen Âge. Débats autour de Jürgen Habermas*, edited by Patrick Boucheron and Nicolas Offenstadt, Paris, Presses Universitaires de France, 2011, pp. 119-130.

JUDDE DE LARIVIÈRE 2015

EAD. 'Religion civique et ordre social à Venise (XVᵉ-XVIᵉ siècles)', in: *La cité cultuelle. Rendre à Dieu ce qui revient à César*, edited by Ariane Zambiras and Jean-François Bayart, Paris, Karthala, 2015 (Recherches internationales), pp. 15-41.

KANTOROWICZ 1957

KANTOROWICZ, Ernst H. *The King's Two Bodies: A Study in Mediaeval Political Theology*, Princeton, Princeton University Press, 1957.

KIPLING 1998

KIPLING, Gordon. *Enter the King: Theatre, Liturgy, and Ritual in the Medieval Civic Triumph*, Oxford-New York, Oxford University Press, 1998.

KNAPTON 1998

KNAPTON, Michael. '«Nobiltà e popolo» e un trentennio di storiografia veneta', in: *Nuova Rivista Storica*, LXXXII (1998), pp. 167-192.

KNOX 1990A

KNOX, Dilwyn. 'Ideas on Gesture and Universal Languages, c. 1550 - c. 1650', in: *New Perspectives on Renaissance Thought: Essays in the History of Science, Education and Philosophy in Memory of Charles B. Schmitt*, edited by John Henry and Sarah Hutton, London, Duckworth, 1990, pp. 101-136.

KNOX 1990B

ID. 'Late Medieval and Renaissance Ideas on Gesture', in: *Die Sprache der Zeichen und Bilder. Rhetorik und nonverbale Kommunikation in der frühen Neuzeit*, edited by Volker Kapp, Marburg, Hitzeroth, 1990 (Ars rheotirca, 1), pp. 11-39.

# GIOVANNI FLORIO

KNOX 1993
ID. 'Giovanni Bonifacio's *L'arte de' cenni* and Renaissance Ideas of Gesture', in: *Italia ed Europa nella linguistica del Rinascimento / Italy and Europe in Renaissance Linguistics. Atti del Convegno internazionale. (Ferrara, Palazzo Paradiso, 20-24 marzo 1991). 2*, edited by Mirko Tavoni, Ferrara, F. C. Panini, 1993, pp. 379-400.

LAZZARINI 2009
LAZZARINI, Isabella. 'Il gesto diplomatico fra comunicazione politica, grammatica delle emozioni, linguaggio delle scritture (Italia, XV secolo)', in: *Gesto – immagine tra antico e moderno. Riflessioni sulla comunicazione non-verbale. Giornata di studio (Isernia, 18 aprile 2007)*, edited by Monica Salvadori and Monica Baggio, Rome, Quasar, 2009 (Antenor Quaderni, 16), pp. 75-94.

LAZZARINI 2015
EAD. *Communication and Conflict: Italian Diplomacy in the Early Renaissance, 1350-1520*, Oxford, Oxford University Press, 2015 (Oxford Studies in Medieval European History).

LUCIOLI 2017
LUCIOLI, Francesco. 'Roncalli, Giovanni Domenico', in: *Dizionario Biografico degli Italiani. 88*, Rome, Istituto della Enciclopedia Italiana, 2017, <https://www.treccani.it/enciclopedia/ricerca/Roncalli,-Giovanni-Domenico/>, accessed March 2023.

MARANINI 1931
MARANINI, Giuseppe. *La costituzione di Venezia. 2: Dopo la Serrata del Maggior Consiglio*, Florence, La Nuova Italia, 1974.

MENNITI IPPOLITO 1986
MENNITI IPPOLITO, Antonio. 'Le dedizioni e lo stato regionale. Osservazioni sul caso veneto', in: *Archivio Veneto*, CXVII/162 (1986), pp. 5-30.

MORPURGO 1878
MORPURGO, Emilio. 'Le Rappresentanze delle popolazioni di terraferma presso il Governo della Dominante', in: *Atti del Regio Istituto Veneto di Scienze, Lettere ed Arti*, s. V, IV (1878), pp. 869-888.

MUIR 1977
MUIR, Edward. *Civic Ritual in Renaissance Venice*, Princeton, Princeton University Press, 1977.

MUIR 2000
ID. 'Was There Republicanism in the Renaissance Republics? Venice after Agnadello', in: *Venice Reconsidered: The History and Civilization of an Italian City-State, 1297-1797*, edited by John Martin and Dennis Romano, Baltimore-London, The Johns Hopkins University Press, 2000, pp. 137-167.

MUIR – WEISSMAN 1977
ID. – WEISSMAN, Ronald. 'Social and Symbolic Places in Renaissance Venice and Florence', in: *The Power of Place: Bringing together Geographical and Sociological Imaginations*, edited by John A. Agnew and James S. Duncan, Boston, Unwin Hyman, 1989, pp. 81-104.

MULRYNE – ALIVERTI – TESTAVERDE 2015
*Ceremonial Entries in Early Modern Europe:. The Iconography of Power*, edited by James R. Mulryne, Maria Ines Aliverti and Anna Maria Testaverde, Abingdon-New York, Routledge, 2015 (European Festival Studies: 1450-1700, 1).

MULRYNE – DE JONGE – MORRIS – MARTENS 2019
*Occasions of State: Early Modern European Festivals and the Negotiation of Power*, edited by James R. Mulryne, Krista De Jonge, Richard L. M. Morris and Pieter Martens, Abingdon-New York, Routledge, 2019 (European Festival Studies: 1450-1700, 6).

MULRYNE – WATANABE-O'KELLY – SHEWRING 2004
*Europa triumphans: Court and Civic Festivals in Early Modern Europe*, 2 vols., edited by James R. Mulryne, Helen Watanabe-O'Kelly and Margaret Shewring, Aldershot, Ashgate, 2004.

MURPHY 2016
MURPHY, Neil. *Ceremonial Entries, Municipal Liberties and the Negotiation of Power in Valois France, 1328-1589*, Leiden-Boston, Brill, 2016.

MUSATTI 1888
MUSATTI, Eugenio. *Storia della Promissione ducale*, Padua, Tipografia del Seminario, 1888.

NEU 2010
NEU, Tim. 'Rhetoric and Representation. Reassessing Territorial Diets in Early Modern Germany', in: *Central European History*, XLIII/1 (2010), pp. 1-24.

NEVOLA 2013
NEVOLA, Fabrizio. 'Review Essay: Street Life in Early Modern Europe', in: *Renaissance Quarterly*, LXVI/4 (2013), pp. 1332-1345.

NICCOLI 2007
NICCOLI, Ottavia. 'Gesti e posture del corpo in Italia tra Rinascimento e Controriforma', in: *Micrologus*, XV (2007), pp. 379-398.

NUBOLA 2001
NUBOLA, Cecilia. 'Supplications between Politics and Justice: The Northern and Central Italian States in the Early Modern Age', in: *Petitions in Social History*, edited by Lex Heerma van Voss, Cambridge, Cambridge University Press, 2001 (International Review of Social History, supplement, 9), pp. 35-56.

O'CONNELL 2016A
O'CONNELL, Monique. 'The Multiple Meanings of Ritual: Orations and the Tensions of Venetian Empire', in: *Rituals of Politics and Culture in Early Modern Europe: Essays in Honour of Edward Muir*, edited by Mark Jurdjevic and Rolf Strøm-Olsen, Toronto, Centre for Reformation and Renaissance Studies, 2016 (Essays and Studies, 39), pp. 91-110.

# GIOVANNI FLORIO

O'CONNELL 2016B
EAD. 'Voluntary Submission and the Ideology of Venetian Empire', in: *I Tatti Studies in the Italian Renaissance*, XX/1 (2017), pp. 9-39.

ORTALLI 2002
ORTALLI, Gherardo. 'Entrar nel Dominio: le dedizioni delle città alla Repubblica Serenissima', in: *Società, economia, istituzioni. Elementi per la conoscenza della Repubblica Veneta. 1*, Verona, Cierre, 2002, pp. 49-62.

PANZERA 2012A
PANZERA, Cristina. 'Francesco Sansovino e l'umanesimo veneziano, Parte I. La fonte nascosta della retorica epistolare e dei modelli di lettere', in: *Italianistica. Rivista di Letteratura Italiana*, XLI/2 (2012), pp. 21-48.

PANZERA 2012B
EAD. 'Francesco Sansovino e l'umanesimo veneziano, Parte II: un progetto editoriale tra tradizione e veneziana libertas', in: *Italianistica. Rivista di Letteratura Italiana*, XLI/3 (2012), pp. 11-33.

PINETTI 1929
PINETTI, Angelo. 'Nunzi ed ambasciatori della Magnifica Città di Bergamo alla Repubblica di Venezia', in: *Bergomum*, XXIII/1 (1929), pp. 33-57.

PITKIN 1967
PITKIN, Hanna Fenichel. *The Concept of Representation*, Berkeley-Los Angeles, University of California Press, 1967.

POVOLO 1994
POVOLO, Claudio. 'Centro e periferia nella Repubblica di Venezia. Un profilo', in: *Origini dello Stato. Processi di formazione statale in Italia fra medioevo ed età moderna*, edited by Giorgio Chittolini, Anthony Molho and Pierangelo Schiera, Bologna, il Mulino, 1994 (Annali dell'Istituto Storico Italo-Germanico in Trento. Quaderno 39), pp. 207-221.

POVOLO 1997
ID. *L'intrigo dell'onore. Poteri e istituzioni nella Repubblica di Venezia tra Cinque e Seicento*, Verona, Cierre, 1997.

POVOLO 2006A
ID. 'Un sistema giuridico repubblicano: Venezia e il suo stato territoriale (sec. XV-XVIII)', in: *Il diritto patrio. Tra diritto comune e codificazione (secoli XVI-XIX)*, edited by Italo Birocchi and Antonello Mattone, Rome, Viella, 2006, pp. 297-353.

POVOLO 2006B
ID. 'Un rapporto difficile e controverso: Paolo Sarpi e il diritto veneto', in: *Ripensando Paolo Sarpi. Atti del Convegno internazionale di studi nel 450° anniversario della nascita di Paolo Sarpi*, edited by Corrado Pin, Venice, Ateneo Veneto, 2006, pp. 395-416.

## CELEBRATING THE PRINCE FROM AFAR

POVOLO 2008
ID. 'La piccola comunità e le sue consuetudini', in: *Tra diritto e Storia. Studi in onore di Luigi Berlinguer promossi dalle Università di Siena e di Sassari*, Soveria Mannelli, Rubbettino, 2008, pp. 591-642.

RAU 2019
RAU, Susanne. *History, Space, and Place*, Abingdon-New York, Routledge, 2019.

RAVEGNANI 2013
RAVEGNANI, Giorgio. *Il doge di Venezia*, Bologna, il Mulino, 2013 (Universale Paperbacks il Mulino, 654).

RODRÍGUEZ MOYA – MÍNGUEZ CORNELLES 2016
*Visiones de un imperio en fiesta*, edited by Inmaculada Rodríguez Moya and Víctor Mínguez Cornelles, Madrid, Fundación Carlo De Amberes, 2016.

ROSPOCHER 2013
ROSPOCHER, Massimo. 'La voce della piazza. Oralità e spazio pubblico nell'Italia del Rinascimento', in: *Oltre la sfera pubblica. Lo spazio della politica nell'Europa moderna*, edited by Massimo Rospocher, Bologna, il Mulino, 2013 (Studi e ricerche, 666), pp. 9-30.

ROSPOCHER – SALZBERG 2013
ROSPOCHER, Massimo – SALZBERG, Rosa. 'An Evanescent Public Sphere: Voices, Spaces, and Publics in Venice during the Italian Wars', in: *Beyond the Public Sphere: Opinions, Publics, Spaces in Early Modern Europe (XVI-XVIII)*, edited by Massimo Rospocher, Bologna, il Mulino, 2012 (Annali dell'Istituto Storico Italo-Germanico di Trento. Contributi, 27), pp. 93-114.

RUSSELL – VISENTIN 2007
*French Ceremonial Entries in the Sixteenth Century: Event, Image, Text*, edited by Nicolas Russell and Hélène Visentin, Toronto, Centre for Reformation and Renaissance Studies, 2007.

SALZBERG 2013
SALZBERG, Rosa. *Ephemeral City: Cheap Print and Urban Culture in Renaissance Venice*, Manchester, Manchester University Press, 2014.

SARPI 2001
SARPI, Paolo. *Consulti. 1: I consulti dell'interdetto, 1606-1607*, edited by Corrado Pin, Pisa-Roma, Istituti editoriali e poligrafici internazionali, 2001.

SCROCCARO 1986
SCROCCARO, Carla. 'Dalla corrispondenza dei legati veronesi: aspetti delle istituzioni veneziane nel secondo Quattrocento', in: *Nuova rivista storica*, LXX (1986), pp. 625-636.

SINDING-LARSEN 1974
SINDING-LARSEN, Staale. *Christ in the Council Hall: Studies in the Religious Iconography of the Venetian Republic*, Rome, L'Erma di Bretschneider, 1974 (Acta ad archaeologiam et artium historiam pertinentia, 5).

# GIOVANNI FLORIO

ŠPOLJARIĆ 2018
ŠPOLJARIĆ, Luka. 'Power and Subversion in the Ducal Palace: Dalmatian Patrician Humanists and Congratulatory Orations to Newly Elected Doges', in: *Neo-Latin Contexts in Croatia and Tyrol: Challenges, Prospects, Case Studies*, edited by Neven Jovanović, Johanna Luggin, Luka Špoljarić and Lav Subaric, Vienna, Böhlau, 2018, pp. 81-104.

URBAN 1998
URBAN, Lina. *Processioni e feste dogali: Venetia est mundus*, Vicenza, Neri Pozza, 1998.

VAN GELDER 2018
VAN GELDER, Maartje. 'The People's Prince: Popular Politics in Early Modern Venice', in: *The Journal of Modern History*, XC/2 (2018), pp. 249-291.

VAN GELDER 2019
EAD. 'Ducal Display and the Contested Use of Space in Late Sixteenth-Century Venetian Coronation Festivals', in: MULRYNE – DE JONGE – MORRIS – MARTENS 2019, pp. 167-195.

VARANINI 1992
VARANINI, Gian Maria. 'Il giurista, il comune cittadino, la Dominante: Bartolomeo Cipolla legato del comune di Verona a Venezia', in: *Comuni cittadini e stato regionale. Ricerche sulla Terraferma veneta nel Quattrocento*, edited by Gian Maria Varanini, Verona, Libreria Editrice Universitaria, 1992, pp. 361-384.

VARANINI 2011
ID. 'La Terraferma veneta del Quattrocento e le tendenze recenti della storiografia', in: *1509-2009. L'ombra di Agnadello. Venezia e la Terraferma*, edited by Giuseppe Del Torre and Alfredo Viggiano, Venice, Ateneo Veneto, 2011, pp. 13-63.

VENTURA 1993
VENTURA, Angelo. *Nobiltà e popolo nella società veneta del Quattrocento e Cinquecento*, Milan, Unicopli, 1993.

VIALLON 2008
VIALLON, Marie. 'La procession ducale à Venise: un rite urbain pour montrer sa puissance', in: *Cahiers d'études romanes*, no. 18 (2008), pp. 39-54.

VIGGIANO 2013
VIGGIANO, Alfredo. 'Politics and Constitution', in: *A Companion to Venetian History, 1400-1797*, edited by Eric R. Dursteler, Leiden-Boston, Brill, 2013, pp. 47-84.

VISCEGLIA 2001
VISCEGLIA, Maria Antonietta. 'Il viaggio cerimoniale di Carlo V dopo Tunisi', in: *Dimensioni e problemi della ricerca storica*, no. 2 (2001), pp. 5-37.

# Celebrating the Prince from Afar

Wintroub 2006

Wintroub, Michael. *A Savage Mirror: Power, Identity and Knowledge in Early Modern France*, Stanford, Stanford University Press, 2006.

Wolters 1987

Wolters, Wolfgang. *Storia e politica nei dipinti di Palazzo Ducale: aspetti dell'autocelebrazione della Repubblica di Venezia nel Cinquecento*, Venice, Arsenale, 1987, pp. 246-255.

# TRADITIONAL MUSIC
# IN SEVENTEENTH-CENTURY OPERAS 'ALLA VENEZIANA':
# INTERSECTIONS IN THE ITALIAN SOUNDSCAPE

*Nicola Usula*
(UNIVERSITÉ DE FRIBOURG)

AMONG THE MAIN MUSICAL ELEMENTS of the mid-seventeenth-century Venetian soundscape, *opera in musica* was one of the most important and idiomatic, to such an extent that it contributed to redefining the entertainment system of the city[1]. Soon after the pioneering experiments at the Teatro S. Cassiano in 1637, other Venetian theatres started to house operas, and during the first two decades of their activity they produced a total of about seventy-five works[2].

While the impresarial system stabilised in Venice, the rise of touring opera companies contributed to the dissemination of operas 'alla veneziana' to the rest of the peninsula, allowing the very first widespread diffusion of the genre[3]. After some very limited early migrations[4], operas such as *La finta pazza* (G. Strozzi and F. Sacrati, Teatro Novissimo, 1641) and *Giasone* (G. A. Cicognini and F. Cavalli, Teatro S. Cassiano, 1649) played a fundamental role in spreading elements of the Venetian soundscape outside Venice. These works allowed audiences from all over Italy and beyond to come in contact with some significant portions of the city's

---

[1]. For helping me to enhance my work, I owe a debt of gratitude to Lorenzo Bianconi, Valeria Conti, Ignazio Macchiarella, Margaret Murata, and James O'Leary and Peter Hauge for their unparalleled linguistic and musicological help.

[2]. See BIANCONI – WALKER 1984; ROSAND 1991; BIANCONI 1991; WHENHAM 2004; GLIXON – GLIXON 2006; SELFRIDGE-FIELD 2007.

[3]. For the early phenomenon of operatic dissemination see BIANCONI – WALKER 1975.

[4]. For example, *La Delia* (G. Strozzi and F. Manelli) premiered in 1639 at Teatro Ss. Giovanni e Paolo, and was revived in Bologna (1640), Genoa (1645) and Milan (1647). The main source I used to identify the sources available online for each libretto edition is the database *CORAGO*, edited by Angelo Pompilio.

soundscape, creating a network in which the Italian peninsula shared a common taste for opera, albeit with some local peculiarities[5].

However, the trajectory from Venice to the rest of Italy was not the only one drawn by these works. An analysis of the extant librettos and scores from this early period reveals that Venetian operas contain direct quotations from another musical context, outside the opera houses. These pieces could be identified as elements from the musical worlds that now call *folk music*, *urban music*, or *popular music*. However, in this study I will use the term *traditional music*, because it better underlines the relationship between the contemporary audience and a certain well-recognised common music tradition, both urban or rural, which, in any case, was well known by composers and operatic audiences[6]. One would expect to find mainly indigenous Venetian elements in this kind of example, and this would strengthen the idea that through operas even traditional music components of the Venetian soundscape could be exported. However, my analysis produced other results. It seems that these quotations refer primarily to a probably pan-Italian soundscape, or better, to an already shared concept of traditional music that in the middle of the century looks to have been unanimously perceived as extraneous to the art music world.

In the present study, I will analyse some extracts from mid-seventeenth-century operas 'alla veneziana' that present (1) local elements such as Venetian locations for some scenes' backgrounds (usually Piazza San Marco) and passages in Venetian dialect, as well as (2) traditional pieces out of context, or 'traditional-like' compositions, for example *canzonette*, *filastrocche* and dances. In the final section (3) I will give an account of the results of this study.

## THE VENETIAN SOUNDSCAPE IN VENETIAN OPERAS

### Contents and Images from Venice

Some early Venetian operas reveal a strong relationship with the city in which they were conceived. This connection concerned their subjects — which were often linked to the historical and mythical roots of the city, like the Trojan War and the Roman Republic — as well as their contents[7]. Venetian librettos, in fact, were filled with the ideologies that originated from the Accademia degli Incogniti, and sometimes with direct references to the city of Venice[8].

---

[5]. See BIANCONI 1991, pp. 190-204. One of the most important studies on the early modern Venetian soundscape is HOWARD – MORETTI 2009.

[6]. See LEYDI 1991; MACCHIARELLA 1994; PEGG 2001; PORTER 2001; MAGRINI *ET. AL.* 2001; HAMM – WALSER – WARWICK – GARRETT 2013.

[7]. Many studies pointed out the relationship between Venetian opera and Venice: a comprehensive bibliography on this topic is in ROSAND 1991, pp. 125-144.

[8]. For this Accademia, see MIATO 1998, and CONRIERI 2011.

Ill. 1: G. Giorgi Tedesco, engraving after the stage set by G. Torelli for *Il Bellerofonte* (Prologue) by V. Nolfi and F. Sacrati, Venice 1642 (from Nolfi, *Il Bellerofonte, folio* edition, copy in I-Vc, 497).

Furthermore, this phenomenon of indigenisation sometimes also involved visual aspects. Some extant scenery shows explicit Venetian landscapes, as for example those by Giacomo Torelli for *Il Bellerofonte* by Vincenzo Nolfi and Francesco Sacrati (Venice, Teatro Novissimo, 1642)[9]. In this opera, during the prologue, Neptune from his sea-chariot promises Innocence (with a lamb) and Astrea (with a lion and a scale) the coming of a city «gloriosa e superba», invoking the appearance of Venice[10]. The engraving by Giovanni Giorgi Tedesco after Torelli's scenery (Ill. 1) shows, indeed, a realistic view of Piazza San Marco from the Venetian lagoon, commented on by Giulio del Colle within the 1642 *folio*-edition of the libretto[11]:

---

[9]. Score lost, libretto in I-Bc (Lo.4941): Nolfi 1642a. For the main bibliography about this opera see Milesi 2000 and Cecchi 2017.
[10]. Nolfi 1642a, pp. 20-21.
[11]. Libretto in I-Vc (497): Nolfi 1642b, in folio, p. 9.

At the behest of Neptune, the model of the city of Venice came out from the sea. It was so lovely and vividly crafted that everyone claimed it was a technical masterpiece. The picture of St Mark's square tricked the eye with its public buildings for they were so realistically reproduced; and everyone was more and more delighted by the trick, and, in front of the depicted square, they almost forgot about the true one in its real position.

(D'ordine suo [i.e. di Nettuno] viddesi sorger dal mare in modello la città di Venezia, così esquisita e vivamente formata che la confessò ognuno un sforzo dell'arte. Ingannava l'occhio la piazza con le fabriche publiche al naturale immitate, e dell'inganno ognor più godeva, scordandosi quasi per quella finta della vera dove realmente si tratteneva.)

Similarly, in the last lines of *La prosperità infelice di Giulio Cesare dittatore* by Gian Francesco Busenello (unknown composer and unknown premiere) the city of Venice appears as a place of future prosperity. The same Neptune promises to Libertà (Freedom) the birth of a Heaven on earth: «una cittade gloriosa e grande | [...] Venezia sarà detta | questa città suprema e trionfante | che renderà famose | le adriatiche sponde [...]» (a city glorious and great [...] Venice will be the name of this supreme and triumphant city that will make the shores of the Adriatic Sea famous [...]). Furthermore, the city appears onstage on scale («una picciola forma | di Venetia felice») for Jupiter's will, and the opera finishes with the choir «Viva, Venezia, viva!» (Long live Venice)[12].

### Venetian Dialect

The direct reference to Venice in early operas 'alla veneziana' can be traced also via the language of certain passages in librettos, since, as with the early Roman operatic tradition (and later also in the Florentine, Milanese and Neapolitan contexts), the contact between operas and their birth-city was also perpetuated by the dialect[13].

In 1649, on the occasion of the Venetian performance of Giacinto Andrea Cicognini and Francesco Lucio's *Orontea* at the Teatro SS. Apostoli, the drunk comic servant Gelone

---

12. Libretto printed only ten years later in BUSENELLO 1656, fourth libretto: *La prosperità infelice di Giulio Cesare dittatore*, (copy in I-Bc, Lo.7001) pp. 1-64, at 62-64 (passage quoted in BELLINA 2000, p. 369). The premiere of this opera is dated 1646 in IVANOVICH 1681, whose unreliability is well-known (WALKER 1976).

13. The first Roman opera with passages in dialect is possibly *Primavera urbana col trionfo d'Amor pudico* by Ottaviano Castelli with music by Angelo Cecchini, performed in 1635 during the Carnival. Score lost, libretto in I-Rvat. See MURATA 1995, p. 92; and for Castelli in general, DI CEGLIE 1997. For the mid-century operas in Florence, Milan, and Naples see WEAVER – WEAVER 1978; LEVE 1998; MICHELASSI 2000; DAOLMI 1998; LANFOSSI 2012; D'ALESSANDRO 1984; FABRIS 2007.

blended fiction and reality by singing in Italian and then in Venetian dialect in scene I.12[14]. This intervention by the drunk character shows a very irregular metric structure, which strictly depends on his temporarily altered state. Furthermore, the connection between off-stage reality and on-stage fiction is strengthened by the 'local' imagery of Gelone's lines, which link the indigenous Venetian audience with its own geographical context (e.g., the references to 'Murano' and the boats)[15].

| GELONE | Ferma là, | Stop! |
|---|---|---|
| | ferma là, | Stop! |
| | non urtar... | Quit shoving... |
| | non urtar: t'ucciderò! | Quit shoving or I'll kill you! |
| | Saldo in barca: irato è 'l mar, | Don't rock the boat: the sea's rough |
| | e 'l buon vin mi fa buon pro... | and the good wine is a benefit for me... |
| | O che caldo | Oh what a heat |
| | [...] | [...] |
| | O che caldo maladetto, | Oh what a cursed heat, |
| | poss'io morire... | shall I die... |
| | ...s'io non ho Murano in petto. | ...if I have not Murano in my heart! |
| | [...] | [...] |
| | Oè, oè, barca, oè! | Hey, hey, you on the boat, hey! |
| | Guarda, guarda dove vai! | Watch where you're going! |
| | Ohimè, ohimè: | Alas, alas: |
| | la nave ha percosso*, | The boat has struck, |
| | la poppa si apre, | the stern is smashed, |
| | si squarcia la prora, | the prow is shattered, |
| | la vela si rompe, | the sail is torn, |
| | il remo si spezza, | the oar is broken, |
| | l'antenna è divisa! | the mast is split in two! |

&ast;. The printed libretto presents the *lectio* 's'apre', but since the metric context is made up of *senari*, I correct the original *quinario* by avoiding the elision of *i* and inserting a *dialefe*.

Although this opera is set in Egypt, Gelone, while standing on the *Marina* (seashore) of the Red Sea, believes he is on a boat sailing on the Venetian lagoon. Moreover, in his alcoholic vision, he thinks his boat is involved in a shipwreck and is going to sink. From then on, he looks at the smashed stern, the shattered prow, and so on; therefore his most genuine and intimate

---

14. This character has been thoroughly studied in BROWN 2000.
15. From CICOGNINI 1649B, pp. 27-28 (libretto in D-Mbs, L.eleg.m. 2785).

language surfaces in the following lines, bringing on stage a realistic sound-picture of the city in Venetian dialect[16]:

| GELONE | Ah, ah, ah, ah, ah, ah, scoppio di risa. | I burst out in laughter! |
| | Bestia, ti ridi? | Bumpkin! you laugh? |
| | Vostù zugar, | Do you want to joke, |
| | brutto animal, | stupid yokel? |
| | che te traggo in canal? | I'll throw you in a canal! |
| | E là chi me dà man? | Hey, who will help me? |
| | Chi me conduse? | Who will lead? |
| | Menego, | Domenico, |
| | Bortolo, | Bortolomeo, |
| | bestie, | yokels, |
| | portéme luse. | bring me some light! |

Paolo Fabbri pointed out that this example is one of the very rare cases in which a Venetian seventeenth-century libretto presents a passage in Venetian dialect, and this rarity seems not to be accidental[17]. The characters that sing in dialect were the legacy of those that already in the Commedia dell'arte were regionally well recognisable by their language and inflections, and we find them also in late seventeenth-century operas throughout Italy[18]. However, mid-century Venetian operas did not contain these language peculiarities most likely for the literary roots of the new genre. Generally, both *favole pastorali* and tragedies avoided indigenous dialectal elements, and, similarly, *drammi per musica* tended to limit any linguistic transfer from outside to inside the theatres. Therefore, in these works we can hardly recognise some features from the city's particular sound context. Venetian operas, in fact, were inclined to create links between the audience's usual soundscape and the music onstage, though not from a local perspective.

## THE ITALIAN SOUNDSCAPE IN THE VENETIAN OPERAS

### *Canzonette and filastrocche*

The examples of traditional music quotations traceable in early operas 'alla veneziana' are different from one another, although they all share the peculiarity of being slightly difficult

---

[16]. I thank Silvia Urbani for helping me in clarifying the meaning of these lines.

[17]. FABBRI 1990, pp. 89-90.

[18]. For example, the case of the comic Calabrese character in the Neapolitan late seventeenth-century operas is studied in TEDESCO 1995. For the relationship between Commedia dell'arte and the early operatic world see the recent HILL 2015; and WILBOURNE 2016.

## Traditional Music in Seventeenth-Century Operas 'alla Veneziana'

to find for the contemporary musicologist. For some of them I could identify some original sources outside the operatic world, and more specifically among previous dances, nursery and traditional rhymes. However, most of the cases I found concern apparent references to traditional music: cases in which the quotation seems likely because of its musical features, or because it is preceded by expressions that seem to refer to a well-known piece.

I could identify the traditional origins of two *canzonette*, the first of which is in *Giasone* by Giacinto Andrea Cicognini and Francesco Cavalli. This opera, staged in 1649 at the Venetian Teatro San Cassiano, was one of the most performed operas of the century[19]. It was such a powerful medium for the transmission of the Venetian operatic taste that, from then on, in coeval operas, copying some scenes or some characters from it became very common[20].

In this opera, we find a quotation from the traditional music in the comic scene II.10, in the encounter between Demo and Oreste, servants of the king Egeo and the queen Isifile respectively. In this scene, the stutterer Demo comes ashore after a shipwreck and tries to tell Oreste about his ruinous incident. He is still in shock and his complex stuttering contributes to the efficacy of the comic dialogue. While pointing at the sea, he struggles to explain to his interlocutor that he had swallowed some seawater, with the lines «dopo aver là be-, | là be-, là be-, là be-» (after having 'la be-'), which should be completed as «dopo aver là bevuto» (after having swallowed [seawater] there [in the sea]). However, his companion Oreste uses the repeated syllables «là be-» to start a rounded *canzonetta* — immediately joined by Demo, too — that presents the same first syllables but develops as «La bella traditora» (The fair traitress, lines 1527-1531)[21].

| | | |
|---|---|---|
| DEMO | Io, dall'onde sbattuto, | I, scrambled from the waves, |
| | dopo aver là be- | after having there fai- |
| | là be- là be- là be- | there fai-, there fai-, there fai-, |
| | | |
| ORESTE | 'La bella traditora... | 'The fair traitress... |
| DEMO | ...che m'ha rubato il cor, | ...that has stolen my heart, |
| | col guardo mi innamora | with her eyes enchants me |
| | e mi fa star di fuor. | and makes me lose my mind. |
| ORESTE | La bella traditora...' | The fair traitress...' |
| | | |
| DEMO | [*Indicando il mare.*] | [*Pointing at the sea.*] |

---

[19]. See BIANCONI 1991, p. 196; CARPANI 2008; GLIXON 2013; LIN 2015. The extant sources for this opera (*c.* 45 libretto editions and 12 manuscript scores) are listed in CICOGNINI – CAVALLI forthcoming.

[20]. See some examples in LANFOSSI 2012, pp. 20-27, and ANTONUCCI – BIANCONI 2013, pp. ix-x.

[21]. CICOGNINI 1649a, p. 70 (libretto in I-Vnm, Dramm.3456.3). Modern edition of this 'seconda impressione' is in GRONDA – FABBRI 1997, pp. 107-207 and 1816-1817.

| Dopo aver là bevuto, | After having swallowed [seawater] there, |
| lo spirito nel mar lasciai disciolto [...] | I left my spirit dispersed in the sea [...] |

This piece's structure in *settenari piani* and *tronchi* with an alternate (*axaxa*) rhyme scheme, together with its musical shape, suggests its traditional origins. The musical configuration of this interpolation is very clear and schematic: in a harmonic context based on G minor, the sung melody presents a period of two symmetrical phrases, which are split in two halves that respectively end on the dominant and on the tonic (Ex. 1). Furthermore, the melodic line of the first phrase, although distributed between two vocal parts, shows a parabola shape, with a climax and anti-climax. It starts with an ascending leap of a fourth from dominant to tonic (in Oreste's part), and keeps rising until the upper dominant (in Demo's part), and, in the second semi-phrase it comes back to the tonic[22].

Ex. 1: Extract from *Giasone* by G. A. Cicognini and F. Cavalli (score in I-Vnm, fol. 95r).

---

[22]. Score in I-Vnm (It. Cl. IV, 363 =9887).

# Traditional Music in Seventeenth-Century Operas 'alla Veneziana'

An extra-operatic composition seems to be the ancestor of Cavalli's 'La bella traditora'. It is a galliard by an anonymous author, which is titled *La traditora* and is documented already in some early sixteenth-century manuscript sources with lute music[23]. This composition was so famous during the early baroque era that it was copied and printed all over Europe, becoming a dance formula that was set to music for different instruments and ensembles[24]. The following version in four parts comes from a manuscript collection of *Gallyardes and Neapolytans Songes* dated around 1550, preserved in the Henry Fitzalan collection of the British Library in London (Ex. 2)[25].

Ex. 2: Extract from the galliard *La traditora*, in *Gallyardes and Neapolytans Songes* (four partbooks in GB-Lbl, fol. 5v in all the volumes).

Apart from the time indication and the different ensemble, this version of *La traditora* differs from the one in *Giasone* in one main respect: in the galliard the harmonic sequence of the first two phrases does not end on the tonic as in Cavalli's score, but always on the dominant. Nevertheless, as I show in the following music example (Ex. 3), this harmonic change seems to be more superficial than substantial. Together with the coincidence of the general key in the two sources, not only the melodic profile but also the very notes of both versions correspond. It seems that Cavalli, although changing the harmonic progression, simply presented the melodic quotation without distorting it, allowing the audience to recognise immediately the external musical link[26].

---

[23]. See Brown 2001; Moot 1978; and mainly Ness – Kolczynski 2001. In the latter the authors give evidence of the presence of *La traditora* already in a manuscript source dated 1533-1544 preserved in D-Mbs (Mus. Ms.1512). Early printed sources for this piece (from 1545 to 1592) are in Brown 1967, *ad indicem*.

[24]. The sixteenth-century sources that contain music titled *La traditora* are countless. However, many different compositions present this title. For example, in a *frottola* for four voices by Ludovico Fogliano, we find a piece that starts with the words «La traditora la vòl ch'io mora», but this is very different from the one quoted in *Giasone*. The composition is a *centone* that contains several traditional music quotations and starts with the words «Fortuna d'un gran tempo». It was published into the Ninth book of *frottole* printed by Ottaviano Petrucci in 1508, and was studied already in 1939 in Jeppesen 1939.

[25]. Source in GB-Lbl (Royal Appendix MS 59-62, four partbooks: Cantus, Altus, Tenor, Bassus). I thank Florian Amort for digitizing this source in London for me.

[26]. A similar direct quotation is a *Bergamasca* starting with the words «Franzeschina me garbada» sung by Zanni in *L'Egisto, overo Chi soffre speri* by Giulio Rospigliosi, Virgilio Mazzocchi and Marco Marazzoli (Rome

Ex. 3: Structural comparison between *La bella traditora* from *Giasone* and the galliard *La traditora*.

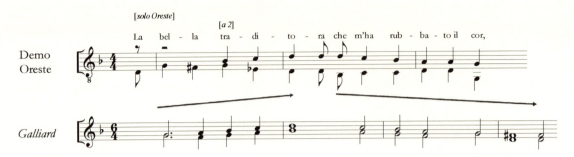

I found another direct quotation of a traditional piece in a libretto composed outside Venice, although by a poet whose operatic apprenticeship was Venetian. I refer to *L'Almonte* by Antonio Draghi with music (lost) by Giuseppe Tricarico[27]. The libretto of this opera, printed in Vienna in 1661 for the premiere, contains a direct reference to some traditional music during the scene III.6. Here the comic character Gelone, «servo parasite» (parasite servant), sings to bide his time, while his master Almonte and Pallante are sleeping onstage. After singing the first two lines of a *canzonetta* that starts with the words «La bella Margherita», he stops, because — as he says — it is «troppo trita» (it has been sung too many times)[28].

| GELONE | La bella Margherita | The beautiful Daisy |
|---|---|---|
| | l'è bianca quanto un fior... | is white like a flower... |
| | ma questa è troppo trita: | but this song is too trite: |
| | voglio mutar tenor. | I want to change style. |
| | | |
| | Io canterò, se non mi date fretta, | I will sing, if you do not rush me, |
| | un'aria nova in su la spagnoletta. | a new song on the *spagnoletta* dance-theme. |

---

1637 and 1639, see MURATA 2007, pp. 94-96. The modern transcription of the libretto is in ROSPIGLIOSI 1998, p. 94; and the facsimile edition of the manuscript of this opera held in I-Rvat (MS Barb. lat. 4386) is in ROSPIGLIOSI – MAZZOCCHI – MARAZZOLI 1982, fols. 114v-115v.

[27]. The Riminese Draghi sang the part of the comic bass Bato in *Le fortune di Rodope e di Damira*, by Aurelio Aureli and Pietro Andrea Ziani, performed in 1657 Carnival at the Teatro S. Apollinare in Venice (information in AURELI 1657, p. 9, copy in D-Mbs, P.o.it. 100). The traces of his Venetian activity are presented in MONALDINI 2000, pp. 21-28. An overview of the literary compositions by Draghi is in SALERNO 2000; and a critical edition of his extant secular librettos is in preparation at the University of Vienna: NOE – USULA forthcoming. The career of Giuseppe Tricarico in Rome, then Ferrara and finally Vienna is studied in DEISINGER 2006; and DEISINGER 2009.

[28]. DRAGHI 1667, fol. G$^2$v (copy in I-Rn, 35.5.A.15.6).

## Traditional Music in Seventeenth-Century Operas 'alla Veneziana'

Unfortunately, the score for *L'Almonte* is lost, but we find the quotation of the music for *La bella Margherita* in at least two other vocal compositions from the same period: one cantata and a late seventeenth-century *dramma per musica*, for both of which the music survives.

The cantata appears in a manuscript source preserved in Naples, from a chronological point of view probably close to Draghi and Tricarico's work. It is a composition for soprano and continuo attributed to Francesco Provenzale (Naples, before 1624-1704) that starts with the line «Squarciato appena avea con strali d'oro»[29]. This work is a complex 'patchwork', in which the famous *Lamento della regina di Svezia* (Lament of the Queen of Sweden) is interpolated with a number of traditional songs[30]: among others *Fra Iacopino, Gallo di mona fiera, È morto Saione, Chi t'ha fatto queste scarpette* (*La Girometta*)[31]. The use of *La bella Margherita* in this cantata is quite similar to that in *L'Almonte*, since in both cases it links two different musical worlds. However, in the cantata, the gap between the historical background of the lament and the character of the traditional song is much broader than in the comic scene with Gelone. In the Neapolitan composition, indeed, in a context of serious narrative, dealing with the desperation of the Queen of Sweden for the death of the king Gustavus II Adolphus, the singer abruptly switches to a different musical style and contents. Therefore, the final result is intentionally outrageous in regard to the mournful character of the story.

*La bella Margherita* in this cantata presents some features that could be easily recognised as 'traditional'. Firstly, it shows a fragmentary and irregular structure in two tripartite phrases (▪), then it presents a syllabic configuration of the sung part, and the close repetition of the first short semi-phrase 'La bella Margherita' (that in both cases ends with a perfect cadence). Finally, it presents a passage with the nonsensical lyrics «fa lalì lalera»; and an opening ascending skip of a fourth (Ex. 4).

The second vocal piece that presents a reference to *La bella Margherita* is much later: *Gli equivoci in amore, overo La Rosaura* opera by Giovani Battista Lucini and Alessandro Scarlatti that premiered in Rome in 1690 (Palazzo della Cancelleria)[32]. During the scene II.1 of this

---

[29]. This cantata is copied in a music manuscript held in I-Nc (33.4.12[b] - ex Arie 47; Cantate ibride 9, pp. 25-56), and it has been studied in GIALDRONI 1987, pp. 132-135, 139-141 and 147-150; and FABRIS 2007, pp. 187, 196-200, 207 (n. 19) and 260. See also the entry dedicated to this composition in *CLORI*, no. 4688.

[30]. The dramatic *topos* of the lament in the seventeenth-century opera is studied in BIANCONI 1991, pp. 204-219; and ROSAND 1991, pp. 361-386.

[31]. *La Girometta* appears also in the second *intermedio*, *La fiera di Farfa*, added to the 1639 Roman revival of *L'Egisto, overo Chi soffre speri* by Rospigliosi, Mazzocchi and Marazzoli. See ROSPIGLIOSI 1998, p. 118; and ROSPIGLIOSI – MAZZOCCHI – MARAZZOLI 1982, fol. 200r-v. This traditional song originated already in the early sixteenth century and was quoted by many composers until the nineteenth century. See the essay 'Come il Girometta divenne la «Girometta»', in: LEYDI 1991, pp. 220-227.

[32]. A copy of the libretto's *editio princeps* (LUCINI 1690) is held in I-Bc (Lo.6316). Instrumental and vocal parts in A-Wn (Suppl. Mus. 01086). A list of the surviving sources for this opera is in BOYD – PAGANO – HANLEY 2001, and the edition of the first two acts of the opera by Robert Eitner is in LUCINI – SCARLATTI 1885.

Ex. 4: Extract from the cantata 'Squarciato appena avea con strali d'oro', music by F. Provenzale (?) (manuscript in I-Nc, pp. 28-29).

opera, the protagonist Rosaura suffers for love, and confesses her sorrow to her lover's servant, Lesbo. She complains with the words «Peno, né son gradita» (I grieve, and I am not desired), then the comic character — rapidly changing topic — sings 'La bella Margherita', the lines of which perfectly rhyme with the ones sung by Rosaura[33].

| | | |
|---|---|---|
| Lesbo | Si potrebbe sapere in fin cosa vi duole? | Finally, would it be possible to know what does hurt you? |
| Rosaura | Peno, né son gradita, e non l'intendi ancor? | I grieve, and I am not desired, and do you still do not understand? |
| Lesbo | 'La bella Margherita l'è bianca quanto un fior.' | 'The beautiful Daisy is white like a flower.' |
| Rosaura *si alza* | Lesbo, - | Lesbo, - |
| Lesbo | Signora mia! | Milady! |
| Rosaura | - non peno più: io sto meglio che mai. | - I do not suffer anymore: I have never felt so well. |

In this case, the reference is not similar to that of *La traditora* in *Giasone* or that of *La bella Margherita* in the Neapolitan cantata. In *La Rosaura* we notice, in fact, a strict interpenetration between the music quotation and Scarlatti's music. Rosaura's lament and Lesbo's intervention do alternate in a musical and dramatic *fluxus* without interruptions, although the composer clearly distinguishes the musical *affetti* of their respective passages. Rosaura's bars have their own painful and angry characterisation, and Lesbo's passage maintains a 'traditional' character, even if it shows the traces of Scarlatti's manipulation (Ex. 5).

---

[33]. Lucini 1690, p. 27.

Ex. 5: Extract from *Gli equivoci in amore, overo la Rosaura* by G. B. Lucini and A. Scarlatti (parts in A-Wn).

From a structural, melodic, and harmonic point of view, the music for *La bella Margherita* in *La Rosaura* maintains the ascending skip of a fourth at the very beginning, the immediate repetition of the first semi-phrase, the ascending line, and the prosody of the last phrase's start («l'è *bianca* quanto un fior»). However, the composer integrates this quotation into the musical texture of the scene, and, more than simply importing that music material, he adapts it. His main goal was both stimulating the effect of extraneousness and quoting, thus suggesting to the audience a musical picture from outside the theatre.

The literary and poetic status of *La bella Margherita* was so low that its text was often quoted with negative connotations. For example, Salvator Rosa in his second *satira* titled *La poesia* — composed during the 1640s, but published at the end of the century — quoted *La bella Margherita* while complaining about the lack of poetic inspiration in Italy at that time. He addressed some lines to contemporary poets, counselling them to learn a job that could feed them, so they could freely sing *La bella Margherita* as they pleased[34].

During the eighteenth century we still find critiques of 'La bella Margherita', and the persistence of this negative perception reveal much about its popularity[35]. Furthermore the name 'Margherita' in some cities — for example in Naples — was often associated with prostitutes[36], so we can only vaguely imagine the likely strength of such a musical quotation in the operas. For example, the quotation of this traditional piece during the 1692 Roman performance of *La Rosaura* at the Teatro Capranica created a documented big sensation. It was so disturbing to the cardinal Pietro Ottoboni, that he tried «sottomano di farla levare» (to have it deleted under the table), perhaps because of its vulgar allusion, or because it seemed to refer to one of his affairs at that time with a singer named Margherita[37].

*Likely and Unlikely Quotations of Vocal Pieces*

Two samples from Cavalli's works could be taken into consideration for possible, though doubtful, quotations. In these cases some music-materials could belong to a traditional musical context, because they present elements that seem peculiar in the traditional musical language. However, they also feature some characteristics that in any case suggest caution in ascribing them entirely to a hypothetically original 'traditional' background.

---

[34]. «[...] Non v'accorgete omai da tanti segni, | che nell'Inferno della povertade | sono l'alme dannate i bell'ingegni?» («After so many signs, do not you realize that in the Hell of misery the best minds are the damned souls?»). «[...] Imparate qualch'arte, onde la vita | tragga il pan quotidiano, e poi cantate | quanto vi par *La bella Margherita*». («Learn to do some job to earn the daily bread, so you can sing *La bella Margherita* as you please»). See ROSA [1664], pp. 30-31; and MONTANARI 2017.

[35]. Also Scipione Maffei, in his 1719 *Dell'antica condizion di Verona*, wrote that «le stampe d'Italia, esiliati gli studi migliori, da cent'anni in qua se la van passando per lo più con "La bella Margherita"» («after refusing the best studies, in the last century the Italian publishers keep loitering with "La bella Margherita"»). See MAFFEI 1790, vol. III, p. 46.

[36]. FABRIS 2007, p. 207, fn. 19.

[37]. Letter in I-Ma (Archivio Falcò Pio di Savoia, B. V.N.483, no. 21, without date) quoted in OVER 2017, pp. 47-49. Some samples of traditional music in eighteenth-century Neapolitan *opere buffe* are in MATTEI 2013.

# Traditional Music in Seventeenth-Century Operas 'alla Veneziana'

In *L'Oristeo* with poetic text by Giovanni Faustini (Venice, Teatro S. Apollinare, 1651), during scene 1.9, Cavalli characterises a comic passage for Oresde with an *ostinato* ascending bass that confers a very strong 'traditional' connotation to the piece. This *arietta*, however, probably did not belong to that musical context, since its musical features, apart from the bass, seem not to be traditional. Its sung part, structured with an insistent *ribattuto* that denies a proper and recognisable melodic profile, together with its repetitions «con voi, con voi» and «o luci, o luci», are clearly idiomatic of the seventeenth-century operatic language (Ex. 6)[38].

Ex. 6: Extract from *L'Oristeo* by G. Faustini and F. Cavalli (score in I-Vnm, fol. 26v).

| Oresde | Occhi belli, | Oh beautiful eyes, |
| | ladroncelli, | little thieves, |
| | di caligini, | black because of haze |
| | di fuligini | and soot, |
| | fatti neri in volta andate | you keep wandering |
| | e di giorno anco rubate: | and steal [hearts] also during the day: |

---

[38]. *L'Oristeo*, pp. 31-32 (copy in I-MOe, 70.F.25.9). This libretto's *editio princeps* is transcribed in Badolato 2012, pp. 51, 352-391. Manuscript score in I-Vnm (It. Cl. IV, 367 =9891).

> con voi, spiriti miei,

> diventare assassino anch'io vorrei.

> Deh, tingermi lasciate

> con il vostro carbone, o luci amate.

> together with you, my spirits,

> I would become a murderer too.

> Please, oh lovely lights, let me dye my eyes

> with the black of your coal.

Another case of apparent quotation comes from the score of *Il Xerse* by Cavalli on a libretto by Niccolò Minato (premiered in Venice, Teatro SS. Giovani e Paolo, 1655)[39]. This opera also contains a passage that for many reasons seems to recall a piece from outside the operatic world. I refer to the *canzonetta* that the comic character Elviro «vestito da vendifiori» (dressed as a flower seller) sings in the scene II.1, soon after the princess Amastre finishes her aria of desperation 'Speranze, fermate' (Hopes, stop). With its disruptive function, the piece by Elviro 'A chi voler fiora' (Who wants flowers?) interrupts the serious moment with something suddenly funny. The language of his lines is intentionally incorrect, since the character is in disguise and speaks the so-called *lingua franca*[40].

ELVIRO

> A chi voler fiora

> de bella giardina!

> Giacinta, indïana,

> tulipana, gelsomina.

> A chi voler fiora

> de bella giardina!

> Hey, who wants flowers

> from a beautiful garden?

> Hyacinths, Indian flowers

> tulips, jasmines!

> Hey, who wants flowers

> from a beautiful garden?

From a musical point of view, this intervention seems to be very simple. Its persistent tonic pedal in the continuo, with only a few moves to the third and the fifth in the vocal part, together with its leaping melodic line, recalls the probably traditional origins of the piece (Ex. 7). However, since Elviro sings in disguise, in a strange Italian, and purposely wants to look as foreign as possible, it is possible that this piece does not belong to the traditional music context, but only imitates some features of its language[41].

---

[39]. MINATO – CAVALLI 2019. Venetian score in I-Vnm (It. Cl. IV, 374 =9898).

[40]. MINATO 1654, p. 24 (copy in I-Bc, Lo.7385). A similar linguistic treatment can be noted in the part of the comic character Scarimagol from Antonio Draghi's (libretto and music) *Vero amor fa soave ogni fatica* (Vienna 1667, music lost, copy of the libretto in CZ-Pu, 9.D.625), edited in NOE – USULA forthcoming.

[41]. The same musical structure characterises many passages in the second *intermedio*, *La fiera di Farfa* inserted in 1639 into *L'Egisto, overo Chi soffre speri* by Rospigliosi, Mazzocchi and Marazzoli. In this piece, many street-cries are set to music with melodic jumps over a tonic pedal in the bass. See for example the music for the lines of the street merchants, «Chi vuol comprare fettucce rare?», «Bicchieri, caraffe a un paolo il pezzo!», «I cappelli di paglia!» («Who wants to buy beautiful strips?»; «Glasses, pitchers, one *paolo* each!»; «Straw hats!»), but also the intervention by the fortune-teller «La ventura, la ventura!» («The fortune! the fortune!»), and many others. I thank Margaret Murata and Barbara Nestola for suggesting me to have a closer look to this *intermedio*.

Ex. 7: Extract from *Il Xerse* by N. Minato and F. Cavalli (score in I-Vnm, fol. 67v).

In one last group of cases, the quotations of traditional music are apparently suggested by their introductory lines, but their text and music show some distance from their likely traditional origins. Among these examples there is *L'Orione* by Francesco Melosio and Francesco Cavalli, composed in 1642 but performed only in 1654 in the theatre of the Royal Ducal Palace in Milan[42]. During this opera, the protagonist unconsciously makes Diana and Aurora fall in love with himself, and thus at the very beginning of the second act he involuntarily attracts the hate of Apollo (Diana's brother), Venere (Diana's enemy), and Amore (Venere's son). After discovering that Titone (Aurora's husband) also detests Orione, his sly servant Filotero addresses the protagonist in the scene II.5 with some comic lines that seem to refer to a well recognisable piece, preceded by the words «Tu sì che puoi cantar *quella* canzona» (Now you can really sing *that* [famous] song). Soon follows a rounded one-strophe *canzonetta*[43]:

| FILOTERO | Or che dici, Orïon? | Now what do you say, Orion? |
| ORIONE | Piango il mio fato. | I cry because of my Fates. |
| FILOTERO | Tu sì che puoi cantar quella canzona: | Now you can really sing that famous song: |
|  | 'Che diavolo sarà? | 'What the devil! |
|  | Sempre Amor la vuol con me, | Cupid always plays a trick on me; |
|  | e finito un mal non è, | one is done, |
|  | ch'un peggior ei me ne fa. | he prepares another even worse. |
|  | Che diavolo [sarà?]' | What the devil!' |

See ROSPIGLIOSI 1998, pp. 116-124, at 116-117; and ROSPIGLIOSI – MAZZOCCHI – MARAZZOLI 1982, fols. 173r-250r, at 177r, 179r, 185r, 191v.
[42]. See the introduction in MELOSIO – CAVALLI 2015.
[43]. *Ibidem*, pp. lxi (ll. 905-911), 53 (bb. 131-150); score in I-Vnm (Cl. IV, 444 =9968).

The aforementioned introductory line to this little composition in *settenari* and *ottonari tronchi* on an enclosed rhyme scheme ($x_7y_8y_8x_8x_7$) seems to suggest the traditional roots of the piece, and it refers to a composition as if it were quoted[44]. However, if on the one hand the dramatic context and the poetic text of this *canzonetta* seem to confirm its traditional origins, then, on the other, its musical structure looks heavily manipulated by Cavalli. He set to music both the introductory line and one phrase of the rounded piece in the same way: this seems a strange choice if one were to assume that he would have wanted to present a well-known piece of music to the audience. Indeed, in this way any effect of sudden recognition and hence any dramatic efficacy is completely negated. Furthermore, some musical features seem to declare openly a deep intervention by Cavalli (if not the piece's Cavallian origins). For example the repeated melodic descending profile of the bass in the introductory line and in the *canzonetta* itself reveals the composer's interference. Similarly, the frequent use of the neighbouring notes as a structural element of the sung part, and finally the general weak melodic and harmonic structure of these few bars suggest that the musical material in this passage has been manipulated by Cavalli (Ex. 8).

The same kind of ambiguity in 'Che diavolo sarà?' can be noted in the scene 1.6 from *La finta pazza* by Giulio Strozzi and Francesco Sacrati, which premiered in 1641 in Venice at the Teatro Novissimo[45]. Here the female protagonist Deidamia sings to the court *musico* Eunuco the lines «vogliam teco dir quella | che ci sembra sì bella» (we want to perform with you that song that is so beautiful to us). Then the invitation is followed by a *canzonetta a tre voci* that starts with the line «Il canto m'alletta» (The singing delights me). Deidamia's introductory lines seem to precede a well-known piece, suggesting that it could contain some traditional elements; however, the hypothetical original music material looks so deeply manipulated in the score as to be unlikely[46].

---

44. The text and the music of this passage are different from the ones in the *arietta* 'E che diavolo sarà' preserved on the Isola Bella (Lago Maggiore) in the music collection of the princes Borromeo (MS.02.03; thanks are due to Lorena Barale, Archivio Borromeo dell'Isola Bella, for providing me with this information): «E che diavolo sarà? | Perché tante bardellette | voglian dar leggi sì strette | al umana libertà? | E che diavolo sarà?». For Borromeo's music collection, see BOGGIO 2004 and USULA 2018.

45. About this opera and its numerous revivals see MICHELASSI 2000; MICHELASSI 2013; USULA 2018.

46. Both the strophes of this *canzonetta* appear in the 1641 Venetian edition of the libretto (ll. 514-519 and 524-529, in MICHELASSI 2013). Only the first one remains in the Feboarmonico version printed in Piacenza in 1644 (ll. 394-399), and in the only surviving score linked to the touring companies' performances, held in I-Bborromeo (MS.AU.298, fols 32v-33r). See STROZZI – SACRATI 2018.

Ex. 8: Extract from *L'Orione* by F. Melosio and F. Cavalli (score in I-Vnm, fols 46v-47r).

| DEIDAMIA | Quando sprigionerai quel canto grato, | When will you produce your pleasant singing, |
| --- | --- | --- |
| | musico addormentato? | sleepy *musico*? |
| | [...] | [...] |
| | vogliam teco dir quella | we want to perform with you that song |
| | che ci sembra sì bella. | that is so beautiful to us |
| | [...] | [...] |
| | *Canzonetta a tre voci* | *Song for three voices* |

EUNUCO, DEIDAMIA e ACHILLE. *A tre.*

(1)     Il canto m'alletta,     The singing delights me,
        la gioia m'abbonda,     the joy replenishes me,
        il suon mi diletta,     the sound amuses me,
        il ben mi circonda:     the prosperity surrounds me:
        ceno, gioco, amoreggio,     I dine, I play, I spoon, shall the aches I will live

| | |
|---|---|
| e 'l mal ch'ho da provar non sia mai peggio. | be no bigger that these. |
| [...] | [...] |

(2)

| | |
|---|---|
| Qui scherzo, qui rido, | Here I joke, I laugh, |
| amor non mi offende: | Love does not bother me: |
| gli credo, mi fido, | I believe him, I trust him, |
| timor non mi prende. | I do not fear. |
| Se non ho senno ho sorte, | When I am not wise, the fortune assists me |
| e sol del mio gioir l'ore son corte. | and my only problem is the shortness of the joyful moments. |

Indeed, this passage's musical features reveal a strong connection to a more learned musical language, although its roots still could be identified as traditional. The basso ostinato with the descending tetrachord that characterises 'Il canto m'alletta' presents a rhythmic and melodic structure with traditional origins (Ex. 9); however, it is worth noting the closeness of the passage «gioco, gioco, amoreggio» by Achille and Eunuco with «io son tua | tuo son io | speme mia | dillo di» in the duet «Pur ti miro | Pur ti godo» with text (and music?) by Benedetto Ferrari, inserted in the extant scores for *L'incoronazione di Poppea*[47]. Thus, this polyphonic passage preserves only a few characteristics of its likely ancestor: undoubtedly, as well as the aforementioned example from *L'Orione*, it is hard to identify it as a direct traditional music quotation[48].

---

[47]. See the famous duet for Nerone and Poppea in the opera by Giovan Francesco Busenello and (who knows to what extent) Claudio Monteverdi (premiere: Teatro Ss. Giovanni e Paolo, Venice, 1643) in the recent critical edition by Hendrik Schulze: BUSENELLO – MONTEVERDI 2017, pp. 256 (ll. 1426-1437) and 170-173 (bb. 349-473).

[48]. We find similar features in two other Venetian operas from the mid-century, both set to music by Cavalli: *La Rosinda* with text by Giovanni Faustini (premiere in 1651), and the already mentioned *Xerse* with libretto by Minato (1655). In both cases, comic characters sing pieces preceded by sentences that suggest their notoriety. However, from a musical point of view both of them do not even sound like traditional ones. In the first case, the comic character Aurilla suggests Vafrillo and Rudione to sing a piece together in the scene III.11. She proposes «Cantiam, cantiamo a tre | "Amor, di nostra fé"» («Let's sing all three "Love, of our faith"»), and to be sure that Vafrillo can sing it, she openly asks him «la sai?» («do you know that?»), and after he answers «La so, la so» («I know it»), Rudione adds «Anch'io vi seguirò» («I will follow you too»). However, the resulting passage 'a 3' has a very refined counterpoint structure, with reiterated syncopations on the word «stringi [i nodi]» («tie the knots») and even groups of four descending semiquavers for the first syllable of the repeated word «spargi» («spread»; in the line «spargi, spargi il tuo mel sui nostri amori», «spread you honey on our loves»). This passage is in *La Rosinda*'s *editio princeps* edited in BADOLATO 2012, p. 425 (ll. 1290-1295), and in the manuscript score held in I-Vnm (It. Cl. IV 370 =9894, fols. 79r-81r). Similarly, the comic characters Clito and Elviro in the scene II.16 of *Il Xerse* sing the passage «A labbra di rose» («to lips of roses») after making sure to know the same 'famous' piece. Clito comes up suggesting «Ora lieti cantiamo» («now let's sing joyfully»), and asks Elviro: «Sai | la canzonetta de la donna avara?» («do you know that song about the stingy [e.g. bashful] woman?»). After the companion's

Ex. 9: Extract from *La finta pazza* by G. Strozzi and F. Sacrati (score in I-Bborromeo, fols. 32v-33r).

positive response, they start the piece; nevertheless, it does not present recognisable traditional features. Apart from the descending tetrachord (A to E) that appears only in the bb. 2-5, the rest of the piece is characterised by a number of imitative passages in long sequences that in no way recall traditional music. See MINATO – CAVALLI 2019; and the Venetian score in I-Vnm (It. Cl. IV, 374 =9898; fols. 110r-111r).

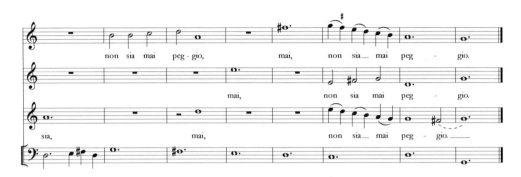

## Traditional Dances

The dance-passages inserted into the Venetian operas, both in the sung and in the instrumental parts, often intentionally evoked the sound of the traditional dance music, and were meant to be recognised as such. Wolfgang Osthoff already highlighted one interesting case in this regard in *L'Egisto* by Faustini and Cavalli, performed at the Teatro S. Cassiano in 1643[49]. In this opera, the crazy protagonist sings the aria 'Io son Cupido' in scene III.9, pretending, in his altered mental state, to be the young god of love. This aria is characterised by a rhythm typical of the sarabande, while the bass evokes the *ciaccona*. However, it looks more like a dance in traditional style than like a direct quotation. In regard to both the text and the structure of the melodic lines in the sung part and in the bass, this piece contributes to strengthen the sense of Egisto's temporary craziness. Furthermore, this example shows how the composer could give a meaningful connotation to an aria that the librettist did not think of as a traditional quotation[50].

| Egisto | Io son Cupido, | I am Cupid |
|---|---|---|
| | che per la terra | and all around the earth |
| | vo mascherato. | I go in disguise. |
| | L'arco dorato | My golden bow |
| | porto nel ciglio, | is in my eyes, |
| | io son vermiglio: | I have ruddy cheeks: |
| | non mi vedete? | can't you see me? |
| | Per vagheggiarmi, | To admire me |
| | donne, correte. | women, come running. |

---

[49]. See Osthoff 1964, p. 48; and Osthoff 2018, p. xxviii. For *L'Egisto*'s *editio princeps* see Badolato 2012, pp. 48-49 and 116-161. The two extant scores are held in I-Vnm (Cl. IV, 411 =9935) and A-Wn (Mus. Hs.16452).

[50]. The text of the aria 'Io son Cupido' is ediyed in Badolato 2012, p. 155, ll. 1588-1596; and the music is present in both the surviving scores (I-Vnm, fol. 90r; and A-Wn, fols 105v-106r).

Ex. 10: Extract from *L'Egisto* by G. Faustini and F. Cavalli (copy in I-Vnm, fol. 90r).

Sometimes the reference to some traditional dance was suggested by the librettist, but the composer disregarded it. This is what happens in *La Didone* by Busenello and Cavalli (Teatro S. Cassiano, 1641)[51]. In scene III.2, the poet refers to two dances when Iarba meets two Damigelle (damsels) and gives them proof of his temporary madness. Here the male character sees some imaginary flies flying around his head and sings that they dance the canary-dance («la canaria»), but the Damigella II answers him that his brain (instead of the flies) is flying and beating the rhythm of a *ciaccona*[52]. Cavalli did not adopt the musical suggestions by Busenello and set this passage to music without any reference to the quoted dances, in a simple recitative style[53].

Ex. 11: Extract from *Didone* by G. F. Busenello and F. Cavalli (score in I-Vnm, fol. 95v).

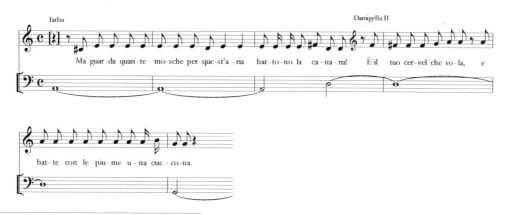

---

[51]. BUSENELLO – CAVALLI forthcoming; score in I-Vnm (It. Cl. IV, 355 =9879).

[52]. See HUDSON – LITTLE 2001. Quotations of traditional dances in the early operas 'alla veneziana' appear also in the librettos by Benedetto Ferrari. For example, at the end of the second Act of his *La ninfa avara* (The stingy [e.g. chaste] nymph, music lost), the character Lilla anticipates the closing instrumental piece with the line «danziamo al suon dell'onda una corrente» («Let's dance a courante together with sound of the waves»). See BADOLATO – MARTORANA 2013, p. 167, l. 612.

[53]. The text of this passage is extracted from the score in I-Vnm (fol. 95v), and is confirmed by the 1656 Venetian edition of the libretto, printed into BUSENELLO 1656, second libretto: *La Didone*, pp. 1-80: 58.

| IARBA | Ma guarda quante mosche per quest'aria | Look how many flies in the air |
|---|---|---|
| | battono la canaria! | beat the rhythm of the canary! |
| DAMIGELLA II | È il tuo cervel che vola, | [What you see is not flies:] it is your brain that flies |
| | e batte con le piume una ciaccona. | and with its wings beats the rhythm of a *ciaccona*. |

One of the most important and famous traditional references in an opera 'alla veneziana' is the passage in dance-style sung by Valletto in the scene 1.6 of *L'incoronazione di Poppea*[54]. After accusing Seneca of bad faith, the adolescent complains about the recommendations, which the philosopher dispenses as if they were «misteri» (mysteries), while, according to the boy, they actually are «canzoni» (songs, i.e. nonsenses, mockeries)[55].

| VALLETTO | M'accende pure a sdegno | This painter of detailed and beautiful concepts |
|---|---|---|
| | questo miniator de' bei concetti; | turns me to indignation; |
| | non posso stare al segno, | I cannot stay calm |
| | mentr'egli incanta altrui con aurei detti. | while he enchants others with his golden sentences. |
| | Queste del suo cervel mere invenzioni | These mere inventions of his intellect |
| | le vende per misteri, e son canzoni. | he sells as mysteries, while they are songs. |

In the surviving scores to *Poppea* the last word of this passage is set to music in a traditional dance-style music, more specifically a *ciaccona*, which immediately recalls to the audience the traditional roots of the musical moment. This bass was used in some compositions by Monteverdi — such as in the madrigal *Zefiro torna e di soavi accenti*, and in the passage sung by Iro in *Il ritorno d'Ulisse in patria*, on the words «chi lo consola?» (scene III.1)[56]. The case of *Poppea*, however, seems to be more meaningful. The melodic and rhythmic structure of this *ciaccona* gives the word «canzoni» a strong and unexpected musical characterisation with traditional roots that strengthens the concept of low esteem that Valletto expresses against Seneca's words. Apparently, for the composer no other musical connotation than a traditional dance style could demonstrate the change of direction towards a demeaning sense[57].

---

[54]. The complex textual tradition of *L'incoronazione di Poppea* is studied in CHIARELLI 1974; CHIARELLI 2011; CURTIS 1989; FABBRI 1993; ROSAND 1994; CARTER 1997; CARTER 2002, pp. 263-296; ROSAND 2005; ROSAND 2012; BIANCONI 2009; USULA 2019.

[55]. This passage is present in the 1656 libretto printed into *Delle ore ociose* by Busenello and edited by Lorenzo Bianconi in BUSENELLO – MONTEVERDI 2011, pp. lxxv-xciii: lxxix (ll. 351-356). Extant scores in I-Vnm (It. Cl. IV, 439=9963; fol. 31r) and I-Nc (Rari 6.4.1; fol. 29r).

[56]. *Zefiro torna* appears for the first time in 1632 in the collection *Scherzi musicali, cioè arie et madrigali in stil recitativo con una ciaccona a 1 et 2 voci* (only extant copy in PL-WRu, 50642 Muz.), recently edited in MONTEVERDI 2002, pp. 72-83. Iro's intervention is in the manuscript score of *Il Ritorno d'Ulisse in patria* (only extant copy in A-Wn, fol 104r), edited by Rinaldo Alessandrini in MONTEVERDI 2007, pp. 95-96.

[57]. See OSSI 1988.

# Traditional Music in Seventeenth-Century Operas 'alla Veneziana'

Ex. 12: Extract from *L'incoronazione di Poppea* by G. F. Busenello and C. Monteverdi (?) (copy in I-Vnm, fol. 31r).

## The Quotations of Traditional Music and Their Function

Quoting pre-existing music materials in art music is a very ancient practice and dates back at least to the early fifteenth-century in both sacred and secular music[58]. The original element that Michael Praetorius called 'cantus prius factus' very often had traditional origins, and it played different roles in the history of western music[59].

On the one hand, the principal goal for the interpolation of traditional songs into operatic dramatic plots was usually the creation of an unexpected comic effect. On the other, the use of dances with traditional origins contributed to link contexts where those dances were performed, although very distantly one from the other, like private aristocratic parties and traditional public feasts, as well as institutionalised operatic entertainments. The main function of the traditional music references in seventeenth-century operas seems, in fact, to be the connection between the worlds inside and outside the theatre. These quotations had the power to cross the city-soundscape's layers, but not only spatially. In fact, the persistence of very old traditional pieces, like the early sixteenth-century 'La bella traditora' in the mid-seventeenth-century society, confirms that the connecting attitude of the operatic genre played an important role also from a chronological point of view.

---

[58]. See BROWN 1959.

[59]. Praetorius uses this expression in his *Syntagma musicum* while analysing different typologies of *quodlibet* and their quotations of traditional music; quoted in MANIATES – BRANSCOMBE – FREEDMAN 2001.

# Nicola Usula

However, this attitude to link and to picture spatial, contextual and chronological references in front of the audience was not particular to the operatic genre only. In fact, the main ancestor of *opere in musica*, the regular spoken theatre, developed this function through incidental music long before opera was born[60]. From this point of view, the traditional music quotations in operas played the same role that dances and songs already had on the theatrical stage, revealing that this phenomenon crossed the borders of the two genres, and related to fictional entertainments in general, and to that innate human tendency to reproduce onstage the coordinates of reality.

## List of abbreviations

| | |
|---|---|
| A-Wn | Vienna, Österreichische Nationalbibliothek |
| D-Mbs | Munich, Bayerische Staatsbibliothek |
| GB-Lbl | London, British Library |
| I-Bborromeo | Isola Bella (Lago Maggiore), Archivio Borromeo |
| I-Bc | Bologna, Museo internazionale e Biblioteca della musica |
| I-Ma | Milan, Biblioteca Ambrosiana |
| I-Moe | Modena, Biblioteca Estense Universitaria |
| I-Nc | Naples, Biblioteca del Conservatorio S. Pietro a Majella |
| I-Rn | Rome, Biblioteca Nazionale Centrale |
| I-Rvat | Vatican, Vatican Library |
| I-Vc | Venice, Museo Correr, Biblioteca |
| I-Vnm | Venice, Biblioteca Nazionale Marciana |
| PL-WRu | Wrocław, University Library |

## Bibliography

Antonucci – Bianconi 2013
Antonucci, Fausta – Bianconi, Lorenzo. 'Miti, tramiti e trame: Cicognini, Cavalli e l'Argonauta', in: Cicognini, Giacinto Andrea – Cavalli, Francesco – Apolloni, Giovanni Filippo – Stradella, Alessandro. *Il novello Giasone*, facsimile, edited by Nicola Usula, Milan, Ricordi, 2013 (Drammaturgia Musicale Veneta, 3), pp. vii-xliv.

Aureli 1657
Aureli, Aurelio. *Le fortune di Rodope e Damira*, Venice, Andrea Giuliani, 1657.

---

60. See Savage 2001; Murata 2007; and Lazzi 2002.

# Traditional Music in Seventeenth-Century Operas 'alla Veneziana'

Badolato 2012
Badolato, Nicola. *I drammi musicali di Giovanni Faustini per Francesco Cavalli*, Florence, Olschki, 2012 (Historiae Musicae Cultores, 122).

Badolato – Martorana 2013
*I drammi musicali veneziani di Benedetto Ferrari*, edited by Nicola Badolato and Vincenzo Martorana, Florence, Olschki, 2013 (Historiae Musicae Cultores, 128).

Bellina 2000
Bellina, Anna Laura. '«Brevità, frequenza e varietà»: Cristoforo Ivanovich librettista e storico dell'opera veneziana', in: *Musica e storia*, no. 2 (2000), pp. 367-390.

Bianconi 1991
Bianconi, Lorenzo. *Music in the Seventeenth Century*, English translation by David Bryant, Cambridge, Cambridge University Press, 1987.

Bianconi 2009
Id. 'Indagini sull' «Incoronazione»', in: *«Finché non splende in ciel notturna face». Studi in memoria di Francesco Degrada*, edited by Cesare Fertonani, Emilio Sala and Claudio Toscani, Milan, LED, 2009, pp. 53-72.

Bianconi – Walker 1975
Id. – Walker, Thomas. 'Dalla *Finta pazza* alla *Veremonda*: storie di Febiarmonici', in: *Rivista italiana di Musicologia*, x (1975), pp. 379-454.

Bianconi – Walker 1984
Id. – Id. 'Production, Consumption and Political Function of Seventeenth-Century Opera', in: *Early Music History*, iv (1984), pp. 209-296.

Boggio 2004
Boggio, Enrico. *Il fondo musiche dell'Archivio Borromeo dell'Isola Bella*, Lucca, LIM, 2004 (Cataloghi di fondi musicali del Piemonte, 3).

Boyd – Pagano – Hanley 2001
Boyd, Malcolm – Pagano, Roberto – Hanley, Edwin. 'Scarlatti, (Pietro) Alessandro', in: *Oxford Music Online*, 2001, <http://www.oxfordmusiconline.com>, accessed January 2023.

Brown 2001
Brown, Alan. 'Galliard', in: *Oxford Music Online*, 2001, <http://www.oxfordmusiconline.com>, accessed January 2023.

Brown 1959
Brown, Howard Mayer. 'The *chanson rustique*. Popular Elements in the 15th- and 16th-Century Chanson', in: *Journal of the American Musicological Society*, xii/1 (1959), pp. 16-26.

**Brown 1967**
Id. *Instrumental Music Printed Before 1600: A Bibliography*, Cambridge (MA), Harvard University Press, 1967.

**Brown 2000**
Brown, Jennifer Williams. '«Innsbruck, ich muss dich lassen»: Cesti, *Orontea*, and the Gelone Problem', in: *Cambridge Opera Journal*, xii/3 (2000), pp. 179-217.

**Busenello 1656**
Busenello, Gian Francesco. *Delle ore ociose, Parte prima*, Venice, Andrea Giuliani, 1656.

**Busenello – Cavalli forthcoming**
Id. – Cavalli, Francesco. *La Didone (1641)*, edited by Dinko Fabris and Sara Elisa Stangalino, Kassel, Bärenreiter, forthcoming (Francesco Cavalli: Opere).

**Busenello – Monteverdi 2011**
Id. – Monteverdi, Claudio. *L'incoronazione di Poppea*, facsimile of the Neapolitan score, edited by Lorenzo Bianconi, Milan, Ricordi, 2011 (Drammaturgia Musicale Veneta, 2).

**Busenello – Monteverdi 2017**
Id. – Id. *L'incoronazione di Poppea*, edited by Hendrik Schulze, Kassel, Bärenreiter, 2017.

**Carpani 2008**
Carpani, Roberta. 'Comici, Febiarmonici e Gesuiti a Milano: intrecci e contaminazioni. Problemi della circolazione delle opere di Francesco Cavalli', in: *Musica e Storia*, xvi/1 (2008), pp. 5-39.

**Carter 1997**
Carter, Tim. 'Re-Reading «Poppea»: Some Thoughts on Music and Meaning in Monteverdi's Last Opera', in: *Journal of the Royal Musical Association*, cxxii/2 (1997), pp. 173-204.

**Carter 2002**
Id. *Monteverdi's Musical Theatre*, New Haven-London, Yale University Press, 2002.

**Cecchi 2017**
Cecchi, Paolo. 'Sacrati, Paolo', in: *Dizionario Biografico degli Italiani. 89*, Rome, Istituto della Enciclopedia Italiana, 2017, <https://www.treccani.it/enciclopedia/paolo-sacrati_(Dizionario-Biografico)/>, accessed January 2023.

**Chiarelli 1974**
Chiarelli, Alessandra. '*L'incoronazione di Poppea* o *Il Nerone*. Problemi di filologia testuale', in: *Rivista Italiana di Musicologia*, ix (1974), pp. 117-151.

**Chiarelli 2011**
Id. 'Le fonti dell'*Incoronazione di Poppea* o *Il Nerone*: Appunti in margine', in: Busenello – Monteverdi 2011, pp. xxv-li.

## Traditional Music in Seventeenth-Century Operas 'alla Veneziana'

CICOGNINI 1649A
CICOGNINI, Giacinto Andrea. *Giasone*, Venice, Giacomo Batti, [2]1649.

CICOGNINI 1649B
ID. *Orontea*, Venice, Giacomo Batti, 1649.

CICOGNINI – CAVALLI forthcoming
ID. – CAVALLI, Francesco. *Il Giasone*, edited by Nicola Badolato, Lorenzo Bianconi, Valeria Conti and Nicola Usula, Kassel, Bärenreiter, forthcoming (Francesco Cavalli: Opere).

CLORI
*Clori. Archivio della cantata italiana*, directed by Teresa M. Gialdroni and Licia Sirch, University of Rome Tor Vergata, <http://cantataitaliana.it/>, accessed January 2023.

CONRIERI 2011
*Gli Incogniti e l'Europa*, edited by Davide Conrieri, Bologna, I libri di Emil, 2011.

CORAGO
*Corago. Repertorio e archivio di libretti del melodramma italiano dal 1600 al 1900*, directed by Angelo Pompilio, University of Bologna, <http://corago.unibo.it/>, accessed January 2023.

CURTIS 1989
CURTIS, Alan. '*La Poppea impasticciata* or, Who Wrote the Music to *L'incoronazione* (1643)?', in: *Journal of the American Musicological Society*, XLII/1 (1989), pp. 23-54.

D'ALESSANDRO 1984
D'ALESSANDRO, Domenico Antonio. 'L'opera in musica a Napoli dal 1650 al 1670', in: *Seicento napoletano. Arte, costume, ambiente*, edited by Roberto Pane, Milan, Edizioni di Comunità, 1984, pp. 409-430 and 543-549.

DAOLMI 1998
DAOLMI, Davide. *Le origini dell'opera a Milano (1598-1649)*, Turnhout, Brepols, 1998 (Studies on Italian Music History, 2).

DEISINGER 2006
DEISINGER, Marko. 'Giuseppe Tricarico – Ein Kapellmeister auf Reisen. Von Rom über Ferrara nach Wien', in: *Römische Historische Mitteilungen*, XLVIII (2006), pp. 359-394.

DEISINGER 2009
ID. 'Ein Leben zwischen Musik, Höfischem Zeremoniell und Politik: Zur Biographie und Kompositionstechnik Giuseppe Tricarios', in: *Studien zur Musikwissenschaft*, LV (2009), pp. 7-52.

DI CEGLIE 1997
DI CEGLIE, Roberto. 'Il *Dialogo sopra la poesia drammatica* di Ottaviano Castelli', in: *Studi Secenteschi*, XXXVIII (1997), pp. 338-355.

DRAGHI 1667
DRAGHI, Antonio. *Vero amor fa soave ogni fatica*, Vienna, Matteo Cosmerovio, 1667.

FABBRI 1990
FABBRI, Paolo. *Il secolo cantante*, Bologna, il Mulino, 1990.

FABBRI 1993
ID. 'New Sources for «Poppea»', in: *Music & Letters*, LXXIV/1 (1993), pp. 16-23.

FABRIS 2007
FABRIS, Dinko. *Music in Seventeenth-Century Naples. Francesco Provenzale (1624-1704)*, Aldershot, Ashgate, 2007.

GIALDRONI 1987
GIALDRONI, Teresa M. 'Francesco Provenzale e la cantata a Napoli nella seconda metà del Seicento', in: *La musica a Napoli durante il Seicento. Atti del Convegno Internazionale di Studi (Napoli, 11-14 aprile 1985)*, edited by Domenico Antonio D'Alessandro and Agostino Ziino, Rome, Torre d'Orfeo, 1987 (Miscellanea musicologica, 2), pp. 125-153.

GLIXON 2013
GLIXON, Beth L. 'Behind the Scenes of Cavalli's *Giasone* of 1649', in: *Readying Cavalli's Operas for the Stage: Manuscript, Edition, Production*, edited by Ellen Rosand, Farnham, Ashgate, 2013, pp. 137-152.

GLIXON – GLIXON 2006
EAD. – GLIXON, Jonathan E. *Inventing the Business of Opera: The Impresario and His World in Seventeenth-Century Venice*, Oxford, Oxford University Press, 2006.

GRONDA – FABBRI 1997
*Libretti d'opera italiani dal Seicento al Novecento*, edited by Giovanna Gronda and Paolo Fabbri, Milan, Mondadori, 1997.

HAMM – WALSER – WARWICK – GARRETT 2013
HAMM, Charles – WALSER, Robert – WARWICK, Jacqueline – GARRETT, Charles Hiroshi. 'Popular Music', in: *Oxford Music Online*, 2013, <http://www.oxfordmusiconline.com>, accessed January 2023.

HILL 2015
HILL, John Walter. 'Travelling Players and Venetian Opera: Further Parallels between *Commedia dell'arte* and *Dramma per musica*', in: *Passaggio in Italia: Music on the Grand Tour in the Seventeenth Century*, edited by Dinko Fabris and Margaret Murata, Turnhout, Brepols, 2015 (Music History and Performance: Practices in Context, 1), pp. 131-148.

# Traditional Music in Seventeenth-Century Operas 'alla Veneziana'

HOWARD – MORETTI 2009
HOWARD, Deborah – MORETTI, Laura. *Sound and Space in Renaissance Venice: Architecture, Music, Acoustics*, New Haven-London, Yale University Press, 2009.

HUDSON – LITTLE 2001
HUDSON, Richard – LITTLE, Meredith Ellis. 'Canary', in: *Oxford Music Online*, 2001, <http://www.oxfordmusiconline.com>, accessed January 2023.

IVANOVICH 1681
IVANOVICH, Cristoforo. *Le memorie teatrali di Venezia*, Venice, Nicolò Pezzana, 1681.

JEPPESEN 1939
JEPPESEN, Knud. 'Venetian Folk-Songs of the Renaissance', in: *Papers Read at the International Congress of Musicology Held at New York, Spetember 11ᵗʰ to 16ᵗʰ, 1939*, edited by Arthur Mendel, Gustav Reese, and Gilbert Chase, New York, American Musicological Society, 1939, pp. 62-75.

LANFOSSI 2012
LANFOSSI, Carlo. *Il teatro d'opera a Milano nella seconda metà del XVII secolo. Alcuni esempi di drammaturgia musicale tra storiografia e analisi*, Ph.D. Diss., Cremona, Università di Pavia, 2012.

LAZZI 2002
*Rime e suoni per corde spagnole: fonti per la chitarra barocca a Firenze*, edited by Giovanna Lazzi, Florence, Polistampa, 2002.

LEVE 1998
LEVE, James Samuel. *Humor and Intrigue: A Comparative Study of Comic Opera in Florence and Rome during the Late Seventeenth Century*, Ph.D. Diss., New Haven (CT), Yale University, 1998.

LEYDI 1991
LEYDI, Roberto. *L'altra musica: etnomusicologia. Come abbiamo incontrato e creduto di conoscere le musiche delle tradizioni popolari ed etniche*, Milan, Ricordi; Florence, Giunti, 1991.

LIN 2015
LIN, Thomas. *Giasone's Travels: Opera and Its Performance in the Seventeenth Century*, Ph.D. Diss., Cambridge (MA), Harvard University, 2015.

LUCINI 1690
LUCINI, Giovanni Battista. *Gli equivoci in amore overo La Rosaura*, Rome, Giovanni Francesco Buagni, 1690.

LUCINI – SCARLATTI 1885
LUCINI, Giovanni Battista – SCARLATTI, Alessandro. *La Rosaura* (acts I and II), edited by Robert Eitner, Leipzig, Breitkopf & Härtel, 1885 (Publikation älterer praktischer und theoretischer Musikwerke, 14).

MACCHIARELLA 1994
MACCHIARELLA, Ignazio. 'Appunti per una indagine sulla tradizione non scritta della musica del XVI-XVII secolo', in: *Ceciliana. Per Nino Pirrotta*, edited by Maria Antonella Balsano and Giuseppe Collisani, Palermo, Flaccovio, 1994, pp. 97-109.

MAFFEI 1790
MAFFEI, Scipione. *Opere del Maffei. 3: Dell'antica condizion di Verona*, edited by Andrea Rubbi, Venice, Antonio Curti q. Giacomo, 1790.

MAGRINI *ET. AL.* 2001
MAGRINI, Tullia – PIRROTTA, Nino – PETROBELLI, Pierluigi – ROSTAGNO, Antonio – PESTELLI, Giorgio – WATERHOUSE, John C. G. – POZZI, Raffaele. 'Italy: I. Art Music, II. Traditional Music', in: *Oxford Music Online*, 2001, <http://www.oxfordmusiconline.com>, accessed January 2023.

MANIATES – BRANSCOMBE – FREEDMAN 2001
MANIATES, Maria Rika – BRANSCOMBE, Peter – FREEDMAN, Richard. 'Quodlibet', in: *Oxford Music Online*, 2001, <http://www.oxfordmusiconline.com>, accessed January 2023.

MATTEI 2013
MATTEI, Lorenzo. 'Musica «popolare» e opera buffa: alcune intersezioni', in: *La memoria che vive: musica e cultura popolari in Puglia. Atti del convegno*, edited by Nino Blasi, Vito Carrassi, Vera Di Natale and Pierfranco Moliterni, Bari, WIP, 2013, pp. 51-56.

MELOSIO – CAVALLI 2015
MELOSIO, Francesco – CAVALLI, Francesco. *L'Orione*, edited by Davide Daolmi and Nicola Usula, Kassel, Bärenreiter, 2015 (Francesco Cavalli: Opere, 3).

MIATO 1998
MIATO, Monica. *L'Accademia degli Incogniti di Giovan Francesco Loredan, Venezia (1630-1661)*, Florence, Olschki, 1998 (Studi. Accademia toscana di scienze e lettere La Colombaria, 172).

MICHELASSI 2000
MICHELASSI, Nicola. 'La *Finta pazza* a Firenze: commedie «spagnole» e «veneziane» nel teatro di Baldracca (1641-1665)', in: *Studi Secenteschi*, XLI (2000), pp. 313-351.

MICHELASSI 2013
ID. *La doppia «Finta pazza». Un dramma veneziano in viaggio fra Italia e Francia*, 2 vols., Florence, Olschki, 2013.

MILESI 2000
*Giacomo Torelli. L'invenzione scenica nell'Europa barocca*, edited by Francesco Milesi, Fano, Fondazione Cassa di Risparmio di Fano, 2000.

## Traditional Music in Seventeenth-Century Operas 'alla Veneziana'

MINATO 1654
MINATO, Nicolò. *Il Xerse*, Venice, Matteo Leni, 1654.

MINATO – CAVALLI 2019
MINATO, Nicolò – CAVALLI, Francesco. *Il Xerse*, edited by Hendrich Schulze and Sara Elisa Stangalino, Kassel, Bärenreiter, 2019 (Francesco Cavalli: Opere).

MONALDINI 2000
MONALDINI, Sergio. 'Gli anni ferraresi di Antonio Draghi', in: *«Quel novo Cario, quel divin Orfeo». Antonio Draghi da Rimini a Vienna*, edited by Emilio Sala and Davide Daolmi, Lucca, LIM, 2000, pp. 29-34.

MONTANARI 2017
MONTANARI, Tomaso. 'Rosa, Salvatore', in: *Dizionario Biografico degli Italiani. 88*, Rome, Istituto della Enciclopedia Italiana, 2017, < https://www.treccani.it/enciclopedia/salvatore-rosa_(Dizionario-Biografico)/>, accessed January 2023.

MONTEVERDI 2007
MONTEVERDI, Claudio. *Il Ritorno d'Ulisse in patria*, edited by Rinaldo Alessandrini, Kassel, Bärenreiter, 2007.

MONTEVERDI 2002
ID. *Scherzi musicali a una e due voci (1632)*, edited Frank Dobbins and Anna Maria Vacchelli, Cremona, Fondazione Claudio Monteverdi, 2002 (Edizione Nazionale di tutte le opere di Claudio Monteverdi).

MOOT 1978
MOOT, Linda L. *«La Traditora»: The Progeny of an Italian Dance-Song*, Ph.D. Diss., Philadelphia (PA), University of Pennsylvania, 1978.

MURATA 1995
MURATA, Margaret. 'Why the First Opera Given in Paris Wasn't Roman', in: *Cambridge Opera Journal*, VII/2 (1995), pp. 87-105.

MURATA 2007
EAD. 'Guitar *passacagli* and vocal *arie*', in: *La monodia in Toscana alle soglie del XVII secolo. Atti del Convegno di Studi (Pisa, 17-18 dicembre 2004)*, edited by Francesca Menchelli-Buttini, Pisa, ETS, 2007, pp. 81-116.

NESS – KOLCZYNSKI 2001
NESS, Arthur J. – KOLCZYNSKI, C. A. 'Sources of Lute Music', in: *Oxford Music Online*, 2001, <http://www.oxfordmusiconline.com>, accessed January 2023.

NOE – USULA forthcoming
NOE, Alfred – USULA, Nicola. *«Le fatiche di un povero versificatore». I testi drammatici per musica di Antonio Draghi*, Vienna, Böhlau, forthcoming.

NOLFI 1642A
NOLFI, Vincenzo. *Il Bellerofonte*, Venice, Giovanni Battista Surian, 1642.

NOLFI 1642B
ID. *Il Bellerofonte*, [Venice], n.p., 1642 (in folio edition with engravings).

OSSI 1988
OSSI, Massimo. '«L'armonia raddoppiata»: on Claudio Monteverdi's «Zefiro torna», Heinrich Schütz's «Es steh Gott auf», and other Early Seventeenth-Century *Ciaccone*', in: *Studi musicali*, XVII/2 (1988), pp. 225-252.

OSTHOFF 1964
OSTHOFF, Wolfgang. 'Maske und Musik. Die Gestaltwerdung der Oper in Venedig', in: *Castrum Peregrini*, no. 65 (1964), pp. 10-49.

OSTHOFF 2018
ID. 'La musica della pazzia nella *Finta pazza* di Francesco Sacrati', in: STROZZI – SACRATI 2018, pp. xvii-xxxv.

OVER 2017
OVER, Berthold. 'Spurensuche. Agostino Steffanis vokale Kammermusik in Rom', in: *Agostino Steffani: Europäischer Komponist, hannoverscher Diplomat und Bischof der Leibniz-Zeit. European Composer, Hanoverian Diplomat and Bishop in the Age of Leibniz*, edited by Claudia Kaufold, Nicole K. Strohmann and Colin Timms, Göttingen, Vandenhoeck & Ruprecht, 2017, pp. 41-53.

PEGG 2001
PEGG, Carole. 'Folk Music' (2001), in: *Oxford Music Online*, 2001, <http://www.oxfordmusiconline.com>, accessed January 2023.

PORTER 2001
PORTER, James. 'Traditional Music of Europe' (2001), in: *Oxford Music Online*, 2001, <http://www.oxfordmusiconline.com>, accessed January 2023.

ROSA [1664]
ROSA, Salvator. *Satire dedicate a Settano*, Amsterdam [*recte* Rome], Severo Prothomastix, [1664?].

ROSAND 1991
ROSAND, Ellen. *Opera in Seventeenth-Century Venice: The Creation of a Genre*, Berkeley (CA), University of California Press, 1991.

ROSAND 1994
EAD. 'Did Monteverdi Write *L'incoronazione di Poppea* and Does it Matter?', in: *Opera News*, LIX/1 (1994), pp. 20-23.

# Traditional Music in Seventeenth-Century Operas 'alla Veneziana'

ROSAND 2005
EAD. '*L'incoronazione di Poppea* di Francesco Cavalli', in: *Francesco Cavalli: La circolazione dell'opera veneziana nel Seicento*, edited by Dinko Fabris, Naples, Turchini, 2005, pp. 119-146.

ROSAND 2012
EAD. *Le ultime opere di Monteverdi. Trilogia veneziana*, Italian edition edited by Federico Lazzaro, Milan, Ricordi, 2012.

ROSPIGLIOSI 1998
ROSPIGLIOSI, Giulio. *Melodrammi profani*, edited by Danilo Romei, Florence, Studio Editoriale Fiorentino, 1998.

ROSPIGLIOSI – MAZZOCCHI – MARAZZOLI 1982
ROSPIGLIOSI, Giulio – MAZZOCCHI, Virgilio – MARAZZOLI, Marco. *L'Egisto, overo Chi soffre speri*, facsimile, edited by Howard Mayer Brown, New York-London, Garland, 1982 (Italian Opera, 1640-1770, 61).

SALERNO 2000
SALERNO, Gildo. 'I libretti di Draghi o «Le virtù dell'obbedienza» («[...] chi non diventerebbe poeta per Cesare?»)', in: *«Quel novo Cario, quel divin Orfeo»...*, *op. cit.*, pp. 35-59.

SAVAGE 2001
SAVAGE, Roger. 'Incidental' (2001), in: *Oxford Music Online*, 2001, <http://www.oxfordmusiconline.com>, accessed January 2023.

SELFRIDGE-FIELD 2007
SELFRIDGE-FIELD, Eleanor. *A New Chronology of Venetian Opera and Related Genres, 1660-1760*, Stanford, Stanford University Press, 2007.

STROZZI – SACRATI 2018
STROZZI, Giulio – SACRATI, Francesco. *La finta pazza*, facsimile edited by Nicola Usula, Milan, Ricordi, 2018 (Drammaturgia Musicale Veneta, 1).

TEDESCO 1995
TEDESCO, Anna. 'Note sui personaggi calabresi nell'opera napoletana del Seicento', in: *Fra oralità e scrittura: studi sulla musica calabrese*, edited by Ignazio Macchiarella, Lamezia Terme, A.M.A. Calabria, 1995, pp. 139-151.

USULA 2018
USULA, Nicola. 'One More Gem for «Isabella»: The Score of *La finta pazza* in the Music Collection of Vitaliano VI Borromeo', in: STROZZI – SACRATI 2018, pp. xxxvii-lii.

USULA 2019
ID. '«Qual linea al centro»: New Sources and Considerations on *L'incoronazione di Poppea*', in: *Il Saggiatore musicale*, XXVI/1 (2019), pp. 23-60.

WALKER 1976
WALKER, Thomas. 'Gli errori di «Minerva al tavolino». Osservazioni sulla cronologia delle prime opere veneziane', in: *Venezia e il melodramma nel Seicento*, edited by Maria Teresa Muraro, Florence, Olschki, 1976 (Studi di Musica Veneta, 5), pp. 7-16.

WEAVER – WEAVER 1978
WEAVER, Robert Lamar – WEAVER, Norma Wright. *A Chronology of Music in the Florentine Theater 1590-1750: Operas, Prologues, Finales, Intermezzos and Plays with Incidental Music*, Detroit, Information Coordinators, 1978.

WHENHAM 2004
WHENHAM, John. 'Perspectives on the Chronology of the First Decade of Public Opera at Venice', in: *Il Saggiatore musicale*, XI/2 (2004), pp. 253-302.

WILBOURNE 2016
WILBOURNE, Emily. *Seventeenth-Century Opera and the Sound of the Commedia dell'Arte*, Chicago-London, University of Chicago Press, 2016.

# Forms of Circulation of Musical Knowledge in Eighteenth-Century Italy: Giambattista Martini's *Risposta* to «abate Pavona friulano»

*Elia Pivetta*
(Università di Pavia)

Considering its 'cultural geography' — that is to say, viewing it from the perspective of the places within which cultural phenomena develop — eighteenth-century Italy was a constellation of urban centres which were, albeit to different degrees, desirable destinations for artists, men of letters and prominent figures from all over Europe[1]. Musicians embarked on a Grand Tour through Italy for a number of reasons, but above all the desire to enrich their professional training. The main attraction of some cities was the presence of institutions considered centres for certain fields, particularly the conservatories in Naples, which were favoured destinations for those wishing to study improvisation and composition using *partimento*[2] methods. In other cases, the importance of a city was more closely linked to a single musician. For example, Giuseppe Tartini's teaching was responsible for the prominence of the so-called 'School of Nations' in Padua[3]. The same was true of Bologna, which was frequented throughout the eighteenth century by numerous musicians eager to learn the art of counterpoint under the guidance of Giambattista Martini[4].

In either case, improving one's musical skills required travelling to a city and residing there for a more or less prolonged period, in order either to attend an institution, spend time

---

[1]. See De Seta 2014; Sweet 2012, pp. 1-22; Mellace 2017.

[2]. On Neapolitan conservatories, see Cafiero 2020, pp. 3-42; Sanguinetti 2012, pp. 29-46. The case of Venice was rather particular, since the *ospedali* tended to select experienced maestros to lead their choirs, to guarantee a solid musical training to the *figlie di coro*. See Gillio 2006, p. 158.

[3]. On the 'School of Nations', see Pavanello 2018; Polzonetti 2014.

[4]. On Giambattista Martini's teaching activity, see Pasquini 2007, pp. 145-163.

in the *bottega* (workshop) of a master[5], or simply imbibe the atmosphere. At the end of their apprenticeship, a musician could attempt to pursue an international career[6] or decide to return to their home region for good[7]. The process of knowledge circulation generated by the forging of relationships between musicians also entailed a «transformation of the social individual through their journey, the becoming of someone else by travelling»[8]. As Antoni Mączack has observed, from the end of the sixteenth century onwards, and especially in the eighteenth century, spending time in the cities of Italy became a formative moment in the life of a young artist, a true «crowning glory of their education»[9].

One might now ask what fate was reserved for musicians in culturally peripheral areas, who for any number of reasons were not able to travel and spend time in a cultural centre. In his analysis of European society on the threshold of the French Revolution, Eric Hobsbawm points out how people who lived in rural, or at least less urban environments, «unless snatched away by some awful hazard, such as military recruitment, lived and died in the county, and often in the parish, of their birth»[10]. He is referring above all to those of lower-middle class extraction, but even in Italian upper-class circles not everyone was positively disposed towards the growth in migration made possible by the improvement of communication routes in eighteenth-century Italy. In 1755 the governor of Milan, Beltrame Cristiani, expressed his concern about the number of roads now connecting the Duchy of Milan with the Austrian Empire: «by now there are no more Alps and we Italians ourselves have deprived ourselves on all sides of the barrier that nature had provided for the defence of our freedom [...]»[11]. If these attitudes were common amongst the Italian elite in the middle of the century, one wonders what the real prospects of mobility might have been for an individual without much in the way of economic resources, without the support of rich patrons, and living in a more geographically and culturally peripheral area than Milan, such as Friuli under Venetian rule. In his treatise *Dell'agricoltura* of 1763, the agronomist Antonio Zanon denounced the deplorable state of Friuli, declaring that

---

[5]. The persistence of the practice of 'workshop' learning during the eighteenth century is noted by ARFINI 2011, pp. 120 and 123.

[6]. As for example that of Johann Adolf Hasse after his studies in Naples under Alessandro Scarlatti (circa 1722-1725). See MELLACE 2004, pp. 38-45.

[7]. For example the Italo-Croatian musician Giuseppe Raffaelli (1767-1843), who returned to his home town (Hvar, Croatia) after a brief stay in Padua. See MILOŠEVIĆ 2016, pp. 151-160.

[8]. LEED 1992, p. 251. On the processes of cultural exchange produced by the movement of musicians, see also STROHM 2016, pp. 17-32: 17-18; NIEDEN 2016, pp. 11-31.

[9]. MĄCZACK 1992, pp. 393-395.

[10]. HOBSBAWM ²1995, p. 10.

[11]. «Ormai non vi sono più Alpi e noi altri italiani medesimi ci siamo privati da ogni parte della barriera che la natura ci aveva fornito per la difesa della nostra libertà [...]». Letter from Beltrame Cristiani to Giovanni Battista Lorenzo Bogino dated 27 May 1755, in VENTURI 1969, p. 420.

# Forms of Circulation of Musical Knowledge in Eighteenth-Century Italy

«it was a dishonour to our country to abandon such a numerous, meek and docile population to their miserable ignorance»[12].

In this regard, at least in the Italian context, Father Giambattista Martini's private correspondence with dozens of musicians represents a remarkable testimony to how knowledge could be transmitted and acquired even without travelling, and in the absence of a direct relationship with a renowned master. On the one hand, thanks to that «goodness and generosity that all the guests within the walls of San Francesco recognised in him»[13], the writing of letters became for Martini an ideal means to disseminate his cherished knowledge about the art of counterpoint. As can be seen in the following case study, the letters sent by Martini were effective in circulating musical knowledge, enabling his correspondents to learn and to improve their musical skills[14].

In 1770, the *Missæ quatuor vocibus* by the Friulian composer Pietro Alessandro Pavona (1728-1786)[15] emerged from the printing presses of Lelio Della Volpe in Bologna (Ill. 1, p. 184). The publication, in moveable type (*caratteri mobili*) in part books (soprano, alto, tenor, bass and bass *ad libitum* for the organ), comprises four masses composed in the *stile antico* and was the only work that Pavona published in his lifetime.

Born in 1728 in the fortress town of Palmanova, Pavona moved at a young age to Cividale del Friuli, a small town in the Venetian *Terraferma*. Here, having completed his ecclesiastical *cursus honorum*, he joined the local Chapter, first serving as organist (1751) and later, from 1755 until his death, as *maestro di cappella* at the Insigne Collegiata of Santa Maria Assunta.

Information regarding Pavona's musical studies is scarce, and although a later bibliographical tradition has him as a student of the Venetian Bartolomeo Cordans (1698-1757), no documentary evidence survives in support of this[16].

---

[12]. «Non fu molto onore alla nostra patria l'abbandonare una così numerosa, mansueta e docile popolazione alla loro [*sic*] miserabile ignoranza». See Donati 1996, p. 178.

[13]. Pasquini 2007, p. 146.

[14]. The role assumed in the eighteenth century by the letter as an instrument for the circulation of learning has already been pointed out by Ronconi 1998, pp. 229-236. Moreover, from the second half of the century onwards, some Italian literati vehemently emphasised the scientific value of private correspondence between learned men, even advocating for such correspondence to be published, especially if it had a high content of erudition and doctrine. The phenomenon is discussed by Forner ²2020, pp. 143-162.

[15]. I have examined the exemplar now preserved in I-CF, P047.09. The signature refers to Zanini 2000. The complete title of this work is: *Missæ quatuor vocibus concinendæ cum Basso pro Organo ad libitum*, Bologna, Lelio Della Volpe, 1770. More details about Pavona's biography are offered by Zanini – Nassimbeni 1995, pp. 11-44, Zanini 2009.

[16]. The thesis that Pavona was a pupil of Bartolomeo Cordans is generally traced back to Giovanni Battista Candotti (1809-1876), also *maestro di cappella* in Cividale from 1845 until his death. In a letter of 22 January 1846 sent by Candotti to François-Joseph Fétis, the Friulian composer declares to the French musicologist that the four *Missae* printed by Pavona in 1770 «can stand alongside those of his master Cordans». See Colussi 2014, pp. 206-209.

# CANTUS.

# MISSÆ

QUATUOR VOCIBUS CONCINENDÆ CUM BASSO
PRO ORGANO AD LIBITUM.

DICATÆ

*Illustrissimis, & Reverendissimis D. D.*

## DECANO CANON. ET CAPITULO
## CIVITATEN.

A PETRO ALEXANDRO PAVONA

EJUSDEM ECCLESIÆ MUSICÆ PRÆFECTO.

BONONIÆ

Typis Lælii a Vulpe Instituti Scientiarum Typographi. 1770.
*SUPERIORUM PERMISSU.*

ILL. 1: Pietro Alessandro Pavona, *Missæ quatuor vocibus* [...], Bologna, Lelio Della Volpe, 1770, I-CF, P047.09.01, 1r.

# Forms of Circulation of Musical Knowledge in Eighteenth-Century Italy

It is however documented that on 2 June 1761 he «asked permission [from the Chapter of Cividale] to be allowed to leave the service of the church for fifteen days to go to St Anthony's in Padua»[17]. On this occasion he probably had the opportunity to meet Giuseppe Tartini and attend his legendary violin lessons, and could well have composed some violin sonatas[18]. Other than this brief stay in Padua, there is no record of any direct contact with famous masters, or even with some of the better trained local musicians who could have helped him reach the level required of a *maestro* at the main church of Cividale. Even if it is true that this city «never represented such a substantial demographic nucleus that it could aspire to become an economic pole of attraction for the entire region»[19], in the eighteenth century it boasted a lively cultural tradition. The *cappella musicale* of Santa Maria Assunta dominated the city's musical life, and the *maestro* was required to compose and conduct all the music necessary for its numerous liturgies. These included masses, psalms, antiphons and hymns, both strictly contrapuntal for voices alone or *concertati* with instruments. Pietro Pavona was a prolific and industrious composer, as evidenced by the hundreds of manuscript compositions under his name in the archive of the Duomo di Cividale[20], yet for his whole career his activity as a composer remained bound to the Friulian region and to the specific needs of the ecclesiastical institution he served.

On the basis of what has been said so far, the printing of the *Missæ* in 1770 by Della Volpe raises several questions. Anyone consulting the list of musical publications from Della Volpe's printing house will notice that almost all of them are attributable to authors from Bologna, or at least with local connections[21]. Pavona's is one of the very few names seemingly unconnected to the Bolognese context. One might therefore ask how a provincial composer, barely more than self-taught and active only in the Friulian town of Cividale, managed to have his collection of masses published by one of the most important printing houses in Italy, seemingly without connections with Bologna.

---

[17]. «Adimandò permissione [al Capitolo di Cividale] di potersi assentare dal servizio della chiesa per quindici giorni per andare a Padova a S. Antonio». I-CFm, AC F01-54 *Definizioni 1750-1772*, without page numbering.

[18]. This hypothesis is supported by the fact that a large collection of musical manuscripts currently held at the UC Berkeley Library, containing mainly trio sonatas and violin sonatas, also contains three compositions attributed to Pavona (RISM A/II: US-BEb, Italian MS 367, 368 and 369). In 1963, Vincent Duckles noted that the pieces in this impressive *corpus* (around 990 manuscripts) were all works by pupils of Giuseppe Tartini, or at any rate of composers who attended his School. It would therefore seem logical to assume that the three sonatas attributed to Pavona were composed by the musician when he asked the Chapter for permission to travel to Padua in 1761. See DUCKLES 1963, pp. 180-181.

[19]. FRESCHI 2020, p. 296.

[20]. The catalogue of the Cividale music collection (ZANINI 2000) includes around 550 compositions attributed to Pavona.

[21]. See TAVONI – BALATA 1986.

# ELIA PIVETTA

A connection between Pavona and Giambattista Martini, previously put forward as a hypothesis by some scholars[22], can be confirmed by a series of letters preserved in the Museo internazionale e Biblioteca della musica in Bologna. The first of these, undated and unsigned, is addressed to Padre Martini and is attributed to the hand of Marquis Fabio Leandro di Colloredo (1705-1772)[23]. The Marquis, from a family boasting possessions in both Friuli and the Marche, cultivated musical interests and kept up a personal correspondence with Martini[24]. The letter that follows is written on *in-folio* paper and on the *recto* of the first page presents a series of questions to which Martini is invited to respond. The questions refer to a specific piece, preserved in Cividale, that the sender took care to attach, transcribing it in his own hand on pages three and four of the letter.

Memoria

We would like the opinion of the erudite Father Martini on the present composition, found with many others in the Capitular Archive of the Insigne Collegiata of Cividale del Friuli.

1st[:] Approximately when was it written.

2nd[:] If the singers of that time sang it as it is or even added the necessary accidentals in the act of singing, especially at the first chord of the Tone at the resolution of the cadence.

3rd[:] For what reason the author, who was a certain Claudin, did not add the above-mentioned accidentals, one of which even the singers of that time must have believed to be necessary, because it can be seen that a sharp is added afterwards [to the sheet], and by another hand placed under the last note of the Christe in the Canto part.

4th[:] Whether it can also be sung in our times as it is, without detriment to good harmony.

These compositions are in manuscript in large books in the manner of Palestrina, with outlines of rough and coarse board/margins, fortified with iron plates at the edges, and in place of hooks there are two pointed iron ornaments, with an arrow corresponding to an iron point at the opposite side.

The aforementioned reverend father is also requested to have a look at the small composition presented to him by His Excellency, Marquis Fabbio Colloredo,

---

22. ZANINI – NASSIMBENI 1995, p. 37.

23. I-Bc, I.029.060. Fabio Leandro di Colloredo, belonging to the third branch of the Lords of Colloredo, was Marquis of Santa Sofia, commissioner and then papal governor of Forte Urbano (now part of the municipality of Castelfranco Emilia). The little and fragmentary biographical information about him that survives is provided by CUSTOZA 2003.

24. In fact, the Museo internazionale e Biblioteca della musica in Bologna preserves a dozen letters he sent to Father Martini. The entire *corpus* of letters can be consulted at the following website: <http://www.bibliotecamusica. it/cmbm/scripts/lettere/lettere.asp?txtfiltro=colloredo&filtro=md&order=data_ord%2C+lettere.id&image. x=0&image.y=0>, accessed March 2023. See PIVETTA 2022, pp. 71-80.

and, with his usual kindness, to correct it if he finds any solecisms in the counterpoint, which the author will be greatly obliged to do[25].

Ex. 1: transcription of the score in I-Bc, I. 029.060, 2r-v[26].

---

[25]. «Si desidera l'opinione dell'eruditissimo padre Martini attorno alla presente composizione, ritrovata con altre molte nell'Archivio Capitolare dell'Insigne Collegiata di Cividale del Friuli. / 1mo[:] In che tempo all'incirca sia stata fatta. / 2do[:] Se i cantori di quel tempo la cantassero come sta o pure vi aggiungessero gl'accidenti necessari nell'atto di cantarla, specialmente alla prima corda del tuono alla risoluzione della cadenza. / 3zo[:] Per qual ragione l'autore che fu un tal Claudin non vi abbia posti gl'accidenti suddetti, uno de quali anche i cantori di quel tempo convien che l'abbiano creduto necessario, perché si vede deritto posteriormente [al foglio] un diesis, e da altra mano posto sotto all'ultima nota del Christe nella parte del Canto. / 4to[:] Se si possa cantare anche a' nostri tempi così come sta, senza discapito della buona armonia. Queste composizioni sono manoscritte in libri grandi all'uso del Palestrina, con contorni di tavola rozza e grossa, fortificati con lastrette di ferro ai contorni, e in vece di gancetti vi sono due caramelle armate in punta di ferro, con una freccia che corrisponde ad una punta di ferro alla parte opposta. / Resta inoltre supplicato il suddetto reverendissimo padre a degnare di un'occhiata la piccola composizione che li verrà esibita da Sua Eccellenza il signor marchese Fabbio Colloredo, e con la solita sua benignità correggerla se vi ritrovasse solecismi di contrappunto, del che ne sarà molto obbligato l'autore». I-Bc, I.029.060, 1r.

[26]. The transcription of the piece remains faithful to the text as it appears in I-Bc, I.029.060, with the exception of the following interventions: the original clefs of soprano, alto, tenor and bass are replaced with treble and bass clefs; at the beginning of the first system only, the names of the vocal registers have been indicated in

As can be seen, in addition to enclosing the score of the four-voice *Kyrie* that was the subject of the questions above (Ex. 1), the author of the letter asks Martini to take a look at one of his own compositions and check it for contrapuntal mistakes. Before considering the musical questions raised by the *Memoria*, it is worth discussing the issue of who actually wrote the letter. Several facts make it seem unlikely that the author could have been Marquis Colloredo himself.

Firstly, if the writer had been the nobleman, it is unclear why he would have referred to himself in the third person (the score «will be shown to you by His Excellency [...] Fabbio Colloredo»). If Colloredo had written the letter, he would simply have used the first person singular, as well as avoiding a clumsy spelling mistake in his own name («Fabbio», instead of «Fabio»).

Secondly, from the *Memoria* we learn that the author copied the score of the *Kyrie* from some «libri grandi all'uso del Palestrina» (large books in the manner of Palestrina) kept «in the Archivio Capitolare of the Insigne Collegiata of Cividale del Friuli». In the eighteenth century, access to the archive in Cividale was a privilege reserved solely to the archivist of the Collegiate Chapter[27]. Not even the *maestro* was allowed to take out material, but rather had

---

square brackets; bar numbers have been added; the indication of the key and alteration of B♭ has been carried over into all systems.

[27]. On 28 June 1711, an order from the Chapter admonished the archivist, Canon Andrea Minisino, «not to allow any person of any religious or ecclesiastical rank or condition, to allow the transport of books, processes, confinements or the slightest paper from the archive itself» («di non permettere a qualsiasi persona di qual grado

to be content with making «one or even two copies of the music he wished to perform at recurring solemnities»[28]. Other than the archivist, no one was authorised to handle materials or documents on the archive's premises, including scores. Given how closely guarded the holdings of the archive were, it is not clear how Colloredo himself could have procured the score, especially in the absence of documentary evidence testifying to any kind of relationship with the Chapter in Cividale.

Thirdly, whilst the Marquis did discuss musical matters in his correspondence with Martini, the letters bearing his autograph signature never pose questions even nearly technical as those in the *Memoria*[29]. The questions posed in the letter cited above appear too complex to have been formulated by a mere amateur, or in any case by someone without a solid background in counterpoint and composition.

Having established that the author of the *Memoria* is very unlikely to have been Colloredo himself, handwriting analysis can come to the rescue in clarifying the question of attribution. A comparison of the handwriting of the letter with that found in manuscripts in Pavona's hand preserved in Cividale, demonstrates that the true author was, in all probability, the *maestro di cappella* of Cividale, Pietro Alessandro Pavona. Considering first of all the similarity in the bass clefs:

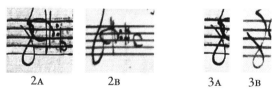

Ill. 2: A) bass clef in I-Bc, I. 029.060 (*Memoria* to Martini), 2v; B) bass clef in I-CF, P052.05, 2r (*De profundis* for choir and orchestra, autograph by Pietro Alessandro Pavona, 1761).

Ill. 3 A) 'curl' in the key armature in I-Bc, I. 029.060, 2v (*Memoria* to Martini); B) 'curl' in the key armature in I-UDc, ms. 3061, 23r (*Pastorale* for organ, autograph by Pietro Alessandro Pavona, undated).

The clef in the autograph (Ill. 2B) is very similar to that which appears in the *Kyrie* in the *Memoria*. Note also the presence of a 'curl' at the end of the brace (Ill. 3A), identifying the key armature of the *Kyrie*: this detail is also found in several of Pavona's autographs (Ill. 3B).

---

o conditione religiosa o ecclesiastica né tanpoco occorrendo al publico medesmo di lasciar trasportar non solo libri, processi, confinationi né minima carta dal archivio medesmo». See I-Cm, AC F01-47, *Definizioni 1701-1712*, 28 June 1711, without page numbering.

[28]. «Una ed anche due copie della musica da lui ricercata per far eseguire nelle ricorrenti solennità». Zanini 1999, p. 487.

[29]. Actually only in I-Bc, I.020.068, Marquis Colloredo discusses musical things with Martini, asking the Bolognese for a copy of his *Gaudeamus omnes in Domino* for his nuns' daughters.

Turning now to alphabetical handwriting, comparing the *Memoria* with an autograph by Pavona dated 1760 (psalm *Cum invocarem* for two choirs and basso continuo, vocal bass part of the first choir) reveals many similarities:

Ill. 4 above: extract from I-Bc, I.029.060, 1r (*Memoria* to Martini); below: extract from I-CF, P055.03, 2r (*Cum invocarem* for two choirs and basso continuo, bass part of the first choir, autograph by Pietro Alessandro Pavona, 1760).

# FORMS OF CIRCULATION OF MUSICAL KNOWLEDGE IN EIGHTEENTH-CENTURY ITALY

The following sequence of images highlights individual alphabetical details taken from the already mentioned manuscripts. On the left are reproductions taken from the *Memoria*[30], on the right are those taken from the *Cum invocarem* autograph[31].

1) capital 'P':

2) lower case 'd' (first manner):

3) lower case 'd' (second manner):

4) capital 'F':

This analysis suggests that the author of the *Memoria* was not the Marquis Fabio Colloredo, but rather Pietro Alessandro Pavona. Colloredo seems to have assumed the role of intermediary; indeed, in the *Memoria* the author states that he would send Martini one of Pavona's compositions, «which will be shown to him by His Excellency [...] Fabbio Colloredo». It is therefore probable that the nobleman sent a letter under his own name to Martini, unfortunately not preserved, along with two 'attachments' from Pavona: the *Memoria* with the questions about the *Kyrie* (by «Claudin») and one of his musical compositions.

The existence of a link between Pavona and the noble house of Colloredo is confirmed by the dedication of one of Pavona's organ sonatas to Violante di Colloredo, one of the Marquis's daughters, who took her vows in 1749 and entered the Major Convent of Cividale under the name of Maria Teresa Costanza[32]. She also corresponded with Martini, and in a letter dated 28 November 1770 asked him for an opinion about Pavona's *Missae*, printed that year in Bologna.

---

[30]. Reproductions from page 1v.

[31]. Reproductions from page 1r, 2r-v and 3r.

[32]. I-UDc, ms. 3178a. That Violante Colloredo took her vows in 1749 is confirmed in a celebratory publication dedicated to her and printed that year: *Raccolta di componimenti poetici per la nobilissima donzella la signora contessa Violante di Colloredo nell'occasione che veste l'abito di S. Benedetto nel monastero maggiore di Cividale del Friuli col nome di Maria Teresa Costanza*, Udine, Giambattista Fongarino, 1749.

> [...] I beg you, moreover, if you would favour me with a gracious reply, to tell me without any consideration whatsoever your opinion about the merit of these four Masses, which Signor *maestro di cappella* [Pavona] had printed for the sole purpose of giving to his Chapter a public testimony of his devotion; this is someone that is very anxious to find ways and means of profiting from, and at the same time nourishes a singular esteem for Your Piety, enjoying various of His works, and makes that price- with the result, justifying, explaining, [which] avariciously demands its admonitions[.] This most devoted of mine prays to you through my beloved Mr Pavona, [who] begs [me] to make you pass on various devout greetings[33].

Although it cannot be affirmed with certainty that Violante Colloredo was a pupil of Pavona, the contact between the two must have been quite close, given that she refers to him as «my beloved Mr. Pavona». When Pavona decided to write to Martini, perhaps also due to the modesty that seems to have characterised his personality[34], he might have preferred to entrust his letter to someone of higher rank (Marquis Fabio Colloredo), who in any case would have been more likely to attract Martini's attention.

\*\*\*

Even if the *Memoria* is not dated, an analysis of the handwriting suggests it is likely to have been written between 1760 and 1770. Comparing the manuscripts above (Ills. 2, 3 and the series of images with the comparison of individual details) with musical autographs from earlier and later in Pavona's career shows that his handwriting changed dramatically over time. For instance, in the composer's will, dated 12 May 1775, the handwriting seems so far removed from that of the *Memoria* that one almost doubts that it is in his own hand[35]. At some point between 1760 and 1770, Pavona could have written to Martini asking for clarifications and an opinion on one of his own compositions, then worked to develop his contrapuntal skills further, before finally having his *Missæ* published by Della Volpe in 1770.

---

33. «La supplico inoltre se mi favorisce di graziosa risposta di dirmi senza verun riguardo la di lei opinione circa il merito di queste quattro Messe, le quali ha fatto stampare il signor maestro di cappella [Pavona] a solo fine di dare al suo Capitolo una pubblica testimonianza della sua divozione; questo è un soggetto moltissimo ansioso di rintracciare modi e maniere de potersi approffittare, e nel tempo stesso nutre per Vostra Pietà singolare stima, godendo varie delle sue opere, e ne fa quel preggio, [che] avaramente esigge le sue ammonizioni [.] Questa mia devotissima la priegarà mediante il mio amatissimo signor Pavona, [il] quale [mi] fà supplica [di] fargliele lesere con li vari devoti saluti». I-Bc, I.003.044k.

34. In 1846, Giovanni Battista Candotti wrote to Fétis: «As for the personal character [of Pavona], here [in Cividale] there are still some old people who knew him who still remember the affability of his manner, the sweetness of his soul and his singular religious piety [...]». See Colussi 2014, p. 208, our translation.

35. The will, written in Pavona's hand, is reproduced in Zanini – Nassimbeni 1995, p. 27.

# Forms of Circulation of Musical Knowledge in Eighteenth-Century Italy

Pavona had to wait some time before receiving a response from Martini. The Museo internazionale e Biblioteca della musica in Bologna preserves two other short missives[36], both undated and unsigned, sent to Martini soliciting a reply to the questions posed in the *Memoria*. Considered in the light of eighteenth-century Italian treatises on epistolography, these two documents are true *biglietti* or notes i.e. «very short letters with nothing not strictly relevant for the purpose of the communication»[37]. *Biglietti* were usually drafted by the personal secretaries of aristocrats, and it is likely that also Marquis Colloredo had at least one in his service. The first note urges Martini to express an opinion on Pavona's composition and to answer the questions concerning «ancient music»:

> The kindest father maestro Martini is requested [to] observe the composition [that] Messer Colloredo brought to him, since the author desires all the corrections, and warnings that the skilful father maestro will find deserving, to the greater light, and profit of the composer.
>
> The said father maestro is also requested [to] express his sentiment on that memory of an ancient music [which] is found in the Archive of the Insigne Collegiata of Cividale in Friuli, wishing to transcribe on the same page his prudent sentiment.
>
> When the aforementioned father maestro is pleased to inform us as to whose music, whether in Mantua or in Venice, he is considering, Messer Colloredo will do him all the pleasure he can, and with the greatest possible commitment to render him service[38].

The second note, shorter than the previous one, also aimed to solicit a reply from Martini. This text, in a different hand to that of the previous note, has been erroneously attributed to the hand of Pavona himself:

> From the very kind father Martini we desire his learned correction of the composition, [which] was presented to him by the marquis Colloredo, work of signor abbate Pavoni, the latter desiring it for his instruction, in the delight he has in composing church music.

---

36. I-Bc, I.029.030; I-Bc, I.009.127.

37. Forner ²2020, p. 21 (our translation).

38. «Il gentilissimo padre maestro Martini è pregato [di] osservare la composizione [che] li recò il messer Colloredo, poiché l'autore dessidera su di essa tutte le correzioni, ed avertimenti che il valente padre maestro troverà possa meritar, a maggior lume, e profitto del compositore. / È pregato pure il detto padre maestro [di] dire il suo sentimento sopra quella memoria d'una antica musica [che] si ritrova nell'Archivio dell'Insigne Collegiata di Cividale nel Friuli, volendo trascrivere nel medesimo foglietto il prudente suo sentimento. / Allorché si compiacerà l'accennato padre maestro d'avisare appresso di chi si trovino, siano in Mantova, o in Vinegia, quelle tali musiche che dessidera, il messer Colloredo li farà tutto il piacere, e con il massimo impegno possibile di renderlo servito». I-Bc, I.009.127.

# Elia Pivetta

Furthermore, he is requested [to] give his skilful and virtuous opinion on that quality of music [which] is found in the ancient books of the Cathedral of Cividale in Friuli, of which the same Marquis Colloredo gave him the memory in writing[39].

The author of this note is highly unlikely to have been Pavona himself. The author misspells his name (calling him «Pavoni») and refers to him as «abbate» (abbot), when Pavona was in fact simply a priest of the Chapter in Cividale. Moreover, the main church in Cividale del Friuli, dedicated to the Assumption, whilst boasting the title of 'Insigne Collegiata', did not at the time have the rank of a cathedral. If Pavona had written the letter, it is hard to explain how he could have made these sort of mistakes. In the absence of firm evidence, it seems likely that a secretary of Marquis Colloredo drafted it.

In any case, Martini did reply eventually and his response is further proof of his lucidity, cultural learning and knowledge of the performance practice of sixteenth-century music.

*Risposta* to the questions of Signor Abate Pavoni

No. 1 There were two French composers under the name of Claudin, the old one, who flourished in the early 1500s, and the young one around 1560. It is therefore necessary to observe whether Claudin the Younger is noted, or Claudin without any addition.

No. 2 The singers of those times were instructed not only in singing, but also in the art of improvising over a cantus firmus, so that they knew the rules about where and when they had to place the accidentals, since it was a rule of counterpoint that the major intervals by their nature have to ascend, and the minor ones to descend, and therefore they did not take care to mark the accidents, except in doubtful or equivocal cases.

No. 3 Claudin did not add the accidentals of ♯ and ♭ for the reasons demonstrated in the previous number.

No. 4 These compositions can be sung also in our times, whenever either the singers are instructed in what has been said above, or the maestri di capella mark the necessary accidents.

Signor abate Pavoni's composition has merit, because in it the author demonstrates that he is learned in the true and essential rules of counterpoint. However, it will become more and more commendable if he ensures that his composition is fuller of harmony, and far from the many unisons with which it is scattered, especially at the beginning of the measure; since, as is well known, unisons

---

39.   «Dal gentilissimo padre Martini si dessidera sua dotta correzzione alla composizione, [che] li fù presentata dal marchese Colloredo, del signor abbate Pavoni, bramandola questi per suo ammaestramento, nella dilettazione c'hà di comporre in musica da chiesa; inoltre è pregato [di] dire il suo valente e virtuoso parere sopra quella tal qualità di musica [che] si trova in antichi libri della Cattedrale di Cividale nel Friuli, di cui al medesimo marchese Colloredo gl'è ne diede la memoria in scritto». I-Bc, I.029.030.

# FORMS OF CIRCULATION OF MUSICAL KNOWLEDGE IN EIGHTEENTH-CENTURY ITALY

cannot produce harmony. It will be very useful for the author to study continuously, and to observe the compositions of Palestrina, in order to instruct himself more and more in the finesse of his art, in which he has had no one who has come to equal him[40].

The first notable aspect of the *Risposta* is the fact that Martini begins dealing directly with musical matters, without initial courtesy formulas of any kind. This could suggest that the *Risposta* was attached to a covering letter, addressed to the Marquis Colloredo.

Martini's first comment («No. 1») is about the identification of the author of the *Kyrie* (score in Ex. 1), «a certain Claudin», and whether it refers to «Claudin the Younger», Claude Le Jeune (c. 1528-1600), or «Claudin the Older», which would refer to Claudin de Sermisy (c. 1490-1562), implied by «Claudin without further addition»[41]. The man in question can be identified as Claudin de Sermisy, a composer active in France in the first half of the sixteenth century. The *Kyrie* is an excerpt from his *Missa Domini est terra*, a work first printed in 1532 by Pierre Attaingnant in his seventh book of masses, the final volume in his monumental collection *Viginti missarum liber*[42]. A parody mass[43], Claudin's *Missa Domini*

---

[40]. «Risposta alle dimande del signor abate Pavoni[:] / N. 1 due maestri di cappella francesi vi sono stati col nome di Claudin, il vecchio, che fiorì nel principio del 1500, e il giovine verso il 1560. Sicché bisogna osservare se sia notato Claudin il Giovine, opure Claudin senz'altro aggiunto. / N. 2 I cantori di que' tempi erano istruiti non solo nel canto, ma [anche] nell'arte di comporre all'improvviso sopra del canto fermo, onde sapevano per regola ove, e quando dovevansi porre gli accidenti, essendovi una regola di contrapunto, che li intervalli maggiori di natura sua vogliono ascendere, e li minori discendere, e perciò non si prendevan cura di segnare li accidenti, se non in casi dubbi, o equivoci. / N. 3 Claudin non ha aggiunto li accidenti di ♯ e ♭ per le ragioni dimostrate al numero precedente. / N. 4 Si potranno cantare simili composizioni anche a' tempi nostri, ogniqualvolta, o i cantori siano istruiti di quanto si è detto sopra, o i maestri di cappella vi segnino li accidenti necessari. / La composizione del signor abate Pavoni ha il suo merito, perché in essa si conosce essere istruito l'autore delle vere ed essenziali regole di contrapunto. Sempre più però si renderà comendabile se procura che sia la sua composizione più piena d'armonia, e lontana da molti unisoni di cui è sparsa, massime in principio di battuta; stanteché, come è noto, li unisoni non possono produrre armonia. Sarà molto utile all'autore lo studio continuo, e l'osservare le composizioni del Palestrina, per sempre più istruirsi nella finezza della di lui arte, nella quale non ha avuto alcuno che sia giunto a eguagliarlo» (I-Bc, I.029.029). This document is named as follows by the bolognese librarian Gaetano Gaspari (1807-1881): *Risposta del p. Martini ad alcune dimande dell'abate Pavona, friulano.* It is contained in a *Zibaldone martiniano* that collects assorted materials, such as letters, opinions and invectives by Martini. The *Risposta* and the whole content of the *Zibaldone* can be consulted online, <http://www.bibliotecamusica.it/cmbm/scripts/gaspari/scheda.asp?id=1680>, accessed March 2023.

[41]. The name Claudin, «without further addition», is in fact the name under which Claudin de Sermisy appears in a miscellaneous collection of motets published in Venice in 1539 by Antonio Gardano, a volume which Martini had in his personal library. See I-Bc, R147.

[42]. RISM B/I: Attaingnant 1532[7]. The *Missa Domini est terra* by Claudin, included in the seventh book, can be found at 21v-22r. See also HEARTZ 1969, p. 249, fn. 39. The mass is edited in DE SERMISY 1977, pp. 112-130.

[43]. The main subject of the *Kyrie* of the mass is identical to that of the motet on Psalm 23 (*Domini est terra et plenitudo ejus*), first published in 1535 in Attaingnant's ninth book of motets (RISM B/I: Attaingnant 1535[9]).

*est terra* circulated not only in printed editions, but also in manuscript copies, amongst them Codex LIII, a choir book currently preserved at the Museo Archeologico Nazionale in Cividale del Friuli[44]. According to Lewis Lockwood, this impressive *librone* was compiled in Cividale around the middle of the sixteenth century by a copyist who seems to have transcribed the music directly from Attaingnant's 1532 print[45], given how «in both Attaingnant and [Codex] 53 the note content is always identical»[46]. This choir book was probably not put together for a specific local purpose, but rather copied at the behest of a member of the wealthy Venetian Grimani family, which between 1517 and 1546 succeeded in having some of its members elected to the throne of Aquileia's Patriarchate[47]. In any case, Codex LIII must have been the source from which Pavona copied Claudin's *Kyrie:* in the *Memoria* he emphasises that the piece is in a «manuscript in large books in the manner of Palestrina, with outlines of rough and coarse board/margins, fortified with iron plates at the edges, and in place of hooks there are two pointed iron ornaments, with an arrow corresponding to an iron point at the opposite side». As can be seen from the pictures below (ILL. 5), Pavona's description of the book corresponds precisely with Codex LIII (ILL. 6).

ILL. 5: I-Cm, Codex LIII, details of the front cover (left) and back plate (right). Note the presence of the two «iron-tipped candies» described by Pavona to Martini.

---

On the cycles of motets published by Attaingnant see BAZINET 2018, pp. 52-53.

[44]. See SCALON – PANI 1998, pp. 196-197.
[45]. LOCKWOOD 1994, pp. 254-260.
[46]. *Ibidem*, p. 260.
[47]. *Ibidem*, pp. 308-311.

# Forms of Circulation of Musical Knowledge in Eighteenth-Century Italy

Ill. 6a: I-Cm, Codex LIII, *Kyrie* from *Missa Domini est terra* by Claudin de Sermisy, 55v.

Ill. 6b: I-Cm, Codex LIII, *Kyrie* from *Missa Domini est terra* by Claudin de Sermisy, 56r.

## Forms of Circulation of Musical Knowledge in Eighteenth-Century Italy

Martini's next remarks address Pavona's second question, regarding «whether the singers of that time sang it as it is or also added the necessary accidentals in the act of singing». Pavona notes that the *Kyrie* is devoid of accidentals, leading him to ask whether it is appropriate to perform the piece «as it stands, without detriment to good harmony». Martini's reply is in two parts: firstly, he points out that «the singers of those times were instructed not only in singing, but also in the art of improvising over a *cantus firmus*»; secondly, he states that sixteenth century singers were guided by a «rule of counterpoint, that the major intervals by their nature have to ascend, and the minor intervals to descend».

The first part of Martini's statement refers to the practice of *contrapunto alla mente*, which consisted in improvising vocal (or even instrumental) lines over a written chant, in accordance with the principles of counterpoint. This practice had its origins by the beginning of the fifteenth century, when the theorist Prosdocimus de Beldemandis wrote his explanatory glosses to a counterpoint treatise by Johannes De Muris[48]. Over the course of the sixteenth century, this practice became increasingly important, such that young singers and instrumentalists were taught it from the earliest years of their studies[49]. *Contrapunto alla mente* was well known to Father Martini, who in the first volume of his *Esemplare* described how it was still practiced in some churches in Rome:

> Among the compositions made by the masters of the art singing over a cantus firmus, singular are those on the Introits, which are used, especially by cathedrals and other churches on the principal solemnities. [The ancients] practised this kind of composition in two ways. The first was that over the noted chant sung mostly by the basses, the other parts would improvise, the sopranos forming a single melody together all, all the altos the same, as well as all the tenors, coming to form with the bass four part counterpoint, as to my great pleasure and admiration I heard sung in 1747 by the papal singers in Rome in the Patriarchal Basilica of S. John on the day of the Ascension of Our Lord Jesus Christ, a way of singing which is called *Contrappunto alla mente*. The rules for composing such counterpoint are set out by Pietro Aaron (*Toscanello in Musica*, book 2, chapter 21) Zarlino (*Instituzioni Harmoniche*, p. 3 chapter 58), Lodovico Zacconi (*Pratica di Musica*, book 2, chapter 34), and by others, but especially by Giovanni Maria and Bernardino Nanini in a manuscript treatise. These rules, learned exactly by the singers, come to form so many counterpoints of improvised music, and must serve as an example, and stimulus to music teachers, and composers to apply themselves more and more to their studies, and take possession of the true rules of their art[50].

---

[48]. Cohen 2002, p. 536.

[49]. See Smith 2011, pp. 131-143; Blackburn – Lowinsky 1993, pp. 61-114.

[50]. «Tra le composizioni fatte da' maestri dell'arte sopra del canto fermo, sono singolari quelle sopra degl'Introiti, che vengono usati, specialmente dalle cattedrali, ed altre chiese nelle principali solennità. In due modi [gli antichi] praticarono questa sorta di composizioni. Il primo fu che sopra del canto fermo cantato per lo più dai

# ELIA PIVETTA

The sixteenth century singer's ability to improvise contrapuntal lines, presupposed a perfect knowledge of the *ambitus* of any given mode, as well as of typical cadential formulas, meaning that they knew where to insert *musica ficta*[51]. This was the reason that the old masters «did not take care to mark the accidentals» in their compositions, «except in doubtful or equivocal cases».

Secondly Martini states that ancient singers introduced accidentals according to the principle that «major intervals by their nature have to ascend, and minor ones to descend». Martini explains this in more detail in the *Breve compendio degli elementi e delle regole di contrappunto* at the start of the first volume of the *Esemplare*. *Regola IV*, in fact, recommends

> [...] to conform to the property and nature of major intervals, which is to ascend, and of minor intervals to descend. These intervals are thirds, sixths, sevenths, major or altered fourths, and augmented or diminished fifths. However, the unisons, octaves and fifths are exempt from this law, being free to ascend or descend as they see fit[52].

Martini's teachings on counterpoint were rooted in the Italian theoretical tradition of the sixteenth century, which had in Gioseffo Zarlino one of its most illustrious representatives. In fact, Martini's *Regola* finds a direct correspondence in Zarlino's *Instituzioni harmoniche*, which states:

> Besides this, imperfect consonances have such a nature that their extremes extend more comfortably and better towards that part which is nearer to its perfection than towards that which is farther from it, because everything naturally desires to become perfect in the shortest and best way it can. Hence the greater imperfect desires to make itself greater, and the lesser has a contrary nature;

---

bassi, le altre parti vi componevano all'improvviso, formando una sola melodia assieme tutti i soprani, l'istesso tutti i contralti, così pure tutti i tenori, venendo a formare col basso un contrappunto a quattro voci, come con mio gran piacere, ed ammirazione intesi cantare nel 1747 dai cantori pontifizi in Roma nella Basilica Patriarcale di S. Giovanni il giorno dell'Ascensione di Nostro Signore Gesù Cristo, qual modo di cantare vien chiamato *Contrappunto alla mente*. Ritrovansi esposte le regole per comporre tal contrappunto da Pietro Aaron (*Toscanello in Musica*, lib. 2 Cap. 21) Zarlino (*Instituzioni Harmoniche* p. 3 Cap. 58) Lodovico Zacconi (*Pratica di Musica* lib. 2 Cap. 34), e da altri, ma singolarmente da Giovanni Maria, e Bernardino Nanini in un trattato manoscritto. Queste regole, apprese esattamente dai cantori, vengono a formare tanti contrappunti di musica all'improvviso, e che devono servire di esempio, e stimolo ai maestri di musica, e compositori a sempre più applicarsi allo studio, e impossessarsi delle vere regole della loro arte». MARTINI 1774, pp. 57-58. For a description of the manuscript treatise by Giovanni Maria and Bernardino Nanino see PASQUINI 2004, p. 314.

[51].   See FROEBE 2007, pp. 13-55.

[52].   «[...] uniformarsi alla proprietà, e natura, degli intervalli maggiori, che è di ascendere, e degli intervalli minori di discendere. Questi intervalli sono le terze, le seste, le settime, le quarte maggiori, o alterate; e le quinte false, o mancanti. Sono però esenti da tal legge li unissoni, le ottave, le quinte, essendo libere di ascendere, o discendere come più le converrà». MARTINI 1774, p. xx.

## Forms of Circulation of Musical Knowledge in Eighteenth-Century Italy

> Therefore the major ditone and the major hexachord [that is, the major thirds and sixths] desire to become major, one coming from the fifth and the other from the octave, and the minor semitone and the minor hexachord [that is, the minor thirds and sixths] love to become minor, one coming towards the unison and the other towards the fifth, as is manifest to all those who are expert in the matters of music and have a sound judgement [...][53].

Thus according to Martini the reason that «Claudin did not add the ♯ and ♭ accidentals» to his *Kyrie* was therefore that the singers of the time knew where to add them without needing them to be marked explicitly in the score.

In response to Pavona's question as to whether the piece could be «sung even in our times as it is» even at the «expense of good harmony», Martini responds pragmatically: given in the eighteenth century it could no longer be taken for granted that singers understood the ancient rules of *contrapunto alla mente*, it would be necessary that «either the singers are instructed in what has been said above, or for the M[aestr]i di Cappella to indicate the necessary accidents».

Having dealt with Pavona's questions concerning Claudin's *Kyrie*, Martini gives his opinion about the «composition of Signor Abate Pavoni», which he received together with the *Memoria*, but about which nothing more is known. Martini's observations suggest that it is likely to have been a contrapuntal piece written in the *stile antico*. He advises Pavona to avoid the «many unisons with which [the composition] is scattered, especially at the beginning of the bar; since, as is well known, unisons cannot produce harmony». This principle of voice leading would make the piece «more full of harmony». It is also worth noting how Martini suggests Pavona taking the works of Palestrina as a model, «in order to instruct himself more and more in the finesse of his art». Martini's admiration for Palestrina can already be seen in his 1747 opinion about the election of the new *maestro di cappella* of the Duomo in Milano[54]. As Elisabetta Pasquini has pointed out, by the time that Martini printed the first volume of his *Esemplare* in 1774, «the primacy of the 'Prince of Music' [...] was beyond doubt», such that «Giovanni Pierluigi da Palestrina [...] was entrusted with much of the responsibility for exemplifying the practice of the ecclesiastical tones»[55].

---

[53].    «Hanno oltre di questo le consonanze imperfette tal natura che i loro estremi con più commodo e miglior modo si estendono verso quella parte, ch'è più vicina alla sua perfezione, che verso quella che le è più lontana, perciochè ogni cosa naturalmente desidera di farsi perfetta con quel modo più breve e migliore che puote. Onde le imperfette maggiori desiderano di farsi maggiori e le minori hanno natura contraria; conciosia che 'l ditono e l'esacordo maggiore [ossia le terze e le seste maggiori] desiderano di farsi maggiori, venendo l'uno alla quinta e l'altro all'ottava, e il semiditono e l'esacordo minore [ossia le terze e le seste minori] amano di farsi minori, venendo l'uno verso l'unisono e l'altro verso la quinta, com'è manifesto a tutti quelli che nelle cose della musica sono periti e hanno il loro giudicio sano [...]». ZARLINO 2011, p. 329. For a practical explanation of this rule see MENKE 2015, pp. 92-93.

[54].    On this episode see TOFFETTI 2014.

[55].    PASQUINI 2004, p. 45.

It is only possible to speculate about the hypothetical role Martini might have played in relation to the publication of Pavona's *Missae* by Della Volpe in 1770. Even in the absence of further surviving letters proving a continuation in the correspondence between the two musicians, we can note that Martini in his *Risposta* declared that «the composition of Signor Abate Pavoni has its merit», and puts this down to the fact that «the author is known to be instructed in the true and essential rules of counterpoint». It is at least plausible that, after the exchange of letters examined here, Martini may have encouraged Pavona to pursue his study of counterpoint, and perhaps submit works of his for printing by Della Volpe. A reserved character like Pavona might not have dared to submit music for publication without the support of a figure of Martini's calibre.

The correspondence between Pavona and Martini is a useful case study. Pietro Alessandro Pavona is a typical example of a composer active in a culturally peripheral context and, with the exception of a brief stay in Padua in 1761, did not have the opportunity to travel to complete his training under the guidance of a renowned *maestro*. In addition to his numerous duties as *maestro di cappella* of the main church in Cividale, as a member of the Chapter he had to comply with a stringent *obbligo di residenza* (obligation of residence), meaning that he was not permitted (by law) to leave the city, other than for short periods[56]. This would have made it difficult for him to gain access to the cultural scenes of the major Italian cities of the time, and profit from the exchange of ideas and learning that benefitted the musicians active in or travelling through them.

Nevertheless, the cultural marginality that could be seen to characterise the life and professional activity of a provincial musician like Pavona should in no way be interpreted as a desire to work in isolation. «These provincial towns were none the less urban for being small»[57], as Hobsbawm states, reminding us how people active in these contexts could still have an intimate desire for self-improvement, and a tangible attraction towards cultural centres. The letter sent by Pavona to Martini is a testament to this: a musician from provincial eighteenth-century Friuli desired to understand the ancient musical heritage in his own archive, wishing to perform it in a more informed manner thanks to the clarifications of a distinguished musician. That Pavona sent a score to Martini also highlights his desire to improve his skills in the art of counterpoint, a language considered indispensable, «an irreplaceable technical and cultural baggage that allows one to face the pitfalls of the profession with complete fluency [...]»[58]. For a

---

[56].    «He shall not depart from the city without a licence from the Chapter» («non doverà partire da la città senza la licenza del Capitolo»), states a note from the *Liber Instrumenti Canipæ* of 1602 with reference to the obligations of the *maestro di capella*. See ZANINI 1999, p. 490.

[57].    HOBSBAWM ²1995, p. 12.

[58].    PASQUINI 2007, p. 153.

# FORMS OF CIRCULATION OF MUSICAL KNOWLEDGE IN EIGHTEENTH-CENTURY ITALY

composer such as Pavona, his exchange of letters with Father Martini probably represented one of few ways he had at his disposal to develop his understanding of counterpoint, and to learn *modi e maniere* (ways and manners) useful for carrying out his duties in the best possible way. Elisabetta Pasquini's notes that the many composers who corresponded with Martini can hardly be considered pupils of his[59]. Certainly this remains true. However, those who wrote to him to obtain an opinion, piece of advice, or a simple clarification, surely considered *him* their master.

The *Risposta* testifies to Martini's desire to transmit the knowledge and erudition he possessed to such a singular degree, not just in the context of a direct and personal relationship between master and pupil, but also to the large number of composers active in peripheral areas, or simply not able to reach him in Bologna. The 'cultural exchange' that took place between Martini and his correspondents through the letters was beneficial for both parties involved: Martini, as master, could share knowledge that he considered important and contribute to its transmission over time. His correspondents gained knowledge, as 'pupils', that assisted them in their musical training.

Martini's activities were central in keeping the art of counterpoint at the heart of the education of musicians in Italy, such that even in the nineteenth century it was still considered of critical importance. In a famous letter dated 5 January 1871 addressed to Francesco Florimo, librarian of the Naples Conservatory, Giuseppe Verdi declared, while declining an offer of the post of director of that institution: «I would have done myself the glory [...] of training the pupils in those serious and severe studies [...]. I would have said to the young pupils: "Practice the Fugue constantly, tenaciously, until you are sated [...]". You will thus learn to compose with confidence, to arrange the parts well, and to modulate without affectation: study Palestrina and a few of his contemporaries [...]»[60].

The hundreds of letters sent by Martini also demonstrate the importance of letter writing in the eighteenth century in the process of the circulation of knowledge: Martini's correspondence could establish fruitful exchanges between musicians active in different contexts, connecting a major urban centre, such as Bologna with the many lively, albeit peripheral, small towns of eighteenth-century Italy.

---

[59]. *Ibidem*, p. 147.

[60]. «Mi sarei fatto una gloria [...] di esercitare gli alunni a quei studi gravi e severi [...]. Avrei detto ai giovani alunni: "Esercitatevi nella *Fuga* costantemente, tenacemente, fino alla sazietà [...]". Imparerete così a comporre con sicurezza, a disporre bene le parti, ed a modulare senz'affettazione: Studiate Palestrina e pochi suoi coetanei [...]». VERDI 2012, pp. 603-604.

# Elia Pivetta

## List of Abbreviations

| | |
|---|---|
| I-Bc | Bologna, Museo internazionale e Biblioteca della musica |
| I-CF | Cividale del Friuli, Archivio capitolare del Duomo di Santa Maria Assunta |
| I-CFm | Cividale del Friuli, Museo Archeologico Nazionale |
| I-Udc | Udine, Biblioteca civica 'Vincenzo Joppi' |
| US-BEm | Berkeley, 'Jean Gray Hargrove' Music Library, University of California. |

## Bibliography

Arfini 2011

Arfini, Maria Teresa. 'Padri musicisti di figli musicisti nella società dei secoli XVII e XVIII. Modalità di trasmissione del sapere musicale', in: *Figure della paternità nell'Ancien Régime*, edited by Paola Bianchi and Giacomo Jori, Turin, Accademia University Press, 2011, pp. 119-137.

Bazinet 2018

Bazinet, Geneviève. 'Singing the King's Music: Attaingnant's Motet Series, Royal Egemony and the Function of the Motet in Sixteenth-Century France', in: *Early Music History*, XXXVII (2018), pp. 45-82.

Blackburn – Lowinsky 1993

Blackburn, J. Bonnie – Lowinsky, E. Edward. 'Luigi Zenobi and His Letter on the Perfect Musician', in: *Studi musicali*, no. 22 (1993), pp. 61-114.

Cafiero 2020

Cafiero, Rosa. *La didattica del partimento. Studi di storia delle teorie musicali*, Lucca, LIM, 2020 (Teorie musicali, 6).

Cohen 2002

Cohen, Albert. 'Performance Theory', in: *The Cambridge History of Western Music Theory*, edited by Thomas Christensen, Cambridge, Cambridge University Press, 2002, pp. 534-553.

Colussi 2014

*Lettere musicali di Giovanni Battista Candotti*, edited by Franco Colussi, Udine, Forum, 2014 (Fonti per la storia della Chiesa in Friuli. Serie moderna e contemporanea, 1).

Custoza 2003

Custoza, Gian Camillo. *Colloredo, una famiglia e un castello nella storia europea*, Udine, Gaspari, 2003.

De Sermisy 1977

Sermisy, Claudin de. *Opera omnia. V*, edited by Gaston Allaire and Isabelle Cazeaux, Holzgerlingen, American Institute of Musicology-Hänssler-Verlag, 1977 (Corpus Mensurabilis Musicae, 52-5).

# FORMS OF CIRCULATION OF MUSICAL KNOWLEDGE IN EIGHTEENTH-CENTURY ITALY

DE SETA 2014
DE SETA, Cesare. *L'Italia nello specchio del Grand Tour*, Milan, Rizzoli, 2014.

DONATI 1996
*Antichi Stati. Repubblica di Venezia. 2: Stati di Terraferma (1700-1797)*, edited by Claudio Donati, Milan, Franco Maria Ricci, 1996.

DUCKLES 1963
DUCKLES, Vincent. *Thematic Catalogue of a Manuscript Collection of Eighteenth-Century Italian Instrumental Music in the University of California, Berkeley Music Library*, Berkeley (CA), University of California Press, 1963.

FORNER [2]2020
FORNER, Fabio. *Scrivere lettere nel XVIII secolo. Precettistica, prassi e letteratura*, Verona, QuiEdit, [2]2020 (Saggi e ricerche. Centro di ricerca sugli epistolari del Settecento, 10).

FRESCHI 2020
FRESCHI, Lorenzo. *I sudditi al governo. Società e politica a Cividale e Gemona del Friuli nel Rinascimento veneziano*, Bologna, il Mulino, 2020 (Istituto italiano per gli studi storici, 76).

FROEBE 2007
FROEBE, Folker. 'Satzmodelle des 'Contrapunto alla mente' und ihre Bedeutung für dem Stilwandel um 1600', in: *Zeitschrift der Gesellschaft für Musiktheorie*, IV/1-2 (2007), pp. 13-55.

GILLIO 2006
GILLIO, Pier Giuseppe. *L'attività musicale degli ospedali di Venezia nel Settecento. Quadro storico e materiali documentari*, Florence, Olschki, 2006 (Studi di musica veneta – Quaderni vivaldiani, 12).

HEARTZ 1969
HEARTZ, Daniel. *Pierre Attaingnant Royal Printer of Music: A Historical Study and Bibliographical Catalogue*, Berkeley-Los Angeles, University of California Press, 1969.

HOBSBAWM [2]1995
HOBSBAWM, Eric John. *The Age of Revolution: Europe 1789-1848*, London, Weidenfeld & Nicolson, [2]1995.

LEED 1992
LEED, J. Eric. *La mente del viaggiatore. Dall'Odissea al turismo globale*, Italian translation by Erica Joy Mannucci, Bologna, il Mulino, 1992 (Biblioteca storica).

LOCKWOOD 1994
LOCKWOOD, Lewis. 'Sources of Renaissance Polyphony from Cividale del Friuli: The Manuscripts 53 and 59 of the Museo Archeologico Nazionale', in: *Il Saggiatore musicale*, I/2 (1994), pp. 249-314.

MĄCZACK 1992
MĄCZACK, Antoni. *Viaggi e viaggiatori nell'Europa moderna*, Italian translation by Renzo Panzone, Rome-Bari, Laterza, 1992.

MARTINI 1774
MARTINI, Giovanni Battista. *Esemplare, o sia Saggio fondamentale pratico di contrappunto. 1*, Bologna, Lelio Della Volpe, 1774.

MELLACE 2004
MELLACE, Raffaele. *Johann Adolf Hasse*, Palermo, l'Epos, 2004 (L'amoroso canto, 1).

MELLACE 2017
ID. 'Italien, Kunstmusik, Das 18. Jahrhundert, Musik, Politik und Geographie, Netzwerk verschiedener Städte', in: *MGG Online*, 2017 <https://www.mgg-online.com>, accessed March 2023.

MENKE 2015
MENKE, Johannes. *Kontrapunkt. 1: Die Musik der Renaissance*, Laaber, Laaber-Verlag, 2015.

MILOŠEVIĆ 2016
MILOŠEVIĆ, Maja. 'From the Periphery to the Centre and Back: The Case of Giuseppe Raffaelli (1767-1843) from Hvar', in: *Music Migration in the Early Modern Age: Centres and Peripheries – People, Works, Style, Paths of Dissemination and Influence*, edited by Guzy Pasiak and Aneta Markuszewska, Warsaw, LiberProArte, 2016, pp. 151-160.

NIEDEN 2016
NIEDEN, Gesa zur. 'Roads «which are commonly wonderful for the musicians». Early Modern Times Musician's Mobility and Migration', in: *Musicians' Mobilities and Music Migration in Early Modern Europe. Biographical Patterns and Cultural Exchanges*, edited by Gesa zur Nieden and Berthold Over, Bielefeld, Transcript, 2016 (Mainz Historical Cultural Sciences, 33), pp. 11-31.

PASQUINI 2004
PASQUINI, Elisabetta. *L'Esemplare o sia Saggio fondamentale pratico di contrappunto. Padre Martini teorico e didatta della musica*, Florence, Olschki, 2004 (Historiae Musicae Cultores, 103).

PASQUINI 2007
EAD. *Giambattista Martini*, Palermo, L'Epos, 2007 (L'amoroso canto, 6).

PAVANELLO 2018
PAVANELLO, Agnese. 'Giuseppe Tartini', in: *Enciclopedia italiana di scienze, lettere ed arti. 9*, Rome, Istituto Italiano della Enciclopedia Italiana, 2018, pp. 249-255.

PIVETTA 2022
PIVETTA, Elia. '«Per sempre più comprovarle la somma stima che fò della di lei persona». Le lettere del marchese Fabio di Colloredo a padre Giambattista Martini', in: *Ce fastu? Rivista della Società filologica friulana*, XCVIII/1-2 (2022), pp. 71-80.

# Forms of Circulation of Musical Knowledge in Eighteenth-Century Italy

Polzonetti 2014

Polzonetti, Pierpaolo. 'Tartini and the Tongue of Saint Anthony', in: *Journal of the American Musicological Society*, LXVII/2 (2014), pp. 429-486.

Ronconi 1998

Ronconi, Giorgio. 'Aspetti della lettera familiare nel Settecento. La corrispondenza tra Egidio e Marco Forcellini e la prima edizione dell'epistolario zeniano', in: *Alla lettera. Teorie e pratiche epistolari dai Greci al Novecento*, edited by Adriana Chemello, Milan, Guerini Studio, 1998, pp. 229-244.

Sanguinetti 2012

Sanguinetti, Giorgio. *The Art of Partimento*: *History, Theory and Practice*, Oxford-New York, Oxford University Press, 2012.

Scalon – Pani 1998

Scalon, Cesare – Pani, Laura. *I codici della Biblioteca capitolare di Cividale del Friuli*, Florence, Edizioni del Galluzzo, 1998 (Biblioteche e archivi, 1).

Smith 2011

Smith, Anne. *The Performance of 16th-Century Music: Learning from the Theorists*, Oxford-New York, Oxford University Press, 2011.

Strohm 2016

Strohm, Reinhard. 'The Wondering of Music through Space and Time', in: *Music Migration in the Early Modern Age: Centres and Peripherie. People, Works, Style, Paths of Dissemination and Influence, op. cit.*, pp. 17-32.

Sweet 2012

Sweet, Rosemary. *Cities and the Grand Tour: The British in Italy, c. 1690-1820*, Cambridge, Cambridge University Press, 2012 (Cambridge Social and Cultural Histories).

Tavoni – Balata 1986

Tavoni, Maria Gioia – Balata, Nicola. 'Dalla Volpe, Lelio Antonio Gaetano', in: *Dizionario Biografico degli Italiani. 32*, Rome, Istituto della Enciclopedia Italiana, 1986, <https://www.treccani.it/enciclopedia/dalla-volpe-lelio-antonio-gaetano_(Dizionario-Biografico)>, accessed March 2023.

Toffetti 2014

Toffetti, Marina. 'Padre Martini e il dibattito sulla varietà degli stili nella musica sacra dei secoli XVI-XVIII', in: *La musica sacra nella Milano del Settecento*, edited by Cesare Fertonani, Milan, LED Edizioni Universitarie, 2014, pp. 65-88.

Venturi 1969

Venturi, Franco. *Settecento riformatore. Da Muratori a Beccaria*, Turin, Einaudi, 1969 (Biblioteca di cultura storica, 103).

VERDI 2012

VERDI, Giuseppe. *Lettere*, edited by Eduardo Rescigno, illustrations by Giuliano Della Casa, Turin, Einaudi, 2012 (I Millenni).

ZANINI 1999

ZANINI, Alba. 'La cappella musicale del Duomo di Cividale', in: *Cividât. 1*, edited by Enos Costantini, Udine, Società Filologica Friulana, 1999, pp. 487-493.

ZANINI 2000

*Archivio musicale capitolare: Cividale del Friuli*, catalogue edited by Alba Zanini, Udine, Centro di Catalogazione e Restauro dei Beni Culturali, 2000.

ZANINI 2009

ZANINI, Alba. 'Pavona, Pietro Alessandro', in: *Nuovo Liruti. Dizionario biografico dei friulani. 2: L'età veneta, N-Z*, edited by Cesare Scalon, Udine, Forum, 2009, pp. 1964-1966.

ZANINI – NASSIMBENI 1995

ZANINI, Alba – NASSIMBENI, Lorenzo. 'Il musicista Pietro Alessandro Pavona «nativo di Palmanova e figlio d'uno di que' benemeriti soldati della Repubblica»', in: *Pietro Alessandro Pavona e la musica sacra a Palma*, [without editor], Palmanova (Udine), Circolo di Cultura 'Nicolò Trevisan', 1995, pp. 11-44.

ZARLINO 2011

ZARLINO, Gioseffo. *L'istituzioni armoniche*, edited by Silvia Urbani, Treviso, Diastema, 2011 (Urania/Specola).

# Urban Spaces and Musical Practices of Neapolitan Female Monasteries between the Seventeenth and Eighteenth Centuries

*Angela Fiore*
(Università di Messina)

## Introduction

Between the seventeenth and eighteenth centuries, Naples appears as a metropolis in which religious buildings abounded to the detriment of civil dwellings. The excessive number of churches and monasteries was a source of surprise to foreigners visiting the city. During the last period of Spanish and subsequent Austrian rule, there was a substantial increase in the number of female religious institutions and the monastic population in a disproportionate ratio to the number of the civil population[1].

By the seventeenth century, there were around 400 religious institutions of which 31 were female monasteries, but the number was destined to increase in the following years.

The various religious buildings in the city played a crucial part in the musical history of Naples; in particular, the cultural liveliness of female cloisters contributed to the city's artistic and spectacular growth. Nunneries were privileged places to ensure an honourable position for the daughters of the nobility destined by vocation or family choice to a cloistered life rather than marriage. The monastery represented the possibility of living in a context with a marked ecclesiastical and social visibility, and it allowed nuns to benefit from the cultural dimension of a community life disciplined by monastic enclosure.

Nunneries were often promoters of devotional practices and centres of musical activities: the documentation within the institutions reveals a constant use of music for both daily liturgical and extraordinary rituals[2].

---

[1]. See Strazzullo 1968.

[2]. Studies conducted on Neapolitan monastic institutions offer sufficient elements through which to understand how monastic life was marked by complex dynamics of social, cultural and religious relations.

One of the main objectives of nuns was to gain visibility in the public space to assert their influence in the city. The organisation of magnificent celebrations contributed decisively to the achievement of this goal. Over the centuries, female religious institutions welcomed the most representative musicians of the city. Musicians active in convents and nunneries mainly had the task of supporting the numerous devotions and principal festivities of the liturgical year with music. In charitable institutions, such as conservatories, musicians also provided musical education to nuns.

As we will see in the following pages, the study of historical and archival sources shows that the musical activity in female cloisters was well organised and firmly established. Female communities were often responsible for producing and commissioning sacred music concerning both the public and private spheres, and through musical production they participated in the creation of the sound identity of Naples[3].

## NUNNERIES IN THE VICEREGAL NAPLES

Like aristocratic courts, female monastic communities were important centres of production, consumption and redistribution of financial and material resources. Over the centuries, many female institutes found themselves accumulating and managing enormous assets, thanks to a dense network of exchanges and relationships with the territory. Monastic centres were also involved in the manufacture of fabrics, sweets and foodstuffs, the proceeds of which constituted an income for the community. However, this *modus vivendi* was in paradoxical contrast with what the post-Tridentine reform had tried to do, separating cloistered life from the outside world[4]. Commercial activity instead contributed to intertwining the cloisters with the economic and social life of the city.

The importance of the monasteries was mainly determined by the relationships they had with exponents of the ecclesiastical hierarchy and the local aristocracy. Archival documentation of renowned institutions such as the monastery of Santa Chiara, the Croce di Lucca, Regina Coeli, San Gregorio Armeno, Donnaregina and San Potito includes prestigious surnames like Pignatelli, Caracciolo and Capece Minutolo. There was also a precise relationship between the

---

See FACCHIANO 1992; ILLIBATO 1985; NOVI-CHAVARRIA 1993; NOVI-CHAVARRIA 2001; GALASSO – VALERIO 2001; VALERIO 2006; VALERIO 2007; RUSSO 1970; HILLS 2004.

3.  This essay derives from my doctoral research conducted from 2011 to 2015 at the University of Fribourg, based on the reconstruction of the musical history of female religious institutions in Naples between 1650 and 1750. The results of the entire project are published in FIORE 2017.

4.  The monastic reform programme was discussed during the Council of Trent. Reintroduction of enclosure, redistribution of cloistered spaces, and behavioural norms were the essential elements of the reform. See GALASSO – VALERIO 2001; CREYTENS 1965, pp. 45-84; BOCCADAMO 1990.

location of the monastery, the presence of family groups within it and membership in one of the capital's 'seats'. Neapolitan noble families were grouped into five seats[5]. As strongholds of the patriciate and administrative bodies of the city government, seats contributed to exercising numerous forms of control over female monastic communities, orienting the criteria of asset management and recruiting women religious.

Abbesses from noble families governed the most prestigious institutes. The family allocated part of its assets to support or create a monastic community and thus controlled, through its daughters, not only the cloisters but strategic political and institutional nodes. Nuns made their monasteries spiritual and cultural centres, while family ties allowed them to play a significant role in the public and city context.

Between 1650 and 1750, there were 43 female religious institutions that undertook remarkable musical activity. Twenty-seven were nunneries of multiple monastic orders subjected to seclusion: seven Benedictine institutes, seven Franciscans, five Dominicans, three Augustinians, three Poor Clares, one Lateran Canoness, and one Carmelite. Instead, charitable institutions without formal cloistered obligation were conservatories, retreats, colleges and hospitals. They attempted to remedy situations of social distress in Naples, hosting the disadvantaged, orphans and poor girls to provide for their education. Each conservatory had a specific purpose: there were institutions destined for disadvantaged girls, orphans with honoured births, poor girls or simple boarders of particular arts corporations. There were sixteen charitable institutions in which musical activity is attested.

Following the monastic reform, the aristocratic families also protected in a certain way the consumption of music by the cloisters. Ecclesiastical authorities believed music could conflict with morality and therefore opposed its too intensive practice. Numerous decrees forbade the use of figured chant, polyphony, the use of instruments other than the organ, and welcoming outside musicians. The ecclesiastical hierarchies aimed to prevent liturgies from resembling secular feasts. Nevertheless, nuns constantly violated restrictions, thanks to the support of their aristocratic families of origin. Ties between patriciate and religious institutions were even more decisive in the monasteries of royal patronage, a type of institution that removed itself from episcopal authority to obey the pope directly through apostolic nuncios.

However, this led to numerous conflicts between secular powers, ecclesiastical hierarchies and nobility, especially since the balance between different parties was made even more precarious by the intervention of authorities such as apostolic nuncios and viceroys[6].

---

5.   The seats, known as *sedili* or *piazze*, were bodies with administrative and political functions that had the task of reconciling the needs of the citizens and the power of the sovereign. There were five noble seats: Capuana, Montagna, Nido, Porto and Portanova. In addition to these, there was also the *Seggio del Popolo*, which included the bourgeois and the working class of the city. The most renowned seats were those of Capuana and Nido.

6.   See Russo 1970; Novi-Chavarria 1993.

# ANGELA FIORE

Their status as royal institutions allowed the monasteries to be more closely linked to the sovereign power, to enjoy benefits and privileges. They had also had more concessions regarding the use of music in ceremonies and became veritable coteries of the city's most representative musicians.

## RITES AND LITURGIES

The musical organisation of celebrations changed according to the economic prestige of the specific devotion, the importance of the various institutions and the noble families supporting them. Some documentary sources give descriptions of the rites and thus provide a visual reconstruction of liturgies, spaces and spectacular apparatuses[7]. Contemporary chronicles often testify to the high quality of the music produced and performed. Moreover, nuns were not passive spectators but were concerned with concretely shaping these events[8]. Some of these institutions simply gathered a few singers and musicians to accompany liturgies, while the main ecclesiastical institutions engaged the prestigious musical groups in the city like the Chapel of the Cathedral of Naples.

Also known as the Chapel of the Archbishop, this was a vocal and instrumental ensemble reporting directly to the archbishop's court. Its task was to satisfy liturgical needs in the countless sacred institutions of Naples. According to the diocesan edicts, the Chapel of the Cathedral and the musicians of the Conservatorio di Gesù Cristo were the only ensembles permitted to play during the liturgies of the Neapolitan sacred institutions, as we can see in the following document:

> Si ricorda alli Signori della Congregazione del Sinodo, chè la S. M. del Cardinal Caracciolo per evitare l'estorsioni, è spese superflue alli Monasteri, è Conservatori soggetti alla sua Giurisdizione, ordinò, chè nelle feste delle loro chiese, anche in occasione di monacazione, ò di altra qualunque funtione, si dovessero servire della musica della Chiesa Arcivescovale, ò pure di quella del Conservatorio di Santa Maria della Colonna detto de' Poveri di Gesù Cristo, come Conservatorio immediatamente soggetto all'Arcivescovo [...][9].

---

[7]. Regarding the musical activity of female institutions in Naples, see CONTI 2003; FABRIS – GRUPPO DI LAVORO 'NAPOLI', pp. 227-281; FIORE 2017.

[8]. The chronicles of the *Gazzetta di Napoli* constitute a rich source of information concerning music and entertainment, reporting on the city's main events, many of which were related to religious institutions. The *Gazzetta* began its weekly publications in 1675 until 1768. See MAGAUDDA – COSTANTINI 2009. In the following pages, documents taken from the *Gazzetta di Napoli* and published in MAGAUDDA – COSTANTINI 2009 will be referred to as GDN.

[9]. Archivio Storico Diocesano di Napoli (ASDN), *Sinodo 1726*. The Chapel of the Cathedral and the Conservatorio dei Poveri di Gesù Cristo were in fact the only musical institutions managed by the Curia.

## Urban Spaces and Musical Practices of Neapolitan Female Monasteries

However, the archbishop's musicians competed on the sacred stage with the prestigious Cappella Reale di Palazzo, an ensemble subordinate to the viceroy, whose task was to accompany religious and mundane ceremonies of the court. Established in 1555, the Royal Chapel gathered around its composers and famous organists such as Jean de Macque, Giovanni Maria Trabaci, Ascanio Majone, Andrea Falconieri, etc.[10]. The viceroyal ensemble also had close ties with various female institutions: in particular, monasteries of royal patronage, supported by the protection of the Viceroys, benefited from the musicians and singers of the Palatine Chapel[11].

Alongside the official musical chapels, there were occasional ensembles composed of musicians from city instrumental groups. Constituted by the chapel master or the organist on duty at the institution, they were assembled and paid according to a specific festive occasion. The composition and size of these ensembles generally reflected the importance of the institution promoting an event and the relevance of the event itself, together with economic reasons and available space[12].

The number of permanent musicians increased during the most solemn festivities with the enrolment of additional artists, also known as *soprannumerari*. During the liturgies, the musical chapel was generally placed in specific spaces made up for the occasion and called *orchesti*. Dates of the liturgical calendar solemnized with music were numerous and different for each institute. Among the moments of the liturgical calendar that most required the intervention of musicians, we find celebrations relating to Advent, Christmas and Epiphany: twelve institutes record expenses for singers and instrumentalists for solemn masses and the Christmas novena[13].

The liturgical year of each institution was crowded with different forms of devotion: the triduum for patron saints, novenas and octaves, a liturgy for a religious profession, a special

---

[10]. See Dietz 1972; Krause 1993, pp. 235-257; Fabris 2001, pp. 235-250; Maione 2005, pp. 309-341; Maione 2015.

[11]. Investigation of the archival sources of monasteries has also produced information that can be useful to map numerically the activity of the monasteries and the workers active in them. The archival data can now be consulted on the platform: <http://musiconapolitano.hkb.bfh.ch/>, accessed January 2023. The database is the result of a project started in 2014 at the University of Fribourg in Switzerland and conducted together with Claudio Bacciagaluppi, with the IT support of Rodolfo Zitellini. The database is dedicated to all music professionals (composers, singers, instrumentalists, librettists, impresarios etc.) whose activity in Naples is documented by published and unpublished archive sources. See also Fiore – Bacciagaluppi – Zitellini 2019, pp. 383-396.

[12]. In addition to the Royal Chapel and the Cathedral Chapel, there were also other permanent ensembles linked to specific religious institutions in Naples. The most prestigious of these was the Cappella Musicale del Tesoro di San Gennaro, an ensemble linked to the cult of San Gennaro. For a detailed reconstruction of the artistic and musical events of the Chapel of San Gennaro, see Columbro – Maione 2008. The Casa Santa dell'Annunziata also had a stable musical ensemble of singers and instrumentalists. On the Annunziata's musical activity, see Columbro 2001, pp. 42-78.

[13]. Regarding the different festivities in Viceroyal Naples, see Fabris 2007; Mauro 2020.

ceremony for a victory, a birth, an aristocratic wedding, were constantly added to the canonical celebrations for Christmas and Easter.

The cult of Mary was particularly felt and celebrated by Neapolitan people. Numerous pious practices in honour of Mary seem to recall the city's bond with the Virgin: five institutes solemnise the feast of the Immaculate Conception, seven that of the Assumption, five the Nativity of the Virgin, three the title of Holy Mary of Grace. The feasts of Our Lady of the Rosary, the Visitation and the Purification of the Virgin, Our Lady of Mount Carmel and Our Lady of Sorrows were also celebrated.

Among the Marian feasts, the Holy Mary of Graces was celebrated on 5 July in the prestigious Santa Chiara cloister and it lasted for a whole month. Each day of the month provided for the exposition of the Blessed Sacrament from morning to evening. Archival documents testify that on the festive day, musical support included «nine voices» several instruments and a choir «with two registers». In the following days, the ensemble dwindled into «four voices, four violins, cello, lute and contrabass». The rite continued with the Exposition of the Sacrament until 10.30 pm during which motets and symphonies were performed. The pomp of this festivity and the music lasted until the late hours and did not fail to provoke the indignation of the archbishops, in some cases forcing the closure of the monastery[14].

The liturgical and musical ceremony for the Holy Mother of Sorrows was also particularly solemn. At the Conservatorio della Solitaria, artisans set up gilded altarpieces, ephemeral machines, and altars adorned with canopies, silk or paper flowers. The participation of celebrities such as the castrato Matteo Sassano is documented. Furthermore, Neapolitan female institutions intensified scenic and spectacular apparatuses during the celebrations of Holy Week. Despite the penitential spirit that this liturgical moment was supposed to entail, there was a long succession of lavish liturgies throughout the Lenten period up to Easter Sunday. As many as twenty-one institutions record expenses for music for the preparation of sepulchres, processions and re-enactments of the Passion of Christ.

## Processions

Travelling spectacles and expressions of popular faith, processions constituted one of the greatest moments of public representation for all the city institutions involved. The richness of the liturgical vestments, the use of sumptuous apparatuses and sound architecture not only aimed at arousing the astonishment of the people but also contributed to the symbolic construction of the power underlying events themselves. Some of the most significant city processions saw the active involvement of female institutions.

---

14. Archivio Storico di Napoli (ASN), *Corporazioni religiose sopprese*, f. 2579.

# Urban Spaces and Musical Practices of Neapolitan Female Monasteries

The evocative Good Friday procession, known as the 'Solitaria's Procession', was organised by the Conservatorio della Solitaria, a charitable institution for the orphaned daughters of Spanish soldiers stationed in Naples[15]. Nuns provided the organisation and supported the expense of the imposing procession that wound its way through the streets of Naples on Good Friday night. Carlo Celano in his chronicles refers to «a very devout procession with the mysteries of the Holy Passion» with «two thousand lighted torches and perhaps more» in which the main city authorities took part[16]. Even Jean Jacques Bouchard in his renowned *Voyage dans le royaume de Naples* was struck by the charm of this ritual:

> Après ces battans, suivent / quantité de faquins tous vestus de longues aulbes de toile et la face couverte, qui portent les uns au bout de longues perches de grans chaudrons pleins de poix, graisse et huile alumez, les autres des cierges de cire blanche au bout de certaines cannes fendues en quattre, et entourent tout le mystere, au devant duquel marche un choeur de musique, et au derriere le cavalier *il quale conduce il misterio*, avec tous ceus qu'il a invitez, ayants tous un cierge allumé en main. En ce mesme ordre suivent tous les autres mysteres [...][17].

As Bouchard writes, the procession was enriched by processional 'mysteries', artistic depictions of the passion and death of Christ, which stood on a shaped wooden base called *vara*, made either of wood or papier-mâché. The mysteries were inspired by classical iconography and sacred scriptures. Statues were often embellished with precious silver ornaments and elaborate floral compositions to enhance their beauty. The procession was attended by the viceroy and the court, all the high city authorities including the military corps, clerics and priests. In addition, a host of *battenti*, accompanied the procession wearing hoods and armed with scourges, added physical mortification to the prayer, as a sign of penitence and participation in the passion of Christ.

Finally, musicians and singers from the Royal Chapel and 'fleets' of the male conservatories accompanied the procession. Female nunneries used to establish real partnerships with the four male city conservatories, to secure the presence of the 'sons' during the celebrations. The task of these children, organised in 'fleets' or 'flotillas', was not always music-related: they often acted as simple ornaments. They could be dressed as angels or wear clothes of various styles[18].

---

[15]. The Conservatorio di Nostra Signora della Solitaria, also known as Soledad, guaranteed the guest girls an education based not only on Christian doctrine and the womanly arts but also on learning music. This institution, forgotten for decades, must have had its importance in Viceroyal Naples. Research conducted on the materials in the institution's archive has led to clarifying the role of the Conservatorio della Solitaria in the cultural life of Naples. Reference is made to Fiore 2017, pp. 203-216.

[16]. Celano 1974, p. 588.

[17]. Bouchard 1977, pp. 189-190.

[18]. For example, on the feast of the Nativity of Mary, celebrated at the monastery of San Potito on 8 September, the presence of «the Red Children» or children with «country clothes» is attested.

The duty of the nuns was to provide for every need of the procession: to call artisans to «dress and undress the mysteries»; to purchase candles; to arrange refreshments for children of the conservatories; to engage the Viceroy's musicians[19].

The use of music and musicians during the procession is unfortunately only briefly mentioned in the archive documents, without precise details, allowing us only partially to imagine the sound performance of this nocturnal procession.

Another event with a symbolic charge was the Corpus Domini procession, one of the central moments of Neapolitan devotion. Rites of Corpus Christi began with the celebration of a solemn mass in the Cathedral. At the end of the liturgy, the Blessed Sacrament was carried through the streets of Naples under a processional pallium, a sort of canopy, made of a rectangular cloth supported by eight poles. The magnificent procession lasted six hours. It started from the Cathedral and, passing through the city centre, touched the main city squares, ending at one of the most prestigious cloisters: the monastery of Santa Chiara.

The first significant moment of the procession was in the Piazza della Selleria, also known as the Piazza del Pendino, the seat of the Seggio del Popolo, where a sumptuous catafalque was erected and music was performed by the main musicians of the city chosen by the Seggio del Popolo[20]. The various stages of the procession included musical accompaniment by musicians from the Royal Chapel, as evidenced by bank records of the Banco di Napoli Historical Archives, which repeatedly document the presence of musicians from the Palatine ensemble such as Giuseppe de Majo or Nicola Fago[21]:

> A Don Giuseppe Brunasso d. Cento e per esso a Don Nicola Tarantino
> [Fago] per tanti che ha improntato una nota esibitali di diversi Instromenti di Fiato,
> e Voci, che hanno servito nella Musica fatta il giorno del Corpus Domini prossimo
> passato per la festa da esso fattasi, com'Eletto del Fedelissimo Popolo [...][22].

The monastery of Santa Chiara was the final stage of the procession. At Santa Chiara, a solemn mass was celebrated, with the presence of the viceroy, the most important city authorities, the army and the court[23].

---

19.    See FIORE 2017, app.doc. pp. 309-335.

20.    The Sedile or Seggio del Popolo, dating back to the thirteenth century, although not having a direct administrative function, played the role of 'spokesperson' of the citizens and was the absolute protagonist in the festivals in the square or religious processions. See NAPPI 2001, pp. 100-120.

21.    The Historical Archive of the Istituto Banco di Napoli (ASBN) holds today the accounting records of the seven ancient Neapolitan credit institutions. These are credit instruments and policies used for payments by public and private institutions and individuals. See COTTICELLI – MAIONE 2015.

22.    *Ibidem*, app. doc. ASBN, BSA, 11/I/1736.

23.    The Corpus Christi procession followed this route: Archbishopric, Vico delle Zite, Sant'Agostino alla Zecca, Strada della Selleria, Strada dei Cortellari, Largo di Porto, Santa Maria la Nova, Montoliveto. After the

## Urban Spaces and Musical Practices of Neapolitan Female Monasteries

Between the seventeenth and eighteenth centuries, the monastery of Santa Chiara was one of the most prestigious monasteries in Naples. The institution was founded by King Robert of Anjou and his wife Sancia of Majorca[24]. It was Queen Sancia herself who drew up the constitution of the religious community, inspired by the cloistered rules given to the Poor Clares of San Damiano by Innocent IV. The designation of the monastery of Santa Chiara as the seat of the state ceremonies, coronations and royal burials meant that it became a tangible sign of royal power over the centuries. The consecration of the monastery as a royal institution took place in 1317 with the official dedication to the Holy Body of Christ, but already in Angevin documents of 1321, it was referred to simply by the name of Santa Chiara. Corpus Domini represented the institution's main feast and therefore a particular lustre was accorded to it. Already in 1536, Father Giacomo d'Ancona, General of the conventuals in charge of the spiritual guidance of the institution, complained about the worldly character of the ceremonies organised by the Poor Clares. For example, Giacomo d'Ancona pointed out that during the feast of Corpus Christi too many secular persons entered the monastery of Santa Chiara where «too much music» was played[25].

King Robert of Anjou, being particularly devoted to the Eucharistic cult, asked and obtained from the Pope, with a papal brief, that during the feast of Corpus Domini, the procession would leave the archbishopric and enter the monastery of Santa Chiara. Then, the Blessed Sacrament was to be exhibited in it for eight continuous days.

Therefore, following the rites of Corpus Christi on Thursday, an octave was organised, with the Blessed Sacrament exposed to the adoration of people for eight days. Each day included the perpetual exposition of the Blessed Sacrament and the celebration of vespers with the concluding *Pange lingua* sung by the children from the Conservatorio della Pietà de' Turchini.

Although there are few and only generic indications regarding the musical part of the ceremony, the cloister documentation records the participation of children from the Conservatorio of Pietà de' Turchini during vespers and the engagement of musicians from the Royal Chapel for the solemn procession and mass. The Poor Clares also organised a small procession inside the monastery courtyards, also accompanied by music, which was used to carry the Blessed Sacrament into the church. The octave was to be quite solemn, as some public

---

solemn mass at Santa Chiara, the procession resumed its route along Strada Trinità Maggiore, Piazzetta Nilo, Via Nilo, Largo dei Girolamini before returning to the Cathedral. See NAPPI 2001; DE FREDE 2005. Information on the Corpus Domini procession can be found in the ceremonials of the court of Naples, which report in detail chronicles of the celebrations of this feast from the sixteenth century until the reign of Charles of Bourbon (1734-1759), making it possible to study the evolution of the liturgy and to understand the importance conferred on the ritual over the centuries by different rulers. See ANTONELLI 2012; ANTONELLI 2014.

24. The monastery of Santa Chiara was a double monastery housing the Poor Clares and the Franciscan Friars. See PANE 1954; GALLINO 1963; VALERIO 2006; D'ANDREA 1987; GAGLIONE 2007, pp. 127-209.

25. MIELE 2001, p. 97.

# ANGELA FIORE

notices testify, reporting that the «Religious Ladies of Santa Chiara [...] are always admired, especially in the current Octave of the Holy Sacrament with continuous Music with several choirs, Panegyrics, and with other demonstrations until night»[26]. The accounting records of the monastery add details regarding the amount incurred on Corpus Christi. For example, in 1736 expenses for the festivity amounted to 1863 ducats:

> Per la Musica oltre l'estraordinario della sera, che si ponerà al suo luogo ed oltre quello si carica al Vicariato d. 528. [...]
> Per convito di Messe, stampa d'Indulgenze, Figliuoli della Pietà, e serventi d. 55.
> E per la Processione dell'Ottava con Altar alla porta, Trombette, rinfresco, e parato, spese in tutto il triennio d. 85
> Somma d'esito per detta Festività del Santissimo d. 1863[27].

## THE CULT OF SAINTS

Countless celebrations were linked to the cult of saints, whose patronage was invoked through commemorative celebrations, triduum and novenas. The feast of San Potito fell on 14 January. Several documents refer to an «extraordinary music» organized by the Benedictine nuns of the homonymous monastery with the use of «special violins». In a chronicle of 1720, the *Gazzetta di Napoli* reports that «the music, both in the first and second vespers and in the morning of that festivity, was performed by the best voices and musicians of this capital» with the participation of «the celebrated and virtuoso musician, Marquis Matteo Sassano»[28].

Even on the feast of San Benedetto, the presence of famous musicians is documented, whose nuns note the nicknames with which they were best known:

> In marzo [...] san Benedetto [...]
> Dato al sig. Aquilano per le due vesperi e Messa d. 4
> Dato al sig. Traschilio e sig. Battestino d. 8
> Dato per diece Istromenti d. 20
> Dato alli Poveri di Giesu Xristo d. 9 [...]
> Dato a chi a tirato li Mantici d. 0.1.10
> Dato per affitto di un organo d. 1.2.10[29]

---

[26]. ASN, *Corporazioni religiose soppresse*, f. 2556, cc. 63-64, 1736.

[27]. Biblioteca di Santa Chiara, *Conti del Badessati* (1733-1736).

[28]. GDN, 23 January 1720 (2).

[29]. ASN, *Corporazioni religiose soppresse*, f. 2943. The 'Aquilano' corresponds to Domenico Melchiorre, musician of the Royal Chapel; the 'Battestino' could probably be identified with the German cellist Jean-Baptiste Stuck, who, in the eighteenth century, was in the service of the Countess of Lemos.

# URBAN SPACES AND MUSICAL PRACTICES OF NEAPOLITAN FEMALE MONASTERIES

Likewise, St Benedict, the patron saint of monasteries under Benedictine rule, was celebrated by the monasteries of Donnalbina and San Gregorio Armeno, with sung masses and processions.

In addition to titular saints of the orders and patrons of the city, most of the festivities were organized to celebrate the saints of which some monasteries kept the relics[30]. For example, at the end of the sixteenth century, the Benedictine nuns of San Gregorio Armeno were custodians of the head of St Stephen; the head of St Blaise; part of the wood of the cross of Christ; the arm of St Laurence; the arm of St Pantaleone; the blood of St Stephen; the chain of our St Gregory[31]. Therefore they celebrated with solemnity:

> [...] cinque giorni festivi con musica e panegirici a 3. Febraro la festività di S. Biaggio Vescovo e Martire a 21. marzo la festività di S. Benedetto a 29 ag.o la festività della decollazione di S. Gio: Batta a 21 sett.e la festa di S. Matteo Apostolo a p.mo ott.re la festa di S. Gregorio Armeno titolare del Mon.rio [...][32].

In particular, the festivity of Saint Blaise included five days with «musici extraordinari», «voci aggionte» and «instromenti»[33].

The solemn mass dedicated to Saint Blaise was introduced by an «impressive procession with thirty or forty lit torches, accompanied by different kinds of sounds and an infinite number of people». The procession accompanied the head of the «glorious Saint Blaise» through the city[34]. The cult of Saint Blaise of Sebaste in Armenia was particularly felt in the south of Italy. It was in fact the Armenian nuns of San Gregorio Armeno who had fostered the devotion in Naples of the saint invoked for throat diseases. The feast included two characteristic moments: the procession of candles and the blessing of the loaves of bread on 3 February. Following the procession, two candles are held in a crossed position over the throats of the faithful and small loaves of bread were blessed and distributed to the people, in memory of the most popular miracle of the Saint: the healing of a child freed from suffocation caused by a fishbone stuck in his throat with a piece of bread.

The festivities of St John the Baptist were pervaded by folkloric elements. Celebrations for the feast of St John the Baptist were a travelling spectacle through the streets with a series

---

[30]. At the end of the sixteenth century, the nuns of San Gregorio Armeno disputed for a long time with the Benedictine nuns of San Potito for possession of the relic of St John the Baptist. Not only matters of prestige were at stake, but also economic revenues that could be derived from the veneration of the relics by the people.

[31]. CARRINO 2013, pp. 113-114.

[32]. SPINOSA – PINTO – VALERIO 2013, Appendice A, p. 803.

[33]. ASN, *Corporazioni religiose soppresse*, f. 3356.

[34]. The passage is taken from Fulvia Caracciolo's memoirs. CARRINO 2013, p. 63.

219

of impressive scenic apparatuses: processions, *tableaux vivants*, sacred representations, and pantomimes in which the female monasteries themselves took part[35].

Three institutes had been custodians of the St John's precious blood that was annually subject to liquefaction: Santa Maria di Donnaromita, Sant'Arcangelo a Baiano and San Gregorio Armeno. Therefore, the patronage of the celebrations was contested between the three institutes. The dispute did not refer only to the patronage of devotion, but it was especially due to economic gains that could be derived from the veneration of the relics by the faithful.

Two dates were linked to the Saint: the celebration of his birth on 24 June and his beheading on 29 August. On these dates, the liquefaction of the blood took place. These two solemn occasions included the traditional visit of the viceroys, with the participation of renowned singers such as Domenico Gizzi. We find mention of him in an account book of the monastery of Donnaromita:

> Al 3 settembre detto 1729 pagato per la Musica in occasione che il signor
> Vice Re e Vice Regina e suoi signori figli vennero a vedere la Reliquia di San Giovanni
> Battista alle sottoscritte persone sono cioè:
> Pagato al Mastro di Cappella dell'Arcivescovado d. 1
> Pagato per numero 4 Istrumenti d. 2
> Pagato alla prima voce Gizij d. 1.2.10
> Pagato alla seconda voce Don Diego del Vasto d. 1 [...][36].

The *Gazzetta di Napoli* mentions the feast of St John in 1717 at Donnaromita, emphasising the presence of Matteo Sassano: «the church was richly decorated with four choirs of selected musicians, the first and second vespers were celebrated, and in the morning the renowned marquis Matteo Sassano was there to sing [...]»[37].

Rich festivities were also organised in the city of St Clare, from 10 to 12 August. The Poor Clares of the monastery of Santa Chiara had recognised the solemnity of this Saint as a feast of precept for the whole city of Naples. Between the late seventeenth and mid-eighteenth centuries, an impressive triduum was organized. The statue of St Clare, kept in the Cathedral of Naples, was carried in procession to the monastery of Santa Chiara on 10 August. On arrival at the church, the Royal Chapel intoned a solemn *Te Deum*. The place of the ceremony was set up «with silver drapes» and «golden fringes» that adorned the space intended for musicians. When the statue entered the church, the Royal Chapel of the Palace sang the *Te Deum* «continued by its musicians accompanied by a great shot of 300 firecrackers». The following day, vespers

---

[35]. See MEGALE 2013, pp. 387-414.

[36]. ASN, *Corporazioni religiose soppresse*, f. 4009. This document is also cited in BACCIAGALUPPI 2010, p. 71.

[37]. GDN, 31 August 1717.

# Urban Spaces and Musical Practices of Neapolitan Female Monasteries

and a mass sung «by resounding music for four choirs» were scheduled and the church was «cluttered with the Church by every class of people»[38].

On the feast day, 12 August, another sung mass was celebrated with music in the presence of the viceroy and the highest city authorities. Late at night, the feast ended with a procession of the statue of St Clare in the inner courtyard of the monastery. Finally, on 13 August, with a new procession composed of friars, cantors, and children of the Pietà de' Turchini, the precious statue was brought back to the Cathedral[39].

## Dynastic Events

Female cloisters also fervently participated in the various celebrations of the court or aristocratic families. Festive celebrations dedicated to the aristocracy rather than the royal house made it possible to strengthen ties and alliances. Thus, births, baptisms and weddings of viceroys involved solemn masses. A *Te Deum* of thanksgiving was sung for the recovered health of members of the aristocracy. Processions and solemn funerals were instead organized for the death of sovereigns, members of aristocratic families and clergy.

Particularly heartfelt were all the events connected with the new king of Naples, Charles of Bourbon, seen as the liberator from Austrian oppression and misrule. On 10 May 1734, the new sovereign made his triumphal entry into Naples, greeted by a jubilant crowd on which he showered gold coins. The procession passed through the city centre, greeted by great jubilation from the people.

Numerous city institutions participated in this event: for example, the Benedictines of Santa Patrizia lit their monastery continuously for three evenings, «and sang the *Te Deum* with highly chosen music [...]»[40]. The Poor Clares of Santa Chiara note that on the day of entry of the King and for all three following evenings, in the streets adjacent to their monastery oboes, hunting horns, flutes, bassoons and trumpets resounded and there was a continuous sound of bells[41].

After settling in Naples, Charles of Bourbon visited the most significant institutions in the city, including the monastery of Santa Chiara. To gain the new sovereign's favour and

---

[38].   ASN, MS, f. 2555.

[39].   ASN, MS, f. 2554, a detailed explanation of the proceedings of the triduum can be found in the nella *Relazione distinta del modo con cui siasi ottenuta la Festa di Precetto per la nostra gloriosa Santa Chiara e delle pompe festive praticate in quest'anno 1729*. In the 1729 celebration, the chapel master was Nicola Fago.

[40].   GDN, 25 May (5).

[41].   ASN, *Corporazioni religiose soppresse*, f. 2555, app. pp. 254-255, this is the *full report of everything that took place on the occasion of the happy entry of the new King Charles of Bourbon with the functions that then took place and the expenses incurred* [...].

attention, the nuns had sent numerous gifts to the court, receiving in return the privilege of a visit to the monastery and its gardens on 20 May 1734.

Because of the extraordinary nature of the event, nuns provided not only decorations for the church but also for the courtyards and outdoor spaces as far as the largo del Gesù. The Poor Clares describe these moments as follows[42]:

> Dalla parte laterale vi si fece un ben disposto orchesto a due registri per la lunghezza de' palmi sessanta, finché fosse stato capace per musica à quattro cori. [...] [all'esterno] si pose una corte di trombe di caccia, oboè, flauti, e fagotti, quale col suono festivo delle campane anticiparono i [...] segni di giubilo. Finalmente verso le ore ventidue e mezza giunse sua maestà [...]. S'incamminò verso l'Altar maggiore osservando ogni intorno [...] facendosi trambusto da musici una strepitossissima sinfonia con tutte sorti di istrumenti, con la direzione del maestro di Cappella Niccolò Tarantino. Appena giunto al suo posto, dal nostro M. Padre Guardiano Don Alessio di Roma, con l'assistenza delli due Padri Confessori [...] e con dodeci cantori vestiti di cotta e Chierico schierati con buon ordine, fatta prima riverenza a sua Maestà s'intuonò il Te Deum corrisposto dà scelta musica à quattro cori de' primi virtuosi qui si ritrovano, e dà grande sparo di mortaretti [...][43].

The nuns also hoped to host the solemn coronation of Charles of Bourbon as King of Naples, planned for the summer of 1734. Since the monastery of Santa Chiara was, therefore 'Casa Regia' as well as «luogo capacissimo» and «veneratissimo» by the Pope, nuns were quite certain to obtain this concession from the future king as well. However, the coronation ceremony of Charles of Bourbon as King of the two Sicilies took place only on 3 June of the following year at the Cathedral of Palermo[44].

A few years later, in 1737, Maria Amalia of Saxony became betrothed to Charles of Bourbon. The wedding ceremony was publicly announced at the end of October 1737. The wedding celebration then took place in Dresden on 8 May 1738. The 14-year-old Maria Amalia married Charles of Bourbon by proxy. As early as January 1738, numerous thanksgiving ceremonies took place to announce the marriage: the nuns of Santa Chiara sang a solemn

---

[42]. Evidence of the event is also to be found in GDN, 25 May 1734 (1): «La M. del nostro re, avendo risoluto d'osservare i luoghi più cospicui di questa capitale, giovedì 20 del corrente mese dié principio dal rinomatissimo suo R. monistero di S. Chiara [...]; e in fatti verso le ore ventidue e mezza, portatasi sua maestà in detta chiesa [...], entrò in quella, sotto l'armonioso concerto di scelta musica a quattro cori e di altri suoni ivi preparati e, giunto sullo strato, s'intuonò il Te Deum da quel guardiano, padre Alessio da Roma, corrisposto da' musici [...]».

[43]. ASN, *Corporazioni religiose soppresse*, f. 2555.

[44]. The coronation of Charles of Bourbon was organized for the summer of 1734, not long after his entry into Naples. The opposition of the Roman court, favourable to the Austrian imperialists, advised postponing the ceremony to avoid incidents with the Papacy. This was celebrated on 3 June 1735 in Palermo Cathedral. See RENDA 1978, p. 187.

# Urban Spaces and Musical Practices of Neapolitan Female Monasteries

*Te Deum* in their church «with music, magnificent apparatus and continuous prayers»[45], «pompous apparatus» and «extraordinary music»[46] at San Potito, while the «inexplicable devotion» to the «invincible monarch» of the nuns of Santa Maria Maddalena, was sealed by a «rich altar of silver by the light of several torches [...] *Te Deum* and a solemn mass with several choirs of chosen music [...] in thanksgiving to the Highest for the established marriage of His Majesty with the Most Serene Royal Princess of Poland [...]»[47].

The wedding was also celebrated in other city institutions, such as the conservatory of the Solitaria, by the nuns of Santa Maria Egiziaca and at the monastery of Ss. Pietro and Sebastiano.

The various pregnancies of Queen Maria Amalia also saw the participation of the women's cloisters. The Solitaria sang a solemn *Te Deum* for the birth, in 1740, of Maria Isabella Antonia, while the nuns of Santa Chiara sang a solemn *Te Deum* for that of Maria Josefa Antoinette, who died shortly afterwards[48]. For the birth of Prince Philip, the Conservatorio dei Santi Filippo e Giacomo celebrated a «grand mass [...] with several choirs of music and an unfailing *Te Deum* in thanksgiving»[49]. Nuns of the Conservatorio dell'Arte della Lana celebrated the birth of little Charles, destined to become Charles IV, continuator of the Spanish branch of the Bourbons «with apparatus, exposition of the Blessed Sacrament, sung mass, music and great firing of firecrackers»[50].

***

In conclusion, monasteries and conservatories contributed to the development of spectacular liturgical musical traditions. In this sense, their contribution to the cultural life and festive organization of the city can be compared to that of more celebrated Neapolitan institutions, such as the Tesoro di San Gennaro, the Royal Chapel, and the theatres, to which many more studies refer. Considering the contribution of the monastic communities' sound activity to the city's musical landscape allows us to broaden the perspective of musical historiography. This unravels a significant part of the history of Neapolitan music in which women have played a leading role.

---

[45].  GDN, 7 January 1738 (2).

[46].  GDN, 21 January 1738 (5).

[47].  GDN, 4 February 1738 (1).

[48].  GDN, 15 March 1740 (3); GDN, 23 January 1742 (4).

[49].  GDN, 18 July 1747 (3).

[50].  GDN, 26 November 1748 (2).

# Angela Fiore

## Bibliography

Antonelli 2012
Antonelli, Attilio. *Cerimoniale del viceregno spagnolo e austriaco di Napoli. 1650-1717*, Crotone, Rubbettino, 2012.

Antonelli 2014
Id. *Cerimoniale del viceregno austriaco di Napoli. 1707-1734*, Naples, Arte'm, 2014.

Bacciagaluppi 2010
Bacciagaluppi, Claudio. *Rom, Prag, Dresden Pergolesi und die Neapolitanische Messe in Europa*, Kassel, Bärenreiter, 2010.

Boccadamo 1990
Boccadamo, Giuliana. *Una riforma impossibile? I papi e primi tentativi di riforma dei monasteri femminili di Napoli nel '500*, Rome, Dehoniana, 1990.

Bouchard 1977
Bouchard, Jean-Jacques. 'Journal: Voyage dans le royaume de Naples', in: *Œuvres de Jean-Jacques Bouchard. 2*, edited by Emanuele Kanceff, Turin, Giappichelli, 1977.

Carrino 2013
Carrino, Candida. *Le monache ribelli raccontate da suor Fulvia Caracciolo*, Naples, Intra Moenia, 2013.

Celano 1974
Celano, Carlo. *Notizie del bello dell'antico e del curioso della città di Napoli (1692) con aggiunzioni di Giovanni Battista Chiarini (1856-60)*, edited by Atanasio Mozzillo, Alfredo Profeta and Francesco Paolo Macchia, Naples, Edizioni scientifiche italiane, 1974.

Columbro 2001
Columbro, Marta. 'Le fonti musicali nella Conservatoria del patrimonio storico, artistico ed archivistico dell'ex Reale Casa Santa dell'Annunziata di Napoli', in: *Fonti d'archivio per la storia della musica e dello spettacolo a Napoli tra XVI e XVIII secolo*, edited by Paologiovanni Maione, Naples, Editoriale Scientifica, 2001, pp. 42-78.

Columbro – Maione 2008
Columbro, Marta – Maione, Paologiovanni. *La Cappella musicale del Tesoro di San Gennaro di Napoli tra Sei e Settecento*, Naples, Turchini, 2008.

Conti 2003
Conti, Carla. *Nobilissime allieve: della musica a Napoli fra Sette e Ottocento*, Naples, Guida, 2003.

Cotticelli – Maione 2015
Cotticelli, Francesco – Maione, Paologiovanni. 'Le carte degli antichi banchi e il panorama musicale e teatrale della Napoli di primo Settecento: 1726-1736', in: *Studi Pergolesiani / Pergolesi Studies 9*, edited by Francesco Cotticelli and Paologiovanni Maione, Bern, Lang, 2015, pp. 659-759.

## URBAN SPACES AND MUSICAL PRACTICES OF NEAPOLITAN FEMALE MONASTERIES

CREYTENS 1965
CREYTENS, Raymond. 'La riforma dei monasteri femminili dopo i Decreti Tridentini', in: *Il Concilio di Trento e la riforma tridentina*, Rome, Herder, 1965, pp. 45-84.

D'ANDREA 1987
D'ANDREA, Gioacchino Francesco. 'Il monastero napoletano di S. Chiara secondo i registri dell'Archivio di Stato di Napoli', in: *Archivum Franciscanum Historicum*, LXXX (1987), pp. 39-78.

DE FREDE 2005
DE FREDE, Carlo. *Il Decumano maggiore da Castel Capuano a San Pietro a Maiella: Cronache napoletane dei secoli passati*, Naples, Liguori, 2005.

DIETZ 1972
DIETZ, Hanns-Bertold. 'A Chronology of Maestri and Organisti at the Cappella Reale in Naples, 1745-1800', in: *Journal of the American Musicological Society*, XXV/3 (1972), pp. 379-406.

FABRIS 2001
FABRIS, Dinko. 'La Capilla Real en las etiquetas de la corte virreinal de Nápoles durante el siglo XVII', in: *La Capilla Real de los Austrias. Música y ritual de corte en la Europa moderna*, edited by Juan José Carreras and Bernardo José García, Madrid, Fundación Carlos de Amberes, 2001, pp. 235-250.

FABRIS 2007
ID. *Music in Seventeenth-Century Naples: Francesco Provenzale (1624-1704)*, Aldershot, Ashgate, 2007.

FABRIS – GRUPPO DI LAVORO 'NAPOLI' 2005
ID. – GRUPPO DI LAVORO 'NAPOLI' DELL'UNIVERSITÀ CA' FOSCARI. 'Dal Medioevo al decennio napoleonico e oltre: metamorfosi e continuità nella tradizione napoletana', in: *Produzione, circolazione e consumo. Consuetudine e quotidianità della polifonia sacra nelle chiese monastiche e parrocchiali dal tardo Medioevo alla fine degli Antichi Regimi*, edited by David Bryant and Elena Quaranta, Bologna, il Mulino, 2005, pp. 227-281.

FACCHIANO 1992
FACCHIANO, Annamaria. *Monasteri femminili e nobiltà a Napoli tra medioevo ed età moderna*, Altavilla Silentina, Edizioni Studi Storici Meridionali, 1992.

FIORE 2017
FIORE, Angela. *'Non senza scandalo delli convicini': pratiche musicali nelle istituzioni musicali femminili a Napoli 1650-1750*, Bern, Lang, 2017 (Publikationen der Schweizerischen Musikforschenden Gesellschaft, 58).

FIORE – BACCIAGALUPPI – ZITELLINI 2019
EAD. – BACCIAGALUPPI, Claudio – ZITELLINI, Rodolfo. 'Musico Napolitano: Chances and Perspectives of Research for a Neapolitan Biographical Index', in: *Paisagens sonoras urbanas: História, Memória e Património*, Évora, Publicações do Cidehus, 2019, pp. 383-396.

GAGLIONE 2007

GAGLIONE, Mario. 'La basilica e il Monastero doppio di S. Chiara a Napoli in studi recenti', in: *Archivio per la Storia delle Donne. IV*, 2007, pp. 127-209.

GALASSO – VALERIO 2001

GALASSO, Giuseppe – VALERIO, Adriana. *Donne e religione a Napoli. Secoli XVI-XVIII*, Milan, Franco Angeli, 2001.

GALLINO 1963

GALLINO, Tommaso Maria. *Il complesso monumentale di S. Chiara in Napoli*, Naples, Pontificio Istituto Superiore di Scienze e Lettere S. Chiara dei Frati Minori, 1963.

HILLS 2004

HILLS, Helen. *Invisible City: The Architecture of Devotion in Seventeenth-Century Neapolitan Convents*, Oxford-New York, Oxford University Press, 2004.

ILLIBATO 1985

ILLIBATO, Antonio. *La donna a Napoli nel Settecento: aspetti dell'educazione e dell'istruzione*, Naples, D'Auria, 1985.

KRAUSE 1993

KRAUSE, Ralph. 'Documenti per la storia della Real Cappella di Napoli nella prima metà del Settecento', in: *Annali dell'Istituto Italiano per gli studi Storici*, XI (1993), pp. 235-257.

MAGAUDDA – COSTANTINI 2009

MAGAUDDA, Ausilia – COSTANTINI, Danilo. *Musica e spettacolo nel Regno di Napoli attraverso lo spoglio della «Gazzetta» (1675-1768)*, Rome, Ismez, 2009.

MAIONE 2005

MAIONE, Paologiovanni. 'Il mondo musicale seicentesco e le sue istituzioni: la Cappella Reale di Napoli (1650-1700)', in: *Francesco Cavalli: La circolazione dell'opera veneziana nei Seicento*, edited by Dinko Fabris, Naples, Turchini, 2005 (I Turchini saggi, 2), pp. 309-341.

MAIONE 2015

ID. '«La Real Azienda»: la cappella musicale di Napoli tra Sei e Settecento', in: *I Quaderni del Conservatorio Domenico Cimarosa di Avellino*, no. 1 (2015), pp. 57-68.

MAURO 2020

MAURO, Ida. *Spazio urbano e rappresentazione del potere: le cerimonie della città di Napoli dopo la rivolta di Masaniello (1648-1672)*, Naples, FedOA-Federico II University Press, 2020.

MEGALE 2013

MEGALE, Teresa. 'Teatro e spettacolo nella Napoli vicereale: modelli e ritualità', in: *Fiesta y Cerimonia en la corte virreinal de Napoles (siglos XVI y XVII)*, Madrid, Centro de Estudios Europa Ispanica, 2013, pp. 387-414.

# Urban Spaces and Musical Practices of Neapolitan Female Monasteries

Miele 2001

Miele, Michele. 'Monache e monasteri del Cinque-Seicento tra riforme imposte e nuove esperienze', in: Galasso – Valerio 2001, pp. 91-138.

Nappi 2001

Nappi, Eduardo. 'Antiche feste napoletane', in: *Ricerche sul '600 napoletano. Saggi e documenti*, Naples, Electa, 2001, pp. 100-120.

Novi-Chavarria 1993

Novi-Chavarria, Elisa. 'Nobiltà di seggio, nobiltà nuova e monasteri femminili in Napoli in età moderna', in: *Dimensioni e Problemi della Ricerca Storica*, no. 2 (1993), pp. 84-111.

Novi-Chavarria 2001

Ead. *Monache e gentildonne. Un labile confine. Poteri politici e identità religiose nei monasteri napoletani, sec. XVI-XVII*, Milan, Franco Angeli, 2001.

Pane 1954

Pane, Roberto. *Il chiostro di Santa Chiara in Napoli*, Naples, L'arte tipografica, 1954.

Renda 1978

Renda, Francesco. 'Dalle riforme al periodo costituzionale 1734-1816', in: *Storia della Sicilia. 6*, edited by Rosario Romeo, Naples, Società editrice Storia di Napoli e della Sicilia, 1978.

Russo 1970

Russo, Carla. *I monasteri femminili di clausura a Napoli nel secolo XVII*, Naples, Istituto di Storia Medievale e Moderna, 1970.

Spinosa – Pinto – Valerio 2013

Spinosa, Nicola – Pinto, Aldo – Valerio, Adriana. *San Gregorio Armeno. Storia, architettura, arte e tradizioni*, Naples, Fridericiana Editrice Universitaria, 2013.

Strazzullo 1968

Strazzullo, Franco. *Edilizia e urbanistica a Napoli dal '500 al '700*, Naples, Berisio, 1968.

Valerio 2006

Valerio, Adriana. *Istituti religiosi femminili a Napoli dal IV al XVI sec.*, Naples, Voyage pittoresque, 2006.

Valerio 2007

Ead. *Istituti religiosi femminili a Napoli dal 1600 al 1861*, Naples, Voyage pittoresque, 2007.

# Ritualising a Resilient City:
## Soundscape, Collective Performances and Construction of Urban Imaginary

*Maria Rosa De Luca*
(Università di Catania)

THIS STUDY ADOPTS the methodological perspective of urban musicology, an approach which is meant to interpret music in the physical, symbolic, social and cultural context of the city[1]. It problematises the reconstruction of the framework of relationships which underlies the various urban musical customs, according to an interpretative model based on concepts such as image, space, landscape and representation. As a result, the focus of the historian tends to shift from the individual to communities. These latter occupy (both physically and acoustically) and shape the urban area through civil customs that over time identify the peculiar features of the city. Here the relationship between rituality and music appears very close[2].

The central question of this methodological approach is the concept of the urban scene. Relevant to a historiographical model which aims to create the sense of an historical narration, in the constant interaction between spatial context and social and cultural usages, the urban scene comes into being when a part of the urban area presents a significant density of communicative phenomena, based on an interaction of people, institutions and means. This concept emphasises the social and symbolic value of tangible physical places. It reflects, however, the complexity of relationships based on conflicts and mediations within an organised system such as that of the

---

[1]. On the interrelation between urban history and historical musicology, the monographic issue of 'Urban History', XXIX/1 (2002), and, in particular, the article by CARTER 2002, remains a benchmark. In the same research field are the contributions by CARRERAS 2005 and GAUTHIER – TRAVERSIER 2008. Research progress is tracked by the volume KNIGHTON – MAZUELA-ANGUITA 2018: especially CARTER 2018 and FABRIS 2018.

[2]. Following Strohm's pioneering work on the city of Bruges (STROHM 1985), on Jaca by Marín (MARÍN 2002), on Milan by Kendrick (KENDRICK 2002), and on Cuzco by Baker (BAKER 2008).

city. In urban scenes, the meaning of a cultural component such as music becomes substantial and enriching. It is no longer an accessory element, but an essential component of a complex network of relationships and meanings.

## SCENES FROM A REBUILT CITY

Based on these essential concepts, the aim of this present study is to reflect on the interaction between ritual and city space. My aim is to understand how a collective (civic or religious) liturgy can unfold within the public space and transform it. Bringing places of power to the street or the square means entering into a dialogue constructed among those who organise the ritual, those who perform it and those who witness it. In accordance with this objective, I focus on the city of Catania in the eighteenth century. My enquiry aims to observe how the form of this city has been improved and reorganised over the centuries according to the configuration of the festive celebration of St Agatha, patron saint of Catania. The feast employs various types of symbolic and ritual (not exclusively musical) practices. Among these, the procession with the relics of St Agatha throughout the city to some extent reshaped the town plan during the reconstruction that occurred after two natural disasters, one being the eruption of Mount Etna in 1669 and the other the massive earthquakes of 1693. Ecclesiastical chant and instrumental music may have played an important role in the reconstruction of 'urban scenes' as ideal places for collective performance.

Catania was entirely rebuilt following the earthquake. Indeed, the eighteenth century represents the city's century of rebirth. Elected as an emblem, the motto *melior de cinere surgo* expressly summarises the image of a city rising magnificently from the rubble of the *horribile tremuoto* of 1693[3]. A 'liturgy of memory guides' the main institutional actors (senate, religious orders, nobility) to rebuild churches, convents and palaces 'now as then' over a period of forty years. And thus, Catania became a protagonist of the Enlightenment *renovatio* in the cultural scene of the Kingdom of Naples and Sicily. What are the reasons for this? The recent studies, drawn on notarial and accounting sources[4], present the history of the city and its territory as a significant paradigm of resilience. According to these accounts, the reconstruction of the city would have taken place over several stages: a first one, in the years following the earthquake, and a second and larger one, starting between 1710 and 1720 and peaking in the 1760s, before slowing down, with sporadic recoveries, from 1770 onward[5]. The city elites, namely the numerous

---

[3].  See RELAZIONE 1693, c. 213*r*.

[4].  I refer to the project on the history of Catania, directed by Giuseppe Giarrizzo, with the publication of the following four volumes: AYMARD – GIARRIZZO 2007; SCALISI 2009; IACHELLO 2010; GIARRIZZO 2012.

[5].  See PAGNANO 2010, pp. 71-87.

religious orders in the territory, a rather dynamic noble class, as well as a vibrant professional bourgeoisie, are the elements that set the pace for the rebuilding project that distinguishes the entire early eighteenth century. As for the reconstruction, these three orders were favoured by the general provisions dictated by the government of Madrid in May 1693 on the exemption of *gabelle* (i.e., tallages) to be granted to the earthquake-struck cities[6]. The data relevant to the urban population that, on the basis of economic recovery, had increased from 16,000 to over 25,000 in over three decades (between 1714 and 1747), are quite interesting[7]. However, in the course of this process of rebirth (or perhaps resilience), a significant role is played by the 'memory' of the city routes linked to a rituality consolidated since the mid-sixteenth century and institutionalised during the long Spanish rule[8]. The spatial hierarchy and the privileged places of the itineraries emerge from the demand for a rebuilding project of the city patronised by the elites governing the territory; a programmatic plan that wanted to see Catania rise magnificently from the rubble like a phoenix both in ritual and celebration. The urban planning choices of the architects of the reconstruction (nobles and ecclesiastics who rebuilt under the directions of Giuseppe Lanza, Duke of Camastra, delegate of Viceroy Francisco Uçeda, and of Bishop Andrea Riggio, consecrated by Innocent XII) strove to remake the functionality of the previous urban layout with the need to modernise the public space[9]. These choices required the final erasure of the city's ancient medieval layout in favour of an orthogonal scheme based on the intersection of two major road axes, via Uceda and via Lanza (today via Etnea and via di Sangiuliano), at the intersection of the Quattro Canti (an ambitious as well as impossible replica of Palermo's Ottangolo) and the Platea magna (Piazza del Duomo) where the via del Corso and via di San Filippo (today via Vittorio Emanuele and via Garibaldi) converged[10]. The markedly orthogonal subdivision of the urban terrain by means of preferential street axes re-proposes a centrality of functions (civil, religious, cultural) in the vast space over which the cathedral towers. When the reconstruction was completed, a magnificent *representation* of

---

6. See Condorelli 2011, pp. 286-287.

7. Longhitano 1998, p. 153.

8. For these aspects of urban ritual, I refer to De Luca 2012.

9. For the city's rebuilding project, see Dato 1983, pp. 23-112; Magnano di San Lio 2010, pp. 31-49; Condorelli 2006, pp. 799-816.

10. The plan of post-earthquake Catania is an example of «paleo-rationalist urban planning that, when considering the functional hierarchies of its parts, goes beyond the scenographic modules of late Baroque town planning. Many experiences filter out into this plan: Philip ii's directions, focused on the geometric partitioning of cities; the experience of the Sicilian-founded cities of the sixteenth and seventeenth centuries; the symbolism of street crosses superimposition on the pre-existing pattern, like in Messina and Palermo; the recall of the Spanish *plazas majores* and the Parisian *places royales*. The plan [...] may not have been the subject of a graphic since its shape derives from the network of main streets drawn on the rubble field — tying in a straight line two urban gates with the cathedral facade (the streets S. Filippo and Uceda) and drawing two others to intersect the Uceda street (the course and the Lanza street, however not hexagonal to the Uceda) [...]». Pagnano 2010, p. 72.

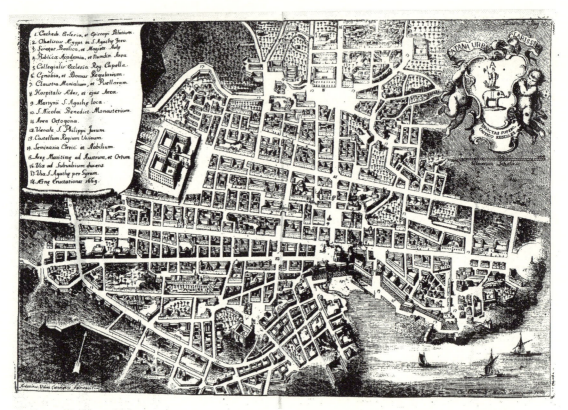

Ill. 1: Antonino Vacca - Antonio Gramignani, *Catania Urbs Clarissima*, in: Amico 1760.

the ancient opposition between civil power (with the rebuilding of the Senatorial Palace) and religious power (with the construction of the cathedral and the seminary of the clerics), which which over the course of previous centuries had traced a moment of synthesis in the worship of St Agatha (the city's patron), was presented here (Ill. 1).

## Urban Space, Ritual and Celebration

The feast of St Agatha in Catania is the celebratory occasion to which the economic resources and organisational energies of both religious and civil power are channelled. The celebration in itself makes explicit the complex ceremonial of the performance requiring the feast to be conceived, at least apparently, in two different ways by the Church and the Senate: for the former, as a means of pursuing ends of moral and religious edification; for the latter, as a moment of legitimation of its government over the territory (but, in reality, the true intentions of both agreed in the emblematic representation of a closed and hierarchically organised society in the festive protocol). The civic and religious significance of this celebratory occasion is

# Ritualising a Resilient City

confirmed by the economic patronage of the city's Senate as well as by the recognition granted to it by the Catanese church that had made it a crucial point in the liturgical calendar, with no fewer than two significant dates: one in the winter season, namely on 5 February (the anniversary of the Saint's martyrdom) and one during the summer, in the month of August (the translation of the Agatine relics from Constantinople to Catania in 1126). The main celebrations took place in February: they started on February 1, peaked between February 3 and 5 and «lasted for the space of fifteen days»; preparations began «four to six months beforehand»[11]. The phases were dictated by the ceremonial drawn up in 1522 by Alvaro Paternò, who had fixed the event's scenic and ritual details[12]. The nodal points of the complex celebratory apparatus involving the city in its spaces within and outside the town walls were: in the first two days, the processions of the main city authorities (Captain of Justice, patrician and jurors) who headed to the cathedral to pay homage to the saint; and on the third day, the so-called «procession of the luminaria», the offering of votive candles (strictly extinguished) to the patron Saint by the city's major institutional actors as a sign of homage and devotion[13].

The overpowering sacred *facies* of seventeenth-century Catania is revealed by the description given by Pietro Carrera:

> First the six beaters of the drums lead the procession, followed by the orphans dressed in white, the Capuchins, the Discalced from the Third Order of St Francis, those of the Holy Trinity, the Paulines, the Carmelites, the Augustinians, the Friars Minor Conventual of St Francis, the Zoccolanti, and the Dominicans. Then follows the clergy with a huge candle of a weight of almost 63 pounds, the only one carried lit on this day among all the other candles [...]. Lastly come the canons of the Collegiate, the canons of the Cathedral and the Bishop[14].

This first group was followed by a second one that gathered representatives of the various arts and crafts guilds; each of them participated with a particular votive candle, the so-called *Gilio*, a kind of *machina* where «sacred scenes, ecclesiastical histories, princes, kings, choirs of

---

[11]. See Carrera 1639-1641, p. 508; another effective description of the seventeenth-century Agatine feast is in Guarneri 1651, pp. 189-242.

[12]. The transcription of Alvaro Paternò's *Liber cerimoniarum* may be read in Di Liberto 1952.

[13]. The word 'luminaria' should not be applied to lit candles, since the procession was done in broad daylight and with the candles extinguished, but to the offering of wax by the citizens to illuminate the altar of St Agatha.

[14]. All parts in inverted commas are taken from Carrera 1639-1641, p. 512: «prima fan capo a detta processione i sei battitori de' tamburi, dopo i quali seguono gli orfanelli vestiti di bianco, i cappuccini, gli scalzi del terzo ordine di S. Francesco, quei della Santissima Trinità, i paulini, i carmelitani, gli agostiniani, i minori conventuali di S. Francesco, i zoccolanti, e i domenicani. Indi segue il clero con un gran cero, ch'è di peso di libre quasi 63, il qual solamente fra tutti gli altri ceri, che in questo giorno vi sono, si porta acceso [...]. Vengono ultimamente i canonici della collegiata e i canonici della cattedrale e il vescovo».

angels, acts of martyrdom and various events mostly pertaining to the history and greatness of the Saint»[15] were depicted. At the close of the procession, the magistracies and representatives of civil power paraded. The fourth day of the feast was dedicated to the procession of the Agatine relics carried on a kind of coffin (the so-called *bara* or *fercolo*)[16] around the town walls. The fifth day exclusively provided the celebration in the Church with the exposure of the precious reliquary bust on the shrine of the cathedral[17].

Music was an essential ingredient in the spatial and scenic architecture of the solemnity. For the occasion, the musical chapels of Messina, Augusta, Piazza Armerina, Francofonte, and Biancavilla, cooperated to mobilise musicians and form vocal and instrumental groups to take part in the procession of the so-called *Gilii*. Indeed, a prescriptive ritual required each *Gilio* to be accompanied by «instruments of sound and music» and a chorus of singers to declaim the victorious and miraculous deeds of the Saint. Thus, it was that «all the players, who with their instruments, whatever they may be, come to play in honour of the feast, hundreds of them concur, and therefore a vague variety is enjoyed, and at times novelty of rare instruments that kindle and increase the triumph of the Saint»[18]. Framing the occasion is a set of not strictly devotional events, such as the famous *Palio* race taking place on «the second day of February», the use of fireworks during processions, or as recalled by Giovan Tommaso Longobardo in his *Trionfo. Poema della festa di S. Agata*, the shouts of exultation and joy (*olè*) of the many devotees who pulled with great effort the rope of the silver coffin containing the effigy of the Saint[19].

---

[15]. *Ibidem*: «scene sacre, historie ecclesiastiche, principi, re, chori di angeli, atti di martirio et eventi varii per lo più spettanti all'historia e grandezza della Santa».

[16]. The Italian term *fercolo* comes from the Latin *fercŭlum*, and so from the verb *ferre* (i.e. to carry), and it is already found in Ancient Rome, referring to a little bed or litter upon which the statues of the gods were placed during processions, or the remains of the enemies were set in triumph as a prize of war. By metonymy, *fercolo* denotes what is carried in procession per se as a sign of victory, thus — especially in a religious context — the term itself symbolically represents the saint or the divinity that is carried through the streets of the city.

[17]. See DE LUCA 2012, p. 6. It is worth mentioning that two seventeenth-century musical sources related to the feast of St Agatha found in Catania mention the motet *O Catanensis gloria*, included in the anthology by Michele Malerba — *maestro di cappella* of Catania cathedral during the bishopric of Bonaventura Secusio (1609-1618) — entitled *Sacrarum Cantionum quae binis, ternisque vocibus concinuntur, cum basso ad organum* (Venice, Magni, 1614), and the motet *Quam pulchrae sunt mammae tuae*, which is part of Antonio Ferraro's anthology entitled *Sacrae cantiones quae tum unica, tum duabus, tribus, ac quatuor vocibus concinuntur, liber primis* [...], *cum basso pro organo* (Rome, Zanetti, 1617). These two printed exemplars allowed us to shed light both on the musical genre performed in Catania in the early seventeenth century and on the channels of circulation of music in Sicily.

[18]. CARRERA 1639-1641, pp. 520-521: «tutti i suonatori, che co' suoi strumenti, qualunque essi siano, vengono a suonare in honor della festa, ve ne concorrono le centinaia, perciò si gode una vaghissima varietà, e talhor novità di rari strumenti, i quali accendono e accrescono il trionfo della Santa».

[19]. LONGOBARDO 1628, p. 94.

## RITUALISING A RESILIENT CITY

In the August event, the translation of the Agatine relics from Constantinople to Catania was celebrated. In the later 1700s this occasion was recognised by both the liturgical and civil calendars[20]. The liturgical feast included exposure of the Agatine bust on the high altar and the procession of the relics inside the cathedral, a mass and the solemn vespers[21]. The civil feast included a procession through the streets near the cathedral and the performance of a sacred drama in the *Piano degli Studi* set up on a wooden stage in front of the gate of the oldest University in the Kingdom of Sicily, the *Siciliae Studium Generale*.

## 1769: THE CITY AS A THEATRE

As previously mentioned, the aim of this paper is to observe how the shape of the city of Catania was improved and reorganised in the course of its reconstruction, according to the configuration of the St Agatha celebrations. In the scenic architecture of the feast, religious processions shape urban space and make the symbolic cohesion of the community visible, as the inhabitants of a territory physically and acoustically occupy it and shape it through public practices that, over time, outline contexts of cultural production and fruition. Here the relationship between ritual and music is very close: it plays a primary role in both outdoor and indoor festive ceremonial. It is a fundamental element in the intellectual game of perception and figuration of the city decorum[22].

The touchstone for such a scenario is the chronicle titled *Distribuzione de' giorni festivi Dedicati alla Solennità della Gloriosa Vergine e Protomartire Catanese S. Agata da farsi in questo corrente Anno 1769*, a rich and detailed programme of the Agatine celebrations for the one hundredth anniversary of the lava eruption of 1669; it was an opportunity for the city Senate to exhibit its ability of mobilising forces and carefully arranging the spatial and scenic construction of the feast in order to trace the aesthetic horizon where the rebirth of the city might be placed. The city's Patricians offered:

> [...] constant thanks to the Most High and to such a great Interceding Patron with demonstrations of jubilation and gaiety [...] with magnificent ceremonial splendour, as a sign of thanksgiving, homage, gratitude and love [...], for six continuous days,

---

[20]. See OFFICIA 1770, pp. iii-viii and OFFICIA 1792, pp. v-viii. The calendar of festive occasions approved by the Catanese Senate in the second half of the 1700s is reproduced in the *Perpetua votivarum supplicationum quae a S.P.Q.C. quotannis peraguntur tabula* of 1761 affixed to the right-side wall of the Catanese Senate Palace. The text of the *Tabula* can be read in RASÀ NAPOLI 1900, pp. 308-310.

[21]. See TOSCANO DEODATI 1959.

[22]. On this particular aspect see DE LUCA – SANFRATELLO 2019.

with happy applause, with stunning apparatuses, with unique parties in adventurous remembrance of the obtained liberation[23].

The setting arranged in the urban space inside the town walls in August 1769 was therefore a hyper-text of the political, civic and religious apparatuses present in the Etnean territory: a city designed as an *en plein air* stage where a collective performance might be staged. The scenographic details transformed part of the urban space into a large 'theatre of wonders': an immense mobile representation of the city's devotion realised through the use of «several Theatres of Invention» (also called *transparent*, that is, painted canvases illuminated from behind) depicting the stages of St Agatha's life, erected in front of the main convents, monasteries, churches and confraternities (Monastero di S. Chiara, Confraternita di S. Giovanni Battista, Monastero delle moniali della SS. Trinità, Convento di S. Agostino, Convento dei Reali Padri di S. Francesco d'Assisi, Convento di S. Benedetto, Convento di S. Giuliano, Confraternita dei preti sotto titolo dell'Addolorata, Chierici regolari minori di S. Michele, Monastero delle moniali di S. Agata, Monastero delle moniali di S. Placido, S. Agata alle sciare)[24].

Playful and competitive elements (horse races, illuminations) alternated with the solemn moments of processions and mass celebrations in the cathedral. The fulcra of the city's rituals were the processions and parades. They redesigned the urban space and made the symbolic cohesion of the community visible in the scenic architecture of the feast, which included magnificent illumination at the most important road junctions (Piano del Duomo, Piano dell'Università, Quattro Canti, Porta del mare, Porta di Aci and Porta Ferdinanda) equipped «with noble furnishing, magnificent tapestries and pompously adorned very rich apparatus» in view of such an «admirable and playful spectacle», due to the presence of «various machines and pyramids of different architecture» which «well arranged and very rich in light» were placed in front of the Palazzo dell'Università, Palazzo del Senato, Piazza San Filippo, in front of the Ospedale S. Marco, in the Piano della Loggia in front of the cathedral and in the Piano dei Quattro Cantoni (Ill. 2 = Tav. 1, p. 237)

The role of music appears functional and fundamental. Happy entertainments presented by the «virtuosi», who played «various pairs of instruments to keep the people's cheerfulness alive at all times» were replicated throughout the celebrations in the «orchestre» (i.e., *wooden*

---

[23].  All parts in inverted commas are taken from Avviso 1769 (in I-CATc, Misc. A.299.47): «sempre grazie all'Altissimo ed a sì grande Interceditrice Padrona con dimostranze di giubilo e di allegrezza [...] con magnifica pompa, in segno di ringraziamento, e di omaggio, di gratitudine e di amore [...], per lo giro di sei giorni continui, con lieti applausi, con ricchissimi apparati, con singolari festini l'avventurosa ricordanza in rendimento della ottenuta liberazione».

[24].  Apart from these, in the mid-seventeenth century, about 43 lay companies and/or confraternities were established under the statutory aim of participating in religious processions and/or carrying out charitable works. See De Luca 2012, p. 12.

# Ritualising a Resilient City

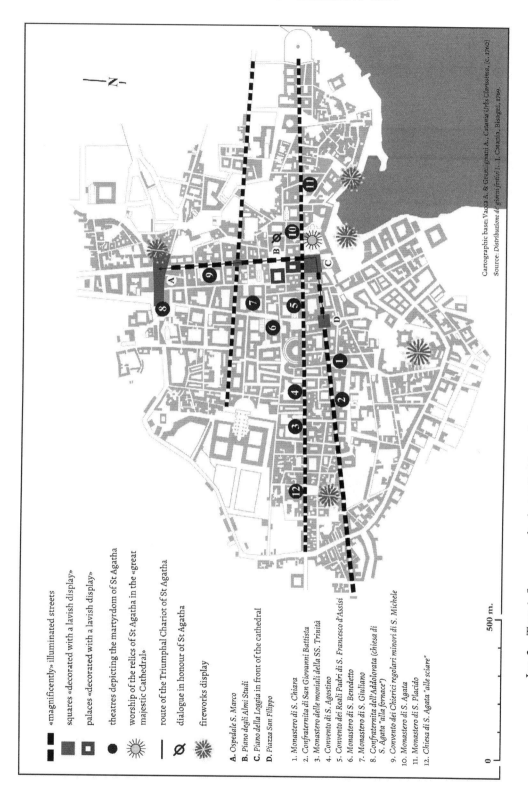

Ill. 2 = Tav. 1: Street map displaying details on the scenic architecture of the feast reported in Avviso 1769.

Ill. 3: Jean Claude Richard de Saint-Non, *Palazzata alla Marina*, acquaforte e bulino da *Voyage pittoresque ou Description des royaumes de Naples et de Sicilia*, Paris, 1781-1786.

*boxes*) in front of the Palazzo Senatorio; a performance on the Piano degli Almi Studi of «an allusive Dialogue in honour of St Agatha» composed for the occasion and performed by selected «virtuosi» with the participation of the entire nobility and the people; the triumphal chariot followed by the «numerous crew of the instrumentalists of the Senate», inside of which were «several choirs of voices and instruments», spread melodic songs in honour of the glorious St Agatha over the six days of the festival. The varied locations of the urban scenes for the theatre in music appears significant: while the musical events dedicated to the sacred (the Dialogue) took place in front of the Palazzo degli Studi, the melodrama was staged in the Piano della Marina, where a wooden theatre was probably erected «for the musical operas to be there represented by chosen virtuosi» (Ill. 3).

This was not a random choice; the enhancement of this part of the event was linked to the importance of the architectural backdrop of the magnificent facade of the Palace of Ignazio Paternò Castello, the fifth Prince of Biscari (1719-1786). The basic points of his ambitious political-cultural programme[25] were the construction of the Catanese harbour and

---

25. For a profile of Ignatius v Prince of Biscari and his ambitious programme, see De Luca 2012, pp. 86-98.

Ill. 4: *Porta Ferdinanda in Catania*, incisione da V. Cordaro Clarenza, *Osservazioni sopra la storia di Catania cavate dalla storia generale di Sicilia*, Catania, Riggio, 1835.

a promenade at the Marina, as sumptuous as the one in Palermo, and the erection of the Porta Ferdinanda[26] (Ill. 4).

Built in 1768 to the design of the Polish architect Stefano Ittar (1724-1790) on the occasion of the wedding of Ferdinand III of Bourbon to Maria Carolina of Habsburg (hence the name Porta Ferdinanda), its structure is majestic and harmonises with the city's architectural style, due to the presence of the bi-chromatism of black and white stone. It encapsulates a number of signs with a strong symbolic value: from the elephant of the Platea magna to the phoenix, i.e. the mythological bird rising from its ashes. Looking at the top of the monument today, we glimpse a large clock. Originally, however, one could admire a large cameo engraved with the portraits of Ferdinand and Maria Carolina. Popular narratives reveal that the Prince of Biscari wanted to build the door at that very spot, so that the two rulers could grasp, when looking from the arch down along Via San Filippo (later Strada Ferdinanda), the prospect of St Agatha's cathedral. However, it is reasonable to assume that the orthogonal cut of that artery was merely another aspect of the rebuilding project of the city, which in placing the symbol of the phoenix on top of the majestic gate sanctioned its own rebirth and sealed an important stage in its history.

---

[26]. About the construction of *Porta Ferdinanda*, see DATO 1983, pp. 113-117.

## Maria Rosa De Luca

## 1799: The Urban Mobilisation of the Sacred

The image of the city of Catania we get from reading the *Avviso al pubblico*[27] for the extraordinary feast of 1799 is again that of a magnificent urban theatre apparently set up specially for the customary summer celebrations for the Agatine festivity. Actually, the occasion was meant to be a tribute to Ferdinand III and Maria Carolina for the reconquest of the Kingdom of Naples and Sicily, which took place following the tragic events that had suddenly occurred between 1798 and 1799, and that were the cause of the two sovereigns' forced exile to Sicily[28]. Figuratively speaking, the anonymous writer of the *Notice* (perhaps Canon Giovanni Sardo)[29] traced the origin of the Bourbon victories over the French to the protection of Heaven, without neglecting to emphasise the decisive role played by the city of Etna in the positive resolution of the events: through the constant prayers of its inhabitants and loyalty to the Bourbons, Catania would obtain the intercession of its holy martyr Agatha for the achievement of a happy outcome.

The *Avviso* recalls the 1769 festive protocol. The literary text is emphatic and pompous and describes the shared participation of the entire social fabric in the Agatine rite around which the city devotion revolves. After all, the defensive strategy of the Senate and Cathedral had been set on the devotional practices in order to cope with the point-like rise of the Jacobin conspiracies that had found favour with the most advanced elements of the city's elites. In fact, between 1796 and 1799, it was the clergy that carried the greatest weight in the anti-Jacobin propaganda: under directives from the viceregal government, Bishop Corrado Deodato Moncada promulgated several edicts to draw the attention of the faithful to the calamitous events. Numerous Tridua were called in all churches, convents and monasteries, with the Exposition of the Blessed Sacrament and the celebration of solemn votive mass *in tempore belli*.

Thus if, on the one hand, the echo of the Bourbon victories over the French troops justified the 'extraordinary' celebration of the Agatine feast, on the other hand, the modalities related to the organisation of the event consolidated the employment of Catania's devotion as a real *instrumentum regni* for both the Senate and the Cathedral. Let us now turn our attention to the festive protocol encapsulated in the *Avviso* in order to derive the urban scenes that help us to recognise the role and functions of music in Catania at the turn of the nineteenth century.

In the first part of the text, the anonymous writer describes the scenic framework of the festival. It is based on a set of urban furnishings consisting of:

---

[27]. See Avviso 1799 (in I-CATc, U.R. Misc.A5.10): it reads transcribed in full in De Luca 2012 (Appendix 4).

[28]. About Jacobinism in Sicily, see D'Alessandro – Giarrizzo 1989, pp. 614-626.

[29]. An analysis of the *Avviso* gives no indication as to the author of the text; however, the following handwritten annotation on the title page reads «Giovanni Sardo author».

# Ritualising a Resilient City

1. «Machines and representations that throughout the duration of the feast will administer very rich matter of pleasure and edification», placed in the main road junctions of the city (Piazza del Duomo; Quattro Cantoni; Piazza della Porta di Aci; Piazza di S. Filippo). These are scenic designs in a still largely baroque style in terms of their grandeur and pomp but updated with the most innovative trends of the neoclassical style (this can be guessed, for example, from the expressions «on the Greek taste» and «very elegant Greek-style design»)[30]. Therefore, a Temple of Victory about 15 meters high was placed in the former Platea magna, to the left of the Cathedral: «of circular figure and Corinthian order, supported by 18 columns, terminated by a Dome embracing many elliptical openings, adorned with festoons and tablecloths on the Greek taste». It probably contained inside the depiction of Ferdinand III and Maria Carolina in the company of Faith while receiving from the hands of Victory respectively a laurel wreath and a cross. Images relating to the four seasons were placed in each of the Quattro Canti, while in the Piano della Porta di Aci a scenography «in masterfully painted paper» depicted the liberation of Naples by Admiral Nelson. Finally, a «magnificent apparatus» consisting of four pyramids graced each of the four corners of Piazza S. Filippo (see Ill. 5 = Tav. 2, p. 242).

2. A series of sixteen «Religious Demonstrations» of the martyrdom and apotheosis of St Agatha placed before churches, convents and monasteries in the city. Compared with the 1769 feast, these are no longer transparencies but «superbly decorated theatres», or life-size statues, probably in mixed media, as was already customary from the seventeenth century onward for nativity scenes and *Passiones*[31]. Embellished with illustrative epigraphs and designed to represent the salient moments of the Agatine martyrdom, as well as the miracles performed by the Saint during the eruptions of 1444 and 1669, they were placed before: Monastero di S. Chiara, Monastero di S. Maria dell'Ajuto, Monastero della SS. Trinità, Convento di S. Agostino, Convento di S. Francesco, Monastero di S. Benedetto, Monastero di S. Giuliano, Chiesa di S. Agata alla fornace, Convento dei Minoriti, Monastero di S. Agata, Monastero di S. Placido, Chiesa Collegiata.

3. A triumphal chariot «76 palms high [about 19 meters] and of a most elegant Greek design, brilliant in its gilding and consecutive friezes adorning it» represented a majestic mobile scenic apparatus. Inside one could admire a depiction of the two sovereigns kneeling in thanksgiving before the patron Saint. Its route was also planned according to the main urban scenes: Piazza del Duomo, Piazza S. Filippo, Quattro Canti up to the Porta di Aci, which represented the northern limit of the city.

---

[30]. All quoted parts are from Avviso 1799.
[31]. See Beddington – Caragliano 1997; Isgrò 1981, pp. 361-398.

241

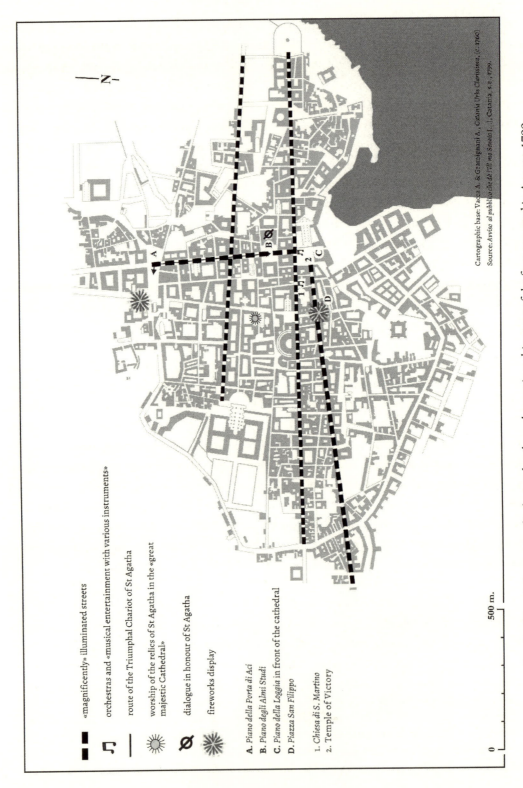

Ill. 5 = Tav. 4: Street map displaying details on the scenic architecture of the feast reported in Avviso 1799.

## RITUALISING A RESILIENT CITY

In the second part of the *Avviso*, the learned reviewer goes into detail about the articulation of urban ceremonial. It is in this part of the text that we can grasp some information about the event's musical accompaniment. In fact, the *Avviso* informs us that choral music accompanied the chariot in procession through the main streets and squares on the second day[32]; musical entertainments of the «virtuous lords of the city» would take place every evening in the Temple of Victory (Piazza Duomo); solemn celebrations in the church, with the intonation of the *Te Deum*, would be attended by civil and religious authorities in gala attire; and the Pontifical Mass and exposure of the Agatine relics would be held «with the most touching music both vocal as well as instrumental».

The activities in the urban space were intertwined with musical events: in the *Piano degli Studi* on the evening of the first day (around 5 p.m.) «a magnificent orchestra, lit by wax, and full of virtuosi *nostrali* and *forestieri* (locals and strangers)», sang an oratorio entitled *Il fonte di Orebbe*, based on a poetical text by Niccolò Maria Paternò Castello, Baron of Recalcaccia (brother of Prince Ignazio v Paternò Castello), and with the music of Giuseppe Geremia[33]; a «musical entertainment of the finest taste» followed the same evening in the Temple of Victory (Piazza Duomo – Porta del Mare) «to represent a continuation of delight to the lovers of harmony». On the second day, the parade of the triumphal chariot from Piano della Porta di Aci to Piazza S. Filippo was sounded by the voices of «a squad of Musicians» that sang «the happiest symphonies as choral music». On the third day, the sounds of the Senate Band accompanied the Bishop and Captain to the *Palio*, that is, to the so-called «race of the Barbarians»; then, the civil and religious authorities returned to the Piano degli Studi to watch the encore performance of the sacred drama and the parade of the triumphal chariot from Piazza di S. Filippo to Porta di Aci, always accompanied «with the same music». On the fourth day the procession of the sacred body of St Agatha «escorted by all the Congregations, Regular and Secular Clergy, Chapter of the Collegiate, and of the Cathedral, Bishop and Senate» would travel along the streets of the western part of the city; a new musical entertainment in the Temple of Victory was the fulfillment of the evening (see ILL. 5 = TAV. 2, p. 242).

Alongside the regular flow of the festive organisation, the city also hosted musical performances in Palazzos aimed at solemnising the extraordinary event that included the presence of the two sovereigns in Catania. The encomiastic cantata *Napoli riacquistato* performed in the Palazzo of Francesco Paternò Castello of the Dukes of Carcaci in the

---

[32].    The poetry text of one of the choral compositions is transcribed in DE LUCA 2012 (Appendix 4, p. 177).

[33].    The libretto of the sacred cantata titled *Il fonte di Orebbe* is reported in I-CATc U.R.Misc.A.4.36; the musical score has not been found. The Catanese composer Giuseppe Geremia (1732-1814) studied in Naples at the Collegio of S. Maria di Loreto, a pupil probably of Francesco Durante. From 1769, Geremia is active in Catania as *maestro di cappella* in the Cathedral, a post he held until his death: see DE LUCA 2012, pp. 67-71.

presence of the royal couple should be placed in this framework. It is a melodious allegorical dialogue between the Simeto River (the allegorical figure of Catania) and the Sebeto River (the allegorical figure of Naples), on a text by Giovanni Sardo with music by Emanuele Nani from Malta. This dialogue sketched the nostalgic atmosphere in which the Catanese nobility took leave of Ferdinand III and Maria Carolina before their final return to Naples.

## The *voyageurs'* Perception

The long days of the Agatine feast are also confirmed in the literary descriptions referring to the Catania stage of the *grand tour*. Through the effectiveness of the representation and its consolidation into a meaningful image, the *récits* of the *voyageurs* contribute to building the identity of the 'great Catania' and to popularising it, tracing and spreading a European model of city. As a side note in the description of Catania and its treasures, we can also find the visitors' observations on music, an implicit element of the local culture: these may be found in the accounts of Riedesel, Münter, Goethe, Saint-Non, Houel and many others[34].

Jean Houel (1735-1813) was a French painter, engraver and architect, who sojourned in Sicily from 1776 to 1779, and had the opportunity to attend both festive occasions in honour of St Agatha: he provided an insightful report of the first one, especially aimed at capturing the scenic aspects of the festive protocol in the outdoor spaces; as far as music is concerned, Houel's attention focuses mainly on the sounding of the opening ceremony of the *Palio*, where «les tambours, les trompettes, les hautbois, les bassons» stand out, and of the third day of the festivities (the parade of the triumphal chariot), in which the Senate's band corps parades, composed by «quatre timbaliers, six trompettes, tous à cheval»[35] (Ill. 6, p. 245).

Houel's observations are confirmed in the dictate of the Senate ceremonial used in Catania in the second half of the eighteenth century (dated 1761, unpublished): therein, the regular presence of an instrumental ensemble formed by «drums trompettes and piffare» in royal uniform for festive occasions is prescribed[36]. Regarding the summer Agatine feast, Houel gives us an interesting account of the performance he had attended in 1786:

> This one is celebrated on August 19: it is not really as beautiful as the first one [*scil.* the one in February] and lasts for only two days. On the evening of the first day, the facade of the Royal Palace of Studies, marked on the Catania plan with No. 3, is magnificently illuminated. When [I] attended it, a triumphal arch had been

---

[34]. Regarding the journey in Sicily, see Di Matteo 1999-2000. About the *grand tour*, see also De Seta 2001; Beaurepaire 2006, pp. 31-49.

[35]. Houel 1785, pp. 10-16.

[36]. See Cerimoniale Senato 1761 (ms. in I-CATu, MSU8 formerly Arm.3.14), c. 14ff.

Ill. 6: Jean-Pierre-Louis-Laurent Houel, *Interno della Cattedrale di Catania adornata per la festa di Sant'Agata, con partenza del reliquario per la processione*, acquatinta da *Voyage pittoresque des isles de Sicilie, de Malte et de Lipari*, Paris, 1782-1787.

erected in front of the palace, where twenty-five musicians had taken their places. A large enclosure of seats and benches built around the triumphal arch and crowded with the public, offered a most pleasant sight. Many Priests and Religious could be recognised there. All the carriages of the city were gathered there. At the beginning of this night festival, booklets were distributed with the concert program. It was music especially composed for the feast and it was a great success. [...] The same evening the whole city was illuminated with a great profusion of street lamps. The large streets had the most pleasant perspective.

In the square, that is, on the parvis of the Cathedral indicated as V in the plan, a theatre had been erected in honour of St Agatha. An episode from the life of St Agatha was there performed with some kind of carved and painted puppets. A street full of adorned stores had been set up near the theatre, stretching all around the square: they were filled with every object of the most glittering kinds, whose brilliance was enhanced by the abundant illumination. All this splendour distracted one from detecting the rather bad taste of the decoration on this pleasant evening. A very large crowd of the public flocked from everywhere, crowding in without commotion, which enabled everyone to enjoy this brilliant show easily and with pleasure[37].

According to the French engraver's interpretation, two performances took place during the summer feast of St Agatha: one in the Piano degli Studi, the other in the former Platea magna; they took place in the evening and followed different modalities. In the first case, it was a sacred drama (a musical oratorio); in the second, a dramatisation of the martyrdom story of Agatha adapted for a puppet theatre (also called in Sicily *teatro dei pupi*)[38]. The two events

---

[37]. HOUEL 1785, p. 16: «Questa si celebra il 19 agosto: non è davvero bella come la prima [*scil.* quella di febbraio] e dura solo due giorni. La sera del primo giorno si illumina in modo magnifico la facciata del Reale Palazzo degli Studi, segnato sul piano di Catania col n. 3. Quando [vi] ho assistito, di fronte al palazzo era stato eretto un arco di trionfo, dove avevano preso posto venticinque musicisti. Attorno all'arco di trionfo era stato costruito un grande recinto di sedili e di banchi, che affollati di spettatori offrivano un gradevolissimo colpo d'occhio. Vi si riconoscevano molti Sacerdoti e Religiosi. Tutte le carrozze della città erano lì riunite. All'inizio di questa festa notturna, furono distribuiti dei libretti col programma del concerto. Era musica composta apposta per la festa ed ebbe un grande successo. [...] La stessa sera tutta la città fu illuminata con grande profusione di lampioni. Le grandi strade avevano la prospettiva più gradevole. / Nella piazza, cioè sul sagrato della Cattedrale indicato V in pianta, era stato eretto un teatro in onore di sant'Agata. Vi si rappresentò un episodio della vita di sant'Agata con delle specie di marionette intagliate e dipinte. Presso il teatro era stata realizzata una strada di botteghe decorate, che si estendevano tutto attorno alla piazza: erano colme di ogni oggetto dei tipi più luccicanti, il cui brillio era aumentato dall'illuminazione abbondante. Tutto questo splendore non permetteva proprio di rilevare il leggero cattivo gusto della decorazione di questa piacevole serata. Una folla grandissima di spettatori affluì da ogni dove, affollandosi senza tumulti, il che permise a ciascuno di godere agevolmente e con piacere di questo spettacolo brillante».

[38]. In the last thirty years of the eighteenth century, the custom of setting up «casotti» (mobile wooden constructions used as theatres) became widespread in Sicily, but especially in Palermo: see MAIORANA 2008.

may have had different audiences: the *parterre* of the sacred drama in the Piano degli Studi was more select (the presence of «many Priests and Religious», the carriages, as well as the distribution of the librettos suggests this in descriptive terms); the public attended the show «with the puppets», which was a popular entertainment (as is implied by the details of the scenario: shops around the square with «slight bad taste of decoration» and the intervention of a very large crowd of spectators who «flocked from everywhere»).

The literary narratives and musical sources allow a comparison with Houel's *récit*. They confirm the custom of staging a sacred drama for the Agatine summer celebrations in the Piano degli Studi (or Piano del Duomo)[39]. The poetic compositions (which were quite varied in their terminology: dramatic composition, music drama, oratorio, dialogue, cantata, theatrical feast) relate mostly to biblical and hagiographic subjects, that is, ones based on the story of St Agatha. They are structured in one or two parts (with no subdivision into scenes), following the model of the Metastasian oratorio, especially widespread in Naples in the second half of the century, and feature the usual alternation of recitatives and arias (almost always musically tripartite, of two stanzas of usually isometric verses). With regard to the quality of the poetry texts, the feast of St Agatha is linked to the literary accounts of the leading contemporary intellectuals in Catania, some of whom were engaged in the activities of the *Siciliae Studium Generale* and academic conferences, such as Girolamo Pistorio, Giovanni Sardo, Mario Montesano Marziano[40]. The composition of the music, however, must be credited to the city's two chapel masters, Giuseppe Geremia and Vincenzo Tobia Bellini[41]. A hypothetical estimate of the orchestral forces employed on such occasions may be obtained through a comparison of the instrumental ensemble that can be inferred from a composition by Giuseppe Geremia intended for the feast of St Agatha and the size of the performing ensemble described by Houel (about twenty-five instrumentalists). Let us take, for example, the musical text of the sacred drama *Il ritorno di Tobia alla casa paterna*, composed by Geremia for the August St Agatha's feast in 1773 (Piano degli Almi Studi) and repeated in 1777 (Piano del Duomo)[42]. On the frontispiece of the libretto, the work appears described as «Componimento drammatico», while on the cover of the manuscript as a «Serenata a quattro voci e più strumenti»; the use of the term 'serenata' (frequent in poetic-dramatic compositions for St Rosalia celebrations in Palermo)[43]

---

[39]. See De Luca 2012, Appendix 2, years 1772-1799: out of twenty-five titles traced, twenty report the Piano degli Studi and five the Piano del Duomo as the performance location.

[40]. Biographical profiles of Sardo, Pistorio and Montesano Marziano are available in Percolla 1842, *ad voces*.

[41]. Vincenzo Tobia Bellini (1744-1729), an Abruzzese composer, had settled in Sicily in the late 1760s after studying at the Conservatory of S. Onofrio in Naples. In Catania, he was active as a chapel master for the Senate and the noble family Paternò Castello of the princes of Biscari: see De Luca 2012, pp. 67-71.

[42]. See *ibidem*, Appendix 2, years 1773 and 1777.

[43]. See Tedesco 2007 and Tedesco 2018.

referred to a model of dramatic cantata, scenically performed in open spaces and usually after sunset, entrusted to an ensemble of voices and instruments. However, we have no further evidence to confirm this performance practice in Catania, but for Houel's interpretation, which confirms the performance of the sacred drama in the late afternoon and the presence of a scenic apparatus (the triumphal arch). The poetical text of the *Ritorno di Tobia* (unknown author, probably a local poet) presents a short drama entrusted to four characters (Tobiolo, Angelo, Anna and Tobiah: Soprano, Soprano, Alto, Tenor, respectively); the instrumental ensemble consists of strings, winds and *basso continuo*[44]. As for the structure of the opera, the traditional opening symphony (a tripartite ABA' Introduction) is followed by a dramatic action that unfolds in a regular succession of *recitativi secchi* or *accompagnati* and arias *con da capo*. The sacred drama is completed by a final chorus that is given the task of intoning the allegorical subject matter. If, according Houel's description, we agree with the assumption that the total number of instrumentalists was 25, the instrumental arrangement would hypothetically be as follows: seven first violins, seven second violins, two oboes, two horns, two trumpets, two cellos, two double basses, and a harpsichord[45]. As it is easy to guess, these festive occasions did not exclusively involve performances in the city's outdoor spaces but were accompanied by the liturgical musical services that graced the celebrations in the places of worship.

In the chapter about Catania, Houel also describes a festival of an ancient peasant tradition that took place in the countryside adjoining the urban area: this was the feast of the wheat harvest, a festivity linked to the cult of the goddess Ceres:

> In the countryside surrounding the city, after the harvest, the peasants celebrate a folk festival, a kind of orgy in thanksgiving for the good harvest. Some young men open the procession with dances and evolutions; they are followed by a man beating a drum astride a donkey; five or six other people follow behind, also riding this peaceful animal, and holding long sticks to which sheaves of wheat are attached. Between them is another man, who on the same mount carries a large banner that waves majestically, moved by the wind. Next comes a young woman dressed in white and seated on a donkey; she is surrounded by many men on foot who carry on their heads and arms wheat sheaves as if they want to homage her. A multitude of peasants follow the procession in droves while *playing various instruments*[46].

---

[44].  The manuscript score of the sacred drama *Il Ritorno di Tobia* is preserved in I-CATm, MM-9/72-28.

[45].  Some accounts of the celebrations in honour of St Rosalia in Palermo confirm the same number of instrumentalists employed for the performance of serenades and oratorios: TEDESCO 2008, p. 397.

[46].  HOUEL 1785, p. 101: «Nelle campagne che circondano la città, i contadini celebrano, dopo la mietitura, una festa popolare, una specie di orgia, in ringraziamento del buon raccolto fatto. Alcuni giovani aprono la processione con balli ed evoluzioni; li segue un uomo che batte un tamburo a cavalcioni di un asino; cinque o sei altri, che montano anch'essi questo pacifico animale, vengono dietro impugnando lunghi bastoni ai quali sono

Ill. 7: Jean-Pierre-Louis-Laurent Houel, *Festa della mietitura*, acquatinta da *Voyage pittoresque des isles de Sicilie, de Malte et de Lipari*, Paris, 1782-1787.

Houel emphasises the very ancient origins of this now lost custom in deference to the rites of Ceres: the young woman depicts this goddess, to whom the peasants offered the crops they received on account of her generosity, and accompanied the performative rite with musical instruments (Ill. 7).

In this regard, it is definitely worthwhile to mention the account of the feast reported by the English Anglican priest John James Blunt (1794-1855) during his journey to Sicily in the early nineteenth century. In 1823, Blunt wrote a long description of the feast, underlining the power of Agatha as patron saint of Catania, who sheltered the city from the violence of the nearby volcano[47]. By comparing the presence of Christian patron saints (e.g. St Peter, St Lucy, St John) — providing a strong protection over modern cities such as Rome, Syracuse, Enna

---

attaccati fasci di grano. In mezzo a loro un altro uomo, sulla stessa cavalcatura, porta un grande stendardo che sventola maestosamente, mosso dal vento. Viene poi una giovane donna vestita di bianco e seduta su un asino; la circondano molti uomini a piedi che portano sulle teste e sulle braccia mannelli di grano che sembrano volerle offrire in omaggio. Una moltitudine di contadini segue a frotte il corteo *suonando diversi strumenti»*.

[47]. See Blunt 1823, pp. 56-84: the diary is an account of Blunt's two journeys to Sicily in 1818-1819 and 1820-1821.

and Catania — with the influence of tutelary deities of the past (i.e. Mars, Diana and Ceres, respectively) replaced later by the ecclesiastical authority, Blunt focuses on the crucial refuge allegedly granted by St Agatha and the miracle of her veil against the massive eruption of 1669 that destroyed several areas around the city of Catania. In fact, Blunt suggests a deep connection between the festival ceremonies of St Agatha and the ancient cult of Ceres (i.e. Demeter, in ancient Greek mythology), e.g. the horse race that was among the entertainments of the feast of Ceres, which in the past began the ceremonial of St Agatha on the 1st of February. On the third day, Blunt describes the employment of twenty-one «clusters of monstrous wax candles»[48], at that time already called *cerei* or *candelore*, namely large decorated wax candles nowadays characterised by a strong Sicilian Baroque style, offered as sign of devotion of the citizenship to the Saint and placed in the square of «Porta di Aci». In addition, this kind of votive offering was (and today still is) provided by workers gathered within craft unions, such as the ones representing craftsmen including shoemakers, tailors, greengrocers, ice merchants (these no longer found today), bakers, carpenters, etc. As in the case of the horse race, offering a certain number of wax candles was among the actions that could be done to give honour to Ceres. They could be seen as an emblem of the pines that the goddess is believed to have taken and lit with the fire of Mount Etna when she crossed Sicily in search of her daughter Persephone who had been carried off by Hades. According to Blunt, a reasonable interpretation of such similarities between these two traditional ceremonies might be found in the centuries-old ideological conflict between the pagan and the Christian system, whereby the people of Catania at a certain point decided to compromise, by maintaining some pagan ceremonies and agreeing to no longer call «Ceres» but «St Agatha» their object of praise. While looking for analogies or differences between the Catanese feast and the Eleusinian Mysteries, Blunt describes the various stages of the ceremony in honour of St Agatha, focusing on the behaviour shown by the faithful, such as the way they shouted at the Saint with the expression of praise «viva Sant'Agata!», or danced for her whilst wearing the traditional white costume (that is called *saccu*, i.e. a sort of tunic), or how they handled the procession of the *fercolo* by carrying the *cerei* or *candelore* (in the past *Gilii*) through the streets of the city.

In conclusion, Blunt also describes a sound experience in Catania that coincides with the Agatine festive and devotional ritual. It is markedly ostensive and is based on a strong sense of belonging, expressed through an urban community ritual, namely the procession. This ritual involves the city, which becomes the actual celebratory space. Agatha's incorruptible body appears as a remnant of her sacred status. The Saint is carried in procession by other bodies, who display their devotion through tests of strength, of resilience to fatigue, interspersed with songs and prayers in a collective performance that has its roots in a very ancient past. Music

---

[48]. Regarding the offer or the employment of light, illuminations or wax candles within the framework of urban ceremonies, see VAN DER LINDEN 2019.

# RITUALISING A RESILIENT CITY

plays a large part in this urban spectacle. Sonic gestures have always been powerful sources of symbolic representation in the context of celebrations of religious ceremonies and rituals. Over time, musical activities have shaped internal and external spaces, in which cultural production and symbolic representation are carried out. This is even more significant when repetitive traditional practices contribute to shape the space sonically.

## SOURCES

AMICO 1760
AMICO, Vito Maria. *Lexicon Topographicum Siculum. 3*, Catania, Pulejo, 1760.

AVVISO 1769
*Distribuzione de' giorni festivi Dedicati alla Solennità della Gloriosa Vergine e Protomartire Catanese S. Agata da farsi in questo corrente Anno 1769*, Catania, Bisagni, 1769.

AVVISO 1799
*Avviso al pubblico che dà l'Ill.mo Senato della Chiarissima e Fedelissima Città di Catania pell'imminente Solennità della Gran Vergine e Martire S. Agata nell'agosto del 1799*, Catania, 1799.

CARRERA 1639-1641
CARRERA, Pietro. *Delle memorie historiche della Città di Catania. 2*, Catania, Rossi, 1639-1641.

CERIMONIALE SENATO 1761
*Del modo e osservanza che si costuma nelle processioni così ordinarie come straordinarie di tutto l'anno, dove interviene il Senato, e come in caso l'intervenisse il Prelato* (ms. in I-CATu, Fondo universitaria, segnatura MSU8 [*olim* Arm.3.14]).

GUARNERI 1651
GUARNERI, Giovanni Battista. *Le zolle historiche catanee*, Catania, Rossi, 1651.

LONGOBARDO 1628
LONGOBARDO, Giovanni Tommaso. *Il trionfo. Poema della festa di S. Agata Vergine e Martire nella città di Catania*, Catania, Rossi, 1628.

OFFICIA 1770
*Officia propria Sanctorum Ecclesiae Catanensis* [...] *jussu domini D. Salvatoris Vintimilii*, Catanae, Typis Seminarii, 1770.

OFFICIA 1792
*Officia propria Sanctorum Ecclesiae Catanensis* [...] *jussu domini D. Conradi M. Deodato de Moncada*, Catania, Pastore, 1792.

## Maria Rosa De Luca

RELAZIONE 1693
*Relazione dell'orribile terremoto. Seguito nell'Isola di Sicilia il dì 11 gennaio 1693. Colla nota delle Città e Terre, sprofondate, de' mari. E luoghi che hanno patito e con tutte le particolarità più degne di essere registrate. Aggiuntovi l'Orazione contro il terremoto*, Rome, Bisagni, 1693.

### BIBLIOGRAPHY

AYMARD – GIARRIZZO 2007
*Catania. La città, la sua storia*, edited by Maurice Aymard and Giuseppe Giarrizzo, Catania, DSE, 2007.

BAKER 2008
BAKER, Geoffry. *Imposing Harmony: Music and Society in Colonial Cuzco*, Durham-London, Duke University Press, 2008.

BEAUREPAIRE 2006
BEAUREPAIRE, Pierre-Yves. '«Grand Tour», «République des Lettres» e reti massoniche: una cultura della mobilità nell'Europa dei Lumi', in: *La massoneria*, edited by di Gian Mario Cazzaniga, Turin, Einaudi, 2006 (Storia d'Italia - Annali, 21), pp. 32-49.

BEDDINGTON – CARAGLIANO 1997
*Capolavori in festa. Effimero barocco e largo di Palazzo (1683-1759)*, edited by Charles Beddington and Renata Caragliano, Naples, Electa, 1997.

BLUNT 1823
BLUNT, John James. *Vestiges of Ancient Manners and Customs: Discoverable in Modern Italy and Sicily*, London, Murray, 1823.

CARTER 2002
CARTER, Tim. 'The Sound of Silence: Model for an Urban Musicology', in: *Urban History*, XXIX/1 (2002), pp. 8-18.

CARTER 2018
ID. 'Listening to Music in Early Modern Italy: Some Problems for the Urban Musicology', in: KNIGHTON – MAZUELA-ANGUITA 2018, pp. 25-49.

CARRERAS 2005
CARRERAS, Juan José. 'Música y ciudad: de la historia local a la historia cultural', in: *Música y cultura urbana en la edad moderna*, edited by Andrea Bombi, Juan José Carreras and Miguel Ángel Marín, València, Universitat de València, 2005, pp. 17-51.

CONDORELLI 2006
CONDORELLI, Stefano. 'The Reconstruction of Catania after the Earthquake of 1693', in: *The Second International Congress on Construction History (Queens' College, Cambridge University, 29th March - 2nd April 2006). 1*, edited by Malcom Dunkeld *et al.*, Exeter, Short Run Press, 2006, pp. 799-816.

CONDORELLI 2011
ID. *«U tirrimotu ranni». Lectures du tremblement de terre de Sicile de 1693*, Ph.D. Diss., Paris, École des Hautes Études en Sciences Sociales-Paris, 2011.

D'ALESSANDRO – GIARRIZZO 1989
D'ALESSANDRO, Vincenzo – GIARRIZZO, Giuseppe. *La Sicilia dal Vespro alll'Unità d'Italia*, Turin, UTET, 1989 (Storia d'Italia, 16).

DATO 1983
DATO, Giuseppe. *La città di Catania. Forma e struttura 1693-1833*, Rome, Officina Edizioni, 1983.

DE LUCA 2012
DE LUCA, Maria Rosa. *Musica e cultura urbana nel Settecento a Catania*, Florence, Olschki, 2012 (Historiae Musicae Cultores, 123).

DE LUCA – SANFRATELLO 2019
EAD. – SANFRATELLO, Giuseppe. 'Shaping Sacred Spaces: The Feast of St Agatha and the Development of Its Urban Rituality', in: *Quadrivium. Revista Digital de Musicologia*, no. 10 (2019), pp. 1-10.

DE SETA 2001
DE SETA, Cesare. *L'Italia del Grand Tour, da Montaigne a Goethe*, Naples, Electa, 2001.

DI LIBERTO 1952
DI LIBERTO, Rosalia. 'La Festa di S. Agata a Catania nel «Cerimoniale» di Alvaro Paternò (sec. XVI)', in: *Archivio Storico per la Sicilia Orientale*, s. IV, XLVIII/1-3 (1952), pp. 19-27.

DI MATTEO 1999-2000
DI MATTEO, Salvo. *Viaggiatori stranieri in Sicilia dagli Arabi alla seconda metà del XX secolo*, Palermo, ISSPE, 1999-2000.

FABRIS 2018
FABRIS, Dinko. 'Urban Musicologies', in: KNIGHTON – MAZUELA-ANGUITA 2018, pp. 53-68.

GAUTHIER – TRAVERSIER 2008
GAUTHIER, Laure – TRAVERSIER, Mélanie. 'Introduction', in: *Mélodies urbaines. La musique dans le villes d'Europe (XVIᵉ-XIXᵉ siècles)*, edited by Laure Gauthier and Mélanie Traversier, Paris, Presses de l'Université Paris-Sorbonne, 2008, pp. 11-21.

GIARRIZZO 2012
*La città moderna, la città contemporanea*, edited by Giuseppe Giarrizzo, Catania, DSE, 2012.

HOUEL 1785
HOUEL, Jean-Pierre-Louis-Laurent. *Voyage pittoresque des isles de Sicilie, de Malte et de Lipari. 3*, Paris, s.e. [= de l'impremerie de Monsier], 1785.

# MARIA ROSA DE LUCA

IACHELLO 2010
*La grande Catania. La nobiltà virtuosa, la borghesia operosa*, edited by Enrico Iachello, Catania, DSE, 2010.

ISGRÒ 1981
ISGRÒ, Giovanni. *Festa teatro rito nella storia di Sicilia*, Catania, Cavallotto, 1981.

KENDRICK 2002
KENDRICK, Robert L. *The Sounds of Milan (1585-1650)*, Oxford, Oxford University Press, 2002.

KNIGHTON – MAZUELA-ANGUITA 2018
*Hearing the City in Early Modern Europe*, edited by Tess Knighton and Ascensión Mazuela-Anguita, Turnhout, Brepols, 2018 (Epitome musical).

LONGHITANO 1998
LONGHITANO, Gino. *Studi di storia della popolazione siciliana. I Riveli, numerazioni, censimenti (1569-1861)*, Catania, CUECM, 1998.

MAGNANO DI SAN LIO 2010
MAGNANO DI SAN LIO, Eugenio. 'Maestranze ed architetti nella Catania del Settecento', in: IACHELLO 2010, pp. 31-49.

MAIORANA 2008
MAIORANA, Bernadette. *Pupi e attori ovvero l'opera dei pupi a Catania. Storia e documenti*, Rome, Bulzoni, 2008.

MARÍN 2002
MARÍN, Miguel Ángel. *Music on the Margin: Urban Musical Life in Eighteenth-Century Jaca (Spain)*, Kassel, Reichenberg, 2002.

PAGNANO 2010
PAGNANO, Giuseppe. 'Melior de cinere surgo. Catania 1693-1790', in: IACHELLO 2010, pp. 71-87.

PERCOLLA 1842
PERCOLLA, Vincenzo. *Biografie degli uomini illustri catanesi del secolo XVIII*, Catania, Pastore, 1842.

RASÀ NAPOLI 1900
RASÀ NAPOLI, Giuseppe. *Guida e breve illustrazione delle Chiese di Catania e sobborghi, con tutte le epigrafi latine tradotte in italiano e con l'aggiunta dei nomi dei Pontefici romani da S. Pietro ai di nostri con l'anno della loro elezione e tabella cronologica dei Vescovi di Catania*, Catania, Galati, 1900, pp. 308-310.

SCALISI 2009
*L'identità urbana dall'antichità al Settecento*, edited by di Lina Scalisi, Catania, DSE, 2009.

STROHM 1985
STROHM, Reinhard. *Music in Late Medieval Bruges*, Oxford, Clarendon, 1985.

TEDESCO 2007
TEDESCO, Anna. 'La serenata a Palermo alla fine del Seicento e il Duca di Uceda', in: *La serenata tra Seicento e Settecento: musica, poesia, scenotecnica. 2*, edited by Niccolò Maccavino, Reggio Calabria, Laruffa, 2007, pp. 550-562.

TEDESCO 2008
EAD. 'Aspetti della vita musicale nella Palermo del Settecento', in: *Il Settecento e il suo doppio. Due correnti nella Sicilia del XVIII secolo*, edited by di Mariny Guttilla, Palermo, Kalós, 2008, pp. 391-401.

TEDESCO 2018
EAD. 'Shaping the Urban Soundscape in Spanish Palermo', in: KNIGHTON – MAZUELA-ANGUITA 2018, pp. 165-176.

TOSCANO DEODATI 1959
TOSCANO DEODATI, Alfonso. *Catania e Sant'Agata*, Catania, Ospizio di Beneficenza, 1959.

VAN DER LINDEN 2019
VAN DER LINDEN, Huub. 'Blinding Light and Gloomy Darkness. Illumination, Spectatorship, and the Oratorio in Baroque Rome', in: *The Grand Theater of the World: Music, Space, and the Performance of Identity in Early Modern Rome*, edited by Valeria De Lucca and Christine Jeanneret, Abingdon-New York, Routledge, 2019, pp. 96-111.

# LA MUSICA COME PERSECUZIONE.
## L'INQUINAMENTO MUSICALE NELLE CITTÀ ODIERNE

*Giuseppina La Face*
(UNIVERSITÀ DI BOLOGNA)

L'ARGOMENTO CHE MI ACCINGO A PRESENTARE — l'inquinamento musicale nei contesti urbani — è ben noto[1]. Esso ha una dimensione storica. Basti ricordare il 'Severo' che nel *Contrasto musico* di Grazioso Uberti (Roma 1630) lamenta l'abuso di musiche che nelle chiese, nei palazzi, nei monasteri e per le strade di Roma distolgono gli animi da ogni concentrazione e compunzione. Oppure le lagnanze che il giovane Leopardi manifestò alla sorella Paolina nel dicembre 1825: a Bologna, acquartierato in una stanzetta contigua al Teatro del Corso, gli toccava sorbirsi sera per sera voci e suoni dello spettacolo di là dal muro. La pubblicistica ottocentesca eresse a stereotipo critico la nozione che, in mano a Rossini (a Parigi variamente soprannominato 'Signor Tambourossini' o 'Monsieur Vacarmini') o a Berlioz (caricaturato mentre dirige un «Concert à mitraille»), le moderne orchestre sinfoniche e teatrali fossero divenute apparati acusticamente micidiali. Potremmo ripercorrere l'intera storia dell'arte musicale sotto il profilo del costante incremento del volume fonico, e dunque del sempre più ampio raggio di diffusione del «suono umanamente organizzato»[2].

Qui mi limiterò a trattare la questione in prospettiva sincronica, nella realtà odierna, nell'incidenza che essa esercita sulle vite degli individui e della collettività, con una speciale attenzione alle ricadute psicologiche. La concentrazione sull'attualità si giustifica anche in ragione di un'evoluzione tecnologica che ha introdotto innovazioni dirompenti nel fenomeno, e di conseguenza nel suo impatto. Ne parlerò tra poco.

Incomincio riportando quattro titoli tratti da giornali italiani, tutti risalenti al giugno 2019 (ossia nell'imminenza del convegno *The Global City: The Urban Condition as a Pervasive Phenomenon*, Bologna, 11-14 settembre 2019):

---

[1]. Rimando *en bloc* a CUOMO 2004.

[2]. È questa («humanly organized sound») la ben nota definizione di 'musica' fornita da John Blacking nel primo capitolo del suo trattatello: BLACKING 1986, pp. 3-31.

- *il Resto del Carlino*, domenica 9: «Ogni notte è l'inferno, me ne vado».
- *la Repubblica*, martedì 4: «Palermo, residenti contro il Conservatorio: "Chiudete le finestre per suonare". A luglio ci sarà l'insonorizzazione di tre aule, intanto i residenti protestano contro l'istituto: "Non riusciamo a dormire"».
- *RavennaNotizie.it*, domenica 9: «Aggrediti musicisti durante le prove per Ravenna Festival al CISIM di Lido Adriano: 3 in ospedale».
- *Quotidiano Nazionale*, martedì 18: «Movida di sangue. "Abbassa quella musica". E uccide il barista».


Sono solo quattro dei tanti titoli che, soprattutto tra primavera e autunno, annualmente compaiono sui nostri giornali cartacei e online. I primi tre denunciano reazioni di fastidio e conseguente impulso all'aggressività in tre situazioni differenti; il quarto riporta un grave fatto di sangue. Il fattore comune sta nel riferimento a emissioni musicali in contesti urbani e nell'effetto nefasto che le conseguenti immissioni esercitano su cittadini non coinvolti nella produzione o fruizione di quelle musiche. Esaminiamoli.

Primo caso. Un giovane, un lavoratore ammogliato con prole, non riesce più a dormire e vivere serenamente nel proprio appartamento per via del 'cerimoniale' collettivo che ogni notte si celebra nella piazza vicina. Un cerimoniale nel quale senza dubbio molti si riconoscono, e che ha non trascurabili ricadute economiche a vantaggio degli esercizi commerciali che lo promuovono, ma che per altri comporta danni in termini di salute, tranquillità, valore di mercato dell'immobile.

Il secondo caso. Gli abitanti di un condominio protestano nei confronti degli alunni di un conservatorio. I discenti hanno il diritto/dovere di studiare ed esercitarsi per ore e ore ogni giorno. Ma il vicinato è tormentato dalla reiterazione incessante della musica, magari proveniente da aule diverse in una cacofonica, babelica simultaneità. Qui non si tratta di un 'cerimoniale' notturno, bensì di semplice studio, diurno e diuturno, in un'istituzione didattica che, riconosciuta dall'ordinamento scolastico, avvia gli iscritti verso l'esercizio professionale dell'arte musicale. Eppure il disturbo c'è, ed è grave.

Il terzo caso. Alcuni cittadini, esasperati, addirittura malmenano i percussionisti del Ravenna Festival. Come nel caso di Palermo, è evidente che i musicisti, chiamati a esibirsi in un festival internazionale di spicco, hanno tutte le ragioni per provare e riprovare il loro pezzo. Ma di riflesso i residenti, estranei all'evento sonoro, sono nevrotizzati dall'assidua esposizione al clangore e al tintinnio penetrante degli idiofoni, al tellurico rimbombo dei membranofoni.

Il quarto caso. Un pensionato si sente perseguitato dai suoni (e dagli schiamazzi) di un chiosco lì vicino. Snervato, sfoga la propria impotenza sparando al proprietario del gazebo. Questo caso è più simile al primo: il 'cerimoniale' nevrotizza il singolo che ad esso non partecipa né aderisce, ed anzi si ribella con esiziale violenza.

## LA MUSICA COME PERSECUZIONE

In tutti e quattro i casi, dunque, l'arte dei suoni, anziché produrre piacere, benessere, letizia dell'anima, diventa fomite di nervosismo, fastidio, aggressività. Se nel 1489 la musica era per Marsilio Ficino «consolazione delle fatiche e pegno di vita duratura» (*De triplici vita*, II, XV)[3], e nel 1859 Schopenhauer la denominava «panacea di tutti i nostri mali» (*Die Welt als Wille und Vorstellung*, libro III, § 52), nei casi riportati accade tutto il contrario. C'è abbrutimento, disperazione, al limite psicosi. A dire il vero, un filosofo del Settecento aveva intuito gli effetti deleteri dell'arte musicale (ch'egli considerava peraltro un'arte di rango inferiore). Immanuel Kant così si esprimeva nella *Critica del giudizio* (§ 53): «Alla musica è propria quasi una mancanza di urbanità (*ein gewisser Mangel an Urbanität*), specialmente per la proprietà che hanno i suoi strumenti di estendere la loro azione al di là di quel che si desidera», ossia sul vicinato, «per cui essa in certo modo s'insinua e va a turbare la libertà di quelli che non fanno parte del trattenimento musicale; il che non fanno le arti che parlano alla vista, perché basta rivolgere gli occhi altrove, quando non si vuol dare adito alla loro impressione»[4]. Kant aveva inoppugnabilmente ragione. La musica difetta di urbanità quando invade spazi che non le sarebbero concessi, e da consolazione può allora facilmente trasformarsi in tormento.

Tale congenita 'inurbanità' delle emissioni musicali può poi essere decuplicata dall'abuso, cioè dall'uso smodato, debordante e persistente che se ne fa; ed è centuplicata, ai giorni nostri, dall'uso invadente dei mezzi di amplificazione. Nel suono, anche il più dolce e soave, è sempre presente un quoziente di aggressività. Gli psichiatri lo sanno bene. Lo dice in maniera lampante Eugenio Borgna: «Un suono *si stacca*, come acqua che scaturisce da una fonte, dalla sua sorgente sonora, mentre un colore *aderisce* all'oggetto. Il contenuto di una percezione visiva *resta* insomma al suo posto, mentre quella di una percezione uditiva *si muove* e si avvicina. Un suono ci insegue e ci assale: non ci si può 'difendere' se non dopo essere stati afferrati»[5].

La nostra società — qui parlo in particolare dell'Italia, ma il fenomeno è generalizzato — indulge oggi all'uso massiccio delle emissioni musicali negli spazi urbani (e all'occasione anche in contesti rurali o balneari). Ne risulta, al limite, una vera e propria forma di *inquinamento*: luoghi pubblici, bar, ristoranti, negozi, supermercati, mezzi di trasporto, piazze, parchi, locali d'intrattenimento sono, più spesso sì che no, invasi dalle musiche: il che può innescare polemiche roventi. Ora, se la musica può in tanti casi diventare persecuzione, se le abitazioni assediate dalle 'cerimonie' musicali circostanti possono tramutarsi in 'case nemiche' per chi vi abita, se il singolo può sentirsi dilaniato da un 'cerimoniale' al quale altri partecipano ma che egli non desidera, ciò dipende da vari fattori[6]. Ne elenco qualcuno.

---

3.  FICINO 1991, p. 161.

4.  KANT 1963, p. 192.

5.  BORGNA 1999, pp. 33-46: 43.

6.  Sulle esecuzioni all'aperto si veda MONARI 2013. Il saggio, ben documentato, affronta numerose implicazioni sociologiche e antropologiche del *soundscape*, ma accenna solo di sfuggita agli effetti deleteri dell'inquinamento musicale'.

1. La musica, la più squisitamente temporale fra tutte le arti, occupa *spazio*: spazio fisico e spazio psichico. Occupa il proprio spazio — lo spazio di chi la fa e la ascolta — e in più, come dice Kant, invade lo spazio del prossimo: uno spazio altrui. Così facendo può intaccare, occupare, ridurre e restringere quella zona privata, fisica e psichica, che è essenziale per la vita dell'Io e per la vita di relazione. Nel caso, ad esempio, della musica di sottofondo essa può inserirsi nello spazio comunicativo condiviso da più persone, e colonizzare, oltre i luoghi, lo spazio privatissimo della mente, della psiche.

2. Si dà per scontato che la musica piaccia: che piaccia sempre e dappertutto e a chicchessia. Questa credenza risale a un'idea immediata e diffusa, a un luogo comune inveterato: la musica unisce, aggrega, affratella. È vero che la musica può unire, può aggregare, può affratellare, ma solo chi da essa vuole essere unito, aggregato, affratellato: ossia unisce chi in quella data musica e in quel dato momento e in quel dato luogo si riconosce. In forza di ciò la musica segrega chi, forse soltanto in quell'occasione, in essa non voglia riconoscersi. In tal caso, la musica di un gruppo diventa *ipso facto* il nemico potenziale o attuale degli individui che in quel gruppo non sono inseriti né intendono inserirsi.

3. Manca nella nostra società la coscienza che le emissioni musicali producono inquinamento, e che esso non sia equiparabile *sic et simpliciter* all'inquinamento acustico generico, ossia al *rumore*, all'eccesso di rumore. L'inquinamento musicale è subdolo, perché particolare e ambivalente è il fattore inquinante. Essendo la musica, a differenza dal rumore, un 'linguaggio organizzato', un discorso dotato di una sua cogente logica, essa impatta sul sistema limbico e induce, soprattutto mediante metro e ritmo, una pervasiva e imperiosa attivazione senso-motoria: anche un minuetto di Mozart o una ballata di Georges Brassens possono risultare insopportabili, se in quel momento non si è psichicamente disposti a seguirne, con attenzione oppure anche distrattamente, il discorso e il decorso.

4. A questi tre punti si aggiunge un quarto fattore, dal portentoso effetto moltiplicatore: la riproduzione del suono e la sua amplificazione per via elettrica ed elettronica. Nel corso del Novecento questo fattore ha modificato alla radice, macroscopicamente — o dovremmo forse dire macrofonicamente —, la produzione e la recezione di musica, nonché le modalità d'ascolto e le abitudini fruitive. R. Murray Schafer[7] ha impartito al fenomeno un nome suggestivo: 'schizofonia'. La parola designa «la frattura esistente tra un suono originale e la sua trasmissione o riproduzione elettroacustica». L'innovazione ha avuto conseguenze estetiche e sociali enormi: «Dopo l'invenzione delle apparecchiature elettroacustiche per trasmetterli e conservarli,

---

[7].  R. Murray Schafer si può considerare l'iniziatore dei *soundscape studies* con i volumi *The New Soundscape: A Handbook for the Modern Music Teacher* (SCHAFER 1969) e *The Soundscape: Our Sonic Environment and the Tuning of the World* (SCHAFER 1977).

260

## LA MUSICA COME PERSECUZIONE

tutti i suoni [...] possono venire amplificati e diffusi ovunque o essere immagazzinati»[8]. Ne sono scaturite due conseguenze assai incisive: se da un lato la registrazione sonora consente di riprodurre le emissioni musicali in spazi e momenti diversi da quelli della loro produzione originaria, e dunque di reiterarle *ad libitum*, dall'altro l'amplificazione tecnica ne aumenta a dismisura l'impatto acustico, e dunque l'invadenza. Aumentano così i danni potenziali delle emissioni musicali eccessive o invasive; si aggiunge violenza a violenza dilatando l'ambito di espansione del suono, investendo così fasce sempre più ampie di potenziali succubi. La semplice abolizione degli amplificatori abbasserebbe *ipso facto* i livelli dell'inquinamento musicale, e dei danni che ne derivano. Ma d'altra parte molte musiche dei giorni nostri esistono soltanto in virtù dell'amplificazione, non ne possono proprio fare a meno. E purtroppo un convincimento rudimentale assai diffuso reputa che, quanto più alto è il volume, tanto più interessante, aggregante ed eccitante sia l'evento musicale.

Ci sono poi nell'abuso di musica in luoghi pubblici effetti nefasti inavvertiti, che non risaltano immediatamente. Ne indico due. Il primo: l'abuso di musica cui siamo sottoposti àltera l'ascolto, riducendolo a indistinta esperienza sensoriale in cui tutto finisce per apparire eguale a tutto. È l'esatto contrario di ciò che occorre per fruire e godere scientemente la musica, qualsiasi musica: una discriminazione avvertita, non una sottomissione supina. Il secondo effetto ne discende: se si ottunde la capacità di ascolto, essenziale allo scambio razionale e sentimentale tra gli individui, si mette in crisi la relazione fra noi e gli altri. Tale mancanza di attenzione agli 'altri', tale difficoltà di corrispondenza ed empatia fra simili tocca talvolta, nella nostra società e negli ambienti più disparati, punte drammatiche.

Il termine 'inquinamento musicale' ha fatto la sua comparsa in musicologia nel 1975 con il pamphlet di Peter Jona Korn, *Musikalische Umweltverschmutzung: polemische Variationen über ein unerquickliches Thema*[9]. Sul piano intellettuale il fenomeno interessa beninteso i musicologi, ma ha vaste implicazioni interdisciplinari. Non è facile da concettualizzare, giacché si basa su una serie di antinomie. La più appariscente è questa: se la musica in quanto produzione culturale va sostenuta e tutelata, come giustificare un 'inquinamento' che va invece contrastato[10]? Altre antinomie non meno problematiche si compendiano in altrettante diadi

---

[8]. SCHAFER 1977, pp. 131 e segg. L'autore introdusse il termine ed elaborò il concetto nel capitolo 'Schizophonia' (SCHAFER 1969, pp. 43 e segg.). Da parecchi decenni e in molte lingue il termine è correntemente in uso, tanto nel discorso musicologico quanto nella pubblicistica, ma non ha finora trovato accoglimento nei lessici generali come *Oxford English Dictionary*, il *Grande Dizionario italiano dell'uso* di Tullio De Mauro (1999, con i supplementi 2003 e 2007), il supplemento 2004 del *Grande Dizionario della lingua italiana* (Battaglia-Sanguineti) o lo Zingarelli 2016. Anche questo ritardo è un indizio di quanto i fenomeni qui trattati fatichino a trovare udienza nella coscienza comune.

[9]. KORN 1975 (e successive ristampe).

[10]. *Cfr.* GOLA 2004.

concettuali: ne sintetizzo alcune. Suono/rumore: la musica, intesa come antitesi al rumore, nel momento in cui inquina si riduce essa stessa a 'rumore'. Quantità/qualità: la quantità di rumore o di suono è misurabile in decibel, quindi accertabile, la qualità del disturbo arrecato è invece per sua natura opinabile, dunque controvertibile[11]. Soggettivo/oggettivo: la medesima musica può produrre nello stesso momento euforia o rilassatezza in chi desidera ascoltarla, rabbia o stress in chi non la vorrebbe udire. Individuale/collettivo: il profitto dell'esercente che mediante un piano-bar all'aria aperta attira gli avventori è di certo propizio allo sviluppo della sua attività produttiva (e indirettamente, attraverso la tassazione, alla società *at large*), ma nel contempo arreca un danno — in termini di quiete, riposo, libertà, salute — alla collettività viciniore che se ne sente oppressa, violentata, frustrata.

---

[11].    La giurisprudenza italiana riconosce oggi il 'danno esistenziale', fattispecie che per la sua sottigliezza e per l'importanza che riveste nel campo qui indagato merita una succinta illustrazione (ringrazio l'avv. Ilaria Simoncini per la gentile comunicazione): «Il danno esistenziale è quella figura di danno creata dalla giurisprudenza e dalla dottrina per la sentita esigenza di colmare, nel sistema risarcitorio del danno alla persona, tutelata espressamente dall'art. 2 della Costituzione, il vuoto lasciato tra le due figure del danno morale e del danno biologico. Il danno esistenziale assicura quindi tutela risarcitoria a fronte di quei comportamenti illeciti che non integrano un fatto di reato e non hanno cagionato al danneggiato una lesione all'integrità psicofisica, accertabile con criterio medico-legale, ma nondimeno hanno menomato o fortemente compresso la estrinsecazione della sua personalità nei rapporti con il prossimo, con l'ambiente o rispetto alle attività della vita, in modo da ledere i diritti costituzionalmente tutelati dal citato art. 2 della Costituzione. Si parla di compromissione delle attività realizzatrici della persona umana con incidenza negativa sulla vita della vittima; sul punto si richiama il *dictum* delle Sezioni Unite del 2008 (Cass., sez. un., 11 novembre 2008, n. 26972), le quali hanno in proposito precisato che: (*a*) in presenza di reato (è sufficiente che il fatto illecito si configuri anche solo astrattamente come reato), superato il tradizionale orientamento che limitava il risarcimento al solo danno morale soggettivo, identificato con il patema d'animo transeunte, ed affermata la risarcibilità del danno non patrimoniale nella sua più ampia accezione, anche il pregiudizio non patrimoniale consistente nel non poter fare (*rectius* nella sofferenza morale determinata dal non poter fare) è risarcibile, ove costituisca conseguenza della lesione almeno di un interesse giuridicamente protetto, desunto dall'ordinamento positivo, ivi comprese le convenzioni internazionali (come la convenzione europea per la salvaguardia dei diritti dell'uomo), e ciò purché sussista il requisito dell'ingiustizia generica secondo l'art. 2043 c.c., la tutela penale costituendo sicuro indice di rilevanza dell'interesse leso; (*b*) in assenza di reato, e al di fuori dei casi determinati dalla legge, pregiudizi di tipo esistenziale sono risarcibili purché conseguenti alla lesione di un diritto inviolabile della persona. Prima ancora, nel 2006, le sezioni unite avevano ritenuto il danno esistenziale consistere nel pregiudizio di natura non meramente emotiva ed interiore, ma oggettivamente accertabile, provocato sul fare areddituale del soggetto, che alteri le sue abitudini di vita e gli assetti relazionali che gli erano propri, inducendolo a scelte di vita diversa quanto alla espressione e realizzazione della sua personalità nel mondo esterno; in altri termini, nel "danno conseguenza della lesione", sostanziantesi nei "riflessi pregiudizievoli prodotti nella vita dell'istante attraverso una negativa alterazione dello stile di vita" (Cass., sez. un., 24 marzo 2006, n. 6572)». In dottrina *cfr.* Pozzo 2004, pp. 187-199; e per la fattispecie del «danno esistenziale da inquinamento ambientale, che altera le normali abitudini della vita ed influisce sulle normali attività quotidiane causando depressione, ansia ed irritazione», si veda Linguanti 2017, pp. 325-360: 337-342. Ampi aggiornamenti in Maistrelli 2023.

## La musica come persecuzione

Noi musicologi possiamo soltanto descrivere il fenomeno e additare il problema. Esso è troppo sfaccettato, e invoca tante diverse professionalità e competenze a largo raggio, perché possa essere affrontato (e men che mai contrastato) da una disciplina come la nostra.

Innanzitutto l'inquinamento musicale interpella la *medicina*. I medici devono sensibilizzare l'opinione pubblica su anatomia, fisiologia e patologia di quell'organo mirabile ma delicato che è l'orecchio, nonché sulle connessioni che lo legano al sistema limbico, dunque al sistema emotivo. A loro spetta di sottolineare i rischi che l'abuso di musica comporta per l'orecchio, ma anche per la psiche. Non solo: i medici devono denunciare, al fine di prevenirli, i danni cui si va incontro in alcuni ambienti di lavoro. Penso, per esempio, ai commessi di certi supermercati sottoposti da mane a sera a un continuo bombardamento sonoro; oppure ai lavoratori delle discoteche, esposti a volumi sonori massacranti. A pro dei lavoratori dovrebbero attivarsi anche i sindacati, e vigilare con severità su tali problematiche[12].

Il fenomeno, con le sue implicazioni, interpella poi le due sfere dell'*economia* — l'uso pubblico di musica, e l'abuso in cui esso degenera, muove interessi economici cospicui[13] — e del *diritto*. Da quasi trent'anni il riferimento obbligato è in Italia la legge quadro sull'inquinamento acustico, numero 447/1995, nella quale peraltro la fattispecie dell'inquinamento musicale *non* è contemplata, essendo essa assorbita e assimilata *tout court* all'inquinamento acustico. Alla legge quadro hanno fatto seguito svariati atti normativi[14], nonché pronunciamenti della Corte di Cassazione, sulla difesa dell'ambiente e della salute, la zonizzazione acustica dei Comuni, la tutela civilistica[15].

Ricade sulla Pubblica Amministrazione un compito arduo: essa deve garantire per un verso la tutela della quiete pubblica e della salute che, secondo l'art. 32 della nostra Costituzione, è «fondamentale diritto dell'individuo e interesse della collettività»; per l'altro, deve consentire lo sviluppo di attività produttive che apportino beneficio economico al consorzio civile, senza che però le emissioni musicali, piacevoli per alcuni, devastino la quiete di chi — lavoratore,

---

[12]. Alcune norme del d.lgs. 81/2008 si occupano specificamente dell'inquinamento da rumore negli ambienti di lavoro.

[13]. *Cfr.* Candela 2004.

[14]. In particolare il d.lgs. 194/2005, che recepisce la direttiva 2002/49/CE, si applica al rumore nell'ambiente esterno, non a quello abitativo. Un decreto recente è il d.lgs. 17 febbraio 2017, n. 42, che reca «disposizioni in materia di armonizzazione della normativa nazionale in materia di inquinamento acustico». Il lettore trova un quadro compendiario della normativa di riferimento in Linguanti 2017, pp. 352-356.

[15]. Per un primo approccio si veda Caravita – Cassetti – Morrone 2016; il capitolo x riguarda l'inquinamento acustico (pp. 147-156), che peraltro non contempla la fattispecie dell'inquinamento musicale. Per la tutela dal disturbo delle occupazioni o del riposo delle persone ci si riferisce *in primis* all'art. 659 del codice penale; per tali aspetti si rimanda a Pelissero 2019, segnatamente alle pp. 356-368 su 'La legislazione in materia di rumore' e 'La tutela penale dell'ambiente contro l'inquinamento acustico' (autrice Antonella Madeo). Un veloce quadro riassuntivo delle sentenze relative a questo articolo è in Noè 2018, pp. 373-375 (capitolo riguardante il 'Disturbo al riposo e alle occupazioni delle persone').

studioso, degente — ne ha bisogno e diritto. Certo, alla Pubblica Amministrazione si richiede una vera 'quadratura del cerchio', un miracolo di equilibrismo tra opposte esigenze: ma questo equilibrio va invocato, cercato, favorito, realizzato[16]. A tal proposito occorre sottolineare che la questione non riguarda soltanto il *volume* sonoro, il cui valore è esprimibile in decibel (*dB*), ma anche altri fattori incisivi: la *frequenza* dell'evento musicale nel corso della settimana o della stagione, la sua *durata* nell'arco della giornata, l'osservanza dei *limiti d'orario*, assai spesso impunemente trasgrediti (o sanzionati con pene pecuniarie talmente ridotte da perdere la propria efficacia deterrente). Tali fattori possono sfuggire alla rilevazione della cosiddetta soglia di «normale tollerabilità, avuto anche riguardo alla condizione dei luoghi», prescritta dall'art. 844 del codice civile[17], con una espressione piuttosto indeterminata. Nel contempo però essi alimentano un malessere crescente che, nel caso estremo, può sconfinare nello sconvolgimento psichico, fino all'assurda rivalsa personale del napoletano che spara al gestore del gazebo, come s'è visto in apertura.

Oggi un aiuto può e deve venire dall'*ingegneria* e dalla *fisica*. Va incrementata l'ottimizzazione acustica degli edifici, e vanno imposti per gli eventi musicali *en plein air* tutti i dispositivi tecnologici (barriere fonoassorbenti, altoparlanti direzionali, cuffie wireless[18], ecc.) atti a contenere e circoscrivere la diffusione del suono entro gli ambienti e i territori desiderati, senza invaderne altri[19].

---

[16]. Un lavoro prezioso svolgono in questo campo le ARPA (Agenzie regionali per la protezione dell'ambiente) istituite con la legge 61/1994. Le denominazioni variano leggermente regione per regione (in Emilia Romagna, per esempio, è Agenzia regionale prevenzione ambiente energia).

[17]. La giurisprudenza ha individuato il criterio che le immissioni sonore sono da considerarsi intollerabili quando la differenza tra la sorgente rumorosa e il rumore di fondo — un dato, quest'ultimo, variabile in base alla classe d'appartenenza della zona interessata e al periodo di riferimento diurno/notturno (d.p.c.m. 14/11/1997, tabella B) — supera i 3 dB. Ma sempre con riferimento all'art. 844 del codice civile, la Corte di Cassazione civile — con sentenza del 17 gennaio 2011, n. 939, che ha annullato precedenti sentenze — ha però ribadito che «in materia di immissioni [sonore], mentre è senz'altro illecito il superamento dei limiti di accettabilità stabiliti dalla legge e dai regolamenti che, disciplinando le attività produttive, fissano nell'interesse della collettività le modalità di rilevamento dei rumori e i limiti massimi di tollerabilità, l'eventuale rispetto degli stessi *non* può far considerare senz'altro lecite le immissioni, dovendo il giudizio sulla loro tollerabilità formularsi a stregua dei principi di cui all'art. 844 c.c. (Cass. 1418706)»; e che, indipendentemente dall'effettivo superamento del limite di accettabilità decretato per legge, va stabilito in concreto se le immissioni siano «compatibili con lo svolgimento delle ordinarie e quotidiane attività di vita professionale e domestica». *Cfr.* il capitolo VII, su 'Spettacoli, trattenimenti e inquinamento acustico', in: Linguanti 2017, pp. 325-360 (alle pp. 339-342 il testo della sentenza citata).

[18]. Cito due notizie giornalistiche recenti tra tante. Il mensile *Amadeus* del giugno 2019 recava un articolo dal titolo eloquente: '*Sounds of Silence*. Una tastiera, un pianista, dell'alta tecnologia e centinaia di cuffie. Oggi i concerti si ascoltano (e suonano) anche così in modalità wi-fi'. Il 21 luglio *il Resto del Carlino Bologna* annunciava un 'Not Disturb Party' all'aperto in un grande albergo, con tanto di Silent Disco, ossia «una discoteca silenziosa a cui le persone possono partecipare indossando delle cuffie che trasmettono la musica direttamente nelle orecchie».

[19]. *Cfr.* Gabrielli – Fuga 2009.

## LA MUSICA COME PERSECUZIONE

Ma al di là della tutela giuridica preventiva e sanzionatoria, al di là delle ammirevoli conquiste dell'ingegneria, al di là dei richiami dei medici, al di là dell'oculata amministrazione, la difesa dall'inquinamento musicale va affidata nei tempi lunghi a un'*educazione musicale* sensata, ben strutturata, 'forte', saldamente ancorata sul terreno dell'educazione civica[20]. Occorre incoraggiare un'educazione musicale che abitui i discenti a distinguere i diversi generi di musica, li invogli ad ascoltarli anche con le orecchie e la testa degli altri, li istruisca circa le tante e diverse funzioni intellettuali, estetiche e sociali svolte dalla produzione e fruizione di musica, li conduca a percepire la variegata ricchezza del silenzio[21], sia insomma effettiva 'educazione all'ascolto': un ascolto consapevole, critico, selettivo, che offra la possibilità di uno scambio vero, costante, costruttivo e profondo fra gli esseri umani, e con l'ambiente[22]. Spetta al Ministero dell'Istruzione adoperarsi per diffondere questa seria educazione all'ascolto nelle scuole di ogni ordine e grado (così come fa con la Storia dell'arte nell'educare alla visione): alla lunga, è questa la strada più promettente perché il contrasto dell'inquinamento musicale non resti lettera morta. Per ora l'inquinamento musicale è un mero oggetto di disquisizione intellettuale per musicologi, o di protesta civica per chi è esposto alle immissioni sgradite, ma potrà diventare nel prossimo futuro consapevolezza diffusa fra i cittadini di ogni ceto, classe, età, che vorranno prodigarsi per un ambiente e un contesto civile più attento alla qualità del suono, e dunque più vivibile per tutti.

### BIBLIOGRAFIA

BLACKING 1986
BLACKING, John. *Com'è musicale l'uomo*, traduzione italiana di Domenico Cacciapaglia, Milano, Ricordi-Unicopli, 1986, pp. 3-31.

BORGNA 1999
BORGNA, Eugenio. 'L'esperienza allucinatoria nella schizofrenia', in: *Psicopatologia della schizofrenia. Prospettive metodologiche e cliniche*, a cura di Mario Rossi Monti e Giovanni Stanghellini, Milano, Cortina, 1999, pp. 33-46.

CANDELA 2004
CANDELA, Guido. 'Effetti sociali della musica, tra piacere e inquinamento: un controllo economico complesso', in: CUOMO 2004, pp. 201-212.

---

[20]. *Cfr.* CUOMO 2004, pp. 19-26.

[21]. La 'neurofisiologia del silenzio' è venuta di recente alla ribalta in un convegno tenuto a Nocera Umbra (26-28 luglio 2019), promosso dall'Istituto di Ricerca per le Neuroscienze, Educazione e Didattica (RINED) della Fondazione Patrizio Paoletti, in collaborazione con l'Università della Sapienza di Roma e Haifa University. *Cfr.* anche il *Corriere della Sera*, 1° agosto 2019, supplemento 'Salute'.

[22]. Per l'educazione all'ascolto consapevole rimando a LA FACE BIANCONI 2006.

CARAVITA – CASSETTI – MORRONE 2016
*Diritto dell'ambiente*, a cura di Beniamino Caravita, Luisa Cassetti e Andrea Morrone, Bologna, il Mulino, 2016.

CUOMO 2004
*Musica urbana. Il problema dell'inquinamento musicale*, a cura di Carla Cuomo, Bologna, CLUEB, 2004.

FICINO 1991
FICINO, Marsilio. *De vita*, a cura di Albano Biondi e Giuliano Pisani, Pordenone, Biblioteca dell'immagine, 1991.

GABRIELLI – FUGA 2009
GABRIELLI, Tommaso – FUGA, Federico. *Impatto acustico. Accertamenti e documentazione* [...] *Attività ricreative*, Santarcangelo di Romagna, Maggioli, 2009.

GOLA 2004
GOLA, Marcella. 'L'inquinamento musicale è un problema giuridico?', in: CUOMO 2004, pp. 161-170.

KANT 1963
KANT, Immanuel. *Critica del giudizio*, a cura di Valerio Verra, Bari, Laterza, 1963.

KORN 1975
KORN, Peter Jona. *Musikalische Umweltverschmutzung: polemische Variationen über ein unerquickliches Thema*, Wiesbaden, Breitkopf & Härtel, 1975.

LA FACE BIANCONI 2006
*La didattica dell'ascolto*, a cura di Giuseppina La Face Bianconi, *Musica e Storia*, XIV/3 (dicembre 2006).

LINGUANTI 2017
LINGUANTI, Saverio. *Manuale di polizia amministrativa.* [...] *Nuova normativa di impatto acustico* [...] *Aggiornato con* [...] *d.lgs. n. 42/2017 (Modifiche in materia d'inquinamento acustico)* [...], Santarcangelo di Romagna, Maggioli, ³2017.

MAISTRELLI 2023
MAISTRELLI, Annalia. *Il «danno da movida» tra tutela inibitoria e risarcimento del danno*, Trento, Università degli Studi di Trento, 2023 (The Trento Law and Technology Research Group, Student Paper Series, 89).

MONARI 2013
MONARI, Marco. *La piazza che non c'era. Ecologia urbana, paesaggio sonoro cognitivo, luoghi antropici del benessere*, Fano, Aras, 2013.

NOÈ 2018
NOÈ, Gaetano. *Prontuario di polizia ambientale. Violazioni, sanzioni, note operative*, Santarcangelo di Romagna, Maggioli, ⁴2018.

# La musica come persecuzione

PELISSERO 2019
*Reati contro l'ambiente e il territorio*, a cura di Marco Pelissero, Torino, Giappichelli, ²2019.

POZZO 2004
POZZO, Barbara. 'La tutela civilistica: il danno e il suo risarcimento. Profili di diritto comparato', in: CUOMO 2004, pp. 187-199.

SCHAFER 1969
SCHAFER, Raymond Murray. *The New Soundscape: A Handbook for the Modern Music Teacher*, Toronto, Berandol Music, 1969.

SCHAFER 1977
ID. *The Soundscape: Our Sonic Environment and the Tuning of the World*, Rochester (VT), Destiny Books, 1977 [traduzione italiana a cura di Nemesio Ala, *Il paesaggio sonoro*, Milano, Ricordi-Unicopli, 1985].

# Abstracts and Biographies

Valeria De Lucca, *Regulating Sound and Noise in Seventeenth-Century Rome*

Busy early modern cities required authorities to control and regulate sound, noise and silence, to guarantee both the safety of their citizens and an orderly unfolding and occurrence of everyday activities. Attempts to regulate the soundscape of the city, however, were also meant to enact the authorities' political and social agenda, revealing their priorities and anxieties. This chapter considers the ways in which the bans and edicts of seventeenth-century Rome aimed to inflect the sound-print of certain streets, squares or quarters, regulate the behaviour of specific groups of people, and mark occasions of heightened political or religious significance, ultimately shaping the sonic identity of the city.

Valeria De Lucca is Associate Professor of Music at the University of Southampton. Her work on seventeenth-century music and society concentrates on opera, patronage and systems of production in Italy; women patrons and singers, their mobility and strategies of self-fashioning; and aspects of sound, staging and performance in early modern Rome. She is the author of several articles and chapters and a monograph, *The Politics of Princely Entertainment: Music and Spectacle in the Lives of Lorenzo Onofrio and Maria Mancini Colonna* (Oxford University Press, 2020). Together with Christine Jeanneret she is the editor of *The Grand Theater of the World: Music, Space, and the Performance of Identity in Early Modern Rome* (Routledge, 2020).

\*\*\*

Luigi Collarile, *«Ephemerides Itineris Romani»: Experiencing the Sound of Italy in Two Swiss Travel Diaries of the Seventeenth Century*

An hermeneutical approach to two early modern testimonies regarding two journeys to Italy — the first concerning the travel of a Swiss delegation that arrived in Rome in 1661 to plead the cause of a relic, the second the journey of two young Benedictines from the monastery of Einsiedeln who studied in Rome between 1639 and 1641 — provides an interesting perspective on the sonic experience of foreign travellers and their interaction with the sound of the landscape they crossed and, in particular, the complex urban ceremonial of Rome.

Luigi Collarile teaches History of Church Music at the Bern University of the Arts and is currently Research Fellow at the Schola Cantorum Basiliensis (Basel). He studied in Padua, Basel and Fribourg (Ph.D. 2010). He was Research Fellow and Visiting Professor at the Universities of Basel, Rome Tor Vergata, Geneva and Venice. His publications cover different research areas: European sacred music; the musical life of early modern Venice; the soundscape of early modern Italy; music printing and

## ABSTRACTS AND BIOGRAPHIES

publishing and Renaissance music theory. He is a member of the editorial board of the Istituto Italiano per la Storia della Musica (Rome) and the scientific journal *L'Organo* (Bologna).

\*\*\*

UMBERTO CECCHINATO, *Suoni pericolosi. Musica sacra, emozioni e disciplinamento dell'ambiente sonoro nelle chiese venete della prima età moderna*

During the sixteenth century and after the Council of Trent, the widespread use of musical instruments and the performance of secular texts and melodies during celebrations in the churches became one of the objectives of reforming action by bishops in the Italian peninsula. The subject has been treated by music historians for some time, but little has been said about the cultural and social motivations behind these attempts at musical reform. This chapter analyses the decrees concerning sacred music issued during the sixteenth century by the Italian Catholic bishops in the light of recent historical-anthropological literature on the senses and emotions, stressing the connections between reform actions, the disciplining of behaviour in churches and beliefs about the powers of music.

UMBERTO CECCHINATO is a Researcher at the department of Sociologia e studi sociali, Università di Trento and a Research Fellow at the Italian-German Historical Institute, Bruno Kessler Foundation (ISIG-FBK). He is a cultural and social historian, and his studies focus on the connections between festival culture, musical performances and violence in medieval and early modern Europe. He is the editor of medieval normative texts of the Republic of Venice. Before joining the University of Trento, he collaborated on the projects *HOLYLAB, A Global Economic Organization in the Early Modern Period: The Custody of the Holy Land through its Account Books (1600-1800)*, ERC-2020-COG, at the Università di Roma Tre, and *PUblic REnaissance: Urban Cultures of Public Space between Early Modern Europe and the Present* (PURE) funded by the Humanities in European Research Area (HERA), at ISIG-FBK.

\*\*\*

ANGELA FIORE, *Suoni, spazi, identità della Modena estense*

This chapter aims to rediscover and reconstruct the musical landscape of the city of Modena, the seat of one of the most prestigious courts of the Italian Renaissance: the House of Este. During the seventeenth century, Modena became an important musical centre thanks to the Dukes of Este. The court attracted composers and musicians from different parts of Europe and organized magnificent performances. The most significant and intense moment of musical production took place during the reign of Francesco II d'Este (1674-1694). Francesco II enlarged the court orchestra and purchased a large collection of music for the ducal library. At this time, music begins to appear in the public spaces of the duchy and becomes a central part of urban culture. The court itself contributed to the construction of the city's musical identity.

ANGELA FIORE received her Ph.D. from the University of Fribourg, Switzerland in 2015. She is now Researcher in Musicology and History of Music at the Università di Messina, Italy. Her

## ABSTRACTS AND BIOGRAPHIES

research fields include Neapolitan sacred music; the circulation of musicians; the musical production of the House of Este-Modena; and the historical soundscape of early modern cities. For her research she received grants from the Fondazione Pergolesi Spontini Jesi in 2007; the Swiss National Science Found in 2011; the Pôle de recherche-University of Fribourg in 2014; the Jacques-Handschin Prize in 2016; and funding from the American Musicological Society in 2017. Additionally, she held a diploma in violin and specialised in the baroque violin repertoire.

*\*\*\**

GIOVANNI FLORIO, *Celebrating the Prince from Afar: Echoes from the Jubilant Dominions in the Orations to the Newly Elected Doges (XVI-XVII Century)*

The doge's election was a crucial moment in the Venetian civic ritual: the presentation of the new *Serenissimo* to the cheering *popolo* was a performative act that aimed to give substance to the so-called 'myth of Venice' by displaying a well-defined image of republican power and order. This chapter complicates this urban interpretation of the ducal celebration by considering the involvement of the Venetian subject territories in the shaping of Venice's civic ritual. To this end, it takes into account the custom, typical of all the main Venetian subject cities, of celebrating the newly elected doge by sending him a ceremonial embassy appointed to praise him with a congratulatory oration. Mostly printed but largely unexplored, these texts provide significant insights not only regarding the celebrations devoted to the newly elected doges that were performed in — and by — the dominions, but also about the interactions of such ceremonies with the Venetian civic ritual. The rhetorical choices made by the orators aimed to bring to the doge's ears not only the news of the celebrations performed in his honour, but also the echo of their soundscape. Orators aspired to make themselves a living — and resounding — representation of the jubilant dominion, perfectly fulfilling, in this way, their representative function. Sending an embassy to Venice and appointing it to bring to the doge an echo of the celebration performed in his honour was the solution deployed by the dominions in order to cope with the ducal immobility and so with the impossibility of displaying the ritual of recognition of sovereignty so common in other coeval European polities (i.e., joyous entries, ceremonial journeys, triumphs, visits etc.).

GIOVANNI FLORIO earned his Ph.D. in European Social History at the Università Ca' Foscari of Venice in 2014. He is currently a Postdoctoral Researcher at the Università di Padova within the ERC funded project *Risk – Republics on the Stage of Kings: Representing Republican State Power in the Europe of Absolute Monarchies (Late 16th – early 18th Century)*. His work mainly focuses on the political and ceremonial representation of the Venetian subject cities.

*\*\*\**

NICOLA USULA, *Traditional Music in Seventeenth-Century Operas 'alla Veneziana': Intersections in the Italian Soundscape*

During the seventeenth century, operas 'alla veneziana' contributed to the dissemination of the genre throughout the Italian peninsula and beyond the Alps. They were staged for the inauguration

# Abstracts and Biographies

of newly built public theatres far from the Serenissima, slowly spreading a common taste for opera to all Europe. These works presented a number of references to the traditional music that was played outside the theatres, such as nursery rhymes, traditional songs and dances, and their authors exploited these pieces to link the operatic performance to the extra-operatic musical experiences of the audience. One would expect to find mainly indigenous Venetian elements in these kinds of examples, and this would strengthen the idea that through operas even the traditional music components of the Venetian soundscape could be exported. However, the analysis carried out in this study generated other results. It seems that these quotations refer primarily to a likely pan-Italian traditional soundscape, or better, to an already shared concept of traditional music that in the middle of the century looks to have been unanimously perceived as extraneous to the art music world. Venetian operas summarised this sort of dichotomy between high and low, learned and spontaneous, art and traditional music, and used the gap between the two musical worlds toward the same principal dramaturgical goal as the spoken theatre: comic and realistic effect.

Nicola Usula is a Postdoctoral Researcher in Musicology in the field of Italian Opera and Oratorio both in Italy and in Vienna in the seventeenth and eighteenth century. At the core of his production are works on the dramaturgy of music, the philology of music and librettos, together with codicology and music iconography. His main editorial contributions concern philological works on seventeenth-century Italian opera, such as *L'Orione* by Francesco Cavalli (together with Davide Daolmi, Kassel, Bärenreiter, 2015), *La finta pazza* by Francesco Sacrati, *Il novello Giasone* by Francesco Cavalli and Alessandro Stradella (Milan, Ricordi, 2018 and 2013), and *«Cavato dal spagnuolo e dal franzese»: fonti e drammaturgia del "Carceriere di sé medesimo" di Lodovico Adimari e Alessandro Melani (Firenze 1681)* (Pisa, Pacini, 2018). In 2020 he was awarded the prize 'Antonio Feltrinelli Giovani' in the category 'Storia e Cultura della musica' by the Accademia Nazionale dei Lincei in Rome.

***

Elia Pivetta, *Forms of Circulation of Musical Knowledge in Eighteenth-Century Italy: Giambattista Martini's «Risposta» to «abate Pavona friulano»*

By analysing an unpublished case study, this chapter investigates the role played by Father Giambattista Martini's letters in the circulation of musical knowledge. In eighteenth-century Italy, musicians and composers working in culturally peripheral regions were often unable to travel widely, but found in their correspondence with Martini a way to learn and improve their professional skills. Martini's letters also contributed to a widespread diffusion of contrapuntal knowledge, promoting it as a shared cultural background among Italian composers, regardless of the specific geographic areas in which they were active.

Elia Pivetta studied in Udine, where he graduated in Organ at the Conservatory and in Law at the University. He later moved to Switzerland and obtained a Master of Arts in Music Performance in Organ at the Schola Cantorum Basiliensis (Basel), also attending the annual course in Basso continuo. In 2020, he obtained a Master's Degree in Musicology at the Università di Pavia, Cremona. He is about to complete the Specialisation School in Musical Heritage at the Università di Bologna, where he is mainly

## ABSTRACTS AND BIOGRAPHIES

studying the issues of protection, conservation and valorisation of musical manuscripts. He is currently a Ph.D. student in Musicology at the Università di Pavia, Cremona, focusing on the relationship between composition and improvisation in eighteenth-century Venice.

\*\*\*

ANGELA FIORE, *Urban Spaces and Musical Practices of Neapolitan Female Monasteries between the Seventeenth and Eighteenth Centuries*

In the seventeenth and eighteenth centuries, Naples was a primary centre of interest and a radiating point in European music. Religious buildings have played a crucial part in the musical history of the city, through musical practices related to the organization of liturgies and ceremonies. In particular, female religious institutions were often responsible for producing and commissioning sacred music, and archival material has provided information on such institutions with many references to an important musical 'tradition' concerning both the public and private spheres. At all times, monasteries and convents collaborated with the most representative musicians of the city of Naples to embellish the different liturgies or to instruct young women and nuns in music. The comparative study of archival documentation and chronicles also reveals the relationships between the city of Naples and monastic communities, offering numerous details on local traditions and musical practices within the urban context.

\*\*\*

MARIA ROSA DE LUCA, *Ritualising a Resilient City: Soundscape, Collective Performances and Construction of Urban Imaginary*

This study focuses on the urban musical experience in eighteenth-century Catania. Through the methodological perspective of urban musicology, the chapter deals with a paradigmatic case of musical ritualities: the festive celebration of St Agatha. The aim of enquiry is to observe how the form of the city of Catania has been improved and reorganised over the centuries according to the configuration of the feast, which employs various types of symbolic and ritual (not exclusively musical) practices revolving around the celebration of the patron saint. Among these, the procession with the relics throughout the city has to some extent reshaped the town plan. Also, ecclesiastical chant and instrumental music may have played an important role in the (re-)construction of an ideal place for such collective rituality. Nonetheless, the spatial hierarchy and the privileged itineraries derived from the rebuilding project trace a pivotal point in the ritual: the orthogonal subdivision of the urban space gives shape to a city redesigned as a marvellous open-air theatre that annually, according to an ancient ceremonial, hosts a complex visual and sound spectacle on the occasion of the feast.

MARIA ROSA DE LUCA is Associate Professor in Musicology and History of Music in the Department of Humanities at the Università di Catania, where she presides over the master's degree 'Communication of Culture and Performing Arts'. Her research activity involves, above all, the history of music interpreted through the lens of social history and historical soundscape studies. Among her

## ABSTRACTS AND BIOGRAPHIES

publications are the two monographs *Musica e cultura urbana nel Settecento a Catania* (2012) and *Gli spazi del talento. Primizie musicali del giovane Bellini* (2020), the critical editions of *Mottetti sacri* (Napoli, Muzio, 1702) by Alessandro Scarlatti (2012) and *Lilia Campi a 2, 3, 4, 5 e 6 voci* (Roma, Masotti, 1627) by Domenico Campisi (2015) and the volume *Un veneziano in Europa. Teatro e musica nelle carte di Giovanni Battista Perucchini* (2019). She is a member of the Editorial Board of *Musica Docta* and of the Executive Board of *Bollettino di studi belliniani*.

\*\*\*

GIUSEPPINA LA FACE, *La musica come persecuzione. L'inquinamento musicale nelle città odierne*
Music pollution — the syntagm has been attested at least since 1975 [Korn] — is a very special kind of environmental pollution, with which our society is confronted daily. It cannot be *sic et simpliciter* identified with noise pollution, but it is just as harmful. Being catastrophically worsened by sound reproduction and amplification systems, the phenomenon concerns musicologists on a cultural level, as the polluting factor is music as such. However, due to its multiple interdisciplinary connections, such a phenomenon also challenges the responsibilities of medical doctors, lawyers, engineers, psychologists, economists, sociologists, educationalists, environmentalists and administrators. There is a lack of widespread awareness in our society that musical sound emissions in public contexts might produce pollution, and cause disturbance and harm to individuals or communities that are forced to tolerate them without having requested or desired them. In particular, there is a lack of awareness that electronic amplification — which is indispensable to much of today's music — disproportionately increases annoyance to the point of turning it into insidious persecution. This paper intends (1) to offer a concise outline of the general problems relating to musical pollution in urban contexts, pointing out the antinomies that the phenomenon reports; (2) to show how it is essential to tackle these types of pollution phenomena by implementing various and interconnected disciplinary tools; (3) and to reveal that — in order to mitigate them — it is indispensable to cultivate education for 'reflective' and competent listening, and thus to conduct a pedagogical-didactic action over a long period of time, starting from a young age.

GIUSEPPINA LA FACE is the founder and editor-in-chief of *Musica Docta*, an online periodical for Music Pedagogy and Education, as well as the current editor-in-chief of *Il Saggiatore musicale*. She was Full Professor of Musicology and Music History at the Università di Bologna, where, from 2007 to 2018, she headed the Department for Music and Performing Arts, which later developed into the Arts Department. After carrying out research on late fourteenth-century Italian polyphony and Schubert's Lieder, in the past two decades she has made important contributions to research in the fields of Music Pedagogy and Music Education, both in Italy (see, among several other publications, the miscellaneous books *Educazione musicale e Formazione* and *La musica tra conoscere e fare*, Milan, 2008 and 2011) and on an international level, by promoting and coordinating a Study Group *Transmission of Knowledge as a Primary Aim in Music Education* within the International Musicological Society (since 2012). She coordinates the *Rete Universitaria per l'Educazione musicale* (University Network for Music Education) and is a corresponding member of the Accademia delle Scienze in Bologna.

# Index

## A

AARON, Pietro 199, 200
    *Toscanello in Musica* 199-200
ACADEMIES 72, 91, 101-102, 146, 247
    Modena, Accademia de' Dissonanti 91, 101-102
    Paris, Académie de poésie et de musique 72
    Venice, Accademia degli Incogniti 146
AGOSTINI, Pier Simone 99
ALESSIO DA ROMA (padre guardiano) 222
ALLACCI, Leone 93
ALLEGRI, Gregorio 30
    *Miserere* (psalm) 30
ALPS viii, 23, 26, 29, 51, 182
AMORT, Florian 153
ANGLICAN BENEDICTINE CONGREGATION 38, 47
ANJOU, King Robert of 217
APENNINES 26
APOLLO 34, 93, 161
AQUILANO *see* MELCHIORRE, Domenico
ASOLO 66
ASSISI 28, 236
ATTAINGNANT, Pierre 195-196
AUGUSTA (Sicily) 233-234
AURELI, Aurelio 154
    *Le fortune di Rodope e di Damira* (opera) 154

## B

BACCIAGALUPPI, Claudio 213
BAILEY, Peter 15
BAJA Guarienti, Carlo 92
BARATERIO, Francesco 107
BARBARELLA (nun) 64
BARBERINI (family) 27, 37, 40, 44, 47, 93
    Antonio 40
    Francesco 27, 37, 51

Lucrezia 93
Taddeo 44
BASEL ix
BATTAGLIA, Salvatore 261
BATTESTINO *see* STUCK, Jean-Baptiste
BELDEMANDIS, Prosdocimus de 199
BELLI, Ottonello 125
BELLINI, Vincenzo Tobia 247
BELLINZONA 27, 38, 51
    Benedictine residence 51
BELLUNO 113, 117, 122
BELOTTI, Sara 103
BEMBO, Pietro 108
BERGAMO 28, 107, 123
BERGIER, Nicolas 69-70
BERKELEY, Library 185, 204
BERLIOZ, Hector 257
BERNINI, Gian Lorenzo 42
BERTOGLIO, Chiara 60, 74
BIANCAVILLA 234
BIANCHI, Francesco 47
BIANCONI, Lorenzo ix, 145, 168
BISCARI (Sicily) 238-239, 247
BLUNT, John James 249-250
BOGINO, Giovanni Battista Lorenzo 182
BOLLANI, Domenico 77
BOLOGNA vii, 26-27, 38, 60, 69, 96, 145, 170, 181, 183, 185-186, 191, 193, 203-204, 257
    Museo internazionale e Biblioteca della musica 170, 186, 193, 204
    San Francesco, church 183
    Teatro del Corso 257
BON, Andrea 63
BORGNA, Eugenio 259

## INDEX

BORROMEO (family) 38, 67, 70, 74, 78, 162, 170
    Archivio (Isola Bella) 162, 170
    Carlo 38, 67, 70, 74, 78
BOUCHARD, Jean Jacques 215
    *Voyage dans le royaume de Naples* 215
BOURBON (family) 217, 221-223, 239-240
    Charles 217, 221-223
    Ferdinand III 239-240
    Maria Amalia 222-223
    Maria Isabella Antonia 223
    Maria Josefa Antoinette 223
    Philip 223
BRESCIA 28, 77, 120
BRUNSWICK-LÜNEBURG, Charlotte Felicitas of 97
BURCHELATI, Bartolomeo 61
BUSENELLO, Gian Francesco 148, 164, 167-168
    *Delle ore ociose* 168
    *Didone* (opera) 167
    *L'incoronazione di Poppea* (opera) 164, 168
    *La prosperità infelice di Giulio Cesare dittatore* (opera) 148

### C

CAMASTRA 231
CANDOTTI Giovanni Battista 183, 192
CANTON NIDWALDEN (Switzerland) 27
CANTON LUCERNE (Switzerland) 27, 35
CANTON SCHWYZ (Switzerland) 36
CANTON URI (Switzerland) 38
CAPILUPI, Geminiano 90
CAPODISTRIA (today Koper, Slovenia) 110-111, 114, 116, 121, 125
CARACCIOLO, Fulvia 219
CARACCIOLO, Innico 210, 212
CARCACI (Sicily) 243
CARISSIMI, Giacomo 30, 32, 42
CARRERA, Pietro 233
CASTELLI, Ottaviano 148
    *Primavera urbana col trionfo d'Amor pudico* (opera) 148
CATANIA ix, 230-236, 239-241 243-244, 246-250
    *Churches, monasteries and confraternities:*
    Addolorata, preti sotto titolo dell' (confraternity) 236
    Cathedral (church) 231-236, 240-241, 243, 246

Collegiate (church) 233, 241, 243
Minoriti (monastery) 241
S. Agata, moniali di (monastery) 236, 241
S. Agata alla fornace (church) 241
S. Agata alle sciare (church) 236
S. Agostino (monastery) 236, 241
S. Benedetto (monastery) 236, 241
S. Chiara (monastery) 236, 241
S. Francesco d'Assisi, Reali Padri di (monastery) 236, 241
S. Giovanni Battista (confraternity) 236
S. Giuliano (monastery) 236, 241
S. Maria dell'Ajuto (monastery) 241
S. Michele, Chierici regolari minori di (confraternity) 236
S. Placido, moniali di (monastery) 241
Trinità, moniali della (monastery) 236, 241
*Other locations:*
Ospedale di S. Marco 236
Palazzo dell'Università / Palazzo degli Studi 236, 238, 246
Palazzo del Senato / Palazzo Senatorio 232-233, 235-236, 238, 240, 243-244
Piazza del Duomo (Platea Magna, Piano del Duomo) 231, 241
Piazza San Filippo 236, 242
Piano dei Quattro Cantoni 231, 236, 241
Piano della Loggia 236, 242
Piano della Marina 238
Piano dell'Università / Piano degli Almi Studi 238, 242, 247
Porta del mare 236, 243
Porta di Aci 236, 241, 243, 250
Porta Ferdinanda /Ferdinandea 236, 239
Quattro Canti 231, 236, 241
Sebeto (river) 244
Simeto (river) 244
Via del Corso 231
Via di San Filippo 231
Via di Sangiuliano 231
Via Etnea 231
Via Garibaldi 231
Via Lanza 231
Via Uceda 231

# INDEX

Via Vittorio Emanuele 231
University ix
*Other related terms:*
Bara 234
Etna's eruption 1669 230, 235, 250
Fercolo 234, 250
Gilio 233-234
Palio 234, 243-244
Senate 230, 232-233, 235, 238, 240, 243-244, 247
Terremoto / Earthquake 1693 230-231
CAVALLI, Francesco 145, 151, 153, 158-162, 164, 166-167
*Didone* (opera) 167
*Giasone* (opera) 145, 151, 153-154, 156
*L'Orione* (opera) 161, 163-164
*L'Oristeo* (opera) 159
*La Rosinda* (opera) 164
*La traditora* (galliard) 151, 153-154, 169
*Il Xerse* (opera) 160-161, 164
CAVARZERE 114, 122
CATAFALCO 40
CECCHINATO, Umberto viii
CECCHINI, Angelo 148
*Primavera urbana col trionfo d'Amor pudico* (opera) 148
CELANO, Carlo 215
CENEDA 78-79
CENTON, Francesco 123
CHIARELLI, Alessandra 102
CHINEA (coin) 32, 50
CHIOGGIA 113, 115-117, 123
CICOGNA, Pasquale 111, 122-123
CICOGNINI, Giacinto Andrea 145, 148, 151-152
*Giasone* (opera) 152
*Orontea* (opera) 148, 151-152
CIRILLO Franco, Bernardino 70-71
CIVIDALE DEL FRIULI viii, 183, 185-189, 191-194, 196, 202, 204
Benedictine monastery (female) 191
Duomo 185, 194
Insigne Collegiata of Santa Maria Assunta 183, 185, 187-188, 193-194, 204
Museo Archeologico Nazionale 196, 204
CIVRAN, Stefano 63

CHARLES IX, King of France 72
CHRISTINE, Queen of Sweden 155
CLAVELLO, Curzio 121
COLLARILE, Luigi viii
COLLOREDO, Fabio Leandro di 186-189, 191-195
*Memoria* 191-192
COLLOREDO, Violante di (Maria Teresa Costanza) 191-192
COMO 27-28
CONCORDIA SAGGITTARIA 77
CONEGLIANO 80
Ss. Martino e Rosa (church) 80
CONSALVI, Antonio Maria 116
CONTI, Valeria 145
CORDANS, Bartolomeo 183
CORELLI, Arcangelo 99
CORNER (family) 66-67, 77-79
Federico 77
Francesco 66-67, 77, 79
Giorgio 77-79
CORTE DI CASSAZIONE 263-264
CONSTANTINOPLE (today Istanbul, Turkey) 232
COUNCIL OF TRENT viii, 66, 72, 75, 78-79, 81
CREMA 115, 121
CRISTIANI, Beltrame 182
CROWTHER, Victor 102
CURIA (Rome) 27, 212

### D

DA MOSTO, Andrea 109
DA MOSTO, Domenico 64, 66
DA MOSTO, Nicolò 64, 66
DEI, Francesco 63, 65, 79
DEL BENE, Agostino 113, 123
DEL COLLE, Giulio 147
DELLA ROVERE, Giulio Feltrio 74-75
DELLA VALLE, Pietro 47
*Esther* (oratorio) 47
DELLA VOLPE, Lelio 183, 185, 192, 202
DE LUCA, Maria Rosa ix
DE LUCCA, Valeria viii
DE MAJO, Giuseppe (Brunasso) 216
DE MAURO, Tullio 261
DE MURIS, Johannes 198

# INDEX

DEODATO Moncada, Corrado 240
DESCALZO, Ottonello 111-112, 123
DIENER, Martinus 46
DI MARANGONI, Santo 115, 126
DONÀ, Francesco 110, 124-125
DONÀ, Leonardo 110, 113-116, 120, 122-124, 126-127
DONÀ, Piero 63
DOUGLAS, Mary 1
DRAGHI, Antonio 154-155, 160
    *L'Almonte* (opera) 154
    *Le fortune di Rodope e di Damira* (opera) 154
    *Vero amor fa soave ogni fatica* (cantata) 160
DRAGOSITS, Anne Marie 49
DRESDEN 222
DUCKLES, Vincent 185
DURANTE, Francesco 243

### E

EGYPT 149
EINSIEDELN (Schwyz), Benedictine monastery 36-37, 51
ENNA 249
EMILIA ROMAGNA 264
EREMITANI (order) 96
ESTE, d' (family, dukes of Ferrara, Modena and Reggio Emilia) viii, 49, 89-92, 94-97
    Alfonso II 89
    Alfonso IV 91, 96-97
    Cesare I 89-90, 92
    Francesco I 94, 96
    Francesco II 91
    Gianfederico 97
    Ippolito II 49
    Rinaldo I 95, 97
ETNA (mount) 230, 240, 250

### F

FABBRI, Paolo 150
FALCONIERI, Andrea 213
FAGO, Nicola (Tarantino) 216, 221
FANO 28
FARNESE, Orazio 107
FARNESE, Girolamo 37
FAUSTINI, Giovanni 159, 164, 166-167
    *L'Egisto* (opera) 166-167

*L'Oristeo* (opera) 159
*La Rosinda* (opera) 164
FEASTS / OCCASIONS 7, 32, 50, 90, 92
    *Barchette* (Piazza Navona, Rome) 50
    Carnevale (Modena) 92
    Cavalcada Spagnola (Rome) 32
    *Corsa degli Ebrei* (Rome) 7
    Girandola (Rome) 9, 32
    *See also* LITURGICAL CEREMONIES
FEDERICI, Lodovico (di) 120
FELTRE 115
FERRARI, Antonio 99
    *San Contardo d'Este* (oratorio) 99
FERRARI, Benedetto 94, 97, 99, 164, 167
FERRARO, Antonio 234
    *Quam pulchrae sunt mammae tuae* (motet) 234
    *Sacrarum cantionum* (Rome 1617) 234
FÉTIS, François-Joseph 183, 192
FICINO, Marsilio 259
FIORE, Angela viii-ix, 103
FITZALAN, Henry 153
FLECKENSTEIN, Nikolaus 35, 38, 46-47
FLORENCE 26-27, 38
FLORIO, Giovanni viii
FLORIMO, Francesco 203
FOGLIANO, Ludovico 153
FOLIGNO 28
FONTANELLI (family) 100-101
    Archive 101
    Decio 100
    Giulio 100
FORTE URBANO (today Castelfranco Emilia) 186
FRANCOFONTE 234
FRANGIPANE, Cornelio 124-126
FRENCH REVOLUTION 182
FRESCOBALDI, Girolamo 35, 39
FRIBOURG (University) 210, 213
FRIULI 114, 125, 182-183, 185-186, 193-194, 202

### G

GABRIELLI, Domenico 99-100
GAMBERTI, Domenico 96-97
    *Idea di un prencipe et eroe christiano* (1659) 96-97
GAMES 12, 46, 93, 95, 115, 164

# Index

Corda 46
Palla / Pallone 12
GARDANO, Antonio 195
GASPARI, Gaetano 195
GASPARINI, Francesco 100
*La fede tradita e vendicata* (oratorio) 100
GENOA 146
GEREMIA, Giuseppe 243, 247
*Il fonte di Orebbe* (oratorio) 243
*Il ritorno di Tobia alla casa paterna* (oratorio) 247
GESLINO, Pietro 115
GIACOMO D'ANCONA 217
GIANNETTINI, Antonio 99-100
GIANTURCO, Carolyn 102
GIBERTI, Matteo 72, 76, 81
GIORGI TEDESCO, Giovanni 147
GIZZI, Domenico 220
GRAND TOUR 23, 51, 181, 244
GRAZIANI, Girolamo 94-95
*Trionfo della virtù* (opera) 95
GRIMANI (family) 116-117, 123, 196
Marino 116-117, 123
GRISONIO, Francesco 110, 116
GRITTI, Andrea 108
GUALTERUZZI, Ugolino 70
GUILERMO, Biagio 79
GUSTAVUS II ADOLPHUS, King of Sweden 155

## H

HABSBURG, Maria Carolina of 239-240
HASSE, Johann Adolf 182
HAUGE, Peter 145
HOBSBAWM, Eric 182, 202
HOUEL, Jean 244-249
HVAR (Lesina, Croatia) 182

## I

ILLIANO, Roberto ix
ISOLA BELLA (Lago Maggiore) 162, 170

## J

JACOBINISM 240
JANDER, Owen 102

## K

KANT, Immanuel 259-260
*Critica del giudizio* 259
KAPSPERGER, Giovanni Girolamo 47, 49
*Libro quarto d'intavolatura di chitarrone* (1640) 49
KIRCHER, Athanasius 34
Galeria 34
KORN, Peter Jona 261
KÜSSNACHT (Canton Schwyz) 46

## L

LA FACE, Giuseppina ix
LANCELLOTTI, Iacopino 92
LANCELLOTTI, Tommasino 92
LANDI, Stefano 47
LANDSCAPE 23, 29, 50, 109, 113, 147, 223, 229
LANZA, Giuseppe 231
LAZZARINI, Andrea 103
LE JEUNE, Claude 195
LEMOS, countess of 218
LENDINARA 110, 117, 121
LEOPARDI, Giacomo 257
LEOPARDI, Paolina 257
LITURGICAL CEREMONIES
Advent 213
Agatha, Saint (5 February and 19 August) ix, 65, 229-255
Annunciation of Our Lady (25 March) 213
Anthony Abbot, Saint (17 January) 44
Anthony of Padua (13 June) 185
Apollinaris, Saint (23 July) 43
Ascension 199, 200
Assumption (15 August) 42, 194, 214
Beatrice d'Este, Saint (19 January) 99
Beheading of John the Baptist, Saint (29 August) 219-220
Benedict, Saint (21 March) 219
Blaise / Biagio, Saint (3 February) 219
Christmas ix, 213-214, 241
Corpus Domini 62, 216-217
Contardo D'Este, Saint (16 April) 97, 99
Dominic, Saint (3 and 4 August) 45
Easter 13, 50, 214
Epiphany 47, 213

# Index

Exposition of the Blessed Sacrament 214, 217, 219, 223, 240

Francis Xavier, Saint (1 and 2 December) 42, 44

Funerals 47, 96-97, 221

Geminianus, Saint (31 January) 92

Gennaro, Saint (19 September) 213

Gervasio and Protasio, Saints (19 June) 32

Good Friday 215

Gregorio Armeno, Saint (1 October) 210, 219-220

Gregory Pope, Saint (12 March) 44

Holy Mary of Grace (5 July) 214

Holy Trinity 32, 233

Holy Year 13

Holy Week 13, 30, 50, 214

Immaculate Conception (8 December) 214

John the Baptist, Saint, Beheading of (29 August) 219-220

John the Baptist, Saint, Nativity of (24 June) 219

Lent / Quaresima 6, 44, 49-50, 91, 97, 99

Lucy, Saint (13 December) 42, 249

Margherita, Saint (20 July) 36

Mass 11-12, 30, 32, 42-44, 46, 49, 59, 61-67, 70-76, 78, 80-81, 97, 111, 183, 185, 192, 195, 213, 216-219, 221, 223, 235-236, 240, 243

Mass *in tempore belli* 240

Matthew Apostle, Saint (21 September) 219

Maurus, Saint (15 January) 42

Nativity of the Virgin (8 September) 214-215

Novena 97, 213, 218

Othmar, Saint (16 November) 40

Our Lady of Mount Carmel (16 July) 214

Our Lady of Sorrows (15 September) 214

Our Lady of the Rosary (7 October) 214

Palm Sunday 13

Passion of Christ / Passiones 214-215, 241

Pentecost Sunday 30

Peter, Saint 50, 249

Peter and Paul, Saints (28 and 29 June) 32, 50

Potito, Saint (14 January) 210, 215, 218-219, 223

Processions 12, 13, 15, 32, 45, 61, 96, 214-221, 230, 233-236, 243, 248, 250

Purification of the Virgin (2 February) 214

Quarant'Ore 7, 42, 44

Roch, Saint (16 August) 36, 50, 71

Simon and Jude, Saints (27 October) 38

Thomas of Aquinas, Saint (7 March) 45

Visitation of the Virgin (2 July) 214

Vespers 30, 32, 38-40, 42-44, 47, 80, 217-218, 220, 235

Weddings 77, 93, 214, 221-223, 239

Löuw, Johann Melchior 27

London 153, 170

British Library 153, 170

Longobardo, Giovan Tommaso 234

Loreto 28, 93, 243

Lucerne 27-29, 35, 37-38

Lucillo, Sallustio 116

Lucini, Giovanni Battista 155-157

*Gli equivoci in amore, overo La Rosaura* (opera) 155-157

Lucio, Francesco 148

*Orontea* (opera) 148

Lugano 38

Lulier, Giovanni Lorenzo 99

*Santa Beatrice d'Este* (oratorio) 99

Luni (Liguria) 74

## M

Macchiarella, Ignazio 145

Macque, Jean de 213

Mączack, Antoni 182

Madrid 231

Maffei, Scipione 158

Majone, Ascanio 213

Malerba, Michele 234

*O Catanensis gloria* (motet) 234

Malmignatti, Bartolomeo 121

Malta 244

Manelli, Francesco 145

*La Delia* (opera) 145

Manzini, Giulio Giuseppe 99

*San Contardo d'Este* (oratorio) 99

*Santa Beatrice d'Este* (oratorio) 99

Manzuoli, Nicolò 110, 111, 127

Martinelli Braglia, Graziella 102

Martini, Giambattista viii, 181, 183, 186-196, 199-203

Martinozzi, Laura 91, 96

# Index

MAUGARS, André 45
MARAZZOLI, Marco 153, 155, 160
    *L'Egisto, overo Chi soffre speri* (opera) 153, 155, 160
MAZZOCCHI, Virgilio 39, 47, 153, 155, 160
    *L'Egisto, overo Chi soffre speri* (opera) 153, 155, 160
MELCHIORRE, Domenico (Aquilano) 218
MELOSIO, Francesco 161, 163
    *L'Orione* (opera) 161, 163
MENGHINI, Niccolò 42
MENDRISIO 38
MESSINA 231, 234
MILAN 26, 27, 38, 51, 60, 145, 148, 161, 170, 182, 201
    Biblioteca Ambrosiana 170
    Duomo 201
    Theatre of the Royal Ducal Palace 161
    Tomb of St Carlo Borromeo 38
MINATO, Niccolò 160-161, 164
    *Il Xerse* (opera) 160-161, 164
MOCENIGO, Alvise 121
MOCENIGO, Leonardo 79-80
MODENA viii, 27, 72, 89-104
    *Churches and monasteries:*
    Cathedral 90, 92-93, 97
    Cathedral, torre campanaria detta 'Ghirlandina' 92
    Madonna del Parto 97
    Madonna della Ghiara 99
    San Bartolomeo (Gesuiti) 97
    San Carlo Rotondo (chapel) 99
    San Domenico 64
    Sant'Agostino 96
    Santa Teresa (female monastery) 97
    San Vincenzo 97
    *Other locations:*
    Accademia de' Dissonanti 91, 101-102
    Biblioteca Estense 91, 94
    Canalgrande 99
    Collegio dei Nobili 99, 101
    Congregazione teatina di S. Carlo 99
    Gallerie Estensi 103
    Giardino Ducale 92
    Largo Sant'Agostino 92
    Oratorio di San Carlo 91, 99
    Palazzo Comunale 92, 100
    Palazzo della Ragione 92-93

    Palazzo Ducale 92-93, 96, 100-101
    Palazzo Valentini 100
    Piazza Grande 92-93
    Teatro Molza 100
    Teatro Rangoni (later, Teatro Comunale)
    Teatro San Carlo 100
    Teatro San Rocco 101
    Teatro Valentini (later, Teatro Fontanelli) 100
MONTEGNACCO, Massimiliano 114
MONTESANO MARZIANO, Mario 247
MONTEVERDI, Claudio 164, 168-169
    *L'incoronazione di Poppea* (opera) 164, 168-169
MORABITO, Fulvia ix
MURATA, Margaret 1, 8, 145, 160
MORONE, Giovanni 72-73, 81
MUSIC
    Alternatim 40
    Aria 154, 160, 166, 168, 247-248
    Arietta 159, 162
    Bergamasca 153
    Canario 167-168
    Cantata 101-102, 155-156, 243, 247-248
    Canzonetta 146, 150-151, 154, 160-164
    Christmas songs in German 46
    Ciaccona 166-168
    Contrafactum 71
    Contrapunct 185, 188, 192, 195, 200-201
    Contrapunto alla mente 199-201
    Dramma per musica 155
    Favola pastorale 150
    Filastrocca 146, 150
    Frottola 153
    Gagliarda / Galliard 71
    Hymns 40, 185
    Lamento 155,
    Lauda 71, 74-75, 114
    Litanies of the Blessed Virgin Mary 33,
    Mass *L'ombre armato / l'huomo armato* 71
    Mass *La Filomena* 71
    Mass *Hercules Dux Ferrariae* 71
    Miserere 30, 97
    Motet 30, 195-196, 214, 234
    Opera 'alla veneziana' 145-170
    Partimento 181

# Index

Pavana 71

Psalm 39, 71-72, 74, 76, 185, 190, 195

*Salve regina* (antiphon) 38

Sarabande 166

*Te Deum* (hymn) 220-223, 243

*Traditional Songs:*

Chi t'ha fatto queste scarpette (Girometta / Girolmetta) 155

È morto Saione 155

Fra' Iacopino 155

Gallo di mona fiera 155

La bella Margherita 155-158

**Musical Voices and Instruments**

Bassoon 221-222

Castrato 33, 214

Cello 214, 248

Cembalo triarmonico 47

Contrabass 214

Cornetto 59, 80

Discantist 33

Drum / Tamburo 12, 25, 92, 95, 110-112, 114-115, 233-244, 248

Flute 59, 69, 74, 221-222

Horn 221

Lute 153, 214

Oboe 95, 221-222, 248

Organ 34, 39-40, 49, 60, 64, 72-75, 77-79, 81, 183, 189, 191, 211, 218, 234

Piffaro 92

Tibicines 73

Trumpet / Tromba 59, 92-93, 95, 112-115, 218, 221-222

Trombone 79

Violin 80, 90, 185, 214, 218

**Musical Chapels**

Modena, Cappella Ducale 90-91, 94, 97

Modena, Compagnia dei Violini 90

Modena, Concerto degli stromenti 90

Naples, Cappella Musicale del Tesoro di San Gennaro 213, 223

Rome, Cappella Giulia 39

Rome, Collegio Germanico 30, 40, 42-43, 46

Rome, S. Maria Maggiore 33, 44

Rome, Sistine Chapel 30-31, 46

Rome, Venerable English College 38-39, 47, 49

**Murray Schafer**, Raymond 260

## N

**Nani**, Emanuele 244

**Nanino**, Bernardino 200

**Nanino**, Giovanni Maria 200

**Naples** ix, 155, 158, 181-182, 203, 209-213, 215-217, 219-223, 230, 240-241, 243-244, 247

*Churches, monasteries and confraternities:*

Cappella Reale (church) 213

Cathedral (church) 212-213, 216-217, 220-221

Collegio of S. Maria di Loreto 243

Croce di Lucca (monastery) 210

Donnalbina (monastery) 219

Donnaregina (monastery) 210

Regina Coeli (monastery) 210

Montoliveto (church) 216

S. Agostino alla Zecca (church) 216

S. Arcangelo a Baiano (monastery) 220

S. Chiara (monastery) 220-223

S. Gregorio Armeno (monastery) 210, 219-220

S. Maria Egiziaca (monastery) 223

S. Maria di Donnaromita (monastery) 220

S. Maria la Nova (church) 216

S. Maria Maddalena (monastery) 223

S. Patrizia (monastery) 221

S. Potito (monastery) 210, 215, 218-219, 223

Ss. Pietro and Sebastiano (monastery) 223

*Other locations:*

Conservatorio dell'Arte della Lana 223

Conservatorio della Pietà de' Turchini 217

Conservatorio dei Santi Filippo e Giacomo 223

Conservatorio di Gesù Cristo 212

Conservatorio di Nostra Signora della Solitaria (Soledad) 215

Conservatorio di Santa Maria della Colonna (Poveri di Gesù Cristo) 212

Conservatory 203

Istituto Banco di Napoli 216

Largo di Porto 216

Largo dei Girolamini 217

Largo del Gesù 222

Piazza del Pendino 216

# Index

Piazza della Selleria 216
Piazzetta Nilo 217
Strada dei Cortellari 216
Strada della Selleria 216
Strada Trinità Maggiore 217
Via Nilo 217
Vico delle Zite 216
NAPLES AND SICILY, Kingdom of 240
NAVAGERO, Bernardo 73, 76
NELSON, Horatio 241
NEPTUNE 147-148
NESTOLA, Barbara 160
NICOLINI, Bartolomeo 47
NOLFI, Vincenzo 147
  *Il Bellerofonte* (opera) 147

### O

O'LEARY, James 145
O'REGAN, Neil 46
OCHSNER, Kolumban OSB 45
OTTOBONI, Pietro 158

### P

PADUA 28, 107, 111, 113, 120, 123-124, 181-182, 185, 202
  St Anthony, Basilica 185
  Universitas artistarum 113
  University 107
PAINO, Marina ix
PALEOTTI, Gabriele 73
PALERMO 222, 231, 239, 246-248, 258
  Cathedral 222
  Ottangolo 231
PALESTRINA, Giovanni Pierluigi da 30
  *Cum complerentur* (motet) 30
PALLAVICINI, Carlo 100
PALMANOVA 183
PAPAL GUARD 30, 35, 38, 46
PARIS 45
PARMA 27, 74, 94, 96
PARNASSUS 34
PASQUINI, Elisabetta 201, 203
PASTER, Gail Kern 70
PATERNÒ, Alvaro 233,

PATERNÒ CASTELLO (family) 238, 243, 245, 247
  Francesco 243
  Ignazio V 238, 245
  Niccolò Maria 245
PAVANI, Domenico 61-63
PAVAROTTI, Luciano 101
PAVONA, Pietro Alessandro viii, 181, 183-186, 188-199, 201-203
  *Cum invocarem* (psalm) 190-191
  *Missae quatuor vocibus* (1770) 183-184
PEYRAUT, Guillaume 68
PFYFFER, Alexander 35
PFYFFER, Franz 35
PFYFFER Johann Rudolf 35
PIACENZA 27, 38, 74, 162
PIAZZA ARMERINA 234
PILONI, Giorgio 117, 122
PIRANO 114, 122
PISANI DAL BANCO, Geronimo 63
PISTORIO, Girolamo 247
PIVETTA, Elia viii
PO VALLEY 26
POMPILIO, Angelo 145
POPES
  Alexander VIII (Ottoboni, Pietro Vito) 14
  Clemens VIII (Aldobrandini, Ippolito) 89
  Clemens IX (Rospigliosi, Giulio) 7, 30
  Innocens IV (Fieschi, Sinibaldo) 217
  Innocens XII (Pignatelli, Antonio) 231
  Urbanus VIII (Barberini, Maffeo Vincenzo) 40
POVOLO, Claudio 108, 119
POZZOBONELLI, Giuseppe 49
PRAETORIUS, Michael 169
PRIULI, Antonio 121, 124
PRIULI, Girolamo 110, 112, 116-117
PRIULI, Lorenzo 76, 115
PROVENZALE, Francesco 155-156

### Q

QUERINI, Geronimo 59-61, 70, 72, 76

### R

RAFFAELLI, Giuseppe 182
RAMOS DE PAREJA, Bartolomeo 69

# Index

RANGONI, Teodoro 100
RAVENNA 74-75, 258,
    Ravenna Festival 258
    Lido Adriano 258
RECALCACCIA 243
RECANATI 28
REGGIO EMILIA 75, 89, 94, 103
REIMANN, Father Plazidus 36
RELICS 24, 27-28, 35, 219-220, 230, 233-235, 243
    Christ, Wood of the cross of 219
    St Agatha 230, 233-235, 243
    St Blaise, head of 219
    St Gregory of Nazianzus, chain of 219
    St John the Baptist 219-220
    St Laurence, arm of 219
    St Pantaleone, arm of 219
    St Remigius 27-28, 35
    St Stephen, head of 219
    St Stephen, blood of 219
RIGGIO, Andrea 231
RELIGIOUS ORDERS 36, 230-231, 233
    Augustinian 36, 231, 233
    Benedictine 24-27, 36-40, 42-47, 49-51, 211, 218-219, 221
    Capuchin 233
    Carmelite 231, 233
    Discalced from the Third Order of St Francis 233
    Dominican 45, 231, 233
    Franciscan 233
    Friars Minor Conventual of St Francis 231, 233
    Holy Trinity 233
    Pauline 231, 233
    Philippine 34, 44
    Society of Jesu 32, 40-44, 97
    Theatine 44, 99
    Zoccolanti 231, 233
RIMINI 28
ROME viii, 1-3, 5-9, 11-12, 14-15, 23-30, 32-37, 38-47, 49-51, 61, 72, 94, 153-155, 199-200, 222, 234, 249, 257, 265
    *Churches, monasteries and confraternities:*
    Ancient archconfraternity of blacksmiths 10

Blessed Virgin of the Assumption, Congregation of the 42
Collegio Germanico 30, 32, 40, 42-43, 46
Collegio Romano 34, 44, 46
Gesù 40-42, 49
Pantheon (S. Maria della Rotonda) 50
S. Andrea della Valle 44, 47
S. Apollinare 30, 32, 42-43
S. Eligio de' Ferrari 45
S. Giovanni Decollato 45
S. Ignatius 43
S. John in Lateran 42
S. Maria in Vallicella (Chiesa Nuova) 44
S. Maria Maggiore 33, 44
S. Maria sopra Minerva 45
S. Monica 72
S. Onofrio 45
S. Paul outside the Walls 42
S. Peter in the Vatican 32, 35
S. Trinità degli Spagnoli 32
Sistine Chapel 30, 46
*Other locations:*
Campo de' Fiori 50
Castel Sant'Angelo 32
Corso 4
Esquilino 44
Palazzo della Cancelleria 155
Piazza Navona 50
Ponte Rotto 50
Quirinale (gardens) 49
Sapienza 11, 36
Theatre Capranica 158
Trastevere 50
Via di Monserrato 38, 49
Via Ostiense 42
Villa Belvedere 34
RONCALE, Giovan Domenico 112
ROSA, Salvator 158
ROSACCIO, Giuseppe 68
ROSPIGLIOSI, Giulio 7, 153, 155, 160
    *L'Egisto, overo Chi soffre speri* (opera) 155, 160
ROSSANO 74

# Index

Rossini, Gioachino 257
Rovigo 77, 112, 121

## S

Sacchi, Andrea 40
Sacrati, Francesco 145, 147, 162, 165
    *Il Bellerofonte* (opera) 147
    *La finta pazza* (opera) 145, 162, 165
Saint-Didier, Alexandre Touissant de Limojon 61
Sala, Massimiliano ix
Salerno 74
Sancia of Majorca 217
Sanguineti, Edoardo 261
Sansovino, Francesco 107-109
Sardo, Giovanni 240, 244, 247
Sarzana 74
Sassano, Matteo 214, 220
Savallo, Giovan Battista 120
Savioni, Mario 30
Saxony, Maria Amalia of 222-223
Scarlatti, Alessandro 99, 155-157, 182
    *Gli equivoci in amore, overo La Rosaura* (opera) 155-157
Scarpa, Giuliano 116
Schopenhauer, Arthur 259
Selby, Wilfrid 38
Selvatico, Giovan Battista 124
Seripando, Girolamo 72, 81
Sermisy, Claudin de viii, 195, 197-198
    *Kyrie* (mass *Domini est terra*) viii, 195, 197-198
Sicily, Kingdom of 235
Siega, Giacomo 121, 124
Siena 38
Simoncini, Ilaria 262
Soliani, Bartolomeo 102
Solothurn 27, 28
Sound/Sounds
    Artilleries 110, 114
    Archibugi 6, 14-15
    Bombarda 111-112
    Bell / Campana (Ave Maria) 6
    Bells / Campane 6, 25, 29, 93, 110, 111-115, 222

Mortaretto 222
Fireworks 9, 12, 32, 45, 50, 110, 112, 123, 234
Noise viii, ix, 1-16, 25, 29, 50, 110, 112, 114-115, 260, 262-264
Soundscape viii, ix, 1, 3, 9, 12, 15-16, 27, 29, 33, 99, 103, 109, 111-114, 116-118, 121-123, 145, 146, 150, 169, 229, 259-260
Spaccini, Giovanni Battista 92-93
Spoleto 28
St Gallen 38, 40
    Benedictine monastery 40
St Gotthard Pass 26-28, 38
St Urban (Lucerne), Cistercian monastery 35
Stans 27
Stefanini, Giovanni Battista 90
Stradella, Alessandro 99
Strozzi, Giulio 145, 162, 165
    *La Delia* (opera) 145
    *La finta pazza* (opera) 145, 162, 165
Stuck, Jean-Baptiste (Battestino) 218
Swiss Benedictine Congregation 38, 47
Syracuse 249

## T

Tartini, Giuseppe 181
Terni 28
Tiraboschi, Girolamo 101
Tivoli 49
Tomitano, Bernardino 107
Tolentino 28
Torelli, Giacomo 147
    *Il Bellerofonte* (opera) 147
Toscanella, Orazio 110, 112, 117-118
Trabaci, Giovanni Maria 213
Traschilio 218
Trevisan, Giovanni 76, 78
Trevisan, Marcantonio 113-114, 117, 122
Treviso 66-67, 77-79
    *Churches and monasteries:*
    Duomo 79
    Ognissanti 79
    S. Biagio 79

## Index

S. Paolo 79
S. Teonisto 79
Tricarico, Giuseppe 154-155
*L'Almonte* (opera) 154
Trissino, Gian Giorgio 108, 118

### U

Uberti, Grazioso viii, 2, 8, 10, 12, 257
*Il contrasto musico* (1630) viii, 2, 8, 10, 12, 257
Uccellini, Marco 90
Uçeda, Francisco 231
Urbani, Silvia 150
Usula, Nicola viii

### V

Valentini, Giovanni Andrea 100
Valier, Agostino 76
Vecchi, Orazio 90, 93
Venetian Terraferma 76, 110, 112, 183
Venice viii, 26, 28, 36, 51, 107-108, 111, 114, 116-127, 145-148, 154, 159-160, 162, 164, 170, 181, 193, 195, 234
Doge / Prince viii, 107-127
Maggior Consiglio 108, 118-119, 127
Palazzo Ducale 91-93, 96, 100-101, 108
Promissione Ducale 118-119
Senate 107, 116, 119, 127
*Churches and monasteries:*
Frari 63
S. Daniele 64
S. Giorgio Maggiore 36
St Roch and St Margherita 36
S. Zaccaria 63
Salute 62-63
*Other locations:*
Piazza S. Marco 146-147
Theatre Novissimo 145, 147, 162
Theatre S. Apollinare 154, 159
Theatre S. Cassiano 145, 151, 166, 167
Theatre Ss. Apostoli 148
Theatre Ss. Giovanni e Paolo 145, 164
Venier, Francesco 112, 115, 121
Venier, Sebastiano 114, 121
Verdi, Giuseppe 203

Verona 28, 76, 113, 120, 122-124
Viadana, Lodovico 64
Vicenza 28, 77, 108-109, 124
Vida, Giovanni 114, 121
Vidoni (Vidone), Pietro 30, 32
Vigarani, Gaspare 93-95, 100
*Trionfo della virtù* 95
Vincenzo da San Domenico 64
Viterbo 27, 38

### W

Wagner, Johann Georg 24, 26-28, 30, 32-36
*Italienische Sommer- oder Römer Reyss* (1664) 27-28
Weishaupt, Wolfgang osb 24, 36, 51

### Z

Zacconi, Lodovico 199-200
*Pratica di Musica* 199-200
Zanco, Paolo 107
Zanon, Antonio 182
Zarlino, Gioseffo 199-200
*Istituzioni harmoniche* 199-200
Ziani, Pietro Andrea 154
*Le fortune di Rodope e di Damira* (opera) 154
Zianigo 67
Zitellini, Rodolfo 213